FAMOUS AMERICAN CRIMES AND TRIALS

**Recent Titles in
Crime, Media, and Popular Culture**

Media Representations of September 11
Steven Chermak, Frankie Y. Bailey, and Michelle Brown, editors

Black Demons: The Media's Depiction of the African American
Male Criminal Stereotype
Dennis Rome

FAMOUS AMERICAN CRIMES AND TRIALS

Volume 4: 1960–1980

Edited by Frankie Y. Bailey
and Steven Chermak

Praeger Perspectives

Crime, Media, and Popular Culture

Westport, Connecticut
London

Library of Congress Cataloging-in-Publication Data

Bailey, Frankie Y.
   Famous American crimes and trials / Frankie Y. Bailey and Steven Chermak.
      p. cm.—(Crime, media, and popular culture, ISSN 1549-196X)
   Includes bibliographical references and index.
   Contents: Vol. 1. 1607–1859—v. 2. 1860–1912—v. 3. 1913–1959—v. 4. 1960–1980—
   v. 5. 1981–2000.
      ISBN 0-275-98333-1 (set : alk. paper)—ISBN 0-275-98334-X (vol. 1 : alk. paper)—
   ISBN 0-275-98335-8 (vol. 2 : alk. paper)—ISBN 0-275-98336-6 (vol. 3 : alk. paper)—
   ISBN 0-275-98337-4 (vol. 4 : alk. paper)—ISBN 0-275-98338-2 (vol. 5 : alk. paper)
      1. Criminal justice, Administration of—United States—Case studies. 2. Criminal
   justice, Administration of—United States—History. I. Chermak, Steven M. II. Title.
   III. Series.
HV9950.B3 2004
364.973—dc22   2004050548

British Library Cataloguing in Publication Data is available.

Library of Congress Catalog Card Number: 2004050548
ISBN: 0-275-98333-1 (set)
        0-275-98334-X (vol. I)
        0-275-98335-8 (vol. II)
        0-275-98336-6 (vol. III)
        0-275-98337-4 (vol. IV)
        0-275-98338-2 (vol. V)
ISSN: 1549-196X

First published in 2004

Praeger Publishers, 88 Post Road West, Westport, CT 06881
An imprint of Greenwood Publishing Group, Inc.
www.praeger.com

Printed in the United States of America

The paper used in this book complies with the
Permanent Paper Standard issued by the National
Information Standards Organization (Z39.48-1984).

10   9   8   7   6   5   4   3   2   1

Contents

Set Foreword

Famous American Crimes and Trials covers over four centuries, from the colonial era to the end of the twentieth century, in five volumes. In each volume, we introduce the social and historical contexts in which the cases appearing in the volume occurred. We discuss the evolution of the criminal justice system and the legal issues that were dominant during that time period. We also provide an overview of the popular culture and mass media, examining in brief the nexus between news/entertainment and the criminal justice system. In each introduction, we also identify the common threads weaving through the cases in the volume.

Many of the cases featured in these five volumes provide examples of what Robert Hariman (1990) describes as "popular trials," or "trials that have provided the impetus and the forum for major public debates" (p. 1). As we note elsewhere, cases generally achieve celebrity status because they some-how encapsulate the tensions and the anxieties present in our society; or, at least, this has been the case until the recent past. In the last half-century, the increasing importance of television (and more recently the internet) in delivering the news to the public, and the voracious appetite of the media for news stories to feed the twenty-four-hour news cycle, has meant that stories—particularly crime stories—move quickly into, and sometimes as quickly out of, the public eye. So, as we address in volume 5, we now have a proliferation of crime stories that vie for the status of "famous." It remains to be seen whether these cases will have true "staying power" in the same sense as the cases that are still remembered today after many decades or centuries.

Oddly enough, some cases that were celebrated, though attracting a great deal of public attention when they occurred, have now disappeared from

American collective memory. Perhaps some of these cases for one reason or another only touched a public nerve at the time because they resonated with some passing interest or concern, or fit some media theme. Occasionally, such forgotten cases are rescued from the dustbins by a journalist, a true-crime writer, or a historian and undergo a new wave of public attention. That has happened with several of the cases that appear in these volumes. Perhaps the rediscovery of such cases reflects their relevance to current social issues; or perhaps these cases are interesting to modern readers because they are not only enthralling stories but because they occurred in the past and are now entertaining "period" pieces.

We think that the reader will agree that the cases included in these volumes are among the most important of each era. Since space was limited, many famous cases had to be excluded, but many of these have been covered in other books or media. The cases that are included cover each crime, the setting, and the participants; the actions taken by law enforcement and the criminal legal system; the actions of the media covering the case; the trial (if there was one); the final resolution of the case; the relevant social, political, and legal issues; and, finally, the significance of the case and its impact on legal and popular culture.

REFERENCE

Hariman, R. (1990). *Popular trials: Rhetoric, mass media, and the law.* Tuscaloosa, AL: University of Alabama Press.

Series Foreword

The pervasiveness of media in our lives and the salience of crime and criminal justice issues make it especially important to provide a home for scholars who are engaged in innovative and thoughtful research on important crime and mass media issues.

This series will focus on process issues (such as the social construction of crime and moral panics), presentation issues (such as images of victims, offenders, and criminal justice figures in news and popular culture), and effects (such as the influence of the media on criminal behavior and criminal justice administration).

With regard to this latter issue—effects of media/popular culture—as this foreword was being written the *Los Angeles Times* and other media outlets reported that two young half-brothers (ages 20 and 15) in Riverside, California, had confessed to strangling their mother and disposing of her body in a ravine. The story was attracting particular attention because the brothers told police they had gotten the idea of cutting off her head and hands to prevent identification from a recent episode of the award-winning HBO series, *The Sopranos*. As the *Los Angeles Times* noted, this again brought into the spotlight the debate about the influence of violent media such as *The Sopranos*, about New Jersey mobsters, on susceptible consumers.

In this series, scholars engaged in research on issues that examine the complex nature of our relationship with media. Peter Berger and Thomas Luckman coined the phrase the "social construction of reality" to describe the process by which we acquire knowledge about our environment. They and others have argued that reality is a mediated experience. We acquire what Emile Durkheim described as "social facts" through a several-prolonged process of personal experience, interaction with others, academic education, and, yes, the mass media. With regard to crime and the criminal justice system, many people acquire much of their information from the news and from entertainment media. The issue raised by the report above and other anecdotal stories of "copy cat" crime is how what we consume—read, watch, see, play, hear—affects us.

What we do know is that we experience this mediated reality as individuals. We are all not affected in the same way by our interactions with mass media. Each of us engages in interactions with mass media/popular culture that are shaped by factors such as social environment, interests, needs, and opportunities for exposure. We do not come to the experience of mass media/popular culture as blank slates waiting to be written upon or voids waiting to be filled. It is the pervasiveness of mass media/popular culture and the varied backgrounds (including differences in age, gender, race/ethnicity, religion, etc.) that we bring to our interactions with media that make this a particularly intriguing area of research.

Moreover, it is the role of mass media in creating the much discussed "global village" of the twenty-first century that is also fertile ground for research. We exist not only in our communities, our cities, and states, but in a world that spreads beyond national boundaries. Technology has made us a part of an ongoing global discourse about issues not only of criminal justice but of social justice. Technology takes us to events around the world "as they happen." It was technology that allowed Americans around the world to witness the collapse of the World Trade Center's Twin Towers on September 11, 2001. In the aftermath of this "crime against humanity," we have been witnesses to and participants in an ongoing discussion about the nature of terrorism and the appropriate response to such violence.

Frankie Y. Bailey and Steven Chermak
Series Editors

Acknowledgments

We would like to thank the contributors who worked so hard on the individual chapters. The contributors are a very diverse group, but they all share a passion for the cases they tackled. We appreciate their hard work and their willingness to quickly respond to our suggestions for revision. Many of the contributors have published frequently about a case, but they took the approach we requested in these chapters to offer fresh insights into their work. Other contributors had not written specifically about a case but answered our solicitation because they were curious about it. Our thanks to all of them for producing very insightful and entertaining accounts of the most important cases and trials that have occurred throughout the history of the United States.

The staff at Greenwood Publishing contributed significantly to bringing this project to publication. We are especially grateful to Suzanne Staszak-Silva, Senior Editor at Greenwood, for encouraging us to work on this five-volume set. We considered several different ways to approach the organization of the five volumes, and we appreciate her insights and suggestions for organizing the work by historical era. We were both skeptical about being able to cover so many different cases in such a short amount of time, but her energy was contagious and she was able to convince us of the great potential for such a large project. Mariah Krok was the Developmental Editor for the volumes, and we would like to thank her for being such an effective liaison between the contributors and us. We were able to avoid the many problems that can arise from a project with so many different contributors because of her ability to keep us organized. Thanks to Dan Harmon for tackling the very arduous task of tracking down illustrations and seeking permissions.

The staff at Capital City Press was terrific to work with: special thanks to Bridget Wiedl.

Steve's wife was incredibly supportive and interested in the work of this project. Alisha and I welcomed Mitchell into our family during this project. Thanks to him for deciding to sleep through the night on occasion—this is when most of the work got done.

Frankie Y. Bailey and Steven Chermak

Introduction

Steven Chermak and Frankie Y. Bailey

At first glance, the circumstances of the assassination of Senator Robert F. Kennedy appear to be straightforward. After Kennedy won the California presidential primary election in 1968, which would have helped him secure the Democratic Party nomination for president of the United States, he was murdered by Sirhan Bishara Sirhan in the pantry behind the Embassy Ballroom of the Ambassador Hotel in Los Angeles, California. Kennedy had just finished addressing campaign workers and was exiting the ballroom to attend a press conference when Sirhan shot him. The evidence against Sirhan was substantial: he was apprehended a few feet from Kennedy, he had a .22 calibre revolver in his possession, he confessed to shooting Kennedy, he offered a motive, and he said he acted alone (Klaber and Melanson, 1997).

The publicity surrounding Sirhan's trial would rival any of the celebrated cases discussed in this volume. At least two courtrooms were filled by the press covering the trial, and reporters noted that the eyes of the world were focused on Sirhan's trial (Kneeland, 1969). Sirhan's defense attorneys had few legal options because of the strength of the prosecution's case. Sirhan's attorneys argued that he suffered from a diminished capacity and should not be held responsible for his actions (refer to Charles Guiteau in volume 2 for an assassination trial in which the sanity of the offender was an issue). The jury was not persuaded by Sirhan's attorneys, and Sirhan was convicted and sentenced to death.[1] This apparent open-and-shut case provided an outlet for Americans "to purge their own guilt in the violent phenomena that ha[d] plagued the nation these last few years" (Kneeland,

1969, p. 1). The truth, which often gets distorted in famous cases, about what actually happened has since become much less clear.

There are several reasons why the assassination of Robert F. Kennedy and the subsequent trial of Sirhan received such celebrated attention in the press. The Kennedy family's position in America's political life, Sirhan's troubled background and ethnicity, the timing of the event (i.e., Kennedy was likely to be the Democratic Party presidential candidate in 1968), and the boldness of the act are certainly important factors; however, two broader issues require special consideration.

First, Robert Kennedy's assassination was the last in an apparently un-related, but very similar, series of four assassinations—each assassination engaged some critical aspect of the social turmoil that defined the 1960s. In 1963, John F. Kennedy was assassinated, and many referred to Sirhan's trial as "the trial Lee Harvey Oswald never had" (Fosburgh, 1969, p. 1). The assassinations of Malcolm X in 1965 and Martin Luther King Jr. in 1968, which was only two months before Robert Kennedy's death, accentuated the racial conflicts of the decade. Robert Kennedy was a controversial but engaging presidential candidate. One of his campaign promises was to put an end to the U.S. involvement in the very unpopular war in Vietnam. Thus, these four assassinations have helped define how the public remembers this era.

The second factor exacerbating the significance of Robert Kennedy's assas-sination and Sirhan's conviction is the now unresolved issues regarding Kennedy's death. What at first appeared to be a straightforward case and conviction is now considered by some to be a great "failure of American justice" (Klaber and Melanson, 1997). There are many problems with the case against Sirhan that were ignored at his trial, including inconsistent ballistic and forensic evidence, witnesses who have identified Sirhan working in concert with at least one other person, and the destruction and disappear-ance of important physical evidence. These unresolved issues only added to the American public's mistrust of its government during the 1960s, and these issues continue to remain as a source of distress on the American psyche. The facts and the accounts by the government and media, which supposedly explain what happened, are just murky enough to breed an insatiable thirst for the types of conspiratorial accusations that run through Kennedy's assassination and the other assassinations that occurred.

We begin volume 4 with the discussion of Robert Kennedy's assassination because it highlights a consistent theme found in volumes 1–5: a famous case and/or trial is often defined as celebrated by the legal, political, and social environment surrounding the event. Many of the cases discussed in these volumes may have been ignored or received significantly less publicity had they occurred in a different era.

The murder of Fred Hampton, for example, would have been ignored by the national media had it not occurred in the midst of the political protest movements of the 1960s. Hampton's status as a leader within the Black Panther Party—an organization that was openly clashing with government authorities and complaining of police corruption, cover-ups, and abuse—helped influence the importance and representation of his murder in the press.

The national media may have also ignored the case of Francine Hughes. After enduring years of physical abuse, Hughes had set fire to her husband's bed. The case certainly would not have been reconstructed as a popular culture event, if it had not occurred during a period of growing public and political concern for victims of domestic violence. In short, the environment contributes significantly to which cases get promoted to celebrated status, how significant these cases become, and how these cases are represented in the media.

Reciprocally, these famous cases are often how the public comes to understand a historic period. Such cases represent and define the critical issues and events of history. The different cases discussed in these volumes may have achieved celebrated status for various reasons, but public understanding is ultimately influenced by extensive media coverage, public conversation, and the cultural, political, and social changes that occur as a result of these events.

These famous cases impact the public's collective understanding and misunderstandings of what occurred in a particular era. The assassination of John F. Kennedy, which is the lead case in this volume, best represents the public's continuing fascination with a famous case. People who were alive during the assassination of JFK can describe where they were when the assassination occurred, can articulate the crucial facts and circumstances of the case, and may have an opinion or offer their own conspiratorial theory of who killed JFK. The public's memory has been influenced by the great Kennedy mystique, the media coverage, the many books and articles analyzing the case, and popular films depicting the assassination.

Volume 4 covers the famous cases and trials that occurred between 1960 and 1980. Each case provides some evidence of this reciprocal relationship between a famous case and its surrounding environment. In this introduction, we present four critical contextual issues that we believe strongly influenced the types of cases that became famous in this era, how they were presented, and why other cases were ignored by the media. The first contextual issue includes changes in the U.S. criminal justice system and in crime rates. The second is the changing political nature of crime—the shift from liberal, due process values to an emphasis on conservative, crime-control values in the criminal justice system. The third is the cultural, political, and social transformations that occurred between 1960 and 1980, especially during the 1960s. Finally, we discuss relevant media changes and how a greater reliance on television had an impact on the presentation of famous cases and trials.

AN EXPLOSION OF CRIME AND CRIMINAL JUSTICE

The U.S. criminal justice system changed considerably between 1960 and 1980. First, there was a significant change in both the quantity and type of crimes that occurred. Research indicates that between 1960 and 1991, the rate of violent crime increased 500 percent and the level of property crime tripled (McCorkle and Miethe, 2002). In its final report released in 1969, the National Commission on the Causes and Prevention of Violence concluded that violence had risen to alarming levels, was getting out of control, and was doing great harm to domestic tranquility. The report states "whether one considers assassination, group violence, or individual acts of violence, the decade of the 1960s was considerably more violent than the several decades preceding it and ranks among the most violent in our history" (1969, p. 15). The commission also concluded that the high level of violence was "dividing the nation," "jeopardizing our precious institutions," and "poisoning the spirit of trust and cooperation."

Public fear changed dramatically as many thought that the streets were unsafe and that cities, suburbs, and towns were being plagued by violent predators. It is often a famous case—an unexpected assassination, a particularly gruesome predator who strikes many times before being captured, or a homicide without explanation—that fuels the public's fear. The assassination of John F. Kennedy, discussed in chapter 1, is a good example of the impact that high-profile crimes can have on the public's feelings of insecurity. The crimes of serial murderers—Charles Manson, discussed in chapter 8; John Wayne Gacy, discussed in chapter 13; and Ted Bundy, discussed in chapter 14—often catch the public with its guard down: How was one man able to control the minds and actions of so many, convincing "family" members to commit brutal murders? How can someone prey so violently on so many innocent children? How can somebody act so boldly but elude capture and conviction for such a long period of time? Similarly, the Boston Strangler case, discussed in chapter 2, demonstrates how the inability to capture a suspect breeds public concern and fear. Interestingly, this fear often pressures law enforcement to move swiftly, which can often result in mistakes being made. Although many consider the Boston Strangler case closed, there are certainly enough unanswered questions that can lead one to be quite skeptical.

In the 1960s, decisions from the U.S. Supreme Court, which was led by Chief Justice Earl Warren, significantly changed the way those in the U.S.

criminal justice system processed suspects. Although these famous cases are not described in the volume, U.S. Supreme Court cases *Mapp v. Ohio* (applying exclusionary rules to the states), *Miranda v. Arizona* (formulating the now famous Miranda warnings read prior to interrogation), and *Gideon v. Wainwright* (providing indigent suspects with the right to counsel) were decided in the hope of making the criminal justice system more fair and balanced. However, one result of these decisions was a strong public backlash coupled with a belief that people who committed crimes would not be held accountable for their actions.

Important legal decisions often solidify the transformation of an incident into a famous case. The focus of chapter 3 in this volume is on the obscenity trial of Lenny Bruce. Bruce, a comedian and entertainer, tested the boundaries of the First Amendment to the U.S. Constitution, and the result created a legal and public backlash regarding what was considered appropriate speech. The final outcome of Bruce's case, however, was valued more for its cultural impact than for its legal impact.

The third change in the U.S. criminal justice system was its incredible growth as well as a focus on reforming the system and improving law enforcement response to crime. Three major national crime commissions were created for the following purposes: to analyze the nature of crime and violence in society, to recommend measures for reform, and to comfort Americans with the idea that politicians were responding to their fears. These commissions were the President's Commission on Law Enforcement and Administration of Justice ("The Challenge of Crime in a Free Society"), the National Strategy to Reduce Crime by the National Advisory Commission on Criminal Justice Standards and Goals, and the National Commission on the Causes and Prevention of Violence.

Each commission stressed a need for research and analysis to understand the nature of crime in society. These commissions had an incredible impact on how the public regarded the U.S. criminal justice system. They funneled a large amount of money and resources into fighting crime and increased federal involvement into what had historically been considered local law enforcement problems. For example, the Omnibus Crime Control and Safe Streets Act of 1968 created the Law Enforcement Assistance Administration, which allocated $10 billion to law enforcement to fight crime.

THE POLITICIZATION OF CRIME

Crime has always been a political topic. However, the tone and the exploitation of crime for political gains took on new forms during this historic era. Beckett and Sasson (2000) argue that politicians increasingly used law and order discourse to discredit the civil rights movement, calling its leaders lawbreakers and the protests criminal actions. Crime was an important source of political debates, and it was an issue that often swayed voters—it became a way to distinguish candidates. Crime was viewed as a valuable commodity, and whoever was able to own it defined the nature of it and offered suggestions on how best to respond to it.

For example, in the 1964 U.S. presidential campaign, Barry Goldwater, in accepting the Republican Party nomination, said, "the growing menace in our country tonight, to personal safety, to life, to limb, and property, in homes, in churches, on the playgrounds and places of business, particularly in our great cities, is the mounting concern or should be of every thoughtful citizen in the United States." He continued with "nothing prepares the way for tyranny more than the failure of public officials to keep the streets safe from bullies and marauders" (Goldwater, 1964, p. 10). Goldwater pledged that his presidency would focus on fighting crime in the streets. He emphasized that crime, looting, and riots were out of control and that disorder from within is as great a menace as external threats.

Goldwater argued that incumbent president Lyndon Johnson was soft on crime and that the lawlessness that had engulfed the streets of America was caused by a forgiving U.S. Supreme Court, the civil rights movement, and failed social experiments (McCorkle and Miethe, 2002). Although Goldwater was not successful in his bid for the presidency, his strategy was effective in attracting white, middle-class voters (Beckett and Sasson, 2000). The Republican Party used a similar, and this time successful, strategy in the presidential election of 1968 when Richard Nixon defeated Hubert Humphrey. Nixon argued that Humphrey would be soft on crime, and Nixon promised and eventually delivered a war on crime and drugs that shifted the U.S. criminal justice system's focus from fixing society to cracking down on the offender.[2]

Many social problems and social issues are given serious political consideration when used in conjunction with the publicity of a high-profile case. The death penalty is one of society's most contentious issues. Because of concerns about the administration of the death penalty, many jurisdictions no longer used it as a punishment option by the late 1960s, and in 1972, the U.S. Supreme Court in *Furman v. Georgia* declared the death penalty unconstitutional. The public reacted with hostility about the decision, believing that indeed the U.S. criminal justice system was too soft on criminals. State legislators responded to the Court's decision quickly by redrafting legislation for the death penalty to address the Supreme Court's concerns. The Supreme Court examined these legislative changes and reinstated the death penalty in 1976. It was within this legal and political firestorm that

Gary Gilmore, discussed in chapter 10, received national media publicity. It is very likely Gilmore's crimes would have only been of minor significance if he had not been the first person executed after the decision in *Furman*. Gilmore's case provided an opportunity for opponents of the death penalty to highlight the critical arguments against it. Proponents also used Gilmore's case to argue that this brutal murderer should not be spared the ultimate sanction.

The attack on liberal policies that supported defendant rights and reform programs gained considerable momentum in the early 1970s when Robert Martinson published his often cited but misunderstood study of the state of correctional rehabilitation programs in the United States (Martinson, 1974). He stated "nothing works," which added further justification for repealing such rehabilitative programs. Another interesting phenomenon building on this theme was a growing concern for the treatment of victims of crime in the criminal justice system. The women's rights movement, for example, drew attention to the exploitation of women in the criminal justice system. Treatment of victims of rape and domestic violence were of particular concern, and the outcomes of two celebrated cases perhaps signified positive changes that were occurring in society regarding these issues.

The trial of Joan Little, discussed in chapter 11, is quite intriguing because the media coverage was shaped by struggles against racism and sexism that were being fought outside the courtroom. Little, a black woman, killed a white man after he raped her. Advocates and celebrities supported Little and worked to generate publicity in her favor by exploiting their access to the media and participating in public protests. After her acquittal, the public's memory of Little's case quickly began to fade.

The trial of Francine Hughes, discussed in chapter 12, highlighted the treatment of victims of domestic violence in the criminal justice system. Hughes killed her husband by pouring gasoline in his bed and lighting it on fire. Women's rights advocates supported Hughes, using her as an example of what many victims of domestic violence endure. The jury found Hughes not guilty by reason of temporary insanity, and the decision set a precedent for giving serious consideration to battered women's syndrome in such cases. Hughes's case was represented in a made-for-television movie *The Burning Bed*, which aired in 1984 on the first day of National Domestic Violence Awareness Week (see chapter 12).

CULTURAL, LEGAL, POLITICAL, AND SOCIAL FISSURES

It is impossible to thoroughly discuss all of the social and political movements that altered the American landscape in the 1960s. However, it is important to note that the impact of such social and political changes led many Americans to believe that the social fabric binding society together was unraveling. Assassinations, urban riots, and other acts of group violence contributed to concerns about public safety. Protests of civil, political, racial, and social injustices occurred frequently. The United States was losing a very unpopular war amid Cold War concerns, and across the country, college campuses erupted in protest.

Organizations, attorneys, and advocacy groups attempted to define new boundaries of civil rights for women, inmates and defendants, homosexuals, and victims. There was growing suspicion of the government and its attempts to manipulate public perceptions. Watergate was an example of the great lengths an administration would go to achieve its objectives and cover its misdeeds. The Pentagon Papers, secret files, secret bombings, and revelations of the horrors of the Vietnam War only exacerbated these concerns. Not only was society evolving socially and politically during this era, there was also an incredible cultural transformation taking place. Woodstock is still remembered fondly as the best representation of the hippie and drug culture that flourished during this era. These social and cultural movements were weaved into how the media presented this era, and several of the chapters in this volume directly engage these social changes.

The discussion in three chapters (Hampton in chapter 5, Davis in chapter 6, and Little in chapter 11) will provide a look into the state of race relations in the United States after the decision in *Brown v. Board of Education* in 1954. The murder of Black Panther Party leader Fred Hampton provides the best example of the intense confrontations between law enforcement and militant black gangs. Hampton was a leader of the Black Panther Party in Chicago, Illinois. He was killed by police officers who were responding to a tip that Hampton was stockpiling guns. The Federal Bureau of Investigation (FBI) concluded that the Black Panthers posed a threat to national security and instituted a major offensive to infiltrate the organization and discredit them. Hampton and other members of the Black Panther Party were sleeping when the police kicked down the door; however, officers claimed they were assaulted with gunfire. The conflicting accounts of what happened only increased the tensions between law enforcement and the black community.

Angela Davis, discussed in chapter 6, was a high-profile figure well before she was indicted for assisting the Soledad Brothers, black inmates of Soledad Prison in California who were charged with murdering a white guard. Her dismissal from the University of California at Los Angeles (UCLA) for being a member of the Communist Party, her ties to the Black Panther Party, and her efforts in aiding other political causes solidified Davis's position as an important voice for social and political issues. Her visibility increased dramatically when she was charged, but she was later acquitted of conspiracy to commit kidnapping and murder for allegedly supplying guns to assist the Soledad Brothers. Davis continues to be an important voice on race relations in the United States, and she was one of the high-profile figures who supported Joan Little in her trial for killing a male, white jailer.

An unbelievable number of protests and acts of civil disobedience occurred during this era. The war in Vietnam was one of the major sources of protest. It was in the heat of these protests that accusations of the My Lai massacre surfaced. The My Lai massacre was significant because of the scope of the tragedy: hundreds of unarmed civilians had been executed. The case again demonstrated the extent that officials would go to cover-up such tragedies.

Lenny Bruce was another type of protest figure. Bruce, a stand-up comedian, used his comedy to push the limits of what was considered acceptable speech. His powerful words caused such a reaction that prosecutors attempted to silence him by charging him with obscenity. His words, and thus his crimes, are discussed in chapter 3. The trial of the Chicago Seven, discussed in chapter 4, provides a look at how protest was brought directly into the courtroom. The 1968 Democratic National Convention in Chicago, Illinois, which was already spoiled by the assassination of Robert F. Kennedy, was viewed by many national leaders of different movements as a good opportunity to heighten their profiles. The media broadcasted the clashes that occurred between law enforcement and the protestors. Law enforcement's response was an attempt to hold leaders of several movements responsible for the riots. The prosecution was not successful; the defendants were acquitted. However, the trial provided some of the most entertaining moments in the history of courtrooms in the United States.

THE TRANSFORMATION OF THE MEDIA

The cultural, political, and social changes that occurred and the famous cases that accentuated these issues were broadcast to the public in a rapidly changing media environment. Two changes were particularly significant. First, public reliance on television for news and information increased dramatically. Television technology was well developed by the late 1930s, but World War II delayed mass use of this medium. After World War II, the distribution of television sets in American homes increased rapidly, and by early 1960, 90 percent of homes in the United States had a television set (Lange, Baker, and Ball, 1969). Thus, the changes that were occurring in society and the famous cases discussed in this volume were experienced by the American public in a very different way compared with previous years.

Although people were not directly involved in the activities and movements of the period, they felt as though they were part of it. The public viewed the riots, the protests, and the dissent directly, which only added to existing fears and concerns. Television was changing how the public consumed news, how politicians interacted with the public through the media, and how famous cases were presented.

The Attica prison riot, discussed in chapter 9, provides one example of how television shaped the outcome and public understanding of a famous case. A major issue in the 1960s and 1970s was rights for prisoners, and black activists, in particular, tried to heighten social consciousness about the deplorable conditions in prisons. The Attica prison riot was a crucial event influencing reform efforts. Prisoners gained control of the Attica Correctional Facility, a well-known maximum security prison in Attica, New York. Correctional officials attempted to negotiate a peaceful solution. The negotiation committee included legislators, media personnel, a famous defense attorney, and a member of the Black Panther Party. Russell Oswald, commissioner of corrections for New York State, allowed media personnel direct access to the negotiations, and television cameras recorded the activities. The inmates used the presence of cameras as an opportunity to communicate to the public about the deplorable conditions in Attica. As discussed in chapter 9, the presence of cameras resulted in "an explosion of rhetoric." The New York State Commission on Attica, which investigated the riots, concluded that "the admission of newsmen and television cameras . . . not only provided inmates with an unparalleled opportunity to tell the public about prison conditions, but gave them a sense of importance, dignity, and power" (1972, pp. 211–212). The availability of images increased the importance of the Attica prison riots. It was impossible to ignore what was occurring behind prison walls after the media disseminated the images. One result was significant policy changes as activist courts responded to inmate concerns about the quality of life in prison.

The second major issue was the media's self-reflection about how and what issues were covered in the news. Schudson's (1978, p. 161) important discussion of the history of news argues that "in the sixties, as never before, news writing itself was a topic for news coverage." This self-reflection resulted in an indictment of how the media covered news. There was a general acknowledgment that what was covered in the news strongly affected public and political decisions; thus, there should be great care taken when making decisions about news coverage. More importantly, the media came to realize how extensively politicians and other critical sources were attempting to manipulate the media, which resulted in great distortions of the truth. Such manipulation was not unique to this era, but the realization of the intensity of such efforts overwhelmed the media. The media's credibility was directly questioned, and news organizations responded by shifting story-telling strategies, relying on more interpretive reporting, and uncovering distortions of the truth (Schudson, 1978). The Watergate scandal and release of the Pentagon Papers, two incredibly important events of the 1970s, were stunning not only because of the facts of what had occurred but also because of the efforts to control what the media published.

NOTES

1. This sentence was voided when the Supreme Court ruled that the death penalty was unconstitutional in *Furman v. Georgia*, 408 U.S. 238 (1972). Sirhan remains incarcerated in California.

2. The Nixon administration's drug policies were actually somewhat more complex. As a recent *Frontline* documentary, "Drug Wars" (2000) reminds us, Nixon began his presidency with a two-prong approach to the drug problem. At first, he advocated both treatment and law enforcement strategies. It was later, as he faced re-election that he shifted to a "get tough on crime" approach that focused on the drug war to be waged by law enforcement.

REFERENCES

Beckett, K., and Sasson, T. (2000). *The politics of injustice.* Thousand Oaks: Pine Forge Press.

Brown v. Board of Education, 347 U.S. 483 (1954).

Fosburgh, L. (1969, January 19). Sirhan trial: It stirs deep and conflicting emotions. *New York Times.*

Furman v. Georgia, 408 U.S. 238 (1972).

Gideon v. Wainwright, 372 U.S. 335 (1963).

Goldwater, B. (1964, July 17). Transcript of Goldwater's speech accepting Republican presidential nomination. *New York Times*, p. 10.

Klaber, W., and Melanson, P. H. (1997). *Shadow play: The murder of Robert F. Kennedy, the trial of Sirhan Sirhan, and the failure of American justice.* New York: St. Martin's Press.

Kneeland, D. E. (1969, January 6). Trial of Sirhan will open tomorrow. *New York Times.*

Lange, D. L., Baker, R. K., and Ball, S. J. (1969). Violence and the media: A staff report to the national commission on the causes and prevention of violence. Washington, DC: U.S. Government Printing Office.

Mapp v. Ohio, 367 U.S. 643 (1961).

Martinson, R. (1974). What works? Questions and answers about prison reform, *The Public Interest, 35*, 22–54.

McCorkle, R. C., and Miethe, T. D. (2002). *Panic: The social construction of the street gang problem.* Englewood Cliffs, NJ: Prentice Hall.

Miranda v. Arizona, 384 U.S. 436 (1966).

Moldea, D. E. (1995). *The killing of Robert F. Kennedy: An investigation of motive, means, and opportunity.* New York: W.W. Norton.

National Advisory Commission on Criminal Justice Standards and Goals. (1973). *A national strategy to reduce crime.* Washington, DC: U.S. Government Printing Office.

National Commission on the Causes and Prevention of Violence. (1969). *To establish justice, to insure domestic tranquility.* Washington, DC: U.S. Government Printing Office.

New York State Special Commission on Attica. (1972). *Attica: The official report of the New York State Special Commission on Attica.* New York: Bantam Books.

President's Commission on Law Enforcement and Administration of Justice. (1967). *The challenge of crime in a free society.* Washington, DC: U.S. Government Printing Office.

Schudson, M. (1978). *Discovering the news: A social history of American newspapers.* New York: Basic Books.

1

The JFK Assassination: Three Murders, Two Killers, and Four Decades

Kevin F. Wozniak

It was probably the most defining moment in a decade of defining moments, and one's reaction to the assassination of John Fitzgerald Kennedy has served as a kind of political litmus test ever since. Are you pro or antigovernment? Can the government be trusted? Has the government ever lied to the public? Are you satisfied by the official Warren Commission Report that specified a "lone gunman," or are you seduced by a belief in one or more of the dozens of conspiracy theories perpetuated by the press? There have been hundreds of books and movies purporting that Kennedy was killed by the following: the CIA, the FBI, the Secret Service, the KGB, the Mossad, organized crime, organized labor, anti-Castro Cubans, pro-Castro Cubans acting under the direct order of Fidel Castro, pro-Castro Cubans *not* acting under the direct order of Fidel Castro, elements controlled by Vice President Lyndon Johnson, elements associated with the Federal Reserve bank, a clique of New Orleans–based homosexuals, Nazi-sympathizing Texas oil million-aires, various Mexican nationals, various members of the Kennedy family, assorted renegade high-ranking American military officers in Kennedy's entourage, assorted renegade high-ranking American military officers *not* in Kennedy's entourage, the American military-industrial complex in general, or some or all of the above working in tandem to bring forward the mother

The sensational publicity of the assassination of John F.
Kennedy. (Courtesy of Library of Congress)

of all conspiracies. Maybe, as has been suggested on the internet, Aristotle
Onassis' romantic interest in Jacqueline Kennedy led him to plot the murder
of his rival, her husband, JFK. Some wag has even suggested that Jacqueline
Kennedy, Joe DiMaggio, and Arthur Miller conspired to kill Kennedy
because of ire over his alleged affair with Marilyn Monroe. Perhaps many
disparate elements can be demonstrated to have an interest in the death
of any president of the United States who is well-known and controversial
and has many potential enemies. I will relay the verifiable facts in the case,
describe some of the more popular alternative theories, and explore the impact
of John F. Kennedy's death on American culture.

MURDER ONE: DEALEY PLAZA, DALLAS, TEXAS

Friday, November 22, 1963

In the fall of 1963, John F. Kennedy was in political trouble. A legacy
of high-profile failures such as the Bay of Pigs fiasco had caused Kennedy's
approval rating to drop in the political polls, creating apprehension among
the president, his advisors, his party, and his family. Consequently, the
decision to take a campaign swing through Texas was made. This was
acknowledged to be a potentially dangerous move because of the vilification
of Kennedy by militant right-wing groups, anti–civil rights campaigners, and
Cuban exiles. Posters had been displayed throughout Dallas with "Wanted
for Treason" accompanying the president's picture; warnings that the president's life could be in danger had been received from extremists. Therefore,

in an attempt to seek support for his New Frontier policies and with an eye on the 1964 elections, President John F. Kennedy set out on what was planned as a two-day, five-city tour of Texas. This political decision would have extraordinary consequences for American history.

On November 22, 1963, John and Jackie Kennedy awoke in the Hotel Texas in Fort Worth. The day dawned in a misting drizzle, but President Kennedy did not wear a raincoat for his speech in the hotel's parking lot. After the speech, he and his entourage flew to Dallas's Love Field aboard Air Force One. Upon arrival the first couple along with Texas governor John Connolly and his wife Nellie entered the presidential limousine, a stretched and modified dark blue 1961 Lincoln Continental. Kennedy sat in his regular place in the rear seat on the passenger side, next to his wife and directly behind Governor Connolly, who occupied the center jump seat behind Secret Service Agent Roy Kellerman. Nellie Connolly sat in the jump seat next to her husband and directly behind the driver, Secret Service Agent William Greer, who was the oldest member of the presidential security detail. Because of the warm weather, the Secret Service decided not to install the car's transparent plastic bubble top, leaving the limo as an open convertible, a decision with which President Kennedy concurred. Although not bulletproof, the bubble top could serve to partially deflect most projectiles, presenting a more difficult target for potential assassins. The presidential limousine was directly followed by Dallas police officers on motorcycles and by "The Queen Mary," which was an open 1956 Cadillac carrying Secret Service agents with weapons at hand. Vice President Lyndon Johnson's limousine followed behind at some distance. The remainder of the procession consisted of vehicles filled with various dignitaries and the press.

Kennedy's advisors were concerned that Dallas promised to prove a hostile place to visit. Before leaving Washington, DC, Kennedy's secretary Eve Lincoln had warned the president not to go to Texas. The morning of the Kennedys' arrival, the Dallas *Morning News* ran a full-page black-bordered advertisement that sarcastically welcomed the president and accused him of being a tool of international Communism. Paid for by prominent right-wing interests, the ad expressed the dissatisfaction Southern conservatives felt for the young, progressive Democratic president. Despite the overt hostility among the population of Dallas, the motorcade route wound through the city's midtown at midday to give residents the greatest possible exposure to the president. Stopping several times to greet the crowds Kennedy and his entourage continued through town, proceeding toward his luncheon destination, Dallas's Trade Mart. Near the end of the route the motorcade was to pass through Dealey Plaza, a park-like area surrounded by office buildings, before turning on to the Stemmons Freeway for the short trip to the Trade Mart. Kennedy was fated not to keep his luncheon appointment.

At 12:30 p.m. central daylight time, the motorcade slowed to enter Dealey Plaza, making a 120-degree left turn from Houston Street on to Elm Street. The motorcade passed directly in front of the Texas School Book Depository, a seven-floor building containing warehousing space and offices for the educational publishing industry. As the limousine began to accelerate out of the turn, Nellie Connolly noted the crowd's enthusiastic response in this part of the city, turned to President Kennedy, and said, "You can't say that Dallas doesn't love you, Mr. President." "No, you certainly can't," Kennedy replied and resumed waving to bystanders. At that moment, a sharp crack was heard. Most thought it was a firecracker or a backfiring motorcycle, but military veterans and hunters present immediately recognized the sound of rifle fire. Though Dealey Plaza is notorious for strange echo patterns that make it difficult to pinpoint the origin of sounds, a large majority of witnesses placed the sounds as coming from the upper floors of the Texas School Book Depository. Photographic evidence shows bystanders and security personnel pointing to the upper floors immediately after the shots were heard. Incredibly, upon hearing the crack, Agent Greer slowed the Lincoln and looked about rather than driving the president out of danger, giving the assassin an easier target. Another shot rang out, and Kennedy's arms rose into "Thorburn's position," a neurological response to spinal injury in which the victim's fists meet in front of the throat and the elbows become locked straight out to the sides. Computer enhanced silent home movie footage of the assassination, taken by Dallas dressmaker Abraham Zapruder (the famous Zapruder film), clearly shows Jackie Kennedy trying to push her husband's elbow down. A few seconds later, Connolly fell into his wife's arms, a massive hole in the right side of his chest. As the third shot was heard, the top right side of Kennedy's head exploded in a cloud of blood and brain matter. At that moment Agent Clint Hill, running from the follow-up car, grabbed for the handle on the trunk of the Lincoln that was used as a handhold for agents riding on the limousine's rear bumper and nearly fell into the street as Greer floored the accelerator. In the front seat ahead of Connolly, Agent Kellerman grabbed the radio mike and called for an escort to a hospital.

With Agent Hill bent over the trunk and shielding the Kennedys with his body, Greer sped the Lincoln to Parkland Memorial Hospital. It skidded to a stop at the ambulance entrance, and Kennedy and Connolly were carried inside to the hospital's trauma rooms. After approximately twenty minutes of desperate attempts at resuscitation by emergency room chief Dr. Charles Baxter and Drs. Carrico, Jenkins, McClelland, Giesecke, Peters,

Clark, Jones, and Perry, Kennedy no longer had any measurable pulse or respiration. Dr. Perry created a later controversy by cutting a tracheotomy incision directly over the fresh bullet wound in Kennedy's throat. Further efforts were deemed futile, and President John Fitzgerald Kennedy was pronounced dead at 1 p.m. on November 22, 1963. Because the cause of death was deemed to be the massive head wound, the death certificate was signed by the senior neurosurgeon present, Dr. Kemp Clark. Next, a casket and hearse for transporting the late president were ordered from a local undertaker and the late president's body was prepared for removal from the hospital.

Upon receiving news of Kennedy's death, Vice President Lyndon B. Johnson immediately had himself driven to Air Force One in preparation for return to Washington. As acting president, Johnson was not sure if he was putting himself in danger by remaining in Dallas since he did not yet know if Kennedy's killing was part of a conspiracy against the U.S. government. After a telephone consultation with Attorney General Robert Kennedy, it was decided that Johnson would be sworn in as president before Air Force One left Dallas to achieve the most unbroken presidential succession possible. Federal Judge Sarah Hughes was summoned to Air Force One, and after waiting for Mrs. Kennedy and the casket to arrive at the plane, Johnson was sworn in as the thirty-sixth President of the United States at 2:37 p.m. Immediately after the ceremony, Bill Swindal, pilot of Air Force One, took his seat and the Boeing 707 left for Washington.

The nation had been made aware of the assassination, and the press was focused on the arrival of the presidential plane. As Air Force One rolled to a stop, Robert Kennedy climbed aboard unseen, and he and Jackie stepped off the plane together. This had created the impression that Robert Kennedy had been in Dallas with his brother, which had confused the live television audience. The heavy bronze ceremonial casket, which had been damaged in transit, was transferred to a gray U.S. Navy ambulance for transport to Bethesda Naval Hospital in Bethesda, Maryland, where Commander James J. Humes and Commander J. Thornton Boswell, U.S. Navy pathologists, were waiting to perform the autopsy. The autopsy began at about 8 p.m. (official accounts vary) and was completed by 11 p.m., a remarkably quick procedure for a case of this importance. Apparently, pathologists Humes and Boswell were not specifically qualified for forensic procedures. According to Dr. Cyril Wecht, the medical examiner of Allegheny, Pennsylvania, and a noted JFK assassination gadfly, the autopsy was one of the "worst and most botched autopsies ever" (Posner, 1993, p. 302). Wecht noted it was a rushed and incomplete affair due as much to pressure from the Kennedy family as to the inexperience of the pathologists. This shoddy work had given rise to speculations concerning the possibility of evidence tampering and misreporting of findings, which were supposedly to cover-up Kennedy's true injuries and the truth about how he was killed and who actually killed him. The later disappearance of autopsy materials and documents (probably taken by souvenir hunters) has also been cited as evidence of unnamed conspirators covering their tracks. After completion of the autopsy, the body of John F. Kennedy was prepared for burial.

THE FIRST EVIDENCE, THE SECOND MURDER, AND THE PRIME SUSPECT

November 22 and 23, 1963

After the shots were fired, some police officers converged on the area that was in front and to the right of the presidential limousine at the time of the shooting—the area otherwise known as the grassy knoll. A man had been seen running up the sloping hill away from the shooting, and smoke or steam had been seen rising up behind the fence at the top of the knoll. These events caused many assassination researchers to postulate the presence of a shooter on the grassy knoll, which opposed the official findings. The rising steam was first believed to be gun smoke but was later determined to be coming from a hot pipe behind the fence. The fleeing individual was found to be a terrified bystander.

Officer Marrion Baker, who was riding his motorcycle in the motorcade, raced to the front door of the Texas School Book Depository and ran upstairs with depository manager Roy Truly. At the soda machine in the second floor lunchroom, Officer Baker encountered Lee Harvey Oswald, a twenty-four-year-old temporary employee who had been hired by Truly five weeks earlier. A committed Marxist with a history of psychiatric problems, Oswald had defected to Russia four years earlier and had lived in Minsk, Belarus, for a time before returning to the United States with his Russian-born wife, Marina Prusakova.

Oswald had worked as a volunteer for the Fair Play for Cuba Committee, was a great admirer of Fidel Castro, and had qualified as a sharpshooter during his U.S. Marine Corps service. Oswald was a slightly notorious figure in his native New Orleans, Louisiana, due to his political activism—he had made several radio appearances speaking in favor of the Castro revolution. Oswald's anti-American statements at the time of his defection had led the Marine Corps to switch his discharge status from honorable to dishonorable. Oswald's sporadic employment in New Orleans and Marina Oswald's second pregnancy had prompted the couple's relocation to Dallas in September 1963 in an attempt to improve their living conditions.

Truly assured Baker that Oswald was an employee, and Baker continued upstairs from the second floor. Oswald then proceeded calmly downstairs, and he was out the front door of the building less than three minutes after the last shot had been fired.

As he stepped into the pandemonium that followed the shooting, Oswald calmly directed reporter Robert McNeil to a phone, then walked east from Dealey Plaza and boarded a bus driven by Cecil McWatters. When the bus got caught in the traffic caused by police units rushing into Dealey Plaza, Oswald, not wishing to wait, asked for a transfer and left the bus. He then walked two blocks to a taxi stand and hired a taxi to drive him to his home, a rooming house in suburban Oak Cliff. The use of a taxi was highly unusual behavior for the extremely thrifty Oswald. After changing his jacket, Oswald stuck his 38-caliber pistol in his waistband and zipped his jacket to conceal the pistol. It was now approximately 1 p.m.

By this time, the first witnesses in Dealey Plaza had given statements describing Kennedy's murderer. Several individuals indicated that they had seen a thin, balding, smirking man approximately 25 to 30 years of age and about 5 feet 9 inches tall. Witnesses said that he was either standing with a rifle in a window of the sixth floor of the Texas School Book Depository or pointing the gun out of the window at the time of the shooting. Oswald had seemed so calm that some witnesses had believed him to be with the U.S. Secret Service or another security agency. This description, which Oswald fit remarkably well, was transmitted to all Dallas police units as an all points bulletin (APB) within fifteen minutes of the shooting. Shortly before 1:15 p.m., Officer J. D. Tippit stopped his patrol car on Tenth Street in Dallas' Oak Cliff section. Tippit most likely stopped in response to the APB to speak to Oswald who was walking a few blocks from his rooming house. It is a possibility that Oswald's "erratic back and forth movements" may have caught Tippit's attention (Russo, 1998, p. 314). As Officer Tippit got out of the car to speak to Oswald, Oswald pulled the pistol out of his waistband and shot Tippit at least four times. Almost a dozen people witnessed Oswald shoot Tippit. Two of the witnesses ran to Tippit's car, found him dead, and called in the shooting on his police radio at 1:16 p.m. As he ran away emptying shells from the pistol, witness William Scoggins heard Oswald mutter "poor damn cop" or "poor dumb cop." It is thought by most historians that Oswald most likely killed Tippit to avoid arrest for carrying the concealed pistol, which would have been found during the most perfunctory search.

Oswald was in fact arrested as a direct result of the Tippit shooting. A few minutes after the killing, a desperate Oswald, who was running down Jefferson Avenue, heard police sirens and slipped into the lobby of Hardy's Shoe Store. The manager of Hardy's, Johnny Calvin Brewer, noticed Oswald because "his hair was messed up and [he] . . . had been running, and he looked scared" (Warren Commission, vol. 7, 1964, p. 3). After the police cars passed, Oswald left the store and continued down Jefferson away from the direction the police had been heading. Brewer followed the "suspicious" person. Fifty yards away from Hardy's, Oswald, wearing "a panicked look" (President's Commission on the Assassination of President John F. Kennedy, 1964, pp. 10, 14), ran into the Texas Theater without paying. Ticket clerk Julia Postal, after speaking with Brewer, called the police. At least half a dozen patrol cars with fifteen or more officers responded. By this time, an APB had gone out for Officer Tippit's killer, and the Dallas police had "noted . . . [the] similarity in the descriptions of the suspects in the Tippit shooting and the assassination" (President's Commission on the Assassination of President John F. Kennedy, 1964, pp. 1–27).

What seemed to have been an excess number of officers responding has appeared suspicious to certain researchers: How did so many know that the lone assassin would be in the Texas Theater at that time? There is some evidence that the police responded to the APB for Tippit's killer with more alacrity than they had for the Kennedy murder because one of their own had died. The police, responding to the description in the APB, had already raided a nearby library in pursuit of Tippit's killer, and the Texas Theater was only a few short blocks from the site of the Tippit murder. When the police entered the theater, Brewer pointed out the suspect to them. Patrolman M. N. McDonald approached Oswald, who yelled, "Well, it's all over now!" Then Oswald drew his gun with one hand, and struck McDonald with the other. After a brief altercation involving several officers and detectives, Oswald was disarmed, handcuffed, and driven to Dallas police headquarters.

Meanwhile, police had found the sniper's nest on the sixth floor warehouse area of the Texas School Book Depository. A deputy sheriff discovered three empty rifle cartridges near a pile of book cartons in the southeast corner. The pile had screened the corner window from the view of anyone on the sixth floor. This discovery focused attention on the sixth floor. A worn bolt-action rifle was soon found hidden between two rows of boxes on the other side of the floor. After the rifle was found, it was discovered that depository employee Lee Harvey Oswald was missing; he had reported for work that morning and had been seen by Truly and Baker on the second floor immediately after the Kennedy shooting. That morning Oswald had been seen carrying a package made of brown paper, which was later found to be made of the sort of paper readily available to employees of the warehouse, into the building. Oswald had claimed the package contained "curtain rods." This package was found near the three spent shells on the sixth floor, and it is believed that it was used to carry the disassembled rifle into the Texas School Book Depository. No curtain rods were ever found.

After receiving Oswald's description and general information from manager Roy Truly, Captain J. Will Fritz of the Dallas Police Homicide and Robbery Bureau went to police headquarters. Upon arrival, Fritz ordered detectives to proceed to the home of Ruth Paine in Irving, Texas, to arrest Lee Harvey Oswald. Marina Oswald was separated from her violent husband, and she, with their two children, was living with her friend Ruth Paine. Oswald did not live there, but he did stay for frequent overnight visits and kept some of his possessions in Paine's garage. He had listed Paine's house as his residence on his employment application. Captain Fritz was immediately informed by nearby officers that Oswald was already in custody in connection with the Tippit murder.

Oswald denied any involvement in the killings of Kennedy or Tippit, and he denied owning a rifle. He had been identified by witnesses as the Tippit shooter, and he had been carrying a concealed .38-caliber pistol that could have fired the shots that killed Tippit. At 7:10 p.m., Lee Harvey Oswald was formally charged in the death of Officer Tippit.

At 1:30 a.m., after a more extensive interrogation, Oswald was charged with the murder of President Kennedy. Assistant District Attorney Bill Alexander drafted the indictment. Alexander had a somewhat adversarial relationship with the federal agents involved in the investigation. He decided to keep them out of his way in Dallas by having them follow up on a fictitious story in the *Philadelphia Inquirer* that stated Oswald had killed Kennedy as part of a Communist conspiracy. He later concocted a false story with two reporters detailing Oswald's career as an FBI informant. These deliberately misleading stories may have been the origin of some of the conspiracy legends about Oswald's role in the Kennedy assassination.

When arrested, Oswald had been carrying a selective service card in his wallet in the name of "Alek James Hidell." It is thought that the pseudonym had been taken from a combination of Oswald's Russian nickname of "Alik" coupled with a variant of "Heindel" (a Marine he had served with). Marina Oswald has stated that she believed Oswald chose the name "Hidell" because it sounded like "Fidel," an obvious reference to Oswald's hero, Fidel Castro. By 8:00 a.m. on November 23, the FBI had determined that the rifle found on the sixth floor of the Texas School Book Depository had been purchased from a mail order house in Chicago, Illinois, and shipped to a Dallas post office box rented by "A. Hidell." It had been paid for with a money order for $21.45 signed by "A. Hidell." The mail order coupon ordering the 38-caliber pistol used in the murder of Officer Tippit was signed by "A.J. Hidell" and shipped to Oswald's post office box in Dallas. The FBI determined through handwriting analysis that the documents signed by "Hidell" were actually written by Lee Harvey Oswald.

THE HERO AND THE ZERO

Sunday, November 24, 1963

On the morning of Sunday, November 24, Oswald was to be moved to Dallas County Jail because the media's presence in the city jail was disrupting police operations. Despite the fact that anonymous death threats against Oswald had been received by authorities, the decision was made to allow television, newspaper, and radio reporters to cover Oswald being moved to the transfer vehicle in the basement garage of the prison. At 11:21 a.m., a phalanx of detectives emerged from the jail office and escorted Oswald toward the unmarked car to be used for the trip to Dallas County Jail. Suddenly, while millions watched on live television, a Dallas strip-club owner named Jack Ruby jumped out from the crowd of reporters, extended a Colt .38, and yelled, "You killed my president, you rat!" He fired one shot into Oswald's abdomen. Oswald lost consciousness and was taken to Parkland Memorial Hospital where he died at 1:07 p.m. Ruby was tackled by officers, disarmed, and hustled upstairs. To his great surprise, as he expected to be treated as a hero, Ruby was immediately arrested.

There does not seem to be a motive for Ruby's killing of Oswald. By all accounts, on a weekend when many openly expressed and exhibited their sorrow, Ruby was extraordinarily upset, maybe too upset. Friends, relatives, and acquaintances who had face-to-face or telephone contact with him during the weekend of the assassination recalled that he seemed utterly distraught over the president's death almost as if a close family member had died. Ruby sobbed in disbelief while repeatedly asking how "a zero, a complete nothing" like Oswald could possibly succeed in killing the president of the United States. His emotional desolation seemed to have had an element of emotional or mental disturbance. At the best of times, Ruby impressed people with his eccentricities, behaving in ways that appeared to indicate increasing mental instability. Violent, with a hair-trigger temper, which was especially aroused by what he perceived as anti-Semitism (he had been born Jacob Rubenstein and was very proud of his heritage), Ruby had been arrested at least nine times for various charges that included assault and weapons charges. On at least one occasion, he was known to have fired a gun at his former business partner during a chase. Ruby repeatedly stated to police that he had shot Oswald on the spur of the moment and had felt that he wanted to spare Jackie Kennedy from the ordeal of Oswald's trial. Ruby also stated that he wanted to avenge the honor of the city of Dallas and the honor of Jews everywhere.

THE GOVERNMENT RESPONDS: THE WARREN COMMISSION

The new president had to do something. Suppose a hostile foreign government or hostile domestic group was in fact responsible for Kennedy's killing? He needed to know, and he needed to know quickly. On November 29, 1963, Johnson issued Executive Order 11130, which created the President's Commission on the Assassination of President John F. Kennedy (otherwise known as the Warren Commission). U.S. Supreme Court Chief Justice Earl Warren headed a seven-person panel, which had virtually unprecedented power. The Warren Commission was tasked with producing a full report by June 30, 1964, a deadline that proved impractical.

Because President Johnson did not want the impending report to become an issue during the upcoming presidential campaign, he pressed to have the report completed as soon as possible, and the commission's conclusions were finally presented on September 24, 1964. Unfortunately, there had not been enough time for the commission to explore every possible issue in the time allowed, and those on the panel were forced to rely in part on previous investigations by the FBI and the Secret Service. This methodology created gaps in the record, which were treated in the future as big issues by pro-conspiracy researchers.

The most contentious issue was the single-bullet theory. Repeated viewing of the Zapruder film enabled the commission (mistakenly, it turned out) to determine exactly when they thought the shots were fired at the motorcade. Observation of the wounds inflicted and the timing of shots led the commissioners to purpose the "single bullet" or "magic bullet" theory. Simply put, this theory postulates that Oswald's first shot missed; his second, the "magic" shot, entered Kennedy's back, exited his throat, entered John Connally's back, exited his chest, went through his wrist and finally lodged in Connally's thigh; and the third shot blasted through Kennedy's head and killed him. Though essentially proven through computer analysis during the 1990s, the single bullet theory seemed contrived to critics of the commission's theory. In fact, the commissioners themselves had doubts about the theory, debating how best to portray evidence that some believed was conclusive and others thought less so.

Unfortunately, the Warren Commission was mistaken in stating that no evidence of conspiracy was found. There is some evidence, which, although not conclusively indicative of conspiracy, could lead reasonable people to conclude that more investigations were needed. It was oversights like these, usually blamed on the deadline pressures the commission faced, that gave ammunition to the critics who claimed cover-up. Members of the commission rarely, if ever, defended their conclusions or answered questions, which did not endear them to the critics.

THE FIRST TRIAL: YOU DON'T KNOW JACK

Attorney Melvin Belli was satisfied to defend Ruby for free; the publicity he would garner defending Jack Ruby, and the book he would write afterward, would suffice. Unfortunately for Ruby, Belli, a lawyer from California, decided to go with an insanity plea in an attempt to exonerate Ruby rather than have him plead guilty to murder without malice, which carried a maximum sentence of five years.

Belli's defense focused on Ruby's unstable past and his family's history of mental illness. His mother had been institutionalized for mental illness, and when he was a child Ruby had been examined by a psychiatrist. Known for his vicious temper, he had been nicknamed "Sparky" Rubenstein during a stint in a foster home, which had been necessitated by his mother's inability to control him. Ruby's desire to vindicate himself as an avenging hero in the eyes of the world was thwarted by Belli, who undermined his client's dignity in court to the point that many persons in the courtroom and some amongst the prosecution actually felt sorry for Ruby.

Ruby was convicted on March 14, 1964, of the premeditated murder of Lee Harvey Oswald, and he was sentenced to death. In an appeal to the Texas Supreme Court, attorneys Clayton Fowler and Joe Tonahill argued that Ruby could not have gotten a fair trial in Dallas due to the excessive publicity surrounding the case. The appellate court ruled that the defense's motion for a change of venue before the original trial should have been granted, and the court overturned Ruby's conviction and sentence. On October 5, 1966, Ruby was granted a new trial and a change in venue to Wichita Falls, Texas.

From the time of his arrest, there had been a pronounced mental decline in Ruby. Eventually, he did become insane. He became obsessed with the idea that millions of Jews were being murdered in the prison basement, and his turn was coming. He believed that his insanity plea had been a plot concocted because his attorneys had conspired to discredit him in the eyes of the world. Ruby attempted suicide several times, and he was in an agitated state when interviewed by the Warren Commission in the summer of 1964.

In December 1966, Jack Ruby was diagnosed with cancer. Before his retrial could take place, Ruby died of a pulmonary embolism in prison on January 3, 1967.

THE SECOND TRIAL: SHAW LOOKS GOOD
FROM HERE

On January 21, 1969, after twenty-seven months of investigation, the only trial ever conducted of alleged conspirators in the murder of President John F. Kennedy began in New Orleans, Louisiana. Clay Shaw, a prominent New Orleans businessman who founded the International Trade Mart, had been arrested on March 1, 1967. New Orleans District Attorney Jim Garrison charged Shaw with conspiracy to kill President Kennedy. Garrison, a colorful figure with a knack for garnering dramatic publicity, had become interested in Kennedy's murder after his own reelection in 1965. Garrison's original investigation stemmed from two lines of inquiry that had been explored by the FBI in 1963 and 1964.

One lead involved a phone call to authorities from a New Orleans private investigator named Jack Martin. Martin claimed that a fellow investigator named David Ferrie had corresponded with Oswald and had given Oswald instructions in the use of firearms. Ferrie was an eccentric aviator who owned his own plane, a member of the Civil Air Patrol (CAP) during the 1950s, an amateur cancer researcher, and bishop of a radical two-member branch of the Catholic Church. Martin, who knew Ferrie well, decided to connect him to Oswald upon hearing that Oswald was a member of CAP during the same period as Ferrie. Two days after the original call, Martin confessed to the FBI that he had fabricated the story while drunk and had decided to link Ferrie to Oswald in revenge over a personal slight. Despite this admission, Garrison later became convinced that the FBI had failed in their investigation of Ferrie.

New Orleans attorney Dean Andrews provided the second impetus to the Garrison investigation. Andrews, who was primarily an immigration lawyer, claimed to have been contacted on the day after Kennedy's assassination by a mysterious individual named "Clay Bertrand," who asked him to undertake the defense of Lee Harvey Oswald. Andrews could not provide Garrison with any information about Bertrand other than his name, several conflicting physical descriptions, and that Bertrand was bisexual and usually called the attorney when one of his acquaintances was in trouble and needed help. Andrews also claimed Oswald had visited his office, accompanied by several homosexual acquaintances, in connection with legal work Andrews had done for him.

In April 1964, Andrews confessed to the FBI that the entire story was fictitious; Oswald had never contacted him, and there was no such person as Clay Bertrand. The FBI was unable to find anyone who had ever met or even heard of Bertrand. However, in July 1964, while testifying before the

Warren Commission, Andrews again imparted the tale, and he repeated and embellished it again when interviewed by Garrison in late 1966. Andrews eventually admitted he had fabricated the entire story.

In November 1966, Garrison tied the two loose ends together. By claiming that "Clay Bertrand" was actually a pseudonym used by the socially prominent Clay Shaw, a homosexual, Garrison was able to link Shaw to Ferrie, who was also homosexual. After initially questioning Shaw, Garrison decided to drop the investigation against him; however, Shaw reemerged as the focus of suspicion after the death of prime suspect Ferrie on February 22, 1967. Garrison first believed that Ferrie had committed suicide, but the autopsy revealed that a blood vessel had burst in his skull. Ferrie had a history of high blood pressure, and those who knew him believed that strain from Garrison's investigation might have hastened his death.

Garrison's investigation had taken increasingly bizarre turns. For example, unsubstantiated claims were made that Jack Ruby was homosexual and Oswald was bisexual (both were dead by this time). Garrison linked them to known homosexuals Ferrie and Shaw, which Garrison viewed as proof that the president's murder was a homosexual thrill killing. Garrison's "proof" was a witness named Perry Raymond Russo, an insurance salesman from Baton Rouge, Louisiana, who claimed to have known Ferrie and had attended a party with him. On February 27, 1967, Russo was interrogated after being administered sodium pentothal at Garrison's request, and on March 1 he was hypnotized. Over the course of these two occasions, false memories of Shaw, Oswald, and Ferrie plotting the assassination at the party were apparently implanted in Russo's subconscious. Russo's testimony was believable enough to judges at the March 14 preliminary hearing, as they moved to hold Shaw for trial.

During June 1967, an expose on the Garrison probe was aired on NBC. On the show, several witnesses and potential witnesses described attempts by Garrison's staff to coerce testimony buttressing the prosecution's case through bribery and intimidation. Several individuals were offered money or jobs, and two prison inmates were offered deals by Garrison's office in return for perjured testimony. Russo admitted that his testimony at the hearing had been essentially fabricated, and Andrews replied in the negative when asked if Clay Shaw was Clay Bertrand. Shortly after the expose, Garrison's chief investigator resigned and reported to U.S. Attorney General Robert Kennedy that there was no case against Clay Shaw.

In an effort to save face, Garrison began a campaign of media saturation to advance his position. The public willingly believed the romantic image of a lone avenger fighting for justice, which he presented on radio, television, and in print. Garrison, encouraged by the positive response, allowed his theories to grow ever wilder until he was involving Lyndon Johnson, Robert Kennedy, and neo-Nazis backed by Texas oil money. Garrison was also vague about the number of assassins, continually increasing them, until he eventually claimed that more than a dozen took part in Kennedy's assassination.

When the trial of Clay Shaw finally began, Russo downplayed the plotting aspects of the conversations he had overheard at the Ferrie-Oswald-Shaw party, and Andrews admitted that "Clay Bertrand" did not exist. At this point, Garrison brought out witnesses who claimed they had seen Ferrie, Oswald, and Shaw in a car in Clinton, Louisiana, in mid-1963. It appears that these six individuals, known as the Clinton Six, had seen someone resembling Oswald, though they had not come forward until found and questioned by Garrison's investigators. Long after the Shaw trial the Clinton Six were found to be essentially credible by the House Select Committee on Assassinations, but because the committee had sealed the testimony and the original statements obtained by Garrison had not surfaced, it was all but impossible to tell what the witnesses had attested to.

Next for the prosecution was Charles Spiesel, an accountant from New York who claimed that he had attended a party similar to the one Russo described, at which Ferrie, Shaw, and Oswald discussed plans to assassinate Kennedy. On the stand, Spiesel was a less-than-ideal witness. He described how the New York Police Department controlled his thoughts by entering his house disguised as his relatives, which had forced him to fingerprint his own daughter to verify her identity.

Shaw's case went to the jury on March 1, 1969, exactly two years after his arrest. Forty-five minutes later, Clay Shaw was found not guilty of conspiracy to murder John F. Kennedy—but his ordeal was not over. Two days later Garrison arrested him for perjury, claiming Shaw had lied about not being acquainted with Oswald or Ferrie. It took two years of legal struggles and Shaw's life savings to finally get a federal court injunction that prevented Garrison from prosecuting him. Garrison appealed to the U.S. Supreme Court and lost. Shaw filed a multimillion-dollar lawsuit against Garrison, but he died before it could come to trial. Shaw's estate was prevented by law from continuing the suit after his death.

Despite ruining Clay Shaw's life and his own reputation as an investigator, Garrison never gave up. He often stated publicly that he had been on the right track but had been thwarted by the military-industrial complex. In his 1998 book, *On the Trail of the Assassins*, Garrison reiterated the discredited case against Shaw. Shortly before Garrison died in 1992, he felt his views were vindicated when Oliver Stone paid a reported $250,000 to use *On the Trail* as the basis for the film *JFK*.

THE GOVERNMENT RESPONDS AGAIN:
THE HOUSE SELECT COMMITTEE

In March 1975, Abraham Zapruder's film footage of the assassination was aired on national television for the first time. Many in the general public reacted to the "head snap" images, which showed President Kennedy's head moving back and to the left after the third shot. To many in the viewing audience, it appeared that this movement could only have been caused by a bullet striking Kennedy from the front. Because the Warren Commission had concluded that Oswald had fired from behind and above Kennedy's motorcade, a bullet striking from the front could only indicate the presence of a second shooter.

In the spring of 1975, the political climate was right for a reassessment of the Kennedy assassination. President Gerald Ford had called for a new era of honesty in government, and the recent Watergate scandal served to remind Americans that governmental duplicity was a very real phenomenon. Additionally, in its own investigation, the U.S. Senate uncovered evidence that the CIA, with the assistance of organized crime figures, had been involved in assassination attempts against Fidel Castro during the early 1960s. The CIA had not properly informed President Kennedy about the attempts, and the Warren Commission had remained unaware as well, despite the inclusion of former CIA director Allen Dulles as a member of the commission. In April, congressional resolutions were introduced, calling for the reopening of the investigations into the deaths of both John and Robert Kennedy, Martin Luther King Jr., and the attempted assassination of Governor George Wallace. The House Select Committee on Assassinations (HSCA) was established but did little until 1977, when G. Robert Blakely, a law professor with a consuming interest in the mafia, was appointed chief counsel.

The HSCA's forensic panel reviewed the medical evidence and found unequivocally that John Kennedy had been wounded by two shells fired by Oswald's rifle from a point above and behind the president. In a draft of the final report, the HSCA found the Warren Commission's conclusions to be essentially correct. However, at the last minute, the HSCA accepted contentious acoustic evidence that "proved" that a fourth shot had been fired from the grassy knoll. The evidence was a recording of a two-way radio transmission supplied from a Dallas police officer's motorcycle.

The acceptance of the acoustic evidence allowed for renewed speculation about a conspiracy. Blakely decided to follow his suspicions about mafia involvement and named names of possible conspirators, focusing on New Orleans godfather Carlos Marcello, Tampa godfather Santos Trafficante, and former Teamster head Jimmy Hoffa. Though wiretap and surveillance evidence indicated that various organized crime figures disliked the Kennedy brothers and may have been pleased to hear of their deaths, it appears that much of the evidence against the mafia was in the form of unreliable hearsay.

CARVED IN STONE: HISTORY BECOMES CULTURE

Almost immediately after John F. Kennedy was laid to rest, conflicting theories of what occurred began to appear. The first works were based on press accounts of the assassination, and unfortunately some of the original media coverage allowed mistakes, miscommunication, and misleading statements to become a permanent part of the record. It seems that if, as William Manchester said, one naturally "wants to add something to Oswald . . . make him weightier" to infuse Kennedy's death with more meaning, it stands to reason that one would wish to portray a monumental crime as resulting from a significant motivation. Even Jackie Kennedy expressed the wish that her husband would have died at least for the cause of civil rights. So perhaps it is understandable that a distraught nation, dreaming of what might have been, would seize upon the excessive secrecy and manipulative actions of government bodies, the minor unexplained coincidences in the evidence, and the utter senselessness of Oswald's act in an attempt to uncover and understand the "real" (and undoubtedly monumentally significant).

JFK's assassination has become part of American culture. For example, the black convertible in the Zapruder film is familiar—even if the memory of its representation and meaning is lost, the convertible is recognized and its image permanently maintained in photographs or as a cartoon for rock posters and album covers. J.G. Ballard, an English science fiction author, has been remarkably clear on this point. Since the mid-1960s, his work has shown the public's obsession with the imagery and meaning of JFK's assassination. Television shows such as *The X-Files* serve as a reminder to be wary of governmental operatives and "conspiracy theories" while watching "the lone gunman" and "cancer man," who inject people with cancer to kill them. Some speculate the same was done to Jack Ruby to silence him.

After forty years of amateur and professional investigation, no alternative theory has emerged in the assassination of John F. Kennedy that fits the known facts as well as the scenario of Lee Harvey Oswald acting alone. Most, if not all, reputable historians accept this scenario. Hard as it is to accept, random acts of senseless violence can and do cause permanent change and lasting damage. After four decades, we can hopefully begin to accept the verifiable truth about the assassination of President John F. Kennedy.

REFERENCES

Belin, D. W. (1973). *November 22, 1963: You are the jury.* New York: Quadrangle/ *New York Times* Books.

Lifton, D. (1988). *Best evidence.* New York: Carroll & Graf.

Manchester, W. (1967). *The death of a president.* London: Michael Joseph.

NBC News. (1967, June 19). *The JFK conspiracy: The case of Jim Garrison* [Television broadcast]. NBC News Television Broadcast.

Posner, G. (1993). *Case closed.* New York: Anchor Books.

Report of the President's Commission on the Assassination of President John F. Kennedy. (1964). Washington, DC: U.S. Government Printing Office.

Russo, G. (1998). *Live by the sword: The secret war against Castro and the death of JFK.* Baltimore: Bancroft Press.

2

The Boston Strangler:
A Man's Confession
and a City's Unsolved Case

Lindsey Bergeron

THE CRIME, THE SETTING, AND THE PARTICIPANTS

Between 1962 and 1964, at least eleven women were rendered defenseless in the greater area of Boston, Massachusetts, against a vile, yet notorious, serial killer referred to as the "Boston Strangler." This infamous murderer is often classified as America's first contemporary "serial killer" (British Broadcasting Company, 2001). The Boston Strangler case represented the largest string of serial killings since Jack the Ripper in England in the late 1880s (Kelly, 2002). The Boston Strangler would talk his way into the apartments of single women, both young and old, sexually assault most of them, and proceed to strangle the victims to death with a piece of their clothing. For his "signature marking," he often tied stockings or another piece of clothing in a tightly knotted ornamental bow around the victim's neck. Before exiting the crime scene, he positioned the bodies of some victims in sexually obscene positions—this positioning is a common trait of serial killers, especially when sexual assault has been involved. The positioning of the bodies adds a more dramatic effect to the crime scene, sparks media publicity, and gives the killer a feeling of dominance and control. Because the victims of the Boston Strangler were often found spread-eagle and nude, it seemed as though genitalia were "thrust in your face as you came through the doors" (Discovery Channel, 2003).

One of the most controversial issues in the case of the Boston Strangler is the considerable debate about who the Boston Strangler really is. Some people claim that Albert DeSalvo was the Boston Strangler; DeSalvo admitted to killing all eleven victims, as well as two other women who were not originally associated with the Strangler homicides. Others, however, argue that several of the victims following the first homicide were killed as copycat incidents. Regardless of the arguments, the case of the Boston Strangler has never been officially solved.

This chapter examines the victims of the stranglings, the nature of the criminal acts, and the controversy that exists to this day over DeSalvo's admission to being the Strangler. Also included in this chapter are the arguments of others who, for various reasons, still contend that the killer was not DeSalvo; and a discussion of how agents of the U.S. criminal justice system handled this mystifying case, how the media covered the case, and how minute details regarding accounts of the homicides, which were provided by the media, may have enabled copycat killers to commit similar acts or, as in DeSalvo's case, admit to acts that he may not have even committed.

VICTIMS OF THE BOSTON STRANGLER

Table 1 provides basic information about each of the victims. Bardsley and Bell (2003) contend that among the eleven "official" victims of strangulation, six of the women's ages ranged from fifty-five to seventy-five years, and the remaining five victims were notably younger, as ages ranged from nineteen to twenty-three years. Note that Table 1 includes two additional victims: Mary Mullen and Mary Brown, eighty-five and sixty-nine years, respectively. These two women may only be counted as "official" victims in the event that there is accurate information that would deem DeSalvo the one and only Boston Strangler.

The killing spree began on June 14, 1962. Anna Slesers, a fifty-six-year-old physically appealing divorced woman, was found in her apartment brutally strangled to death by way of the belt of her bathrobe. In the months to follow, several other women were killed in much the same way. However, about halfway through the spree, certain characteristics of the victims changed drastically. For example, Sophie Clark, the Strangler's first young victim, differed notably from the previous victims. It seemed as though the Strangler had changed from victimizing older women to younger, more attractive women. Clark, an African American, was the only victim who was not Caucasian. Clark was brutally raped, sodomized, and left for dead; she was

Table 1
Summary of Modus Operandi for the Thirteen Victims

Age	Name	Date of death	Modus operandi (description)
55	Anna Slesers	June 14, 1962	Found with the cord from her housecoat knotted tightly in a bow around her throat. Her housecoat was left open, her legs spread eagle to accentuate her nudity.
85*	Mary Mullen	June 28, 1962	Died of a heart attack in DeSalvo's arms. (Not linked to case until DeSalvo's admittance.)
68	Nina Nichols	June 30, 1962	Strangled by way of her stockings. Blood found in her vagina. Proof of sexual assault. Housecoat left open to accentuate her nudity.
65	Helen Blake	June 30, 1962	Strangled with her own nylon stockings with her bra entwined through them. Found nude and with legs spread apart. Proof of sexual assault. No spermatozoa present.
75	Ida Irga	August 19, 1962	Found strangled in her apartment. Propped up by a pillow placed beneath her buttocks, and her feet were tied to the rungs of a chair. Proof of sexual assault. No spermatozoa present.
67	Jane Sullivan	August 20, 1962	Strangled by way of nylons. Found ten days after her death in the bathtub with head under the spigot. Assumed to have been sexually assaulted by way of a broom.
20	Sophie Clark	December 5, 1962	Strangled with three pairs of nylons. Found spread eagle in living room. Evidence of rape.
23	Patricia Bissette	December 31, 1962	Found in bed with covers up to her chin. Strangled by way of numerous stockings and her blouse. She was vaginally raped, with additional damage to rectum. Bissette was one month pregnant at the time of her murder.

continued

Table 1 (continued)

Age	Name	Date of death	Modus operandi (description)
69*	Mary Brown	March 9, 1963	Found in her apartment, beaten and stabbed. (Not linked to case until DeSalvo's admittance.)
23	Beverly Samans	May 6, 1963	Found nude and spread eagle. Killed by four stab wounds. Handkerchiefs tied decoratively around her neck. No evidence of rape or sexual assault.
58	Evelyn Corbin	September 8, 1963	Strangled by way of nylon stockings. Found with underwear stuffed in her mouth. Spermatozoa present in her mouth.
23	Joann Graff	November 23, 1963	Strangled by way of two nylon stockings. Teeth marks found on her breast, and the outer area of her vagina was blood-spattered and lacerated.
19	Mary Sullivan	January 4, 1964	Murdered in the most grotesque manner of all the strangulations. She was initially strangled by way of a single dark stocking. Next, the stocking was overridden by a pink scarf tied into a large bow under her chin. A card that read "Happy New Years" was positioned to rest against her feet. She was in a sitting position against the headboard with a broomstick protruding out of her vagina and semen dripping from her mouth to her breasts.

*Indicates that these were not necessarily cases linked to the Boston Strangler. These cases are pending on DeSalvo being the Strangler. Note the inconsistencies that these counts portray. Why are there such differences in the modi operandi if these acts were committed by one person?

found hours later by her college roommate. Beverly Samans, another young victim, died as the result of four stab wounds, yet she resembled the previous victims of the Strangler in that she was "decorated" with handkerchiefs around her neck. Although she was found in a sexually obscene position, there was no evidence of sexual assault. Law enforcement officials noted the inconsistencies. The other victims had been strangled, not stabbed, and sexually sodomized. The murder of the Strangler's last victim, nineteen-year-old Mary Sullivan, put the police, public, and top law enforcement over the edge and gave them one mission: to catch the Boston Strangler.

According to Newton (2000, p. 206), "in a sexually motivated murder, the killer's personal fixation determines his [or her] choice of victims." Although the Boston Strangler did focus his/their personal fixation on women, the following questions have been raised: Why did their ages differ so much? Why were some women brutally raped, and others were merely left exposed? Why was one victim as old as eighty-five years and another as young as nineteen years? Newton (2000) argued that these differences seemed to reflect the work of more than one person—a serial killer tends to focus on one type of victim. Therefore, why is it that some people attribute these alleged acts of murder to one person, namely Albert DeSalvo? These questions were divergent parallels that even DeSalvo could not answer. In an interview following his "confession" to being the Strangler, DeSalvo failed to explain such inconsistencies:

Attractiveness had nothing to do with it. . . . When this certain time comes on me, it's a very immediate thing. When I get this feeling, instead of going to work I make an excuse to my boss. I start driving and I start building this image up, and that's why I find myself not knowing where I'm going. ("The Boston Strangler 2003," 2003)

Next, I will examine the life of Albert DeSalvo and explain why some were, and still remain, satisfied to call him the Boston Strangler.

ALBERT DeSALVO: THE BOSTON STRANGLER?

Albert DeSalvo was the product of a broken, abusive, and violent home. DeSalvo was born in 1931, and from a young age he lived with an alcoholic father who regularly physically abused Albert, his siblings, and his mother. His father brought home prostitutes and forced DeSalvo and his siblings to observe the sexual activities, which very possibly predisposed DeSalvo to his insatiably sexually voyeuristic drive and other acts of physical violence (Newton, 2000). DeSalvo also explored his own sexuality at a very early age. In a later interview with F. Lee Bailey, his defense attorney, DeSalvo reported that he was taught fellatio by an older girl when he was nine years old (Bailey, 1971).

When DeSalvo was a juvenile, he was convicted of several crimes, including breaking and entering (Newton, 2000) and assault and battery on more than one occasion (Bardsley and Bell, 2003). The DeSalvo family was very poor. As a result, Albert's father, Frank, educated his children on how to commit crimes to obtain money. DeSalvo's early exposure to deviance and criminality perhaps set the stage for his escalated acts of violence and criminality in the future.

At seventeen, DeSalvo enlisted in the U.S. Army and was stationed in Germany. While stationed overseas, he met his wife, Irmgard, who he brought back to the United States. In 1956, however, he was discharged from the army after he was accused of molesting a nine-year-old girl. Following this incident, DeSalvo and his wife had marital difficulties. He also insisted on having sexual intercourse more than five times per day, and he would depict a very cold demeanor when Irmgard would resist. Their marital problems escalated when their first child was born with a handicap. The child's handicap bothered DeSalvo and disrupted his home life; this frightened Irmgard. She also refused to have sex with DeSalvo, fearing she would bear another child with a handicap. This, in turn, further complicated DeSalvo's life because he had an extraordinarily insatiable sexual thirst that needed to be quenched several times per day. Where or how could he abandon such ravenous desires?

The Measuring Man

In 1961, a few years before the case of the Boston Strangler emerged, a string of peculiar sex offenses began in Cambridge, Massachusetts. These incidents commenced during the same period as DeSalvo's marital problems and were being committed by someone the media called "The Measuring Man." The alleged offender, who was in his late twenties, would knock on apartment doors of young women and inquire if they would like to model swimsuits and formal gowns for a modeling agency with which he claimed to be affiliated. The compensation would be forty dollars per hour, and if the woman was interested, often by way of flattery, he would take out a tape measure, obtain measurements, and fondle the women as he worked. He would tell these women that they would be contacted by telephone if their measurements were appropriate for his agency.

Obviously, none of these women ever received a call because no such agency existed. Ultimately, some of the women contacted law enforcement, and the news media publicized these strange incidents. In mid-March of 1961,

DeSalvo was caught trying to break into a residential home. Without hesitation, he admitted to breaking and entering, and ultimately confessed to being the Measuring Man. He served a two-year jail sentence.

The Green Man

In 1964, about three years after his release from prison on charges associated with being the Measuring Man, DeSalvo was arrested again. However, this time the pending charges were more brutal in nature. DeSalvo's sexual frustration had built up, and he had adopted a more belligerent, violent role. At the end of October 1964, he was convicted of breaking into a woman's home and threatening her with a knife to her throat. He wore green clothing similar to a maintenance man. He stripped off her clothes, used her own garments to tie her legs spread eagle to the bedposts, jammed her underwear into her mouth, and persisted to passionately kiss and fondle his victim. Before DeSalvo escaped the residence, the woman got a good look at his face, and the police sketch matched that of the Measuring Man. DeSalvo was arrested and released on bail (Gambrell, 2001).

His wife showed no sign of bewilderment; Irmgard was fully aware of her husband's inexhaustible allure for sex. His wife, being very understanding about DeSalvo's fixation, urged him to be honest about what happened. DeSalvo initially admitted to assaulting up to four women in various towns in Connecticut within the course of one day, and then he admitted to sexually assaulting women in four states. He claimed to have broken into over 400 apartments, raping some and sexually assaulting over 300 women. However, DeSalvo had the reputation of being a "confirmed braggart" and had the propensity to greatly fabricate many stories and situations. However, Newton attests that "many repeat killers commit various other sex crimes through the years before they 'graduate' to homicide. A pedophile or serial rapist may assault dozens—even hundreds—before he starts killing. For some, murder is the pinnacle of 'achievement,' an end in itself and the only means for sexual release" (2000, p. 205).

The heinous acts of murder committed by the Boston Strangler occurred between June 14, 1962, and January 4, 1964; DeSalvo was not incarcerated during the time the strangulations had occurred (Bardsley and Bell, 2003). Two months after being released from prison for the Measuring Man charges, Anna Slesers, the Strangler's first victim, was killed. DeSalvo remained free until ten months after the last victim was found. DeSalvo was apprehended in November 1964 for charges associated with the Green Man. As the convicted Green Man, DeSalvo, at this point, had not mentioned anything about nor had be been linked to the case of the Boston Strangler.

DeSalvo was admitted to Bridgewater State Hospital for surveillance and assessment by psychiatrists.

While at Bridgewater, DeSalvo came into contact with a precarious criminal inmate, George Nassar. Nassar was in Bridgewater for the gruesome murder of a gas station employee. He had a genius-level IQ and employed the extensive ability of manipulation. DeSalvo and Nassar became close friends at Bridgewater because they were placed in the same area. Nassar informed his defense attorney, F. Lee Bailey, that DeSalvo had admitted to him that he was the "Boston Strangler." Bailey arranged a meeting with DeSalvo to question him about his alleged "admittance" to being the Boston Strangler. After a meeting with DeSalvo, it was agreed that Bailey would be DeSalvo's defense attorney.

In March 1965, DeSalvo's wife received a call from Bailey. He forewarned her that there was going to be a big explosion in the media with reference to her husband (Bailey, 1971). He advised her to assume a different name and leave the area with her children to eschew media exposure. The next day, Irmgard was called back with the news that DeSalvo had confessed to being the Boston Strangler.

Why Did DeSalvo Admit to Committing These Heinous Criminal Acts?

Susan Kelly (2002), who has researched the case of the Boston Strangler, believes that Nassar had manipulated DeSalvo while they were at Bridgewater. The time that had elapsed between when DeSalvo entered Bridgewater and when he committed the murders had given DeSalvo and Nassar plenty of time to converse and plan how to manipulate the media and law enforcement. With Nassar's high IQ and DeSalvo's criminal record, the possibilities were endless. DeSalvo felt burdened with how he was going to provide for his family financially while in prison; he knew he was probably facing life in prison even without the Boston Strangler conviction. There was much speculation about how DeSalvo could sell his story and amass the reward to care for his family even though he could no longer physically be a part of their daily lives. Nassar may have fueled the fire regarding DeSalvo's admittance to being the Strangler. DeSalvo and Nassar were aware of the reward money that would be granted to the person or persons who provided information leading to the capture and conviction of the Boston Strangler. The agreement is speculated as follows: Nassar would turn DeSalvo in, DeSalvo would plead guilty to the murders, and the two would ultimately split the money. This appeared to be a plausible solution to DeSalvo's problem of providing financial support for his wife and children.

In early March 1965, DeSalvo admitted to Bailey that he had committed the eleven alleged acts believed to be committed by the Strangler, as well as two other murders. On Bailey's second visit with DeSalvo, he believed without a doubt that DeSalvo was the killer. Bailey contended:

I became certain that the man sitting in that dimly lit room with me was the Boston Strangler. . . . Anyone experienced in interrogation learns to recognize the difference between a man speaking from life and a man telling a story that he had either has made up or has gotten from another person. DeSalvo gave me every indication that he was speaking from life. He wasn't trying to recall words; he was recalling scenes he had actually experienced. He could bring back the most inconsequential details . . . the color of a rug, the content of a photograph, the condition of a piece of furniture. . . . Then, as if he were watching a videotape replay, he would describe what had happened, usually as unemotionally as if he were describing a trip to the supermarket. (Bardsley and Bell, 2003, p. 2)

Bailey believed that DeSalvo was indeed the serial killer because, among other reasons, he showed no lack of remorse, which is a common trait of serial killers. Newton (2000) attested that the Strangler case was consistent with several criminological sources that indicated serial killers do not use firearms or knives to commit murder. They strive to torture their victim, have power and control over them, and kill them in a consistent way to achieve their goal of "leaving their mark."

Arguments that DeSalvo Wasn't the Strangler

As is the case with many serial killer suspects, not one person who knew DeSalvo alleged that he could have been the Boston Strangler (Bardsley and Bell, 2003). Many of his acquaintances, coworkers, and family members knew DeSalvo to be a decent family man with a gentle and kind spirit, and merely an occasional thief.

In 2002, Kelly wrote a book, *The Boston Stranglers*, which supports the theory that DeSalvo did not murder the eleven women. Kelly believed that while many of DeSalvo's confessions were accurate, he falsified himself as the Strangler. She stated, "The newspapers were an excellent source of information and it's very interesting to me that the details that Albert got wrong in his confession were identical to the details that the newspaper got wrong" (CBS News, February 15, 2001). She further contended that "the circumstances of the killings were so thoroughly and so well documented in the newspapers that anyone who wanted to rid himself of an inconvenient woman, or kill one for the thrill of it, or for any other reason, had a blueprint to do so" (Kelly, 2002, p. 441).

Kelly believes there were numerous dissimilar perpetrators who committed these heinous acts of murder. She acknowledged that DeSalvo did, in fact, admit to killing the eleven women, along with the two other women whose deaths were unrelated to the Strangler murders. However, not one piece of physical evidence tied DeSalvo to any of the murders. Kelly contended that none of the eyewitnesses could correlate DeSalvo's prominent demeanor to any of the crime scenes. Many witnesses cited his dark hair, "beak-like nose," and memorable eyes. However, other eyewitnesses who saw the Strangler more commonly recognized George Nassar, DeSalvo's cellmate at Bridgewater. The eyewitness accounts further supported the argument that DeSalvo was not the only murderer, or even part of the stranglings at all.

In accordance with Kelly's theory, Robert Ressler, a former FBI profiler and criminologist, agreed that it seems highly improbable that only one person could be held accountable for all of the Strangler murders (CBS News, 2001). He stated, "You're putting together so many different patterns here that it's inconceivable behaviorally that all these could fit one individual" (CBS News, 2001).

If DeSalvo was, in fact, the only killer, there are several inconsistencies present in areas that serial killers, especially those who leave their mark, remain unfailingly consistent. The victims represented a diverse female population, representing ubiquitous differences in age, race, and physical attractiveness. Kelly (2002) believed the deviations in the patterns to be so severe that they could not have been the acts of one serial killer. The murderer sexually assaulted some of the women but not all of them. Serial killers have a propensity to opt for and affix to a particular category of victims. Thus, the modi operandi—the way the murders were committed and the individuals who were victims—were not identical, which is quite paradoxical and becomes increasingly imminent when analyzing victim characteristics. I will later examine current DNA evidence that, by way of modern science, further supports the argument that DeSalvo is not the alleged Strangler.

ACTIONS TAKEN BY THE CRIMINAL JUSTICE SYSTEM

More than a year and a half had passed since the first murder, and between June 1962 and January 1964, more than a dozen women met violent deaths. However, a lack of suspects prevented the police from solving the case. Although the public regarded these murders as the act of one individual, the police viewed the case differently. These women were all killed in their own apartments with no signs of forced entry; they were strangled with various articles of clothing; and most, but not all, were sexually abused. The lack of evidence of forced entry indicated that the women voluntarily let the assailant(s) into their homes. The public faulted the police for many things; however, contrary to the fast-paced rhetoric in the Boston area, women were still letting the Strangler into their apartments. Did these women know the assailant(s), or was he deceivingly talking his way into their homes? Because the police had no evidence, few witnesses, and few leads to pursue, they resorted to drastic approaches.

Following the murder of Mary Sullivan, the Strangler's last victim, Attorney General Edward Brooke of Massachusetts wanted the people in the Boston area to know that disentangling the Strangler case was of paramount priority. Because this case spanned across the jurisdictions of five police departments, Brooke's objective was to synchronize a wide assortment of police department activities to enhance the efficiency of law enforcement. These dramatic actions were necessary because different police departments in the area were withholding information from other departments due to covetousness, hostility, and petty feuding. Meeting Brooke's objectives would entail permanently reallocating the use of a task force to work only on the Strangler case.

Assistant Attorney General John S. Bottomly headed the Strangler Bureau Task Force. The task force was led by Detective Phillip DiNatale and Special Officer James Mellon of the Boston Police Department, Lieutenant Andrew Tuney of the Massachusetts State Police, and a "medical psychiatric advisory committee with several well-known experts in forensic medicine" (Bardsley and Bell, p. 2). The goal of the Strangler Bureau Task Force was to work around the clock and pursue every lead that might guide them toward the Strangler. To facilitate the beginning of the task force and to solicit public knowledge regarding the case, a $10,000 reward was offered to any person who presented information contributing to the "arrest and conviction" of the Boston Strangler. The Strangler Bureau had a lot of work to do; there were over 37,000 pages of reports with information to organize and analyze. The forensic experts were in charge of analyzing differences regarding the discrepancies in the modus operandi, and they came to the conclusion that it seemed highly unlikely that one person committed all of the murders. Overall, the Strangler Bureau did collaborate much of the evidence; yet it never successfully convicted any person or persons as the official Boston Strangler.

THE MEDIA

Due to the exposure to earlier serial killers in other countries, namely Jack the Ripper in England in the late 1880s and Vampire of Duesseldorf in Germany in the 1930s, the media had inadvertently fashioned a pervasive apprehension toward publicizing the serial killer phenomenon. Certain names within society are "legendary," as those noted above, in addition to cases such as David Berkowitz, also known as the "Son of Sam."

People in Boston lived in trepidation for two years mainly because newspapers, radio, and television apprehended the story and fueled fires that encouraged widespread panic in the area. Following the first murder, many women lived in a state of constant fear. According to a Discovery Channel documentary, "Boston Strangler: Forensic Evidence" (2003), there was such a vast panic among women in the Boston area that women who previously lived alone moved in with one another, and women set up telephone networks to assure each other that they were all right. An article in *Life* magazine featured how the women in the Boston area were reacting to the fear of becoming a victim of the Boston Strangler. The article portrayed the women of Boston as peering through chained doors and placing bottles inside their apartment door so they could hear the bottles collide if an intruder entered.

The media led the public to believe that the Boston Strangler murders were the work of one murderer only, which was contrary to evidence and opinion of law enforcement. The Discovery Channel documentary contended that the press "rolled all of the crimes into one neat package with a perpetrator known as the Boston Strangler" (2003). The press enjoyed portraying the idea that there was one crazed serial killer on the loose in Boston. Kelly argued that "the killer could also be that the press—particularly the *Record American*—would attribute the crime to the phantom fiend, as would public opinion, which then, as now, was shaped by the media" (2002, p. 441). She also asserted that the media made it appear as though all of the murders were committed with the same modus operandi, which was known not to be the case. Some Boston newspapers publicized the mistakes the police had made, accusing them of being exceptionally incompetent and inefficient in their law enforcement skills and practices.

If DeSalvo was not the Boston Strangler, he may have learned all of the information he "admitted" to from the media. DeSalvo appeared to have had memorized a chart, which was located in several newspapers, that included in-depth details and events. Kelly cited several information sources that DeSalvo possibly utilized to attempt to assume the title of the Boston Strangler (2002). She claimed that the newspaper reports were exceptionally comprehensive; according to Kelly, they included the victim's attire, minutiae of each incident, and other exhaustive details. Kelly theorized that DeSalvo memorized this chart before admitting that he committed the crimes. However, the chart contained both factual and nonfactual information, and DeSalvo allegedly recited both the accurate information as well as the inaccurate information that had been displayed. However, Bailey would argue that by way of his interviews with DeSalvo, DeSalvo could provide exhaustive information about the victims and their residences that only the police and the killer could know (1971).

Kelly claimed that the Suffolk County medical examiner unreservedly circulated information concerning details of victim autopsies. Kelly also contended that because DeSalvo was in so many women's apartments as the Measuring Man and the Green Man, he was familiar with the layouts and allegedly sought out each apartment after the murders.

Kelly contended that many were very eager to solve the Strangler case, and DeSalvo had been provided with in-depth information regarding each victim, so the case of the Boston Strangler would meet its end. She included that Bottomly, a member of the Strangler Bureau, "did knowingly and quite intentionally provide Albert with information about the murders—while he was taking the latter's confession to them . . . which explains why the only version of it [the confession] ever made public was abbreviated and heavily doctored. The full version virtually exonerates DeSalvo" (2002, p. 247). Kelly lastly pointed out that DeSalvo obtained information from Nassar, an inmate of Bridgewater and also a confidant of DeSalvo's. Speculation has occurred and some evidence given that Nassar had, in fact, committed several of the murders in the Boston Strangler case.

By the time that the public believed that the "one and only killer" was behind bars, there was a collective sigh of relief; the moral panic or fear people had for their lives appeared to have ended. The Boston Strangler case had exhausted its media intrigue until DeSalvo and two other inmates escaped from Bridgewater. Another panic loomed as television, radio stations, and newspapers emphasized the seriousness of and the area from where DeSalvo had escaped. According to FBI files and Boston-area newspapers, DeSalvo and two inmates escaped from Bridgewater five weeks after he was imprisoned. The escape of the self-proclaimed "Boston Strangler" has been regarded as the biggest manhunt in Massachusetts state history.

DeSalvo was eventually apprehended. While having coffee with some employees at a uniform shop, he asked, "Can I use the phone? I want to make a call to F. Lee" (Associated Press, 1967, March 7). The employees immediately recognized the name, and they called the police. DeSalvo claimed that he knew all along that the employees knew his identity. The employees were all shocked by DeSalvo's quiet and pleasant demeanor. According to FBI files, he told the employees "to call off the police because he wanted to turn himself in." More than 2,000 people gathered outside the shop to witness his arrest. According to newspapers, DeSalvo escaped from prison to "force public officials to admit that he is the Boston Strangler" (FBI; Associated Press, 1967, March 7).

AN ACCOUNT OF THE TRIAL

Although nobody has formally been on trial for the infamous Boston Strangler murders, DeSalvo admitted with great credibility to committing the strangulations of the eleven victims, as well as two other victims who were not thought to be affiliated with the same case. However, there was no solid evidence on which to try DeSalvo for the thirteen murders. Due to legalities, DeSalvo's confession was unacceptable as evidence. When DeSalvo confessed, he was a patient in Bridgewater and because of the circumstance of his location—being an inmate at a prison and mental hospital— and lack of evidence, this confession could not be used against him. Also, DeSalvo's confession was not considered as solid evidence because there was no physical evidence connecting him to any of the thirteen murders. Also, at the time of the murders, many forensics tests, such as DNA testing, did not exist. DeSalvo was already convicted as the Measuring Man and as the Green Man, and he was already sentenced to life in prison for armed robbery, sexual assault and battery, and breaking and entering.

On January 10, 1967, DeSalvo's trial for the Green Man crimes began. Donald L. Conn led the prosecution, and F. Lee Bailey defended DeSalvo's in Judge Cornelius Moynihan's court.

Bailey advised DeSalvo to plead not guilty by reason of insanity to the sex offenses associated with the Green Man crimes. Thus, DeSalvo was not on trial for the crimes committed by the Boston Strangler, but was being tried for the Green Man crimes. Four victims were present at the trial, and all gave similar accounts of what DeSalvo had done to them. Bailey proclaimed that he "had no doubts that DeSalvo committed the crimes as charged and the only issue was whether the commonwealth could prove that he was not insane at the time" (Bardsley and Bell, 2003, section 17, p. 2). After four hours of jury deliberation, DeSalvo was convicted on ten counts of indecent assault and armed robbery as the Green Man. He was sentenced to life in prison.

Bailey advocated that DeSalvo was in need of psychiatric help, and he strongly believed that DeSalvo could be used as a means to find out what makes people kill. Bailey states, "Society is deprived of a study that might help deter other mass killers who lived among us, waiting for the trigger to go off inside them" (Bardsley and Bell, 2003, section 17, p. 2). Thus, Bailey's goal was to use DeSalvo as a research instrument to get at the heart of what made him kill. Bailey believed, without a doubt, that DeSalvo was indeed the Boston Strangler.

However, why would DeSalvo admit to being a sadistic serial killer who had committed thirteen acts of murder if he did not commit them? Several sources cite that Bailey pressured DeSalvo to plead not guilty by insanity, in essence, to avoid the death penalty.

Another possible explanation is that DeSalvo wanted to become famous as a result of being the Boston Strangler. Because he knew he was already looking at a life sentence in prison and had a wife and children to provide for, DeSalvo could have been "advised" by Bailey to gain a little cash and fame by admitting to this infamous series of murders. It was a means of attaining notoriety and monetary means for his family. Richard DeSalvo, Albert's brother, strongly believes that Bailey took advantage of DeSalvo. Richard DeSalvo claimed that the case helped provide Bailey with fame and a book deal.

DeSalvo, who was known to be a braggart and had adamantly cemented his life sentence, may have believed that he might as well become famous. Dr. Ames Robey, former director of Bridgewater State Hospital and Penitentiary, said, "Albert had a tremendous need to be world famous" (2003).

However, if DeSalvo was not the notorious Boston Strangler, how could he have recalled so many vivid details about the murders and the crime scenes? According to Bailey, DeSalvo could recall, with great accuracy, many minute details known only by law enforcement officials. Bailey stated,

The details of all these cases were bricks adding up to a wall of truth. DeSalvo knew, for instance, that there was a picture of Helen Blake's (victim number three) niece atop her radio. He said he had a cup of coffee with twenty-three-year-old Patricia Bissette, victim number seven. Only the police knew that a half-full cup of coffee had been found in the living room of her Back Bay apartment. He recalled the design of the headboard against which he had placed the body of nineteen-year-old Mary Sullivan. He had to be the Strangler, I thought. He knew too much not to be. (Bailey, 2001, p. 185)

A later interview with Bottomly revealed additional evidence linking DeSalvo to the case. Once again, this was evidence only the police were privy to. As Bailey contended,

Details piled upon details as DeSalvo recalled the career of the strangler, murder by murder. He knew that there was a notebook under the bed of victim number eight, Beverly Samans; he knew that Christmas bells were attached to Patricia Bissette's door. He drew accurate floor plans of the victims' apartments. He said he'd taken a raincoat from Anna Sleser's apartment to wear over his T-shirt because he had taken off his bloodstained shirt and jacket. Detectives found that Mrs. Slesers had bought two identical raincoats and given one to a relative. They showed the duplicate to DeSalvo, along with fourteen other raincoats tailored to different styles. DeSalvo picked out the right one. (Bailey, 1971, p. 204)

Bailey was very vibrant in advocating that DeSalvo committed these acts. The prosecution and the defense attorney were working together, yet the only difference was that the defense was pleading insanity. Bailey wanted to make sure that DeSalvo would not be executed; speculation suggested that Bailey pursued the insanity plea because he was running for the U.S. Senate, and he wanted to make sure that everything with DeSalvo's case was politically and socially correct.

THE FINAL RESOLUTION OF THE CASE

Following DeSalvo's arrest, he was transferred from Bridgewater to Walpole State Prison, where he would serve out his life sentence. It was here that DeSalvo was stabbed to death on November 26, 1973, for allocations not related to the Strangler case. A few days before DeSalvo's death, he contacted Dr. Robey and asked him if he wanted to know the "real story" of the Boston Strangler. Robey answered "of course," and they agreed to meet on November 26. DeSalvo was stabbed repeatedly to death in the heart hours before he was to meet with Robey. DeSalvo's fellow inmates allegedly killed him—DeSalvo was discovered slain in his bed. According to a Discovery Channel documentary (2003), Robey believed that this homicide was directly tied to the case and was more likely an attempt to silence DeSalvo. He died just before he was going to speak the "final truth" to Robey. Did he know something that would incriminate one or more of his fellow prisoners? It seems as though we'll never know for sure.

SOCIAL, POLITICAL, AND LEGAL ISSUES

The case of the Boston Strangler still haunts the greater Boston area. Casey Sherman, the nephew of Mary Sullivan (the Strangler's last victim), concluded that much of the evidence supporting DeSalvo's innocence was never made available to the public. Sherman has spent numerous hours re-examining DeSalvo's confession tapes, police investigations, crime scenes, and DNA evidence, and arrives at the same conclusion: DeSalvo did not do it. He believes that Bailey had manipulated DeSalvo into confessing.

Although the case of the Boston Strangler is almost forty years old, it still continues to captivate and intrigue many as new evidence still surfaces. However, what has been assumed over the past four decades—that DeSalvo was the Boston Strangler—may now be proven not true due to new forensic evidence, which supports Sherman and Kelly's theories that DeSalvo did not commit all, if any, of the murders. Recently, two families, the family of Mary Sullivan and the family of Albert DeSalvo, have formed an anomalous alliance to challenge DeSalvo's culpability. In 2001, Diane Dodd, sister of Mary Sullivan, still did not feel at ease with the case closed and DeSalvo as the murderer. Dodd's instincts kept telling her that they have yet to "find her real murderer."

New evidence had to be gathered for forensic evidence to provide a match to DeSalvo. In late October 2001, DeSalvo's body was exhumed from a grave in Massachusetts and examined at York College in Pennsylvania. To gather new support for Dodd's instincts, she decided to have her sister's body exhumed and re-examined. This second autopsy did reveal some new information, although the body was badly deteriorated. DeSalvo claimed that he had strangled Sullivan with his bare hands, however, the autopsy revealed evidence to the contrary: an unbroken hyoid bone.

James Starrs, forensics expert, said, "We have found evidence and the evidence does not and cannot be associated with Albert DeSalvo" (CBS News, 2000, September 15). Starrs addressed the issue of Sullivan's hyoid bone, stating that if Sullivan would have been strangled by hand, her hyoid bone would likely have been broken. The second finding from the autopsy was hair from the killer found in Sullivan's pubic area; the hair did not match DeSalvo's DNA, which was procured from a DNA sample provided by Richard DeSalvo. Last, DeSalvo claimed he raped Sullivan, yet there was no evidence that she had been sexually assaulted. Starrs concluded, "If I was a juror, I would acquit him with no questions asked."

In 2003, Sherman, Sullivan's nephew, wrote *A Rose for Mary: The Hunt for the Real Boston Strangler*, in which he stated, "He [DeSalvo] did not kill my aunt" (CBS News, 2000, September 15). Sherman, like Kelly, believed that the victims were slain by multiple copycat killers. Sherman claims to know who his aunt's murderer is, and he believes that the murderer may still be at large. Sherman and relatives of DeSalvo have filed a lawsuit to bring the Boston Strangler case to justice and to find the original murderer(s) or, if not, to solve the case in as far as to pronounce that DeSalvo was not the Boston Strangler. Sherman stated, "I never set out to exonerate Albert DeSalvo" (p. 195). He believed that there was no clear or consistent evidence that tied DeSalvo to the case. Sherman also stated, "My goal is to find Mary's killer, and I'm not going to stop until I do" (p. 195).

Sherman strongly believes evidence in the murder of Mary Sullivan pointed to his aunt's ex-boyfriend, Preston Moss. Sherman did research and located a local bar that Moss regularly frequented. Some hair samples were obtained from a baseball cap that Moss had left at the bar. The hair samples, which contained Moss's DNA, were sent to a lab for forensic experts to see if they could obtain a match to the sample found on Sullivan. Sherman contended,

"The DNA test showed the odds were one in five that Moss murdered Mary" (p. 196).

Because Moss had been a suspect in Mary Sullivan's death, he had a lawyer pending from that investigation. Authorities refused to comply with Sherman's request for a blood test to confirm that Moss was Mary Sullivan's killer. Sherman decided to contact Moss himself, using the alias, Wayne Rose. Sherman located Moss, who was now a golf instructor in a city about three hours away from Boston. Sherman as "Rose" contacted Moss for a "golf lesson." After meeting for the lesson, the two were in a golf cart when Sherman identified himself as Sullivan's nephew. Moss grew very defensive and initially refused any comment except "talk to my lawyer." When Sherman asked Moss of his whereabouts the day of Sullivan's murder, he claimed that he was "watching football with his dad and uncle." He persistently claimed over and over that he did not murder Mary Sullivan over forty years ago.

Sherman informed Moss that he knew about the lie detector tests that had never been made available to convict him for the case and about the witnesses such as Sullivan's roommate, Pamela Parker. Moss continued to plead his innocence, and Sherman finally left. Sherman stated, "I concluded that iron bars were not needed to jail Mary's killer. If Moss did it, he was already in a psychological prison. He was being guarded twenty-four hours a day by a conscience that would not let him forget what he had done" (pp. 201–202). Sherman later referenced several sports encyclopedias and uncovered another piece of evidence: "No college or professional football games were played or televised on January 4, 1964" (p. 202), which was the day of Mary Sullivan's murder.

A FINAL CASE FOR DeSALVO

Although he was never officially tried for the Boston Strangler case, however, DeSalvo could explain in exact detail what he did, items in victims' apartments, and the apartments' floor plans. Further DNA evidence is still needed to examine supplementary information regarding DeSalvo's guilt or innocence. DeSalvo contacted a reporter the night before his murder to tell him that he was going to reveal who the real Boston Strangler was, as well as other unsolved mysteries regarding the case. However, because DeSalvo was killed, he never made it to the appointment. Was DeSalvo murdered because someone in prison found out he was going to tell the truth or was DeSalvo hungry for a resurgence of attention regarding the case? It is possible that we may never know the answers to these questions. As the case of the Boston Strangler remains open, there is hope that modern forensic science can uncover the truth and bring justice to the perpetrator(s) and peace to the families of the victims and to the greater Boston area. Sherman claimed that before DeSalvo admitted to the counts of strangulation, police had a "prime suspect" in the case, but they dropped the ideology after DeSalvo's confession. With evidence and his beliefs supporting him, Sherman thinks the police still need to "go after the real killer," who he believes is still alive and residing in the New England area.

If a case similar to this were to happen today, the mere presence of modern-day DNA testing would have proved DeSalvo's guilt or innocence. From a legal standpoint, advancements in forensic testing would have had an impact on the case of the Boston Strangler.

However, if DeSalvo was not the killer, why did these mysterious strangulations cease? Interestingly, DeSalvo composed the following poem a couple of years before his demise:

Here is the story of the Strangler, yet untold
The man who claims he murdered thirteen women,
Young and old.
The elusive Strangler, there he goes,
Where his wanderlust sends him, no one knows
He struck within the light of day
Leaving not one clue astray.
Young and old, their lips are sealed,
Their secret of death never revealed.
Even though he is sick in mind,
He's much too clever for the police to find.
To reveal his secret will bring him fame,
But burden his family with unwanted shame.
Today he sits in a prison cell,
Deep inside only a secret he can tell.
People everywhere are still in doubt,
Is the Strangler in prison or roaming about?

(Kelly, 2002, p. 452)

HOW THE CASE IMPACTED LEGAL AND POPULAR CULTURE

There are several prominent factors relating to the popular and legal cultures of the case of the Boston Strangler. The Strangler's second-to-last victim, Joann Graff, was strangled and raped twenty-four hours after the assassination of John F. Kennedy. The country was already in great upheaval because of the stranglings, and now the nation mourned the president.

Popular cultural parallels exist in the greater Boston area. The Strangler case facilitated the celebrated well-known culture of this infamous New England city. In Boston, tours are available to visit various Boston Strangler sites. Two sites to visit on the tour are the apartment addresses of the first and last victims of the Boston Strangler. They are well-known sites: 79 Gainsborough Street, Back Bay (formerly known as 77 Gainsborough) and 1435 Commonwealth Avenue, Allston.[1]

The Boston Strangler has been characterized as the "first serial killer of the modern era," and vast attention has been raised toward the case. Several movies and documentaries have been made—a horror movie, *The Boston Strangler,* was made in 1968 starring Tony Curtis and Henry Fonda, and various documentaries include *Unsolved Mysteries, 60 Minutes,* and other news programs.

The case of the Boston Strangler has continually resurfaced in the media because of its notorious unknown resolution. The legal culture suffered within its jurisdiction to solve the case even though DeSalvo openly admitted to being the Strangler. Critics have put some blame on the FBI for their eagerness to disentangle the case. The city of Boston and the FBI were jovial in supposing that DeSalvo was the Boston Strangler: His criminal background, admittance to the crimes, and proclaimed accurate knowledge of the crime scenes and strangulation victims. Yet, DeSalvo was never brought to trial because of deficiency in suitable validation of evidence.

The case of the Boston Strangler, though it is not yet resolved, is recognized for its implications in future multiple homicides in the United States. For example, the phenomenon could have possibly resulted in copycat killings. Because the case of the Boston Strangler is so highly recognized and publicized, many more people were made aware of copycat killings which may enable others to commit serial acts of homicide.

FINAL REMARKS

James Starrs, the medical examiner who lead the fight for the DNA testing on Sullivan and DeSalvo's bodies, held a press briefing on December 6, 2001, in Washington, DC. He announced that no DNA present on or within Sullivan's body matched DeSalvo, proclaiming that DeSalvo did not kill the last victim. This made international news as the Times billboard read "ALBERT DeSALVO IS NOT THE BOSTON STRANGLER" on December 7, 2001.

Based on all of the information presented in this chapter, it seems as though consensus has changed from a general belief that DeSalvo was the Strangler to one, as proved by forensic testing, that he may not have been the Strangler. Did DeSalvo commit any of the stranglings? Maybe, but at this point it seems hard to know and more difficult to prove. Sherman concluded; "Until these murders are truly solved, the Boston Strangler case will haunt New England" (p. 204).

NOTE

1. Information about these Boston tours can be found at http://boston. about.com/cstraveltours/index-2.htm.

REFERENCES

Associated Press. (1967, March 7). "Boston Strangler" gives up in store: DeSalvo hunt ends quietly in Lynn, Mass. *The Washington Post Times Herald.* Retrieved September 1, 2003, from http://foia.fbi.gov/desalvo.htm

Bailey, F. L. (1971). *The defense never rests.* New York: The New American Library.

Bardsley, M., and Bell, R. (2003). The Boston strangler controversy. *Crime Library.* Retrieved July 17, 2003, from http://www.crimelibrary.com/serial—killers/notorious/boston

The Boston strangler. (1964, March 6). *Life Magazine.*

Boston strangler: Forensic evidence. (2003, November 8). [Television broadcast]. Washington, DC: Discovery Channel.

Boston strangler 2003. (2003). Retrieved July 17, 2003, from http://www.geocities.com/Hollywood/4003/boston.html

Boston strangler is not says DNA. (2001, December 6). *United Press International.* Retrieved August 22, 2003, from Infotrac database.

British Broadcasting Company. Crime cased closed: The Boston Strangler. Retrieved September 5, 2003, from http://www.bbc.co.uk/print/crime/caseclosed/strangler.shtml

CBS News. (2000, September 15). Strangler case still haunts Boston. Retrieved from http://www.cbsnews.com/stories/2000/09/14/national/main233462.shtml

Falsely Accused: Who is the Boston strangler? (2002, January/February). *The Forensic Examiner, 1,* 47.

Federal Bureau of Investigation. (n.d.). Freedom of information and privacy acts: Albert DeSalvo. Retrieved July 10, 2003, from http://foia.fbi.gov.desalvo.htm

Federal Bureau of Investigation. Freedom of Information and Privacy Acts. Subject: Albert De Salvo, a.k.a. The Boston Strangler. Retrieved September 1, 2003, from http://foia.fbi.gov/desalvo.htm

Frank, G. (1966). *The Boston strangler.* New York: The New American Library.

Gambrell, M. (2001, September). The Boston strangler's confession—truth or fiction? Retrieved September 17, 2003, from http://www.suite101.com/article.cfm/unsolved—mysteries/76305

Kelly, S. (2002). *The Boston stranglers.* New York: Kensington Publishing.

Last Boston strangler victim exhumed for DNA tests. (2000, October 16). *United Press International.* Retrieved August 25, 2003, from Infotrac database.

Newman, M. (2000). *The encyclopedia of serial killers.* New York: Checkmark Books.

Sherman, C. (2003). *A rose for Mary: The hunt for the real Boston strangler.* York, PA: Maple Press.

Strangler in doubt. (2001, December 17). *MacLean's.* Retrieved August 28, 2003, from Infotrac database.

Wuebben, M. (2001, February 15). The Boston strangler. Retrieved July 10, 2003, from http://www.cbsnews.com/stories/2001/02/14/48hours/main272108.shtml

3

Lenny Bruce Obscenity Trial: Free to Be Obscene

Jim Sinclair

Lenny Bruce was a comic felon—ironically, he was both prosecuted by and defended by the privileged and affluent. In his own lifetime, Bruce's speech was censured by conservatives and denigrated by liberals alike. U.S. Supreme Court Justice William Brennan Jr. wrote opinions in obscenity cases, and his view of the First Amendment was central to the Court's decision in *People v. Bruce*. The opinion explains how Bruce was prosecuted, defended, once exonerated on appeal, and how he could have legally been vindicated had he lived longer.

The story of Lenny Bruce has little mention in the recorded history of the First Amendment. There is no celebrated Bruce precedent because his cases have been virtually forgotten, but the following account is of the way that speech plays to people and power. Although the law prosecuted him, the culture acclaimed him after his death. Bruce is now regarded as a hero of free speech and is celebrated in many media forums. He himself attributes his persecution to the prevalence of a certain religious point of view.

LENNY BRUCE AND THE FIRST AMENDMENT

The primary impact of the Bruce trial was related to the First Amendment. The evolution of free speech rights often occurs at the expense of cultural

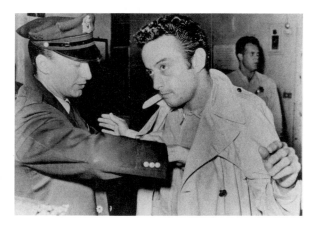

The arrest of Lenny Bruce. (Courtesy of Library of Congress)

outlaws who must be martyred so that their crusades are validated posthumously. This is exactly what happened to Bruce.

The relationship between law and subversive comedy and how Bruce's case was argued is problematic. Bruce's guiding principle was his faith in free speech. He stated, "The First Amendment is . . . the only strength our country has. . . . A country can only be strong when it knows all about the bad—the worst, worst things. When it knows about the bad, then it can protect itself" (Collins and Skover, 2002, p. 9).

Implicit in his statements is a core principle of freedom. If the First Amendment is worth anything, its worth must derive in part from the commitment to protect the cultural outlaw while alive, while offensive, and while extreme to the point of blaspheming all things sacred. Just how that is done, if at all, is what makes the story of *People v. Bruce* relevant.

Lenny Bruce, however, was simply a comic. He did not want to be a martyr for the First Amendment—he just wanted to entertain, free from censorship. His goal was free speech for the living.

Comedy as Commentary

By the time Bruce appeared before a three-person panel of federal appellate judges in 1964, he had been recognized by some critics as some sort of unusual nightclub comedian or oral "poet." *Time* magazine had termed him as a "sicknik" comedian (*Time*, 1959, p. 42). He introduced himself to the panel as "author, lecturer, and social satirist" (de Grazia, 1992, p. 444). He was trying to make a good impression on the judges, so he could persuade them to stop Manhattan District Attorney Frank Hogan and three judges in a criminal court in New York County from sending him to jail for his performance at the Café Au Go Go in Greenwich Village. However, during the time in which he performed his monologues in nightclubs, cabarets, and coffeehouses, Bruce was stopped several times by police in San Francisco, Beverly Hills, Chicago, and New York for being indecent and obscene. Subsequently, Bruce lost the case and was sentenced to four months in jail. The owner of a New York club, the Café Au Go Go, Howard Solomon, was also convicted and fined. After that conviction, no club owner in New York was willing to book Bruce for fear of being arrested, fined, or jailed.

Bruce's nightclub performances were artistic and full of socially relevant, yet controversial, ideas about Catholics, Jews, lesbians, African Americans, white liberals, married couples, and political figures including President Lyndon Johnson, Eleanor Roosevelt, Barry Goldwater, Jackie Kennedy, Dick Gregory, and Francis Cardinal Spellman. During his shows, Bruce would use words like "cocksucker." It was the terminology Bruce employed, rather than the parties against whom his material was directed, that got him into trouble. To indict him it was necessary that his performance be deemed obscene and without social value, based on the social patois he used as a vehicle for his commentary.

The three judges on Bruce's case—John M. Murtagh, J. Randall Creel, and Kenneth M. Phipps—sat regularly on the Criminal Court of the County of New York, and should have been prepared to deal with the subtleties of the law of obscenity as it was expounded by the Supreme Court at this time. Nevertheless, only Creel appeared to acknowledge the complexity of the basic question presented by the prosecution: were Bruce's performances at the Café Au Go Go suppressible obscenity, or were these performances considered speech protected by the First Amendment (de Grazia, 1992, p. 462)? Only Creel dissented from the judgment reached by the majority, in an opinion written by Judge Murtagh, that Bruce was guilty as charged for giving three "obscene, indecent, immoral and impure" performances at the Café Au Go Go (de Grazia, p. 462).

In Murtagh's opinion, he cited examples of obscenity from Bruce's performance such as "ass," "balls," "cocksucker," "cunt," "fuck," "motherfucker," "piss," "screw," "shit," and "tits" (de Grazia, p. 462). Murtagh then identified other monologues of Bruce's that he considered to be "similarly obscene":

1. Eleanor Roosevelt and her display of "tits"
2. Jacqueline Kennedy "hauling ass" at the moment of the late President's assassination
3. St. Paul giving up "fucking"
4. An accident victim who made sexual advances toward a nurse while on the way to the hospital in an ambulance

5. "Uncle Willie" discussing the "apples" of a 12-year-old girl
6. Seemingly sexual intimacy with a chicken
7. "Pissing in the sink" and "pissing from a building's ledge"
8. The verb "to come" with its obvious reference to sexual orgasm
9. The reunited couple discussing adulteries committed during their separation, and the suggestion of a wife's denial of infidelity, even when discovered by her husband
10. "Shoving" a funnel of hot lead "up one's ass"
11. The story dealing with the masked man, Tonto, and an unnatural sex act
12. Mildred Babe Zaharias and the "dyke" profile of 1939

(de Grazia, p. 464)

All three of Bruce's performances that had been cited by the prosecution were found to be obscene, indecent, immoral, and impure within the meaning of Section 1140a of the Penal Law of New York City.

Section 1140a was an archaic statute, and its overlapping adjectives—"indecent, immoral, impure"—had never been clarified through litigation and were vague, inexplicit, and clearly out of harmony with current state and federal laws (Goldman, 1971). No conviction obtained under the Section's catch-all provisions would hold up to the scrutiny of appellate courts; consequently, the only purpose that could be served would be the harassment of the defendant, who would have to spend thousands of dollars to free himself.

The dominant themes of Bruce's performances were deemed to appeal to prurient interests and be patently offensive to the average person in the community, as judged by present-day standards. The performances were lacking in "redeeming social importance," and the monologues were not assessed as being erotic or lust-inciting, yet they "insulted sex and debased it"(de Grazia, 1992, p. 445ff).

The monologues contained "little or no literary or artistic merit. . . . [They were] merely a device to enable Bruce to exploit the use of obscene language. . . . [They were] devoid of any cohesiveness. . . . [They were a] series of unconnected items that contained little social significance. . . . [They were] chaotic, haphazard, and in-artful" (de Grazia, p. 464).

Murtagh's opinion also concluded that it was obscene for Bruce to have "fondled the microphone stand in a masturbatory fashion" during the first condemned performance and to have "turned his back to the audience and moved his hand outward from below his waist in an obvious and crude pantomime of an act of exposure and masturbation" (de Grazia, p. 464). All of this was said to be obscene not because of its capacity to arouse sexual feelings in the audience, but because it was "filth," because "its predominant appeal is to . . . a shameful or morbid interest in nudity, sex, or excretion" (de Grazia, p. 464). He made no effort to support this conclusion, just as the prosecution had made no attempt to prove it.

As mentioned earlier in this chapter, what landed Bruce in jail were the words he chose to use and not the parties against whom they were directed. For the prosecutor to prevail in court, a "Lenny Bruce bit" could be only be dirty words and vulgarity exempt of any redeeming social worth. Bruce's offenses were deemed obscene. Bruce's intention was to challenge the social conventions of speech—he demanded conversational freedom as his constitutional right.

THE GRAPES OF ROTH

U.S. Supreme Court Justice William J. Brennan Jr. said, "The First Amendment does not protect 'speech which is out rightly lewd and indecent'" (Collins and Skover, 2002, p. 25). In the landmark First Amendment case, *Roth v. United States* (1957), Brennan expressed ambivalence about applying First Amendment rights to erotic expression. There were concessions to the power of the states to regulate morality. These concessions were ill-defined as "'narrowly limited classes of speech,' which are not given the protection of the First Amendment. . . . By universal agreement one such exception is speech which is out-rightly lewd and indecent" (Collins and Skover, 2002, p. 27). Brennan wrote the above in a 1953 obscenity opinion for the New Jersey Supreme Court. He had granted that the state's authority to preserve "decency and good order" was encompassing enough to prohibit any show with a "dominant effect" of disseminating "dirt for dirt's sake." He was careful, nonetheless, to specify a range of speech-protective norms to guard against censorship based on a "highly subjective view of morality." Consequently, Brennan raised the following questions in the opinion:

Does every reference to . . . the sex relationship ipso facto classify the presentation as lewd and indecent? Does the presentation become [obscene] if the censor's view is that the subject matter or its treatment is not fit for commercial exhibition to patrons of public places of public entertainment while suitable for presentation before medical societies or under educational or social welfare auspices? Can the presentation be banned in total as lewd and obscene because a part—even a minute part—is coarse, vulgar, or profane? (Collins and Skover, 2002, p. 28)

Ten years later, these were precisely the questions that were raised in the obscenity prosecutions of Lenny Bruce in New York. Unfortunately, in 1953,

Brennan's answer was more rhetorical than useful. When Brennan took his seat on the U.S. Supreme Court, he addressed the same questions and answered them with much of the same ambivalence. He did so in his majority opinion in *Roth v. United States*, the controversial 1957 precedent that contributed to the prosecutions of Bruce and many other transgressors of the prevailing moral code.

The account of *Roth v. United States* is complex, and its nuances and relationship to Lenny Bruce are described here:

Sam Roth, a New York publisher of risqué literature, was sentenced to five years and fined $5,000 for sending an "obscene, lewd, lascivious, and filthy" magazine called *American Aphrodite* through the U.S. mail. David S. Alberts, a Los Angeles book distributor, was placed on a two-year probation on condition of serving sixty days and paying a $500 fine for distributing and advertising such "obscene and indecent" books as *Sword of Desire*, *She Made it Pay*, and *The Business Side of the Oldest Business*. On appeal, both Roth and Alberts conceded to having violated their respective state obscenities laws, although they challenged the constitutionality of those statutes. The two cases were conjoined, and came to be known by the single and famous title, *Roth v. United States*. (Collins and Skover, 2002, p.28)

In the Roth decision, Justice Brennan writes:

This court has always assumed that obscenity is not protected by the freedoms of speech and press. Implicit in the history of the First Amendment is the rejection of obscenity as utterly without socially redeeming importance. There are certain well-defined and narrowly limited classes of speech, the prevention and punishment of which have never been thought to raise any constitutional problem. These include the lewd and obscene ... It has been well-observed that such utterances are not essential parts of the exposition of ideas, and are of such slight social value as a step to truth that any benefit that may be derived from them is clearly outweighed by the social interest in order and morality. (Collins and Skover, 2002, p. 28)

The Court's opinion, as written by Brennan, suggested that obscenity was, by definition, worthless—no analysis or balancing was necessary. For prosecutors, this opinion meant that if they succeeded in branding a book, movie, play, or performance as "obscene," the offender was then convicted. Unfortunately for Lenny Bruce, his case was in the hands of three judges who were all too willing to find that his *shtick* was no essential part of the exposition of important ideas.

In contrast was the liberal interpretation. Charles Rembar remarked with respect to the more liberal side of the opinion: "[Roth] contained within it (nearly hidden and at the same time unnoticed) the seed of future freedom-giving cases" (Collins and Skover, p. 29).

According to Brennan,

Here is the language that inspired that assessment: Sex and obscenity are not synonymous. . . . [Obscene material is] material having a tendency to excite lustful thoughts. . . . All ideas having even the slightest importance—unorthodox ideas, controversial ideas, even ideas hateful to the prevailing climate of opinion—have the full protection of the guarantees, unless excludable because they encroach upon the limited are if more important interests. (*Roth v. United States*, 1957, para 3)

The opinion had its consequences. Brennan indicated that sexual material was no longer labeled obscene outright. Moreover, Brennan suggested that a finding of obscenity hinged on evidence that a work elicited some erotic response. Finally, those messages with sexual material interpolated with social commentary ranked more highly acceptable on the First Amendment scale. For Bruce, the legal opinion would prove encouraging to the minds of some judges appraised of the nuances in his unorthodox and controversial *shtick*. So Justice Brennan's "insoluble enigma" was one that left the judiciary "lost in the wilderness," according to constitutionalists John Nowak and Ronald Rotunda (Collins and Skover, 2002, p. 32). Paradoxically, the Court's opinion in *Roth v. United States* pleased conservatives and liberals alike even as it troubled them. The most memorable portion of the opinion that would find its way into so many state and federal obscenity statutes was Judge Brennans's rather infamous formula for determining obscenity with respect to the material under consideration: (1) whether it could be determined as obscene to the average person; (2) whether it could be determined as obscene after applying contemporary community standards; (3) what was the dominant theme of the material taken as a whole; and (4) whether there were any explicit appeals to prurient interest in the material under question (Collins and Skover, 2002, p. 32).

Each of these four aspects was relevant to Lenny Bruce's case.

First, with respect to the "average person" standard, Bruce's "bits" were not to be judged either by the thin-skinned sensibilities of persons of a bluestocking persuasion or by the more robust sensibilities of nautical types. Identifying the mind-set of the "average person" could have proved to be a intrinsically problematic.

Second, the "contemporary community standards" criterion meant, for example, that Bruce's acceptability in a cosmopolitan locale was not to be governed by the norms of a more rural locale and vice versa. Bruce took his chances when he ventured from San Francisco to St. Louis at a time when mores were fixed in some places and fluid in others. Furthermore, Justice Douglas stated the following in his dissent in *Roth v. United States:* "If the First Amendment guarantee of freedom is to mean anything . . . it must allow protests even against the moral code that the standard of the day sets for the community" (*Roth v. United States*, 1957, footnote 9). Douglas had anticipated the problem Bruce would face—the social contrarians who contest the very community standards by which they will one day be judged.

The third aspect in Brennan's list suggested that Bruce's entire routine could not be considered obscene because of a few phrases that were taken out of context. Accordingly, the work could be considered holistically—an assumption that some of Bruce's future prosecutors would later challenge.

The final determinant was, by far, the most difficult to prove. On the one hand, "prurience" was synonymous with inciting libidinal thoughts. But, buried in a footnote in *Roth v. United States* was a passage that Bruce's prosecutors would stress repeatedly: "Prurience includes 'a shameful or morbid interest in nudity, sex, or excretion' described in a manner going 'substantially beyond customary limits of candor'"(*Roth v. United States*, 1957). With that footnote, the *Roth v. United States* opinion failed to distinguish between what was considered vulgar (i.e., coarse and offensive language) and what was obscene (i.e., sexual immorality)—a dichotomy emphasized by the Supreme Court since 1895.

In June 1957, the U.S. Supreme Court delivered its decision in *Roth v. United States*, which was significant because it helped to liberate the First Amendment as it pertained to obscenity. Three and a half months later, Judge Clayton Horn of the San Francisco Municipal Court issued his sympathetic opinion in *People v. Ferlenghetti*,[1] the first California court decision in which the mandates of *Roth v. United States* for obscenity prosecutions were interpreted.

GOLEM IN GOTHAM

When Bruce was arrested for obscenity for the first time in New York in April of 1964 at the Café Au Go Go in Greenwich Village, it was for a violation of Section 1140a of the New York Penal Code. His arrest and trial was of considerable interest to the media for several reasons.

First, the 1960s was a decade defined by the clash of political, social, and cultural values. Riots, protests, and demonstrations had become prevalent topics in media coverage. Bruce's speech was an important form of protest. Second, the media emphasized individual figures as representatives of particular movements, and Bruce was already a well-known figure before his involvement with the U.S. criminal justice system. Finally, Bruce pushed the limits of protected speech. As society searched for its new boundaries in what was appropriate behavior and expression, the media became the place to explore and thus define these boundaries. The media were also being challenged by Bruce's case: Bruce pushed the First Amendment to its limit, and thus reporters struggled with supporting or condemning a freedom that they so staunchly defended.

At his trial, Bruce was represented by Ephraim London, who argued that the prosecution had not proved that Bruce had violated Section 1140a. Allen Schwarz, one of London's colleagues representing Howard Solomon, claimed that Ella Solomon, coproprietor of the Café Au Go Go, could not be prosecuted under Section 1140a because she was not involved in the management or direction of Bruce's performances.

London offered three fundamental reasons why the complaint against Bruce should be dismissed (Collins and Skover, 2002, p. 216). First, the New York obscenity statute was meant to protect performers like Bruce insofar as it specifically exempted them. London highlighted the text of Section 1140a that explicitly declared that "this statute shall not apply" to anyone "participating in a performance merely as an actor" (Collins and Skover, 2002, p. 216ff). Second, London argued that the statute violated the U.S. Constitution because it was vague. A violation under the statute was inextricably linked to "the corruption of the morals of youth or others" (Collins and Skover, p. 216ff). London contended that the statute was an impermissible standard for obscenity under the 1957 Supreme Court precedent set in *Roth v. United States*. London declared that "The standard must be the average adult of the community," which was in reference to Justice Brennan's formula for determining what was obscene. To identify the mind-set of such a person would be problematic at the very least. For the purposes of the prosecution, the "morals of youth" proviso should be disregarded entirely.

After all bases were argued, Judge Frederick Strong ruled against dismissal of the complaint. The trial was then postponed because Bruce was hospitalized for pleurisy. On May 13, 1964, Justice Gerald P. Culkin of the New York State Supreme Court denied the defense's motion for a jury trial.

The trial convened on Tuesday, June 30, 1964. London replayed his three-point strategy. First, the statutory interpretation argument was, given the precedent of *State v. Wendling* (*People v. Wendling*, 1932), that there would be no prosecution under Section 1140a for coarse and vulgar language alone. London maintained that Section 1140a be limited to monologues that "excite lustful and lecherous thoughts"; otherwise, as the New York Court of Appeals reasoned, it would be obscene "to the language of the street rather than that of the scholar" (Collins and Skover, 2002, p. 217). Second, the facial constitutionality argument stated that the text of the statute penalized that which demonstrably "tends to [the] corruption of morals of youths or others," and this standard violated the U.S. Supreme Court's free speech doctrine.

Although these were legal arguments; they were the kind of legal arguments that, in time, could win Bruce's freedom. For the third point, London argued the *Roth v. United States* obscenity criteria of patent offensiveness judged by contemporary community standards.

In New York, there was little mention of the one-week-old decision in *Jacobellis v. Ohio*, which was the case that London had argued successfully before the U.S. Supreme Court. District Attorney Kuh, the prosecutor, reduced the decision in *Jacobellis v. Ohio* to the obvious proposition that "obscene terms are not within the constitutional protection of the First Amendment" (Collins and Skover, 2002, p. 250). More importantly, he directed the New York judges to the Illinois Supreme Court's recent ruling in *People v. Bruce*: a unanimous bench held that "certain scatological terms somewhat similar to [these here] were vile," and therefore unprotected by the First Amendment (Collins and Skover, p. 250). In effect, Kuh argued that the most relevant law was that of a state court, rather than of the U.S. Supreme Court; that the Illinois decision against Bruce trumped the U.S. Supreme Court decision, which might have saved him.

Kuh had a twofold strategy for his cross-examination strategy. First, there was the focus on the person of Bruce: his character, qualifications, and biases. Second, there was the focus on Bruce's performance: its unity, offensiveness, and social value. In the attack-the-person category, one of Kuh's preliminary strategies was to challenge the expertise of the expert. His favorite attack-the-person stratagem was to reveal any bias in the defense's expert witnesses. The second general category of Kuh's cross-examination involved questions about Bruce's performance, with one notable stratagem within this category being divide and conquer. Kuh would take the offensive words out of context and then judge their worth. He aimed to demonstrate that Bruce's crudities lacked any meaningful artistic value.

Another of Kuh's cross-examination strategies stemmed from Justice Brennan's admonition in *Roth v. United States* that a work, to be judged obscene, must be taken as a whole.

The Office of the State's Attorney created a conundrum. Although obscenity is without any socially redeeming importance, the opposite is not true. An otherwise offensive material cannot be immune from obscenity regulations just because it also contains a nugget of social value or the smidgeon of an idea. The New York prosecution suggested that the correct interpretation of *Jacobellis v. Ohio* must be that as a general rule, a court cannot weigh the merits of a work against the prurient appeal of its sexy parts.

On the one hand, if the decision in *Jacobellis v. Ohio* was to redeem a work that contained an iota of social importance, "there could be no [real] enforcement of the obscenity laws," as the state argued. On the other hand, if the decision in *Jacobellis v. Ohio* was to allow censorship because of the laws or the disgusting manner of expressing otherwise valuable ideas, there could be no real enforcement of free speech guarantees. Obscenity control, after all, is regulation of "manners." Thus, if the First Amendment were to mean anything in the obscenity context, it must protect ideas of value despite the socially unapproved manner of their expression. The question was whether the Illinois Supreme Court would appreciate this conundrum. The effect of obscenity censorship on an open society was the topic (Collins and Skover, 2002, p. 270).

On April 15, 1965, the defense's first fear was realized. On remand from the U.S. Court of Appeals for the Second Circuit, the federal district court in Manhattan dismissed Bruce's first Section 1140a civil rights case against New York prosecutors and judges, *Bruce v. Hogan*. Within eleven days, Edward de Grazia, Bruce's new counsel, filed a petition to the U.S. Supreme Court to review the matter of *Bruce v. Hogan*. The petition raised the following four constitutional questions:

1. Whether the First and Fourteenth Amendments do not guarantee Petitioner the right to deliver dramatic monologues dealing with subjects of topic importance anywhere in the nation regardless of state lines or varying local standards or conflicting state court decisions and whether such a right may not be declared by a federal court
2. Whether the federal courts are powerless to restrain state judicial action when it is being applied against an individual in such a way as to abridge his constitutional right to free speech and deprive him of his livelihood and occupation without due process of law
3. Whether the federal courts are powerless to restrain state law enforcement officials from actions against an individual, taken under color of law, when these acts are abridging his constitutional right to free speech and depriving him of his livelihood and occupation within the due process of law
4. Whether it is not an abuse of judicial discretion for a federal court to decline to enjoin actions by a state court and/or state officials taken under color of law, when these actions are shown to be restraining a person from speaking on subjects having topical interest. (Collins and Skover, 2002, p. 319ff)

On June 1, 1965, the U.S. Supreme Court denied Bruce's petition for certiorari in *Bruce v. Hogan* (*Bruce v. Hogan*, 1965), which was filed on his behalf by Edward de Grazia and Ernst Liebman. Justice Murtagh and his colleagues passed sentence on Bruce on November 4, 1964.

On November 24, Judge Ryan's sentence from March 14, 1963, of one year in jail and a fine of $1,000 on a charge of obscenity committed, was overturned—the sentence stemmed from Bruce's performance at the Gate of Horn in Chicago. The same Illinois Supreme Court that had voted seven-to-zero to sustain Bruce's Chicago obscenity case conviction now voted seven-to-zero to reverse and discharge it. On November 24, 1964, the Illinois appellate justices adduced a per curiam decision. It consisted of a meager 540 words, only a quarter of which might be called all too kindly "legal analysis." It is apparent from the opinions of the majority in *Jacobellis* that "the per curiam decision acknowledged that material having any social importance is constitutionally protected" (Collins and Skover, 2002, p. 301).[2] Then, the Illinois justices openly displayed their lack of respect toward the U.S. Supreme Court ruling:

We would not have thought that constitutional guarantees necessitate the subjection of society to the gradual deterioration of its moral fabric, which this type of presentation promotes. Still, the Illinois Supreme Court conceded begrudgingly "that some of the topics commented on by the defendant are of social importance." Accordingly, the justices are unanimously held that "under [*Jacobellis*] the entire performance is thereby immunized." (Collins and Skover, 2002, p. 301)

THE BLOOD OF THE MARTYR

In New York, the defense's appellate brief for *People v. Solomon*, which was filed eighteen months after the death of Bruce, was nearly one hundred pages long and consisted of eight main arguments. Hellerstein[3] raised challenges under several Amendments to the U.S. Constitution: First Amendment (free speech), Fifth Amendment (self-incrimination), Sixth Amendment (jury trial), and Fourteenth Amendment (due process and equal protection). Among his most colorful arguments were the following:

- The New York obscenity law was unconstitutional as applied to Solomon. Bruce's monologues neither appealed to prurient interest nor were lacking in redeeming social value.

- The state failed to prove a prima facie case that Bruce's acts were contrary to contemporary community standards.

- The New York statute that denied Solomon a right to a jury trial was unconstitutional.

- When Solomon was compelled to turn over and testify about the Café Au Go Go audiotapes. His rights against self-incrimination were violated.

(Collins and Skover, p. 344)

Seymour Krim (1970) made the argument for the artist as outlaw. According to Krim, dissident artists must necessarily exist outside the bounds of the law's protection. Ultimately, the integrity of the artist cannot coexist with the integrity of the law. At some point, art and law must forever be at war if each is to be true to itself. This relationship depends on the notion of the First Amendment that an artist's use of word taboos must be judged, at least in significant part, by community standards. The notion of the community judging art as a matter of law is premised on an idea that is rejected by the legal fraternity, as they believed that an artist's use of word taboos is dissident expression that is not to be judged by community standards. Accordingly, the criminal law could never penalize the artist for transgression of them. By this measure, art and law do not need war, at least not in the facts presented in *People v. Bruce*. When Bruce was irreverent, ribald, raunchy, and tasteless, he was an American with rights. When he was seemingly unrestrained and unrepentant before the judges, Bruce was a Madisonian dissident demanding his constitutional due. Under this view of the First Amendment, comedy of that sort should not be put on trial.

To allow a man or woman to stand proudly on his or her constitutional rights does not mean, of course, that society must or should applaud the expression that gave rise to the need to invoke constitutional protection. There is something very risky about venturing to apply criminal sanctions against such comedians while attempting to remain within the boundaries of a viable and vibrant First Amendment. What *People v. Bruce* revealed was the need to protect dissident comic expression as one would protect political expression. Community standards have always been a potential threat to artistic expression.

Justice Brennan learned a valuable lesson when he found that he could not define obscenity in a manner consistent with the freedoms of free speech: "After sixteen years of experimentation and debate I am reluctantly forced to the conclusion that none of the available formulas [for obscenity] . . . can reduce the vagueness to a tolerable level while at the same time striking an acceptable balance between the protections of the First Amendment . . . [and] the asserted state interest in regulating the dissemination of certain sexually oriented materials" (Collins and Skover, 2002, p. 414).

Brennan was reluctant, but nonetheless willing to extend First Amendment protection to trump most, if not all, obscenity laws. This reluctance can be traced to Brennan's belief that the First Amendment protected political speech, first and foremost. The following statement from his *Roth v. United States* opinion explains his original belief: "The protection given speech and the press was fashioned to assure the unfettered interchange of ideas for the bringing about of political and social changes desired by the people" (Collins and Skover, p. 415).

Thus understood, the First Amendment existed to ensure this enlightenment function, one essential to the well-being of civil society. From that perspective, "prurient interest" expression could be difficult to defend.

Importantly, the various *People v. Bruce* cases illustrate the difficulty of categorical divisions between protected and unprotected expression. Bruce's comedy was a compound expression having both political and so-called indecent elements—his comedy was not simply one or the other.

Professor Harry Kalven of the University of Chicago had represented Bruce in his appeal of conviction in the Gate of Horn obscenity case, and he was keenly aware of the shortcomings of Brennan's opinion in *Roth v. United States*. He saw three major faults with the opinion (Collins and Skover, p. 415ff). First, Roth was predicated on a "two-level theory of free speech." Expression is either protected (e.g., political expression) or unprotected (e.g., obscene expression). The theory was elementary: speech was either valuable or without value. Of course, the theory could easily be applied to the speech in Bruce's acts at the Jazz Workshop and the Café Au Go Go. For example, the theory is concerned with what Kalven called—before he had even met Bruce—the "problem of mixed utterance."

The next problem Kalven identified in Brennan's *Roth v. United States* opinion was the implication that speech should not be protected unless it somehow contributed to the "marketplace of ideas." This rationality-focused aspect of *Roth v. United States* did not portend well for protection of artistic, literary, or other forms of emotive expression. Some of Bruce's comedy, to the extent that it was akin to jazz, could be classified (again believed erroneously under *Roth v. United States*) as outside the sphere of First Amendment protection. Kalven's final concern was that *Roth v. United States* could be interpreted by the government to restrict free speech, which happened in some of the *People v. Bruce* cases, though ultimately *Roth v. United States* and its progeny vindicated Bruce's styles of expression.

Thus, *People v. Bruce* was an ideal case for Kalven to litigate in the Supreme Court. Here was one of the great teachers of free speech who was instructing one of the great judicial defenders of free speech. It gave the professor the perfect opportunity to demonstrate the problematic character of Roth to Justice Brennan and the other members of the Court. More importantly, *People v. Bruce* could be the catalyst to transform the antiquated First Amendment to a modern First Amendment, if only because it depicted both so well. On one hand, it had a societal protest component; on the other hand, it had a sexually indecent component. Combine and protect them both and what results is a First Amendment released from the shackles of eighteenth-century notions of free speech liberty: A First Amendment with bold new breadth. In any event, that is where *People v. Bruce* might have taken the Supreme Court had the case ever been argued there. Also, the Court might have vindicated the First Amendment perspective of Kalven, who said, "We have very few really free spirits, and I think we should cherish all of them" (Collins and Skover, p. 417).

The privilege against compulsory self-incrimination in the Fifth Amendment is one of the fundamental guarantees of American constitutional freedom. The Amendment commands: "No person shall be . . . compelled in any criminal case to be a witness against himself." Essentially, it is a right to remain silent. And when invoked in a courtroom, its exercise cannot be equated with guilt or adverse inference. The Fifth Amendment privilege is a command to the state to prove its own case without any help from the accused. As a criminally accused defendant, Bruce may have benefited from the Fifth Amendment, but as a comedian his future lay with the First Amendment: The right to speak freely and openly. Some of his liberal lawyers seemed not to have full appreciation for Bruce's freedom of speech.

Bruce's struggles for free speech were about precisely the freedoms to say not only what he wanted but also to say things how he wanted. That principle was confirmed by a jury in San Francisco, affirmed by the Illinois Supreme Court, and ultimately reaffirmed by the New York Supreme Court in *People v. Solomon*. It should now become a part of our national law and our culture of free speech. Justice Brennan once counseled that speech be "uninhibited, robust, and wide-open." To observe the status quo is to exercise restraint and to be inhibited. The difficulty lies in that caution, and it will regress into cowardliness and into a willingness to self-censor, especially in the present climate of observing political correctness. When that happens, the prospects for a vibrant First Amendment are weak. From lack of courage, there arises the loss of liberty and once liberty is lost, not much remains.

More than any legal precedents, the possibility of ongoing harassment culminating in death changed the First Amendment culture. The 500 or so comedy clubs in the United States have become free speech zones, which are public places where First Amendment freedom is virtually unrivaled. In March 1977, a ruling in *Pacifica Foundation v. FCC* included the following statement, made by Judge Edward A. Tamm with respect to the Federal Communications Commission (FCC): "Despite the Commission's professed intentions, the direct effect of its order is to inhibit the free and robust exchange of ideas on a wide range of issues and subjects by means of radio and television communications. In fact, the order is censorship, regardless of what the Commission chooses to call it" (Collins and Skover, p. 435). However, in the U.S. Supreme Court, it was adjudged that the medium very much mattered. That is, the breadth of the First Amendment protection was linked to the medium of communication. What was legal in clubs and theaters may not be legal on radio and television.[4]

In 1997, the First Amendment embraced the internet. The question was if the First Amendment would extend its highest level of protection to the internet, or if it would permit government to treat the internet like radio or television. The outcomes of *FCC v. Pacifica Foundation* and *Reno v. ACLU* (Pacifica Foundation, 1978; Reno, 1997) were the Supreme Court's first answers to that question. The American Civil Liberties Union (ACLU) contended the Communications Decency Act of 1996 (CDA), which prohibited the transmission of obscene, indecent, or patently offensive material to any person under eighteen years of age. It was Justice John Paul Stevens who penned the opinion of the U.S. Supreme Court in *Reno v. ACLU*— the same Justice Stevens who had urged his colleagues in *Pacifica Foundation* to treat indecent speech as a constitutionally inferior and a less-protected category of expression. *Pacifica Foundation* had turned on the limited First Amendment protection accorded to broadcasting, but the internet was not broadcasting. Among other reasons, users of the internet were not likely to be surprised by objectionable material, and technological means (such as filtering programs) were readily available to protect children (Collins and Skover, 2002, p. 438).

In 1999, the Parents Television Council and Steve Allen, the famous comedian and television host, ran full-page ads to launch a national decency campaign. Allen had defended Bruce in 1964 in a nationally broadcast interview. He defended his stance, saying Bruce was "different. . . . He was never out for cheap sensationalism and shock laughs. . . . He was a satirist who used the device of stand-up comedy to make often penetrating philosophical observations" (Collins and Skover, p. 442). Steve Allen's conclusion was that the man, his message, and the medium were all different. That conclusion being so, the societal response could be different, even censorial. Mindful of First Amendment liberties, Allen astutely conceded that "the right to produce garbage" is constitutionally protected (Allen, 2001, pp. 222, 313; Holston, 1998, p. E1). In that regard, the comedian reiterated a basic tenet of American constitutionalism, namely, that the Supreme Court only bars the government from censoring speech. It does not, by contrast, bar private citizens or corporations from refusing to give a forum to objectionable expression. If liberal free speech advocates threatened to swamp America with indecency, the liberal remedy to curb such excesses could be found in Allen's agenda. Its foundation rested on the First Amendment notion that more speech—this time, protests against commercially subsidized vulgarity and violence—was better. The motivating belief was that the citizenry would hear both sides of the debate and thereafter rationally determine its own course of private action.

There is a consensus today that the life of Lenny Bruce is a great cautionary tale about why First Amendment freedom must be the rule rather than the exception. His story represents freedom as the default position.

NOTES

1. See Ginsberg (1986): Judge Clayton Horn's decision is quoted and the obscenity standard is made explicit.

2. Profane and vulgar language is not alone considered to be obscene (Collins and Skover, 2002, p. 536).

3. William E. Hellerstein was one of the New York attorneys for Bruce's codefendant, Howard L. Solomon, in the appeal of the Café Au Go Go conviction.

4. FCC order banned radio broadcast of alleged indecent language defining sexual or excretory activities in terms patently offensive by contemporary community standards for the broadcast medium at the time of the day when there is a reasonable risk that children may be in the audience. The order specifically banned seven patently offensive words and constituted censorship under the Communications Decency Act of 1996 (Collins and Skover, 2002, p. 535).

REFERENCES

Allen, S. (2001). *Vulgarians at the gate: Trash TV and raunch radio* (pp. 222, 313). New York: Prometheus Books.

Bruce, L. (1967). *The essential Lenny Bruce.* John Cohen (Ed.). New York: Ballantine Books.

Collins, R. K. L., and Skover, D. M. (2002). *The Trials of Lenny Bruce: The fall and rise of an American icon.* Naperville, IL: Sourcebooks, Inc.

de Grazia, E. (1992). *Girls lean back everywhere: The law of obscenity and the assault on genius.* New York: Random House.

FindLaw for Legal Professionals. (n.d.). U.S. Supreme Court; *Jacobellis v. Ohio* 378 U.S. 184 (1964). Retrieved May 27, 2003, from http://caselaw.lp.findlaw.com/scripts/getcase.pl?court=us&vol=378&invol=184 on

FindLaw for Legal Professionals. (n.d.). U.S. Supreme Court; *Roth v. United States,* 354 U.S. 476 (1957). Retrieved May 27, 2003, from http://laws.findlaw.com/us/354/476.html

Ginsberg, A. (1986). *Howl: Original draft facsimile, transcript and variant versions.* Barry Miles (Ed.). New York: Harper & Row.

Goldman, A. H. (1974). *Ladies and gentlemen—Lenny Bruce!!* New York: Random House.

Holston, N. (1998, November 19). Steve Allen says TV is stuck on the wrong channel. *Star Tribune* (Minneapolis), p. E1.

Kofsky, F. (1974). *Lenny Bruce: The comedian as social critic and secular moralist.* New York: Monad Press.

Krim, S. (1970). *Shake it for the world, smartass.* New York: Dial Press.

Kuh, R. H. (1967). *Foolish fig-leaves? Pornography in and out of court.* New York: MacMillan.

Nowak, J., and Ronal, R. (1955). *Constitutional law* (5th ed.). St. Paul, MN: West.

Pacifica Foundation v. FCC, 556 F.2d 9 (D.C. Cir. 1977).

People v. Bruce, 31 Ill. 2d 459, 202, N.E. 2d 497 (1964).

People v. Wendling, 258 Ny. 451, 454, N.E. 180, (1932).

Reno v. ACLU, 521 U.S. 844 (1997).

Roth v. United States, 354 US 476 (1957).

Sales, G. (1991). *Lenny Bruce originals* [CD.] (vols. 1 and 2). Berkeley, CA: Fantasy Records.

4

The Trial of the Chicago Seven: Stage against the Machine

Stephanie N. Whitehead

> There is hardly a political question in the United States which does not sooner or later turn into a judicial one.
> —de Tocqueville, 1838/1969, p. 270

The trial of the Chicago Seven, or the Chicago Conspiracy Trial, is one of the most important political trials in U.S. history (Lukas, 1969, 24 September). It has also been referred to as one of the most chaotic (Evans, 1994). The Chicago Conspiracy Trial can be described with some certainty, however, as the most entertaining political trial. No matter what characterizations are made of the trial, it stands as a symbol of an era that was torn by political and cultural change (Goldberg, 1987). The trial itself mirrored the political, cultural, and generational tensions that divided many Americans during the late 1960s (Hernandez, 2001). These tensions centered on a young generation who had a vision of a better American society and government. However, the government saw their vision as a challenge and aimed to invalidate this idealist generation with law, order, and punishment. This tension was most visible in the streets as demonstrators frequently clashed with police officers and government officials. However, these tensions also dominated the trial of the Chicago Seven.[1]

The Chicago Seven: Lee Weiner, John Froines, Abbie Hoffman, Rennie Davis, Jerry Rubin, Tom Hayden, and David Dellinger. (Courtesy of Library of Congress)

The trial occurred because of events at the 1968 Democratic National Convention in Chicago, Illinois. Thousands of young people involved in the 1960s social movements descended on Chicago to demonstrate against the war in Vietnam and to promote other social issues. Denied permits to rally by the City of Chicago, the dissidents were thrown out of the parks and descended on the streets where they clashed with a massive force of police officers, the U.S. National Guard, and special army forces. Many individuals, including members of the mass media, were beaten and gassed. The events were broadcast to an American public who saw the collision of a divided America for the first time. Thus, this conflict became a fight for the "heart and soul of America" (Farber, 1987).

The defendants were leaders of major antiwar groups; the youth counter culture, the campus protest movement, and the Black Panther Party. Each group had very different beliefs about American society. When asked whether he had an agreement with the other defendants to come to Chicago for the purpose of promoting violence, Abbie Hoffman stated that the group "couldn't even agree on lunch" (Clavir and Spitzer, 1970). Charged with inciting and conspiring to riot at the Democratic National Convention, the groups banded together to bring their political activism to the courtroom. They even began to call themselves "The Conspiracy" (Epstein, 1970, p. 120).

The individuals involved were a divisive group united by their social protests. Abbot "Abbie" Hoffman and Jerry Rubin were cofounders of the Youth International Movement, or "Yippies." Rennard "Rennie" C. Davis was cofounder of the Students for a Democratic Society (SDS), which was one of the largest campus organizations promoting social justice, and a project director for the National Mobilization Committee to End the War in Vietnam (MOBE) demonstrations in Chicago. David Dellinger was the pacifist chairman of MOBE and editor of *Liberation*, a radical underground newspaper. John Froines was an assistant professor of chemistry at the University of Oregon and a member of MOBE's convention staff. Lee Weiner was also a member of the MOBE convention staff and a teaching assistant at Northwestern University. Tom Hayden was cofounder of SDS and codirector of the convention project. Bobby Seale was cofounder of the Black Panther Party, a black radical group whose main goal was the empowerment of the African American community (Albert and Albert, 1984). The Chicago Seven was eventually acquitted of all charges, but only after a courtroom trial that was, for its time, the "hottest show in town" (Goldberg, 1987).

The dramatic trial of the Chicago Seven has had a lasting impact on American popular culture. In 1987, HBO produced a docudrama based on trial transcripts and featured interviews with the defendants and their attorneys (Goldberg, 1987). Court TV recently produced a documentary based on the events. Numerous books, articles, and commentaries have also described the case. The media made Hoffman and Rubin counterculture icons, and their books that promoted their countercultural ideals became bestsellers.

To completely understand the trial, it must be placed in the context of the era in which it occurred. Although it is easy to take complex situations and simplify them in structured characterizations, I advise readers to keep in mind the complexity of the setting, the actors, and their interrelatedness when reading this chapter. I will discuss several of the events leading up to the trial. Next, I will examine the trial itself and finally, I will examine the role of the media and the trial's place in popular culture.

CRIMINALIZING DISSENT: THE MAKING OF THE CHICAGO SEVEN

The turbulence of the 1960s had its roots in the civil rights movement of the 1950s. Even after the U.S. Supreme Court in *Brown v. Board of Education* in 1954 declared segregation unconstitutional, many states, especially those in the Deep South, were not ready to accept the Court's decision.

Civil rights activists from all over the United States rushed into these areas to protest against government officials and law enforcement officers. Civil rights activists throughout the southern states used civil disobedience in an attempt to force reluctant governments to obey the legal precedent (Beckett and Sasson, 2000).

Many of the Southern officials and law enforcement administrators tried to influence popular opinion against civil rights activists and the movement altogether. They began to characterize the civil rights movement's tactics as criminal, rather than political, acts. Anyone who performed disobedient actions against segregation and black disenfranchisement were viewed as "agitators" and "lawbreakers," and soon this sentiment made its way to Washington. The national stage of politics soon began to regard political dissent and activism as criminal behaviors. Dissent aimed at any form of American government came to be viewed as a criminal action. Activism moved out of the political area and into the criminal one (Beckett and Sasson, 2000).

As the United States entered the 1960s, the protest and crime connection came to be viewed as the reason for the deterioration of society. Conservative leaders such as Richard Nixon and Barry Goldwater explicitly blamed the decline of law and order in American society on the civil rights movement. They argued that the lack of respect those in the movement had for government and law enforcement officials essentially corroded respect of the U.S. government. Soon, law and order rhetoric was heard throughout the country. Conservatives identified the civil rights movement as one of the leading causes of crime in our country. They argued that to counter the movement's corrosive actions, activists would need to be held accountable for their actions and punishments would need to be swift, certain, and severe (Beckett and Sasson, 2000). It is no coincidence that the Chicago Seven were indicted soon after President Nixon took office.

The majority of people in the United States did not view Southern government officials as criminal for not adhering to the decisions of the U.S. Supreme Court. Instead, the crime focus was turned to the activists. This hard-line stance against political dissent had an alternative effect. Instead of diminishing the numbers of activists and movements, their numbers only grew and their actions moved to engulf the entire United States.

By 1968, American youth were voicing their frustrations with society. Blacks were still demonstrating against racial injustice, women were fighting for their liberation from male domination, and many groups joined together to protest the Vietnam War. On campuses and in towns across the nation, those involved in these movements marched in the streets, held sit-ins, and organized festivals to further their respective causes. Brought together by their hope for a better society, most of the groups represented the ideological cliché of hope, love, and peace. However, conservative ideologues were still mounting their war against crime, and activists were the primary enemies of this war (Beckett and Sasson, 2000). Federal, state, and local government officials responded to dissenters in several different ways, and often these responses resulted in violent confrontations between demonstrators and authorities across the United States (Evans, 1994). One of the most memorable and widely televised of these confrontations occurred in Chicago at the Democratic National Convention in 1968 (Schultz, 1972). Before describing this confrontation, it is important to make note of two critical events that had expanded the already brewing tension.

In April 1968, Martin Luther King Jr., one of the leading activists of the civil rights movement, was assassinated in Memphis, Tennessee. Riots broke out in over 168 cities and towns after his murder. Two nights of rioting in Chicago led to the near destruction of many neighborhoods and the deaths of eleven people (Cohen and Taylor, 2000). In a press conference following the events, Mayor Richard J. Daley publicly blamed the police for showing too much restraint during the incidents. Determined not to have these incidents repeated, the mayor reportedly gave orders to police officers to "shoot to kill" arsonists and "shoot to maim" looters (Cohen and Taylor, 2000, p. 455). The law and order position was firmly established in Chicago.

Another important event was the assassination of Robert Kennedy. Kennedy was a promising presidential candidate, and it was believed that if he received the Democratic Party nomination for president he would bring about some of the changes that groups like the SDS and MOBE were advocating. Hours after winning the California primary election for president, Kennedy was assassinated and so were the hopes of many who wanted a candidate who would listen to their ideas (Albert and Albert, 1984). The assassination of Kennedy also led to fears about the safety of other presidential hopefuls, especially at the Democratic National Convention. This fear, coupled with reports of the revitalization of antiwar protesters' plans to march on Chicago, sparked Mayor Daley to take certain measures to ensure that no disruptions would occur during the convention (Farber, 1987). Measures included a massive defensive force of police officers that included eleven thousand nine hundred of Chicago's finest working twelve-hour shifts with battle plans, command posts, and mobile tactical forces. Also, 6,000 specially trained army personnel and 1,000 FBI and Secret Service agents were called in from Washington (Cohen and Taylor, 2000). An additional 6,000 Illinois National Guard troops were on standby (Walker, 1968). The war was ready to be waged; all Chicago needed was the enemy to arrive.

PREPARATIONS FOR THE DEMOCRATIC
NATIONAL CONVENTION

The week of August 21–29, 1968, will always be significant in U.S. history. Hubert Humphrey became the Democratic Party's candidate for president, and millions of Americans watched as a ferocious battle ensued between Daley's security forces and demonstrators.

Planning for the demonstrations had begun earlier in the year. Beginning in February 1968, many organizations met in New York City to determine strategies for Chicago. Many of the groups expressed a growing skepticism about the importance of marching in Chicago. President Johnson's withdrawal from the election, reduced bombing in Vietnam, and the opening of peace talks in Paris made the organizations question the importance of the event. They were also wary of Daley's public statements regarding the restraint of his police force. They knew if they went that violence would surely follow (Walker, 1968). However, after the assassination of Kennedy and the entrance of Vice President Hubert Humphrey into the campaign, many groups felt differently and believed that demonstrating at the convention was now very important (Albert and Albert, 1984; Walker, 1968).

The organizations, including MOBE and the Yippies, were planning separate events to be held in Chicago during the week of the National Democratic Convention. MOBE's goal was to assemble a major antiwar demonstration. The group planned to bring dissident groups, including SDS, from all over the United States to demonstrate against the war in Vietnam (Walker, 1968). Permit negotiations with the City of Chicago began on June 16, 1986, two months before the convention. The primary negotiator for MOBE was Rennie Davis. Davis and other MOBE workers met with David Stahl, the Mayor Daley's administrative officer, on several different occasions. On August 2, 1968, Stahl and Davis met to discuss the group's plan. Davis presented an outline of the plans for convention week and Stahl agreed to keep communications open (Walker, 1968). After many unproductive meetings, however, the group became dispirited with the process and filed suit against the City of Chicago.

The Youth International Party was also unable to obtain permits for their planned Festival of Life. The Yippies were a small group of individuals formed in the aftermath of the 1967 March on the Pentagon. They were the most widely known figures associated with the youth movement of the late 1960s (Boroghkozy, 2001). The group, under the leadership of Hoffman and Rubin, advocated the use of what they called guerilla theater, which was using comedy, play, and theatrics as a new approach to dissent against the government. Their use of entertainment was also a way to manipulate the media as a means of spreading their political messages to a younger generation (Albert and Albert, 1984). As Rubin explained, "[television] is raising generations of kids who want to grow up and become demonstrators" (1970, p. 106). The group believed that having the demonstrations televised across the United States would motivate the country's youth to rebel against the current state of society. Their sway over the media helped propel them into infamy becoming the first American radicals to reach celebrity status (Boroghkozy, 2001).

The Festival of Life was promoted to be a carnival-like party; a convention of the counterculture that would coincide with the Democratic National Convention. The festival offered rock concerts, poetry readings, discussion forums, information exchanges, and workshops. Beginning in February 1968, articles and leaflets were disseminated through underground newspapers to promote the event (Farber, 1987). On March 26, 1968, Yippie representatives met with David Stahl and presented their request for the use of Grant Park (Walker, 1968). Just as with MOBE, communications went back and forth with requests being submitted by both sides. The Yippies joined MOBE in filing suit against the City of Chicago. The suit opened up negotiations, but MOBE ultimately rejected the city's offers. A judgment was made in the city's favor, and only one permit was granted that allowed an afternoon rally at the Grant Park band shell (Walker, 1968). At a press conference on August 4, Hoffman disclosed plans for the festival and stated that the festival would be held even if a permit was not granted (Walker, 1968).

THE WORLD IS WATCHING THE CONVENTION

Beginning August 21, thousands of young people descended on Chicago. Lincoln Park became the meeting ground for those involved in the Festival of Life, and Grant Park became the central command for MOBE (Cohen and Taylor, 2000). The city ordered an 11 p.m. curfew, and police were ordered to clear the park. When individuals refused to leave the park, they were beaten and gassed. Incidents occurred throughout the week. The demonstration leaders and the media were all angered by the police actions. On Tuesday morning, August 25, editors and executives of all major networks and newspapers sent letters and telegrams to Mayor Daley protesting the police actions. Daley responded by holding a press conference stating that there would not be any problems if the news media and other citizens followed police instructions (Farber, 1987). Nonetheless, all would not be well as the struggle escalated on Wednesday, August 26. As the Democratic Party nominations were being decided inside the Conrad Hilton Hotel, thousands of demonstrators who had been forced to leave Grant Park began to gather outside. Thousands marched in front of the hotel and soon met the massive force that Daley had assembled (Cohen and Taylor, 2000). What followed was one of the most horrific scenes of the 1960s.

Protesters were ordered to leave the streets. Some did but not quickly enough. Within minutes hundreds of demonstrators were being arrested, beaten, and maced (Farber, 1987). Many demonstrators tried to run and escape the riotous atmosphere. Many others reacted by fighting with police officers, lighting fires in trashcans, throwing rocks, and smashing windows (Albert and Albert, 1984). As the violence progressed, the demonstrators began to chant, "the whole world is watching," and they were quite right (Farber, 1987, p. 477).

During many of the encounters, members of the press were also battered along with protesters. The press had set up cameras outside the Hilton, and everything that occurred was videotaped. Millions of people had expected to see the nomination of the Democratic Party candidate for president and instead saw violent images. The national media were very outspoken against the violent scenes in Chicago and were also outspoken against Daley's police force (Cohen and Taylor, 2000).

After the smoke cleared, several investigations convened to discern what had contributed to the chaotic event. One report for the National Commission on the Cause and Prevention of Violence titled *Rights in Conflict* concluded that the cause of the violence was random and uncontrolled police violence (Walker, 1968). Daniel Walker, who led the commission and the report was often referred to as the Walker Report, stated that it was the police and not the demonstrators or the media that had initiated the violence and riotous atmosphere. The report, using eyewitness statements, claimed that reporters and photographers were singled out for assault and much of their equipment was destroyed (Walker, 1968).

Mayor Daley charged, from a city investigation of the events titled *Strategy of Confrontation*, that dissidents had planned violence ahead of time. He referred to the demonstration leaders as communists and terrorists (Cohen and Taylor, 2000). He also stated that the news media were naïve and misconstrued in their coverage of the event. He thought that the police and his city had been unjustly criticized and slandered. Daley argued that the demonstrators used the media to set up the violent confrontations and incited the police in front of the media cameras (Farber, 1987). Daley challenged the media stating on national television that they gave revolutionary leaders sympathetic coverage and even referred to those leaders as hippies. He denied that the city's police officers acted in a riotous manner and concluded that it was the behavior of the demonstrators and their manipulation of the media that had contributed to the chaotic events in Chicago (Cohen and Taylor, 2000).

The television coverage was, for many, the first view of the violent division that was taking place in the United States. The television coverage spurred the National Commission on the Causes and Prevention of Violence to hold hearings to determine if the media had contributed to the violence in Chicago. Although the media were cleared of any involvement in the incident, the events in Chicago brought a new debate into the public arena. For the first time, the public began to seriously consider the impact of the mass media on violence and society (Farber, 1987).

There is no doubt that the events surrounding the 1968 Democratic National Convention were complex. There were many people involved, and all had their own agenda contributing to how the situation would unfold. The complexity of the event would soon be simplified by the indictment of eight movement leaders for conspiracy to incite a riot at the convention. The government now had a way to show that the law and order rhetoric was not just talk from Washington.

THE CRIME

The defendants in the case were charged with violating and conspiring to violate the Anti-Riot Act (see Title 18 of the Civil Rights Acts of 1968; Epstein, 1970). Froines and Weiner were also charged with teaching how to use incendiary devices. The U.S. Congress had passed the Anti-Riot Act under the Civil Rights Act of 1968, which made it illegal to use interstate commerce with the intent to incite, organize, promote, or encourage a riot. The act was passed in response to many confrontational and volatile moments in the civil rights and antiwar movements of the 1960s. Before its enactment, rioting and inciting to riot had been considered local law enforcement issues. However, because Washington was now recognizing political dissent as a criminal issue, Congress felt compelled to do something about the growing numbers of activists and movements around the country (Kaul, 1997). The Anti-Riot Act made their behaviors federal crimes and, hence, could enforce harsher punishments for the actions of protesters. The indictment of the Chicago Seven was the first prosecution under this act (Lukas, 1969).

Several members of Congress and the Senate demanded that Attorney General Ramsey Clark prosecute the leaders of the demonstration groups; Mayor Daley also wanted to see them punished. Clark, however, had doubts about the new anti-riot laws. He was unable to uncover any proof that the individuals involved had conspired to incite the riots. He also agreed with Walker's findings and believed that what had occurred was not a conspiracy but a police riot. Clark expressed more interest in prosecuting police officers for their actions than prosecuting the protesters (Farber, 1987).

However, a grand jury was convened to decide whether to prosecute. By the time they had reached their decision, President Nixon was in office. The Nixon administration, along with the new Attorney General John Mitchell, pushed for the charges against the eight organizers (Scheutz and Knedaker, 1988). Nixon was one of the predominate leaders of the law and order position of the early 1960s. Mitchell did not have any of Clark's reluctance and was more than ready to prosecute demonstrators. Nixon hoped to use this trial as a message. If they could convict these seven media-savvy demonstrators, maybe they could put a lid on the protests that were occurring across the United States.

The government, represented by Richard Schultz and Thomas Foran, attempted to prove a collaborative effort by the eight defendants, in which the defendants had encouraged a large number of people to come to Chicago and then had created a situation where these people would riot (Clavir and Spitzer, 1970). The government claimed that three steps were included in this overall plan. First, the defendants used the unpopularity of the war in Vietnam to bring people to Chicago for the purposes of protest. Second, the defendants urged these people to defy the police, city officials, and the convention itself. Finally, they created a situation where demonstrators would meet and confront the police in the streets of Chicago so that a riot would occur. Schultz charged that the defendants assumed specific roles in their plan and that they united and conspired together to encourage people to riot during the convention (Clavir and Spitzer, 1970).

Although the group would eventually call themselves "The Conspiracy," they were not the tightly knit group the government would try to portray (Epstein, 1970). Each group had its own agenda and own purposes for being in Chicago. MOBE was there to speak out specifically on the Vietnam War. The Yippies were there for their Festival of Life and to spread their countercultural ideas. Although they did communicate on problems with permits and other items, there was no specific evidence linking the men together. In fact, Seale had not even met the other defendants prior to their arraignment (Evans, 1994).

THE TRIAL[2]

The trial of the Chicago Seven was one of the most chaotic trials in history (Evans, 1994). Both sides provoked one another, and what is usually a routine event where everyone follows order and procedure had turned into a comedy of errors. The defendants held a blatant disregard for the authority of the judicial system, and Judge Hoffman himself showed no respect toward the defendants and their attorneys. Using the Yippies brand of guerilla theater, the defendants and their attorneys used the five-month trial to mock the judicial system and satire the political climate of the 1960s.

The trial began with Judge Hoffman refusing to grant a six-week continuance to the defendants while their lead counsel, Charles Garry, recovered from gall bladder surgery. Seale, who was very outspoken about the denial to postpone the trial until Garry had recuperated, was then pressured to accept the representation of William Kunstler. Judge Hoffman then ordered bench warrants for four lawyers who had been involved in the preliminary stages of the case. Kunstler stated that the lawyers had never intended to participate in the trial, but they had agreed only to prepare pretrial motions. All four had sent a telegram stating their intent to withdraw from the case to the government. Foran complained that the missing lawyers' conduct was both irresponsible and unprofessional. Judge Hoffman agreed and ordered their appearance before the court, and stated, "My wishes are that a lawyer respects this court" (Epstein, 1970, p. 140). Two of the four lawyers, Michael Tigar and Gerald Lefcourt, were jailed for the incident.[3] The actions of Judge Hoffman created an uproar in the legal community. J. Anthony Lukas (1969), for the *New York Times*, reported that about 125 lawyers filed friends-of-the-court briefs stating that Judge Hoffman's behavior was a mockery of justice. It was also reported that around 150 lawyers representing various groups picketed the court building. Judge Hoffman ultimately dropped the charges against the four men.

The Prosecution

U.S. Attorneys Foran and Shultz presented the defendants as a group of violent instigators who had planned in advance to wreak havoc on the city of Chicago. Their star witnesses were undercover officers who had infiltrated the groups and testified that they observed inciting behavior. Each presented testimony concerning tactics used to incite violence during the demonstrations.

One of the officers, Robert Pierson, posed as a bodyguard for Rubin. Pierson testified regarding speeches made by Seale and Rubin. He testified that Seale specifically told those in the crowd they should arm themselves and take action against the police officers. He also testified that Rubin incited the crowd by yelling, "Kill the pigs! Kill the cops!" (Clavir and Spitzer, 1970, p. 71).

Robert Murray, an undercover police sergeant, observed another incident involving Rubin. Murray claimed that he overheard a conversation between Rubin and an ABC television news reporter. In the conversation, the reporter stated that he was going to leave; however, Rubin called him back stating, "We're going out in the ball field. We want to see what these pigs are going to do about it" (Clavir and Spitzer, 1970, p. 51).

Undercover officer Irwin Bock testified that he met Froines and Weiner in the park. He testified that Weiner told the crowd that they needed more ammunition to fight off the police officers and told the crowd that they needed to get supplies to make Molotov cocktails and to pick a spot and bomb it (Clavir and Spitzer, 1970). The officers testified that they had overheard conversations and were given orders by the defendants that proved that they were indeed trying to cause upheaval and chaos in the city of Chicago.

The Defense

The defense strategy for the trial was to present a "commercial for the counterculture" (Goldberg, 1987, p. 33). It was a strategy that produced more theatrics than evidence. Many well-known figures were called to the stand. Witnesses included civil rights leader Jesse Jackson; folk singers Judy Collins, Arlo Guthrie, and Phil Ochs; poet Allen Ginsberg; LSD guru Timothy Leary; and writer William S. Burroughs. The witnesses recited poetry, sang songs, and gave testimony about the events at the Democratic National Convention. They presented the ideology of the antiwar and countercultural movement in an attempt to show the actual intent of the defendants for being in Chicago (Schultz, 1972). The government objected to much of the testimony that was presented as being superficial and completely irrelevant, although Judge Hoffman did regard them as intellectually stimulating (Schultz, 1972).

The defense, led by attorneys William Kunstler and Leonard Weinglass, even called Mayor Daley as a witness. They were prepared to argue that Daley's shoot-to-kill order was meant to prepare the attitude of the police and the City of Chicago toward antiwar demonstrators during the Democratic National Convention; however, they did not get the chance. Judge Hoffman sustained all objections made by Foran regarding Daley's testimony and the mayor remained, as with all of his appearances, unmarked by the events of 1968 (Schultz, 1972).

The celebrity witnesses lent much to the circus atmosphere in the courtroom. Collins sang her hit song "Where Have All the Flowers Gone." The prosecution repeatedly objected to her outbursts as irrelevant to the case. Foran argued that even though he believed that Collins was indeed a great singer, singing was not proper decorum in a court of law. Judge Hoffman agreed and sustained the prosecution's objection. However, she continued singing. Ginsberg performed mediation exercises that involved reciting some of his poetry and Indian chants. The chants were interrupted by an outburst of laughter by both the spectators of the trial and Judge Hoffman. This outburst resulted in a discussion between the Judge Hoffman, the lawyers, and Ginsberg about the appropriateness of the Sanskrit language being used in the courtroom. Leary discussed the benefit of psychedelic drugs for the benefit of expanding ones consciousness. These and other witnesses tested the patience of Judge Hoffman and the prosecution in many instances. However, it was the actions of the defendants themselves that created the most chaotic experiences.

Rubin and Hoffman were easily the most theatrical, and their symbolic antics led to many laughs in the courtroom. For instance, Rubin and Hoffman entered the courtroom wearing judicial robes. During the trial, they removed their robes and wiped their feet on them in an effort to show their defiance for the court (Epstein, 1970). When introduced to the jury, Hoffman blew kisses at them. After he had taken the stand in his defense, he was asked to introduce himself; he replied that his name was Abbie and he was an orphan of America. When asked where his residence was he claimed that he lived in Woodstock Nation and went on to explain that this residence was a state of mind. When asked his age he replied that he was thirty-three years old, but when asked when he was born, Hoffman replied that psychologically it was 1960. When Weinglass asked Hoffman what had occurred in his life between his actual date of birth and 1960, Abbie replied, "Nothing. I believe they call it an American Education" (Clavir and Spitzer, 1970, p. 153).

The other defendants began to get in on the act. For instance, Hayden shook his fist at the jury. When Judge Hoffman explained to him that his actions were not appropriate for the courtroom, Hayden proceeded to explain that this was his customary greeting. On Seale's 33rd birthday, the defendants presented him with a birthday cake and sang to him. Many of these incidents led to contempt charges against not only the defendants but their attorneys as well. They also made great news for the media. However comedic the actions were in the courtroom, tensions were still apparent. Judge Hoffman would not let the defendants and their attorneys stifle his authority, although they tried to defy and instigate him any chance they could.

Bobby Seale v. Judge Hoffman

Judge Hoffman had his theatrical moments as well. He was extremely antagonistic toward the defendants and their attorneys. The Seventh Circuit Court even noted Hoffman's bias toward the defendants. He would often make insulting comments toward the defense attorneys, overrule almost all of the defense's objections, and was very restrictive on what the defense could present. In one instance, Weinglass attempted to ask defendant Hoffman about certain passages he had written in one of his books. The judge would not allow the question to be asked. When the prosecution asked questions about the same book and presented it to the defendant to read certain passages, Judge Hoffman allowed it (Clavir and Spitzer, 1970). Although Weinglass objected to the ruling, Judge Hoffman would not waiver. This only added to the existing tensions in the courtroom. Tensions peaked on October 30, 1969, in one of the most dramatic moments of the trial.

Seale and Judge Hoffman's animosity grew throughout the trial. From the beginning, Seale argued that he wanted to be represented by Charles R. Garry, a lawyer who had represented others in the Black Panther Party. Garry, who was about to undergo gall bladder surgery before the trial began, was unable to represent Seale and the other defendants at the time. Seale argued repeatedly that the trial should be postponed until Garry was available, and the defense attorneys filed several motions to that effect. Nevertheless, Judge Hoffman repeatedly insisted that Seale was adequately represented. Seale defiantly argued that he was being denied his right to counsel. He consistently denied the representation of Weinglass and Kunstler. He also argued that he was denied his right to cross-examine witnesses because he was without representation (Schultz, 1972). Whenever he was mentioned in the testimony of witnesses, Seale would defiantly argue his points. His daily upheavals were wearing on Judge Hoffman, who, with a dramatic order, instructed the U.S. Marshals to "deal with" the defendant "as he should be dealt with in this circumstance" (Clavir and Spitzer, 1970, p. 162). When they returned to the courtroom, Seale had been handcuffed and leg cuffed to his chair, and his mouth gagged with cloth and adhesive tape. Judge Hoffman instructed the jury not to hold Seale's appearance against him in regard to the charges before him, but that it had to be done to preserve the order of the courtroom.

Finally, after weeks of outbursts and unruly behavior, Judge Hoffman declared a mistrial in the case against Seale. His case was severed from the other defendants. Hoffman also found Seale guilty of sixteen counts of contempt and sentenced him to four years imprisonment (Lukas, 1969). It was in this moment that the Chicago Eight became the Chicago Seven.

The Curtains Close

On February 14, 1970, the jury was instructed and deliberations began. While the jury was in deliberation, Judge Hoffman continued with the contempt proceedings. When these proceedings ended there were no fewer than 159 charges against the defendants and their attorneys. The acts that constituted the charges ranged from playful acts of disrespect such as when the defendants refused to stand when Judge Hoffman entered the courtroom to insulting the authority of the court such as calling the prosecutors Nazis and Judge Hoffman a fascist dog. The longest sentence was handed out to Kunstler. He was convicted of twenty-four charges and sentenced to four years and thirteen days. The appellate court ordered a retrial for the contempt proceedings and concluded that Judge Hoffman should have recused himself from the proceedings due to his personal entanglements with the defendants. (Schultz, 1972). In the retrial of the contempt proceedings, the government reduced the contempt charges to fifty-two and no fines or sentences were imposed.

On February 18, 1970, a verdict was reached and the seven defendants were acquitted of the conspiracy charges. Davis, Hayden, Hoffman, Rubin, and Dellinger were each found guilty of crossing state lines with the intent of inciting to riot and were sentenced to five years in prison, a $5,000 fine, and cost of prosecution. Froines and Weiner were found innocent of all charges. In November 1972, almost two years after the trial, U.S. Seventh Circuit Court reversed the convictions of Davis, Hayden, Hoffman, Rubin, and Dellinger on the grounds that there were many procedural errors in the trial and open hostility toward the defendants. The Seventh Circuit Court concluded that the behavior of Judge Hoffman and prosecutors would have required a reversal of the decision if other procedural errors had not occurred (Goldberg, 1987). Ironically, it was the theatrics of Judge Hoffman and the U.S. Attorneys that were deemed the most outrageous in the courtroom.

THE MEDIA

Media coverage of the Chicago Seven trial was extensive. On the evening news and in daily papers, the antics of the defendants were put in the public spotlight. The gagging of Seale and other controversial trial images appeared in the media. Some reports were sympathetic to the defendants; others were not. The tactics used during the trial were no surprise considering the presence of Rubin and Hoffman. Both had been advocating the use of theatrics and manipulation of the media to get their message across for years, and the trial afforded them the opportunity to use the media to make their political statements. The government may have tried to invoke the image of the defendants as evil and dangerous men, but their manipulation of the media made them cultural icons. Rubin and Hoffman were experts in the manipulation of the media to serve their own agenda. Even before the events in Chicago, they had been in the media spotlight. In several incidents of guerilla theater, they staged events to bring media attention to their cause.

Hoffman, Rubin, and Theater

Rubin and Hoffman's most famous incident brought the New York Stock Exchange (NYSE) to a screeching halt. The duo, along with other Yippies, threw one-dollar bills on the floor of the NYSE, and trading was halted as stockbrokers tried to gather the bills. Their point was to show how greedy America had become (Rubin, 1970). The image of hundreds of rich stockbrokers scrambling for one-dollar bills on the floor of the NYSE showed that greed did run the economic systems in the United States. In October 1967, in what would become one of the most important protests of the 1960s, the March on the Pentagon mobilized 100,000 various antiwar activists. At the demonstration, Hoffman and Rubin declared their intention to levitate the Pentagon and to exorcize it of the evil spirits that were killing both American soldiers and the people of Vietnam. During the Democratic National Convention, the pair nominated a pig, Pigasus, for their presidential candidate (Albert and Albert, 1984).

Rubin and Hoffman often spoke about the Yippie myth. They argued that by making rebellion and the movement entertaining, they could gain more media coverage and expand their audience. In other words, by being unpredictable and comedic, they would be in a better position to sell their ideas to a wider array of individuals. Hence, the Yippies were not really a group, but an idea that would be given meaning by individuals sitting at home watching television. They believed that the youth at home watching demonstrations on television would think of their brand of revolution, as opposed to the images of demonstrators being beaten by thousands of police officers, as something fun and exciting. As Rubin wrote in 1970, "[television] is raising generations of kids who want to grow up and be demonstrators." (Rubin, 1970, p. 106) The media questioned the group often about the difference between a Yippie and a hippie, but they could never get a clear, distinct answer. They left it up to the media and the viewers at home to define their actions. This gave Rubin and Hoffman a mysterious quality that kept the media in awe and wonderment about what the group would do next.

Rubin (1970) also wrote about the manipulation of the media and how television kept them on their toes: "Television keeps us escalating our tactics; a tactic becomes ineffective when it stops generating gossip or interest—news" (p. 107). Rubin and Hoffman believed that, by being more entertaining and provocative, they would generate more airtime. The more airtime they received, the more their revolutionary ideas would expand into the general public. Through their theatrical productions, or guerilla theater, Rubin and Hoffman became countercultural icons, and the trial only solidified their image. Their unpredictable acts were performed for the sake of making a political statement. The media loved them for their entertainment value and their generation of newsworthy events (Gitlin, 1980, p. 174).

Rubin and Hoffman understood the modern motto, "image is everything." Their goal in Chicago was not to cause a riot. Their goal was to change people's understanding of American society (Farber, 1987). They were more interested in changing the minds of the American public than in changing the minds of the politicians inside the Conrad Hilton Hotel. Their presence in Chicago was not to confront the police, the politicians, or even to defy Mayor Daley. It was a symbolic stand against all authority (Farber, 1987).

This symbolic stand was the same goal for their behavior in the courtroom. Judge Hoffman symbolized everything that they were fighting against. They would come to court wearing psychedelic styles, which contradicted the decorum of the courtroom. The courtroom gives an image of order and structure, and this is exactly what the Yippies were hoping to tear down. Their comedic performances and answers to questions were a direct contradiction to everything that a trial embodies.

The Sympathetic Media

The media were a significant part of this case for many reasons. Riots had occurred in other cities across the country. For instance, the race riots that occurred after the assassination of Dr. Martin Luther King Jr. resulted in eleven deaths, millions of dollars in property damage, and over three hundred arrests in one day. The riots at the Democratic National Convention did not even come close to the damage that was done after the King assassination riots. At the 1968 Democratic National Convention, over 100 people were hospitalized, and no one was killed. Property damage occurred in one specific area and not all over Chicago. Over 700 protest-related arrests were made during the entire incident (Farber, 1987). The difference in the riots at the Democratic National Convention was that the mass media were present in unprecedented numbers, and many of the media were singled out by police officers and attacked (Cohen and Taylor, 2000). Also, because the riots occurred during coverage of the Democratic National Convention, many more individuals were watching these events on national television.

Mayor Daley's charges that the media were sympathetic to the revolutionaries may have been misleading. Only two of the major networks showed live coverage of the confrontations that ensued between the police and the protestors (Bodroghkozy, 2001). Although attacks on reporters gave media executives initiative to make the unprecedented decision to provide live and unedited coverage of the scenes, the scenes were limited. In reality, very little of the coverage dealt with the young protestors. Bodroghkozy, citing William Small, head of CBS news in New York, notes that of the two networks that broadcast the event live, only 3 percent of the coverage was that of the violence on the street (Bodroghkozy, 2001). Daley's claim that the media were involved with the social movements of the 1960s was also misleading.

The majority of the people involved in the news were professionals with little or no ties to the movement (Cohen and Taylor, 2000).

The events at the Democratic National Convention allowed the majority of the public to view something they had rarely seen. Before these events, the majority of Americans had a disillusioned view of demonstrators. They viewed them all as hippies. This time they saw what it was these demonstrators were facing. The demonstrators' efforts in Chicago were not aimed at concrete changes, as much as they were toward changing people's understanding (Farber, 1987). The theatrical acts in the trial were toward the same end—to create a visual picture of the state in action to shape information for their own purposes. Before 1968, most of the demonstrators were young, black youth; but in Chicago, it was the white, middle class youth who were being beaten and gassed. The public now realized that it was not someone else's children but Middle America's children who were being beaten by the police officers. This realization brought the reality of the social movements much closer to home.

Before the case of the Chicago Seven, the bias of the media had rarely, if ever, been questioned. We take for granted the discussions that are made about the effects of the mass media on society, yet these questions first came about thanks to the Chicago riots and subsequent trial. The media's effect on violence was one of the many discourses that came about after this trial.

THE CHICAGO SEVEN: A LEGACY

No matter the characterizations made, the trial also stands as Rubin so succinctly put it "good theater" (Epstein, 1970, p. 285). It contained everything that makes a theatrical production great: comedy, drama, music, and a cast of characters who gave remarkable performances. The defendants brought their guerilla theater to the government, and the government, in turn, played along.

The flamboyant actions of the defendants in the trial were symbolic of the times in which they occurred. The defendants used the courtroom as a political demonstration (Bodroghkozy, 2001). The younger generation was fighting for a fresh perspective of the world around them; they were on a mission to show the public the reality of the world around them. They wanted to expose the political system for being a theater. In this statement, they argued that the system was not based on a search for the whole truth and nothing but the truth, as they had always been taught. Instead, it was a political mechanism to suppress opposing ideas. The defendants argued that the political system is based on faith and rhetoric instead of objectivity and truth. Using guerilla theater tactics and essentially mocking the system, the defendants and their attorneys hoped to point out the biases within the political arena, and their strategy ultimately paid off. The defendants were acquitted of all charges, and the media gave the defendants a chance to set forth their political agenda (Gitlin, 1980).

THE CHICAGO SEVEN: ICONS OF A REVOLUTION

The trial of the Chicago Seven holds an important place in popular culture. In 1987, HBO made the trial of the Chicago Seven into a movie titled *Conspiracy: The Trial of the Chicago Eight*. Movies about Hoffman have also been made, and his status as the symbol of American rebellion in the 1960s still remains in place today. The trial of the Chicago Seven spurned a theatrical production. Many books have been written about the incident and documentaries and commentaries have abounded. Rubin and Hoffman remain an inspiration to the few who still fight the injustices in the United States. These popular images may make us remember the days of old, however, they are also misleading.

The trial of the Chicago Seven took protest against the government off the streets and into the government's arena: the courtroom. Their comedic performances, celebrity status, and media manipulation made protesting look "cool and fun" to a new generation of dissenters. This image of the 1960s has been romanticized over the years. What most of us remember is the image of flower children and free love, and we tend to forget the dangers that these individuals faced. What looked rebellious and exciting was actually very dangerous. The demonstrators put themselves at great risk by playing in the government's house, but they looked like they were having fun doing it. They eventually succeeded in their endeavor; however, it came at a price. What we are left with is the image, and the message has been lost for many people. However, today there are still those who adhere to the theatrics of the Yippies. In demonstrations across the world, individuals show up in costume and put on plays and skits that poke fun at the government and the state of society. In their actions and theatrics, as well as in their hope for a better future and society, these groups show that the spirit of the Chicago Seven and their social movement allies were not in vain. Their spirit and ideals are still being fought for today.

NOTES

1. The trial began as the Chicago Eight; however, Bobby Seale's case was severed from the other defendants. As a result of a dramatic confrontation with Judge Hoffman, the Chicago Eight became the Chicago Seven.

2. Trial transcripts used in this chapter are from Clavir and Spitzer, 1970.

3. The other two lawyers, Michael Kennedy and Dennis Roberts, had their warrants quashed in San Francisco Federal Court.

REFERENCES

Albert, J. C., and Albert, S. E. (1984). *The sixties papers: Documents of a rebellious decade.* New York: Praeger.

Beckett, K., and Sasson, T. (2000). *The politics of injustice.* Thousand Oaks, CA: Pine Forge Press.

Bodroghkozy, A. (2001). *Groove tube: Sixties television and the youth rebellion.* Durham, NC: Duke University Press.

Clavir, J., and Spitzer, J. (1970). *The conspiracy trial: The extended edited transcript of the trial of the Chicago eight.* Indianapolis, IN: Bobbs-Merrill.

Cohen, A., and Taylor, E. (2000). *American pharaoh: Mayor Richard J. Daley.* Boston, MA: Little, Brown and Company.

de Tocqueville, A. (1969). *Democracy in America.* J. P. Mayer (Ed.) and G. Lawrence (Trans.). Anchor Books. (Original work published 1838)

Epstein, J. (1970). *The great conspiracy trial.* New York: Random House.

Evans, C. (1994). Chicago seven trial: 1969. In E. W. Knappman (Ed.), *Great American trials: From Salem witchcraft to Rodney King* (pp. 586–590). Detroit, MI: Visible Ink Press.

Farber, D. (1987). *Chicago '68.* Chicago: University of Chicago Press.

Gitlin, T. (1980). *The whole world is watching: Mass media in the making and unmasking of the new left.* Berkeley, CA: University of California Press.

Goldberg, S. B. (1987, May). Lessons of the '60s. *American Bar Association Journal, 73,* 32–38.

Hariman, R. (1990). *Popular trials: Rhetoric, mass media, and the law.* Tuscaloosa, AL: University of Alabama Press.

Hernandez, N. (2001, August 31). Reliving the Chicago Seven trial. *The Chicago Lawyer.*

Kaul, A. J. (1997). The case of the Chicago seven. In L. Chiasson Jr. (Ed.), *The press on trial: Crimes and trials as media events* (pp. 147–157). Westport, CT: Greenwood Press.

Lukas, J. A. (1969, 24 September). 8 go on trial today in another round in 1968 Chicago convention strife. *New York Times,* pp. 1, 35.

Lukas, J. A. (1969, 25 September). Trial begins for leaders of '68 Chicago demonstrations. *New York Times,* pp. 1, 39.

Rubin, J. (1970). *Do it!* New York: Simon and Schuster.

Scheutz, J., and Knedaker, K. H. (1988). *Communication and litigation: Case studies of famous trials.* Carbondale, IL: Southern Illinois University Press.

Schultz, J. (1972). *Motion will be denied: a new report on the Chicago conspiracy trial.* New York: William Morrow.

Walker, D. (1968). *Rights in conflict: Convention week in Chicago, August 25–29, 1968: A report.* New York: Dutton.

5

The Murder of Fred Hampton: The Government's Involvement and Cover-up

Laura L. Finley

On December 4, 1969, Fred Hampton, a leader of the Black Panther Party in Chicago, was murdered in his apartment. He was killed by a heavily armed team of Chicago police officers who were responding to an informant's tip about an alleged weapons cache in Hampton's apartment. This was no isolated incident, but part of a targeted effort by the FBI and local police departments across the United States to destroy the Panthers, who were viewed as violent subversives and a threat to the status quo (Churchill and Vander Wall, 1990a).

This chapter describes the declining support of blacks for the nonviolent civil rights movements and the rise of the militant groups in the late 1960s—the Black Panther Party (BPP) was one of the most controversial of the militant groups; this chapter reviews BPP's rise in influence and its positive contributions to the empowerment of blacks as well as a brief history of FBI efforts against black liberation movements; and this chapter discusses the murder of Hampton and concludes with the social, cultural, and political legacy of the BPP in general and the Fred Hampton case specifically.

THE POLITICAL SETTING

By the mid-1960s, legislative victories by the civil rights movement had altered the political and social environment in the United States and, to a

Power to the People poster. One of the many used by the Black Panther Party to increase their public profile and recruit members. (Courtesy of Library of Congress)

degree, offered limited physical and social protection for blacks who spoke out about the conditions they faced (Bloom, 2001). Yet, there was still a great deal of frustration and impatience with the actual effects of the legislative victories. As historian Howard Zinn stated, there was "a small amount of change and a lot of publicity" (1995, p. 456). According to Zinn (2001), even as early as 1963 it was obvious that parts of the South were impermeable to nonviolent tactics. These areas required either violent revolt or federal government intervention.

The violent reaction to the Freedom Summer of 1964 undermined the commitment to integration for some, including the Southern Nonviolent Coordinating Committee (SNCC). In 1966, Stokely Carmichael was elected leader of SNCC. He issued a call for black power and a denunciation of nonviolent tactics (Bloom, 2001). In contrast to earlier phases of the civil rights movement in which many whites played integral parts, some blacks came to believe that no whites could offer them assistance in their efforts to achieve equality. In fact, some blacks embraced segregation as emphatically as white separatists. Murder, beatings, and other forms of harassment of blacks and whites involved in civil rights efforts also contributed to the discontent for many involved or affected. Tensions within the group compounded those from outside. For these reasons, many turned to a focus on Black Nationalism and a much more militant approach to race relations (Bloom, 2001).

Carmichael's approach was much more attractive to Northern ghetto residents than the nonviolent groups were, as they never really felt connected to the previous civil rights efforts with their middle-class orientation (Hayes and Kiene, 1998). By the late 1960s, half of the black population in the United States lived in the North. Because they faced less overt but no less real instances of discrimination, Northerners developed a class consciousness that many in the South lacked (Bloom, 2001). Riots, most notably the 1965 Watts Riots in Los Angeles, helped spur the shift to a more militant approach. There were forty-three racial riots in 1966. The riots served as indication that more than just civil rights were needed to address the grievances of blacks. It became clear to many black leaders that economic disadvantages must also be addressed (Jones and Jeffries, 1998). In fact, the riots resulted in real gains, including funds to fight poverty (Bloom, 2001).

Exacerbating the shift from the nonviolent civil rights movements, the media began to publicize, or rather dramatize, the rift between Martin Luther King Jr.'s nonviolent approach and the militant rhetoric of SNCC leader Carmichael. This shift in focus was exemplified by Carmichael and H. Rap Brown's change of the group's name to the Student National Coordinating Committee, removing the emphasis on nonviolence (Churchill and Vander Wall, 1990b).

THE BLACK PANTHER PARTY

Adopting the symbol of a black panther to distance themselves from the rest of the civil rights movement, Huey Newton and Bobby Seale founded a new political party in Oakland, California, on October 15, 1966, as a response to the growing antagonism between white police officers and the black community (Jones, 1998). They called themselves the Black Panther Party for Self-Defense. The party was modeled after the Black Muslims but had lacked a religious perspective. Party members patrolled the streets of Oakland and protected blacks from police brutality. They also established a ten-point program focusing on economic self-determination ("The Foundation," 2003). Media coverage at the time often portrayed the Panthers as anti-white and hyper-violent (as does much of the contemporary coverage). For instance, after an incident at the California General Assembly, the *Sacramento Bee* reported that they could "accurately be described as anti-white" (Jones and Jeffries, 1998, p. 37). In practice, however, they actually collaborated well with other groups, including organizations supported by whites such as the Peace and Freedom Party (Jones and Jeffries, 1998).

By the summer of 1968, the Panthers had initiated a community education program and an antiheroin program (Churchill and Vander Wall, 1990). Some party members were also outspoken critics of the war in Vietnam. David Hilliard, former Panther chief of staff, compared the party to the Sandinistas of Nicaragua, stressing the role of Panthers as freedom fighters (Pearson, 1997). The Panthers first gained national attention when they marched with arms onto the floor of the California state legislature in an attempt to block the passage of legislation directed at their right to carry guns in public places (Jones and Jeffries, 1998). The Panthers had been "policing the police" and had thought the only effective way to do so was to be armed (Pearson, 1994).

The Panthers and the Media

The Panthers responded to the negative publicity in the mainstream news by using other media to disseminate their message. They employed a group of recording artists known as The Lumpen. Panther Elaine Brown had a deal with Motown Records and recorded "Seize the Time" and "Until We're Free" (Bailey, 2003). "Seize the Time" became the Black Panther Party's national anthem (Brown, 2003). The BPP also published a newspaper—*The Black Panther*—that included news about the party's activities and ideology, as well as stories about the struggles of African Americans and other groups at home and abroad. Initially a monthly publication, *The Black Panther* became a weekly newspaper in January 1968 and did not cease publication until 1980. Not only did this newspaper provide an outlet for their ideology, it also provided a source of income (Davenport, 1998). The inaugural issue dealt with the shooting of twenty-two-year-old Denzil Dowell by a white police officer and the issue of police brutality in general (Abron, 1998). Eldridge Cleaver served as the newspaper's first editor, and during his term the paper reflected his provocative manner. Cleaver was perhaps the most controversial and outspoken of the Panthers. During its peak years of publication, from 1968 to 1972, one hundred thousand copies were sold per week (Jones and Jeffries, 1998).

Conservatives assert that the Panthers recruited "from the most lethal elements in the inner city" (Horowitz, 1995). The Panthers admitted that recruiting and organizing efforts were focused on those they called "The Lumpen," a group of prostitutes, gang members, convicts, and ex-convicts who were not reached by other movements (Churchill and Vander Wall, 1990b). The media also contributed to the Panthers' growth by covering the more radical blacks instead of those who had believed in more nonviolent means. Within two years of the group's formation, they had 5,000 members and chapters in over a dozen cities (Churchill and Vander Wall, 1990b). White liberals, including many in the entertainment business, provided support for the Panthers. Angela Dickinson, Donald and Shirley Sutherland, Leonard Bernstein, and Jane Fonda all offered verbal support. By 1968, according to conservative David Horowitz, the Panthers were taking in $50,000 to $100,000 per month, thanks largely to donations by celebrities (Horowitz, 1995).

The Panthers were a focus of much media attention during the mid- to late-1960s. Both the mainstream and alternative presses carried frequent stories that often emphasized the most controversial and sensationalistic elements of the party (Jones, 1998). In fact, some have argued that the media essentially created the Panthers, giving the group more attention than they were worth because they made good news. An article in *Esquire* magazine stated, "More than any other previous black image, the Panther has been created by television. The medium is a Panther lover" (Jones and Jeffries, 1998, p. 41). Hugh Pearson, in his book *The Shadow of the Panther*, claimed that the media focused on those members who were criminals, which created the image of an alienated black for the public. In addition to the media and the public, the Panthers were also receiving increased attention from the federal government.

COINTELPRO

The white leadership in the United States had long felt threatened by the civil rights movement and its challenge of the status quo. The FBI had engaged in numerous efforts to discredit and dismantle civil rights organizations. A program called COINTELPRO, or Counter Intelligence Programs, had been used effectively against other groups labeled "subversive." COINTELPRO was initiated in 1967 against Black Nationalists. However, the seeds of the anti-black operations had been sown much earlier.

J. Edgar Hoover had authorized efforts to neutralize Black Nationalist Marcus Garvey as early as 1918. The U.S. Justice Department's Bureau of Investigations, forerunner to the FBI, was concerned about the rising number of black militants after World War I, and Garvey's Universal Negro Improvement Association (UNIA) was their primary target. After five years of intensive surveillance, the FBI arranged for Garvey's indictment and conviction on dubious mail fraud charges. Their efforts were effective, as the UNIA was rendered useless without their leader. The FBI also targeted A. Phillip Randolph, head of the Brotherhood of Sleeping Car Porters Union, and W.E.B. Du Bois of the National Association for the Advancement of Colored People (NAACP). Such efforts were justified by Hoover because these groups and individuals were engaged in "subversive activities"; a term he defined in 1940 as the "holding of office in . . . Communist groups; the distribution of literature and propaganda favorable to a foreign power and opposed to the American way of life; agitators who are adherents of foreign ideologies who have for their purpose internal strike [sic], class hatreds and the development of activities which in time of war would be a serious handicap in a program of internal security and national defense" (Churchill and Vander Wall, 1990b, p. 94).

In the 1950s, the FBI began to focus efforts on the Southern Christian Leadership Conference (SCLC), which was established in 1957 by Reverend Dr. Martin Luther King Jr. Despite their seemingly innocent goal of using nonviolent tactics to secure black voting rights in the South, the SCLC and King were still viewed by the FBI as a threat. As King and SCLC's call for desegregation and voting rights for blacks gained increasing support across the United States, the FBI began to actively infiltrate the organization's meetings and conferences. In 1962, they planted five disinformation stories discussing King's alleged communist sympathies, which were never confirmed. Attorney General Robert Kennedy also authorized round-the-clock surveillance of all SCLC offices and King's home. An FBI memo explains the rationale for the surveillance, stating that civil rights "agitators" represent a threat to the "established order" and that "King is growing in stature daily as the leader among leaders of the Negro movement" (Churchill and Vander Wall, 1990b, p. 96).

By 1964, King was established as a civil rights leader, and he was beginning to pursue a more structural agenda for social change. Accordingly, the FBI increased their efforts against him, now attempting not only to discredit him but also to remove him and replace him with someone the FBI considered more "acceptable." The primary means used was a propaganda campaign outlining King's alleged communist sympathies and sexual improprieties. Harassment by the IRS was also used. Anti-King efforts slowed after an effort to publish excerpts from tapes of his trysts with prostitutes failed but continued even after his assassination in 1968 (Churchill and Vander Wall, 1990b).

As King's influence was waning and increasing numbers of blacks were following more militant groups like the Panthers, COINTELPRO efforts shifted as well. An internal FBI memo stated that the goal of the COINTELPRO program was to "prevent the rise of a messiah who could unify and electrify the militant Black Nationalist movement." (Redden, 2000, p. 183) In late 1960, FBI agents began to monitor SNCC meetings. Wiretaps of leaders' phones were authorized in 1965. Also targeted for COINTELPRO efforts were the Nation of Islam and the Organization for Afro-American Unity (OAAU). In addition to discrediting leaders and spreading lies about the various groups, COINTELPRO efforts were also designed to break up or prevent alliances between groups. In some locations, Hoover called on FBI operatives to block media access by black radical groups, saying that "consideration should be given to preclude [black] rabble-rouser leaders of these hate groups from spreading their philosophy publicly or through the communications media" (Churchill and Vander Wall, 1990b, pp. 109–111).

The FBI made good use of informants and agent provocateurs. In 1967, after uprisings in Newark and Detroit, Attorney General Ramsey Clark suggested the FBI expand or establish the use of informants within Black Nationalist organizations. Hoover responded with the institution of the formal anti-black liberation COINTELPRO program in August. By 1968, it was in full swing and had expanded to include forty-one cities (Churchill and Vander Wall, 1990b).

By the fall of 1968, the FBI had identified the organization they felt provided the biggest threat: the Black Panther Party. Hoover was quoted in the *New York Times* stating that "the greatest [single] threat to the internal security of the country" was the Panthers (Caldwell, 1969, December 14). The concern was if the Panthers were able to politicize and mobilize the "brothers in the street," as Huey Newton called them, this mass would be able to effect change. Shortly, thereafter, efforts were made to escalate the COINTELPRO program against the Panthers. Of special concern was an FBI report to President Nixon in 1970 indicating that approximately 25 percent of the black population had great respect for the Panthers, and almost 50 percent of those under twenty-one years old felt this way (Zinn, 1995).

The FBI rationalized that the Panthers were violent and completely ignored their positive contributions. The merger between the Panthers and the SNCC in 1968 concerned the FBI. They quickly initiated an effort to split the two through the media. The FBI created the false appearance that Carmichael himself was an FBI operative, which led the group to expel him in 1970 (Churchill and Vander Wall, 1990b).

COINTELPRO efforts had severely damaged the Black Panther Party by 1970. By then, most of the party's top leadership had been jailed, killed, or exiled. Nevertheless, the FBI launched one more concerted effort to drive a wedge between two party factions. One group supported Eldridge Cleaver, who was exiled in Algeria at the time, and the other followed Huey Newton, who was in jail. The FBI forged anonymous letters that suggested certain members were police infiltrators. After years of harassment, the Panthers, who were founded in part on their animosity toward police, were especially sensitive to this concern. The chance that such efforts might result in a homicide was not lost on FBI leadership. Hoover merely expressed concern that the letters be worded in such a way that they would never be traced. Some murders did occur. For example, in New York, a follower of Cleaver was shot in March 1971, and in April, someone bound *The Black Panther* circulation manager Samuel Napier, a follower of Newton, taped his eyes and mouth shut, laid him face down on a cot, and shot him in the back of the head. At least three other murders were likely linked to this particular COINTELPRO effort (Churchill and Vander Wall, 1990b).

Other COINTELPRO efforts were directed at portraying the Panthers as anti-Semites, with the goal of stopping financial support from wealthy contributors like Leonard Bernstein, conductor of the New York Philharmonic (Churchill and Vander Wall, 1990b).

Much attention was also focused on the Panther's newspaper, *The Black Panther*. According to an FBI document in 1970, "The BPP newspaper has a circulation of . . . [139,000]. It is the voice of the BPP and if it could be effectively hindered, it would result in helping to cripple the BPP" (Churchill and Vander Wall, 1990b, pp. 159–160). The FBI had tried unsuccessfully to get the IRS to close down the paper. They also sent threatening letters to the paper's staff and convinced freight companies to charge the Panthers a higher rate. In all, the FBI has admitted during the years between 1965 and 1971 that it had conducted at least 295 distinct COINTELPRO operations against individuals and organizations advocating black liberation, and 233 were aimed specifically at the BPP. The goal was to essentially crush the BPP (Churchill and Vander Wall, 1990b).

Conservatives, while unable to deny the reality of COINTELPRO, argued it was much more limited in scope and less successful than the Panthers claim. In February 1971, writer Jay Epstein investigated the charges that police and the FBI were collaborating to destroy the Panthers. Epstein concluded, "I think it would be a mistake to say they weren't being harassed, but there is a difference between harassment and genocide. As for the talk of 'genocide,' it wasn't just a case of being overblown; it was false" (Rapp, 1997, p. 25).

FRED HAMPTON AND THE CHICAGO PANTHERS

Fred Hampton impressed many black leaders in the Chicago area as one who was likely to "make it." He earned three varsity letters in high school, received a Junior Achievement Award, and graduated with honors in 1966. He entered Triton Junior College as a prelaw major immediately after graduation. At Triton, he became involved with the NAACP, working to increase the quantity and quality of recreation facilities in black neighborhoods and to desegregate local swimming pools ("Fred Hampton," 2003a). While in high school, Hampton joined the Black Panther Party. He launched and became the leader of the Black Panther Party Illinois chapter in November 1968, when he was twenty years old ("Fred Hampton," 2001). As part of his leadership role, Hampton regularly spoke in the community about the plight of African Americans, and he organized weekly rallies at the Metcalf Federal Building. He worked with a free Peoples Clinic, taught political education classes every morning at 6:00 a.m., and he launched a community control of police initiative, which attempted to provide better oversight of police activities. He played an integral role in establishing the BPP's Free Breakfast Program. Perhaps, his most significant achievement was to mediate a non-aggression pact between the three most powerful street gangs in the Chicago area: the Blackstone Rangers, a black gang; the Young Patriots, a white gang; and the Young Lords, a Puerto Rican gang (Singh, 1998). He first coined the phrase "Rainbow Coalition" to describe the multiracial alliance, a phrase later adopted by Reverend Jesse Jackson ("Fred Hampton," 2001). Hampton once critiqued the BPP's ten-point program, saying they needed to change the focus from whites to capitalists (Hayes and Kiene, 1998).

Initially committed to nonviolence, Hampton began to question the efficacy of that strategy in making social change after he was arrested and convicted of stealing seventy-one dollars worth of candy bars, which he allegedly distributed to neighborhood children. He was sentenced two to five years, but his sentence was later overturned. The experience left him frustrated with the criminal justice system and escalated his concerns about police abuses. He also began to carry guns for the first time. In a 1969 interview with the *Chicago Sun Times*, Hampton made clear his hatred for the police: "I'm not afraid to say I'm at war with the pigs" ("Fred Hampton," 2001), and shortly before his murder, he said, "If you kill a few, you get a little satisfaction. But when you kill them *all* you get complete satisfaction" (Booker, 1997, p. 354).

At the same time, the FBI began to view Hampton as a threat. In 1967, they started a file on him, which was over 4,000 pages long by the time of his death ("Fred Hampton," 2003a). In February 1968, the FBI put a tap on Hampton's phone and also on his mother's phone ("Fred Hampton," 2003b). In 1969, over 100 Panthers were arrested, and there were four raids on Panther headquarters; the last raid was the one in which Hampton was killed ("Fred Hampton," 2001). Based on his leadership qualities and charisma, Hampton was to be appointed chief of staff of the BPP, but he was murdered before assuming that office ("Fred Hampton," 2003b).

The Plot to Kill Fred Hampton

The government supposedly learned that Hampton and other members of the BPP were going to be involved in a "Days of Rage" rally in 1969, which was an "attack on the pig power structure." In reality, neither Hampton nor most of the Chicago BPP supported the rally. National leaders Seale and Newton stressed that spontaneous riots were not the answer (Jones and Jeffries, 1998). This information, however, combined with their general suspicion about the BPP and Hampton's speaking and leadership skills, made Hampton a wanted man in the eyes of the FBI. The Chicago Panthers had long complained that they were targets of the Gang Intelligence Unit and Task Force of the Chicago Police because of their work with local gangs (Grady-Willis, 1998). There was concern that if the Panthers were able to politicize the gang members they worked with, their membership would increase dramatically (Grady-Willis, 1998).

FBI agents in Chicago heard that Jeff Fort of the Blackstone Rangers had some misgivings about an alliance with the Panthers and that he decided to capitalize on them. On January 30, 1969, Hoover authorized an anonymous letter be sent to Fort warning him that the Panthers are "out for themselves, not black people." At the same time letters were sent to various Panthers implying that Fort wanted to "off Hampton" (Grady-Willis, 1998, p. 372). Similar menacing letters that claimed Fort was willing to "blow [Hampton's] head off" were also sent to Hampton (Churchill and Vander Wall, 1990a, p. 65). This effort was obviously not enough, and a more detailed and deadly plan was hatched.

The FBI conspired with the Chicago Police Department to place William O'Neal, Hampton's bodyguard and director of the chapter's security, to spy on the BPP. In exchange for information about Hampton's daily itinerary, the government agreed to drop felony charges pending against O'Neal for car theft ("Fred Hampton," 2001). Interestingly, O'Neal had also been arrested for impersonating a FBI agent (Churchill and Vander Wall, 1990a). He also provided a floor plan of Hampton's apartment and information about the residents. O'Neal was paid over $30,000 between 1969 and 1972, and he received other perks, such as gas money (Redden, 2000). O'Neal encouraged party members to commit armed robberies with explosives he had bought and stored at the request of the FBI (Redden, 2000). "Improving" the amount and variety of weapons the Panthers had was also one of his preoccupations (Churchill and Vander Wall, 1990a). O'Neal attempted to incite the Panthers into committing a variety of violent acts, including the electrocution of interlopers and the construction of an electric chair to punish informers. Fred Hampton rejected both ideas (Churchill and Vander Wall, 1990). Cook County State's Attorney Edward Hanrahan authorized a raid on Hampton's apartment, which the FBI, including Director Hoover, supported ("Fred Hampton," 2003b). The raid was in response to a tip from O'Neal that there was a weapons cache in Hampton's apartment (Singh, 1998).

On the evening of December 4, 1969, Hampton and several party members, including O'Neal, returned to BPP headquarters from a political education class. O'Neal volunteered to make dinner. He slipped a large dose of secobarbital into Hampton's drink. O'Neal left the apartment around 1:30 a.m. Shortly thereafter, Hampton fell asleep. The police version of the story is that they knocked on the door, and the Panthers immediately started shooting. Panthers claim the heavily armed, fourteen-man Chicago police team attacked the apartment at approximately 4:30 a.m. Historian Winston Grady-Willis (1998) stated that the police had an M-1 carbine, a Thompson submachine gun, twenty-five other guns, and an illegally obtained search warrant. They entered by kicking in the front door and then shooting party member Mark Clark—head of the Peoria, Illinois chapter of the BPP—point-blank in the chest (Churchill and Vander Wall, 1990b). Clark had been sleeping in the living room with a shotgun in his hand. Allegedly, his reflexes made him fire a shot before he died. His bullet was later discovered to be the only shot fired at police by Panthers that night. The police shot through the walls of the bedroom where Hampton and his pregnant fiancée, Deborah Johnson (now known as Akua Njeri), were sleeping. Hampton was hit in the shoulder ("Fred Hampton," 2003b). Two officers then entered the bedroom and shot Hampton point-blank in the head. Some reports include one of the officers saying "he's good and dead now" (Churchill and Vander Wall, 1990a, p. 72). The officers dragged Hampton's body out of the bedroom and again fired on the others in the apartment. Panthers Ronald "Doc" Satchell, Blair Anderson, and Verlina Brewer were wounded in addition to the deaths of Clark and Hampton (Churchill and Vander Wall, 1990b). The surviving Panthers were dragged across the street and arrested on charges of attempted murder and assault ("Fred Hampton," 2003a). Although only one accidental shot was fired by the Panthers, the police fired over ninety-eight rounds in Hampton's apartment; each of the surviving members of the BPP were held on $100,000 bonds (Churchill and Vander Wall, 1990b).

THE CRIMINAL JUSTICE RESPONSE

Illinois State Attorney Hanrahan convened a press conference later in the morning in which he announced that the police had been attacked by the violent Panthers and had merely been defending themselves (Churchill and Vander Wall, 1990a). Several days later Hanrahan spoke at another press conference. This time he even praised the officers: "We wholeheartedly commend the police officers' bravery, their remarkable restraint and discipline in the face of this vicious Black Panther attack, and we expect every decent citizen of our community to do likewise" (Churchill and Vander Wall, 1990b, p. 73). Hanrahan also contacted a friend at the *Chicago Tribune* and requested that he run an exclusive on the murders, using the "official" version of events (Churchill and Vander Wall, 1990a). False reenactments were shown on prime-time television and photographic evidence was fabricated to support the self-defense theory promulgated by the state (Churchill and Vander Wall, 1990a).

It was recommended in mid-December that a Federal Grand Jury be empanelled to consider if the raid violated the Panthers' civil rights. Attorney General John Mitchell responded affirmatively. Hanrahan and others coached several officers and the ballistics expert to perjure themselves, however, resulting in an official label of "justifiable homicide" for the murders and no indictments (Churchill and Vander Wall, 1990a). Charges were brought against Hanrahan and a dozen Chicago police personnel for conspiring to obstruct justice, but these charges were dropped in November 1972 when the charges against the Panthers were also dropped (Churchill and Vander Wall, 1990b). It seems that a quid pro quo arrangement was made so that Hanrahan and the officers would remain silent about the FBI's involvement (Churchill and Vander Wall, 1990a).

The murder of two Panthers in the police raid ignited a storm of protest; the deaths of Hampton and Clark helped raise the stature of the party. A nation-wide poll taken one month after Hampton's death revealed that 64 percent of blacks thought the Panthers gave them a sense of pride (Pearson, 1994). The protests were partly due to investigations by certain reporters who had quickly discovered that the photographic evidence being shown was fabricated. Hanrahan responded with yet another press conference and demanded an internal police investigation; the investigation was another sham. In fact, investigators later admitted under oath that "it had been a 'whitewash' and 'the worst investigation' that either had ever seen" (Churchill and Vander Wall, 1990a, p. 74). Further evidence of the outrage about the murders is provided by the attendance at Hampton's funeral, which reached 5,000 people. Reverend Jesse Jackson and Ralph Abernathy, Martin Luther King Jr.'s successor as leader of the SCLC, both eulogized Hampton. A commission including black political leader Roy Wilkins and former U.S. Attorney Ramsey Clark condemned the police in a 1973 report, calling the official violence "most destructive" (Grady-Willis, 1998, p. 373).

The cover-up of the events leading up to and including Hampton and Clark's deaths began immediately. The FBI even brought in an "ace," COINTELPRO manager Richard C. Held, to coordinate the cover-up. The members of the BPP immediately countered these representations of the events of December 4 by opening up the apartment to the public. It was also impossible to overlook the more than 100,000 pages of documents on Hampton and the BPP (Churchill and Vander Wall, 1990b).

Yet, after a total of three "official" investigations, which all extended a clean bill to the government's actions, the only recourse was civil court (Churchill and Vander Wall, 1990a). Families of the Panthers filed a 47.7 million-dollar civil suit against the city, state, and federal government. They finally forced disclosure of O'Neal's identity in 1973, and details about his actions as an infiltrator emerged shortly thereafter (Churchill and Vander Wall, 1990a). The cover-up continued through the civil suit court proceedings, with the defendants recalling very little and being evasive in general. Despite court orders, FBI employees failed to provide the prosecution with pertinent documents regarding their involvement with Hampton. After eighteen months, Federal Judge J. Sam Perry opted to issue directed verdicts for acquittal on all counts, despite the examples of government misconduct (Churchill and Vander Wall, 1990a). The suit was finally settled over a decade later, in November 1982, when District Judge John F. Grady determined there was sufficient evidence of a conspiracy to violate the rights of the Panthers and awarded the plaintiffs 1.85 million dollars in damages (Churchill and Vander Wall, 1990b). Not one of the officers who committed the murders or those who ordered them spent a day in jail (Churchill and Vander Wall, 1990a).

Merely four days after the civil suit, a similar COINTELPRO raid took place in Los Angeles. There the FBI used an infiltrator named Melvin "Cotton" Smith who had, like O'Neal, become director of security for the Panthers. He provided the FBI with a detailed floor plan of the BPP facility to be raided. Forty men from the LAPD's SWAT team, along with over 100 police officers providing backup, took part in the raid on Elmer "Geronimo" Pratt. This time the plan backfired; Pratt was not sleeping in his bed but on the floor next to it. The burst of gunfire, which apparently was supposed to kill him, missed completely. Another difference was that several Panthers were awake and fought off the police for four hours when press and the public arrived on the scene. Six Panthers were wounded and thirteen were arrested. The Panthers were immediately charged with assaulting the police, but the defendants were all acquitted on December 23, 1971. Pratt spent two months in a Los Angeles County Jail until his $125,000 bond was raised (Churchill and Vander Wall, 1990b).

From April to December 1969, police raided Panther headquarters in eight different cities and some headquarters received multiple raids. Frequently, Panthers were arrested on these raids for such offenses as illegal use of sound equipment and possession of stolen goods. The raids often resulted in severe damage to Panther headquarters. During one raid in Philadelphia, police ransacked the building, ripped out plumbing, and chopped up and carted away furniture; Police Chief Frank Rizzo, later mayor of Philadelphia, bragged to the press, "Imagine the big Black Panthers with their pants down" (Churchill and Vander Wall, 1990b, p. 143). Although the efforts of the U.S. criminal justice system to destroy the Panthers did eventually lead to their demise, Hampton's legacy lived on in numerous ways. As he once said, "You can kill a revolutionary, but you cannot kill a revolution. You can jail a liberation fighter, but you cannot jail liberation" ("Fred Hampton," 2001).

FRED HAMPTON'S LEGACY

A scholarship was created in Fred Hampton's name that had been set up by Jesse Jackson and Ralph Abernathy, and Fred Hampton Day was declared in Chicago in 1990 ("Fred Hampton," 2001). In Chicago, Hanrahan's role in Hampton's death was a catalyst for major political upheaval. Hanrahan was defeated in 1972 by a Republican candidate who had earned 60 percent of the African American vote (Jones and Jeffries, 1998).

Hampton's son, Fred Jr., born three weeks after his father's death, also became an activist and leader. By the age of twenty, Fred Jr. was already establishing himself a leader and had become President of the National People's Democratic Uhuru Movement. In 1992, the government indicted him for murder and armed robbery, but he was found not guilty. Allegedly the prosecutor said, "We'll get you." He was brought in again in May 1992, accused of bombing a Korean merchant's store. Despite no evidence of fire or any fire truck ever called to the scene, Hampton was convicted and sentenced to one year for one count of aggravated arson ("Fred Hampton," 2003, para. 3).

No doubt that an important effect of the FBI's surveillance, infiltration, and destruction of the Black Panther Party and other black liberation groups was to solidify wariness about those in authority positions (Blackstock, 1973). This distrust can easily become a vicious cycle: blacks exhibit negative attitudes to the police, which, in turn, leads the police to respond to African Americans negatively. The African American community continues to struggle with many of the same issues that concerned the Panthers in the 1960s. Younger blacks who did not live through the 1960s can point to contemporary examples of police conspiracies and cover-ups against blacks, especially in the inner city. Cases have been documented of police corruption, brutality, and misconduct in New York, Chicago, Detroit, Philadelphia, and New Orleans. Police in New Orleans have been indicted for killing witnesses who were to testify against them (Gibbs, 1996).

The Hampton murder has been commemorated in popular culture. The now defunct band Rage Against the Machine made reference to Hampton's murder in their song, "Down Rodeo."[1]

RENEWED MEDIA AND POPULAR CULTURE INTEREST IN THE PANTHERS

Interest in the Panthers has rekindled in recent years. Books, magazines, newspapers, films, and music have addressed the Panthers and their legacy. Coverage is generally of two types: portraying the Panthers as either heroic soldiers in the fight for black liberation, or cop-killing thugs. The 1989 death of Huey Newton in a drug deal attracted a great deal of attention in the press and furthered the vilification of the BPP, led by former radical David Horowitz (Jones, 1998). For instance, an editorial in the *New York Times* after Newton's death said, "With black berets atop wide afros, leather jackets, shotguns and rifles, [the Panthers] looked like white America's worst nightmare come to life" (Jones and Jeffries, 1998, p. 37). Former Panthers established two newspapers to share the history and contributions of the party (Jones, 1998).

Popular culture has also covered the Panthers as an organization. The 1995 film *Panther* mostly utilized a romanticized version. Produced and distributed by Tribeca, Polygram International, and Grammercy, the film uses some documentary news footage to give a realistic feel to the story of Huey Newton, Bobby Seale, and Eldridge Cleaver. It was adapted for the screen by Mario Van Peebles from a novel written by his father, Melvin Van Peebles. Melvin wrote and directed *Sweet Sweetback's Baadasssss Song*, a film popular with Panthers in the 1970s (Jones, 1998). Conservatives have criticized *Panther* as "an Oliver Stone version of reality" (Horowitz, 1995, p. 16). Horowitz (1995) claimed that Panther leader Bobby Seale had said that 90 percent of the film is inaccurate. Despite the fact that the Panthers were arrested for 349 felonies in 1969 alone, they are depicted as innocent idealists (Horowitz, 1995). *Panther* did stimulate renewed interest in the BPP, but it did not do well at the box office (Jones, 1998). Available with the release of the film was a line of Panther clothing, two "Panther inspired" CDs, and a "Power to the People" sweepstakes where the winner received $1,000 of "personal empowerment cash" (Matthews, 1998, p. 268).

Rap music has also tended to portray the Panthers as visionaries and do-gooders. For instance, rapper Paris, a member of the Nation of Islam and admirer of the Panthers, shared the message of unity and black liberation in his song, "Break the Grip of Shame." His message, like that of the Panthers, is "designed to spark a revolutionary mind-set" (Bernard, 1991, p. 9). The liner notes of his album, *The Devil Made Me Do It,* include a brief history of the BPP as well as biographies of Huey Newton, Bobby Seale, Malcolm X, and other black leaders. MTV refused to air the video for *The Devil Made Me Do It*—where Uncle Sam transforms into Satan—for fear it might "polarize its viewers" (Bernard, 1991, p. 9).

Black Panther Records is headed by David Hilliard, former BPP chief of staff. The goal of the record company, Hilliard says, is to reach a younger generation that does not know much about the Panthers. Hilliard praises the work of Public Enemy and Tupac Shakur, whose mother was a Panther, for raising consciousness about black issues (Bailey, 2003). In 1988, Public Enemy made reference to the Panthers in their song, "Party for Your Right to Fight," which describes COINTELPRO. They also used the Panther slogan, "Power to the People," as the title of a song on their album *Fear of a Black Planet* (Jones, 1998). Others point to the sounds of Digable Planets and Digital Underground as exemplifying the Panther spirit and message (Brown, 2003). "All of Us," by the F.U.G.I.T.I.V.E.S, was released in 2003. The band adopted their name to identify with freedom fighters such as Nat Turner and Harriet Tubman. The song is set against a backdrop of voices that include George Jackson and Fred Hampton (Brown, 2003).

Several former Panthers have written books about the party. Earl Anthony, an FBI informant, was the first to publish his account. Panthers claim most of Anthony's memoir is false. Elaine Brown wrote of her experiences as chair of the BPP from 1974 to 1977, and David Hilliard and William Brent shared their life stories. Conservatives have praised Hugh Pearson's *The Shadow of the Panther* for the accurate portrayal of Panthers as violent thugs. Panthers tend to decry the negative presentation of their group in the book (Pearson, 1994). Pearson blamed this on the "anti-intellectual attitude [that is] rampant in the black community" (Pearson, 1994, p. 69). The renewed interest in the Panthers also prompted the reissue of several out-of-print books that were written by members of the BPP and others (Jones, 1998).

In addition to being memorialized in popular culture, the Panther legacy lives on through The Huey P. Newton Foundation, a non-profit research, education, and advocacy center. It was founded in 1993 in Oakland to honor Newton and the BPP's legacy. The Foundation has published a book, *The Huey P. Newton Reader,* and collaborated on the making of the PBS film, *The Huey P. Newton Story* ("The Foundation," 2003).

Several Panther-like groups were formed in the 1990s. The Black Panther Militia in Milwaukee, Wisconsin, led the way, followed by groups in Dallas and Los Angeles (Jones, 1998).

COINTELPRO REVISITED

The FBI's COINTELPRO efforts against the BPP and others were discovered in March 1971 after a break-in at the FBI Field Office in Media, Pennsylvania. Selected files were released to the underground press (Redden, 2000). Carl Stern of NBC filed a Freedom of Information suit to force the release of more files. The U.S. Department of Justice released some reports in the fall of 1973 that generated a public outcry (Redden, 2000). The controversy eventually led both the U.S. House and Senate to appoint special committees to investigate the federal government's domestic surveillance programs. Known as the Church Committee because it was headed by Senator Frank Church, the committee found that, in addition to the FBI's COINTELPRO programs, other federal agencies were spying on U.S. citizens. For instance, the National Security Agency initiated a "Watch List" in 1967 to gather information about "U.S. organizations or individuals who are engaged in activities which may result in civil disturbances or otherwise subvert the national security of the United States" (Redden, 2000, p. 186). Yet even this investigation was a sham. For instance, the House committee relied on the voluntary participation of federal agencies and even submitted findings to the CIA to see if the CIA wanted anything omitted (Zinn, 1995). The House voted to keep its committee's findings secret. When Daniel Shorr, a CBS newscaster, leaked the report, not only did all the important newspapers refuse to print it, but Shorr was suspended by CBS (Zinn, 1995).

Unfortunately, the Church Committee's findings did not result in the national outcry they should have, perhaps because the Watergate scandal was gaining momentum (Redden, 2000). The intelligence agencies that appeared before the committee all claimed to have ceased their surveillance activities in the early 1970s, yet surveillance of so-called subversives remains, and has intensified in recent years with the passage of the USA Patriot Act after the terrorist attacks on September 11 (Redden, 2000).

Status of the Panther Cases

Some Panthers who were targeted by COINTELPRO programs have been exonerated and released from prison in recent years. The conviction of Geronimo Pratt for the robbery and murder of a Santa Monica teacher was overturned in 1997 after twenty-seven years. Judge Everett W. Dickey overturned the conviction because the prosecution failed to inform the jury that a key witness was also a government informant. In fact, the government continued to withhold information about their informant, Julius Butler, throughout the entire appeals process (Kelly, 1997). Pratt's attorney Johnnie Cochran used FBI COINTELPRO documents and testimony from other Panthers to argue that Pratt was framed by the FBI (Rapp, 1997).

The murder of Fred Hampton demonstrated the lengths to which the federal government will go to suppress those that threaten the status quo. Fear that blacks might unite under a charismatic and efficient leader was a catalyst for state-sanctioned murder. Despite losing the civil suit to the survivors of the attack and the families of the deceased, the government has still accepted no responsibility for Hampton's death. Unfortunately, the FBI's actions against the BPP and other groups are still widely unknown. This is arguably by design, as their conduct would most certainly threaten their credibility with many American citizens. There is still very little oversight of the FBI's domestic surveillance programs. Even when the law does catch up with government officials who abuse their power, the result is often unsatisfactory. For instance, in 1980, former FBI Director L. Patrick Grey and Edward S. Miller, one-time leader of Squad 47—the FBI's New York counterintelligence unit—were convicted of conspiring to "injure and oppress the citizens of the United States" (Churchill, 1999, p.1). Their convictions were due to their involvement in COINTELPRO between 1956 and 1971. Neither Grey nor Miller spent any time in jail; President Reagan pardoned them both during their appeals process in April 1981. Reagan said that he issued the pardons because their actions took place during a turbulent time period, and it was "time to put all this behind us" (Churchill, 1999, p. 1). Yet, no such pardons have been issued to the victims of COINTELPRO. It seems as though the government still feels threatened by black leaders today, as it was discovered in October 2003 that the office of the mayor of Philadelphia, who is black, was bugged.

NOTE

1. Rage Against the Machine's website contains a reading list that includes works by members of the BPP. See "Rage Against the Machine," 2003.

REFERENCES

About the Film Festival. (2003). Retrieved September 17, 2003, from www.pantherfilmfestival.com/about.html

Abron, J. (1998). "Serving the people": The survival programs of the Black Panther Party. In C. Jones (Ed.), *The Black Panther Party reconsidered* (pp. 177–192). Baltimore: Black Classic Press.

Bailey, C. (2003). Ex Black Panther to inject consciousness into rap music. Retrieved September 17, 2003, from http://pub12.ezboard.com/politicalpalace.html

Bernard, J. (1991, May/June). "Rap Panther." *Mother Jones* [electronic version], *16*(3), 9.

Blackstock, N. (1976). *COINTELPRO: The FBI's secret war on political freedom.* New York: Vintage.

Bloom, J. (2001). Ghetto revolts, black power, and the limits of the civil rights coalition. In R. D'Angelo (Ed.), *The American civil rights movement: Readings and interpretations* (pp. 383–407). New York: McGraw-Hill/Dushkin.

Booker, C. (1998). Lumpenization: A critical error of the Black Panther Party. In C. Jones (Ed.), *The Black Panther Party reconsidered* (pp. 337–362). Baltimore: Black Classic Press.

Brown, E. (2003). Notes for "All of us." Retrieved September 17, 2003, from http://www.freethepantherlegacy.com/releases/record.html

Caldwell, E. (1969, December 14). Declining Black Panthers Gather New Support From Repeated Clashes with Police. *New York Times*, p. 64.

Churchill, W. (1999, March 10). Wages of COINTELPRO still evident in Omaha Black Panther case. *ZNET.* Retrieved October 13, 2003, from http://www.icdc.com/~paulwolf/cointelpro/wagecoin.html

Churchill, W., and Vander Wall, J. (1990a). *Agents of repression.* Boston: South End Press.

Churchill, W., and Vander Wall, J. (1990b). *The COINTELPRO papers: Documents from the FBI's secret wars against domestic dissent.* Boston: South End Press.

Davenport, C. (1998). Reading the "voice of the vanguard": A content analysis of the Black Panther Intercommunal News Service, 1969–1973. In C. Jones (Ed.), *The Black Panther Party reconsidered* (pp. 193–210). Baltimore: Black Classic Press.

Fred Hampton. (2001). Retrieved September 15, 2003, from http://www.africanpubs.com/Apps/bios/0213HamptonFred.html

Fred Hampton. (2003a). Retrieved September 15, 2003, from http://www.providence.edu/afro/students/panther/hamptonsr.html

Fred Hampton. (2003b). Retrieved September 17, 2003, from http://www.providence.edu/afro/students/panther/hamptonjr.html

The Foundation. (2003). Retrieved September 17, 2003, from http://www.blackpanther.org/foundation.html

Gibbs, J. (1996). *Race and justice.* San Francisco: Jossey-Bass.

Grady-Willis, W. (1998). The Black Panther Party: State repression and political prisoners. In C. Jones (Ed.), *The Black Panther Party reconsidered* (pp. 363–390). Baltimore: Black Classic Press.

Hayes, F., and Kiene, F. (1998). "All power to the people": The political thought of Huey P. Newton and the Black Panther Party. In C. Jones (Ed.), *The Black Panther Party reconsidered* (pp. 157–176). Baltimore: Black Classic Press.

Horowitz, D. (1995, June 2). Panther movie glamorizes militant black movement. *Human Events, 51,* 21, 16.

Horowitz, D., and Collier, P. (1997). *The race card.* Rocklin, CA: Prima Publishing Co.

Jones, C. (1998). Reconsidering Panther history: The untold story. In C. Jones (Ed.), *The Black Panther Party reconsidered* (pp. 1–24). Baltimore: Black Classic Press.

Jones, C. and Jeffries, J. (1998). "Don't believe the hype": Debunking the Panther mythology. In C. Jones (Ed.), *The Black Panther Party reconsidered* (pp. 25–56). Baltimore: Black Classic Press.

Kelly, M. (1997, August 11–18). "Geronimo!" *New Republic, 217*(6/7), 6.

Legacy. (2003). Retrieved September 17, 2003, from http://www.blackpanther.org/legacynow.html

Matthews, T. (1998). "No one ever asks, what a man's role in the revolution is": Gender and the politics of the Black Panther Party, 1966–1971. In C. Jones (Ed.), *The Black Panther Party reconsidered* (pp. 267–304). Baltimore: Black Classic Press.

Pearson, H. (1994). *The shadow of the Panther.* Reading, MA: Addison-Wesley.

Pearson, H. (1997). Writing about Black Panthers and black people. In P. Collier and D. Horowitz (Ed.), *The race card* (pp. 67–78). Rocklin, CA: Prima Publishing Co.

Rage Against the Machine. (2003). Retrieved September 19, 2003, from http://www.ratm.com

Rapp, C. (1997). *True lies.* In P. Collier and D. Horowitz (Eds.), *The race card* (pp. 13–28). Rocklin, CA: Prima Publishing.

Redden, J. (2000). *Snitch culture.* Los Angeles: Feral House.

Singh, N. (1998). The Black Panthers and the 'undeveloped country' of the left. In C. Jones (Ed.), *The Black Panther Party reconsidered* (pp. 57–108). Baltimore: Black Classic Press.

Ten Point Program. (2003). Retrieved September 17, 2003, from http://www.blackpanther.org/TenPoint.com

Zinn, H. (1995). *A people's history of the United States, 1492–present.* New York: Harper Perennial.

Zinn, H. (2001). The limits of nonviolence. In R. D'Angelo, (Ed.), *The American civil rights movement: Readings and interpretations* (pp. 439–442). New York: McGraw-Hill/Dushkin.

6

The Angela Davis Trial: A Political or a Criminal Trial?

Johnna Christian

Angela Davis was a public figure even before her involvement with the U.S. criminal justice system. In September 1969, Davis became a subject of controversy and debate because of her dismissal and subsequent reinstatement (under a court order) as an assistant professor in the philosophy department at the University of California, Los Angeles (UCLA). The incident received a great deal of media attention because of her membership in the Communist Party (Davis, 1974; Major, 1973). In addition, she was active in political causes and high-profile cases such as the Soledad Brothers (three black inmates charged with killing a white guard), and she was affiliated with the Black Panther Party (Aptheker, 1975).

The Davis case illustrates the intersection between social and political climate, mass media and popular culture, and the U.S. criminal justice system. Her trial was inextricably linked to the social changes, such as the women's movement and antiwar movements, that occurred in the late 1960s and early 1970s. Disenfranchised groups were mobilizing around concerns about equal rights for racial minorities, women, and the poor. Prisoners were viewed as an extremely disadvantaged group because they were poor, mostly black men and were considered to be at the mercy of an oppressive criminal justice system.

FREE ANGELA DAVIS NOW!
NEW YORK COMMITTEE TO FREE ANGELA DAVIS • 29 WEST 15th ST • 7th FLOOR
NEW YORK. N.Y. 10011 • 929 2010

"Free Angela Davis Now!" (Courtesy of Library of Congress)

Before she was charged with a crime, Davis was active in these political movements as an outspoken and high-profile figure who was particularly critical of the criminal justice system. It is within this context that Davis was tried for conspiracy, kidnapping, and murder after a shoot-out in a California courtroom. Although Davis was not in the courtroom at the time of the crime, she was considered an accessory because she allegedly supplied the guns that were used and conspired with the individuals involved to plan the event. After a prolonged trial, preceded by Davis being placed on the FBI's Ten Most Wanted list and evading capture for two months, she was ultimately acquitted of all charges.

Davis's case, however, provides a fascinating context for analyzing the reciprocal nature of the U.S. criminal justice system and the larger social and political environment in which crimes are committed, and how the criminal justice system determines its response. The case also demonstrates how individuals frame crime and justice issues to promote their own interests and points of view. Criminal justice authorities labeled Davis a dangerous fugitive while on the run and a serious criminal after her capture, yet supporters around the world viewed her as a political prisoner and a symbol of government repression of unpopular beliefs (Aptheker, 1975; Major, 1973; Steiniger, n.d.). Many contended that Davis was on trial because she was black, a woman, and a member of the Communist Party. Indeed, media accounts of the crime continually described Davis with adjectives such as black, militant, and Communist.

This chapter discusses Angela Davis's criminal trial with a focus on the crime, setting, and people involved; the criminal justice system's response to the crime; media response to the incident; Davis's trial; the case's relationship to key social, political and legal issues; and the impact of the case on legal and popular culture.

THE CRIME, SETTING, AND PARTICIPANTS

The crimes that Davis was charged with were related to a series of incidents that occurred at Soledad Prison in California. On January 13, 1970, a white guard shot and killed three black inmates and injured a white inmate after a fight broke out in the prison yard (Davis, 1974; Major, 1973). According to Davis (1974), the incident happened after guards deliberately let black, Chicano, and white inmates into the yard together after routinely segregating them during exercise time. Some accounts suggest that the guards knew there would be a fight and that they deliberately allowed it to happen (Davis, 1974; Major, 1973). This was a period of unrest in the California prison system within the prison walls; racial violence was prevalent among inmates, and violence and brutality were perpetrated by the guards (Caldwell, 1970; Davis, 1974; Von Hoffman, 1970).

A grand jury met three days after the incident and determined the shootings were justifiable homicide. After prisoners heard about the grand jury's finding, a white guard was beaten by inmates, and his body was thrown from the third floor tier of the prison (Aptheker, 1975; Major, 1973). Three black inmates—John Clutchette, Fleeta Drumgo, and George Jackson—were charged with first-degree murder for the guard's death. The prisoners became known as the Soledad Brothers, and a wide scale movement was started to aid in their defense (Aptheker, 1975; Davis, 1974; Major, 1973). The Soledad Brothers were considered political prisoners who were symbols of the racism and oppression in the California prison system and in society at large. Protests and rallies were held on the Soledad Brother's behalf, and a defense committee was formed to help fight the charges against them.

Davis became involved in Soledad Brothers defense activities, which she viewed as an extension of the other political causes in which she was involved (Davis, 1974). Davis was an outspoken critic of the California prison system, and she used her position as a public figure to bring attention to brutality against prisoners and repression of their political activity and expression. Davis drew parallels between her dismissal from UCLA for membership in the Communist Party and the Soledad Brothers' position in the prison system (Aptheker, 1975; Davis, 1974; Nadleson, 1972). Davis's speeches on behalf of the Soledad Brothers eventually led the University of California, Board of Regents to dismiss her on the grounds that these activities were "unbefitting a university professor" (Davis, 1974, p. 273).

Davis was tried for a crime that occurred at the Marin County Courthouse in San Rafael, California, on August 7, 1970. This crime was allegedly linked to the Soledad Brothers case. James McClain was on trial for assaulting a guard at San Quentin Prison. Two other inmates from San Quentin, William Christmas and Ruchell Magee, were the witnesses in the crime and were in court to testify. As the trial was getting underway, Jonathan Jackson, the seventeen-year-old brother of one of the Soledad Brothers, George Jackson, who was in the courtroom as a spectator, stood up, held a gun in the air, and said he was taking over (Ginger, 1974). Harold Haley, the presiding judge in the McClain trial, Assistant District Attorney Gary Thomas, and three female jurors were taken hostage. McClain reportedly taped a sawed-off shotgun to Judge Haley's neck (Major, 1973; Nadleson, 1972).

Jackson and the inmates talked about what to do as the incident unfolded, sometimes arguing and disagreeing with each other, indicating that the takeover was not planned out ahead of time (Aarons, 1970; Aptheker, 1975). They used wire to bind the three jurors and Thomas together. The inmates originally had an elderly woman juror in the group of hostages, but she was so frightened that they replaced her with a younger woman (Ginger, 1974; Major, 1973). At one point, a young couple with a baby walked in the courtroom, and one of the inmates was going to take them hostage, but another inmate said they did not want to take any children with them. They also talked to the jurors, telling them not to worry because they would not be hurt (Ginger, 1974). Many accounts report that the inmates yelled at each other as the incident unfolded and that they seemed confused about what they were doing (Aptheker, 1975; Ginger, 1974; Major, 1973).

Judge Haley was ordered to call the sheriff to report that they were being held hostage and that criminal justice authorities should not try to intervene (Ginger, 1974; Major, 1973). Jackson and the inmates led the hostages from the courtroom at gunpoint. They entered a corridor at the courthouse where the sheriff deputies and police officers were; Jonathan Jackson unarmed some of them as the group moved through the corridor and out of the courthouse (Ginger, 1974; Major, 1973). As the group was leaving the courthouse they encountered James Kean, a photographer for the Marin County newspaper, *The Independent Journal* (Major, 1973). One of the inmates told Kean to take all the pictures he wanted, and Kean documented much of the takeover on film. One of the inmates allegedly yelled, "Free the Soledad Brothers by 12:30" as they left the courtroom with the hostages. This was widely reported in media accounts of the incident and was viewed as evidence that the crime was planned and part of a larger radical movement (Aarons, 1970; Caldwell, 1970).

The hostages were led to a rental van that Jackson had parked at the courthouse. As the group tried to escape in the van, they ran into a roadblock set up by San Quentin guards. Corrections officers opened fire on the vehicle, and the gunfire lasted for eighteen seconds (Aptheker, 1975; Ginger, 1974; Major, 1973). Thomas fired Jonathan Jackson's gun and hit Ruchell Magee in the stomach. Thomas was then shot in the back by one of the corrections officers outside of the van (Ginger, 1974). Judge Haley, James McClain, William Christmas, and Jonathan Jackson were killed during the shooting (Aarons, 1970). Magee, a San Quentin prison inmate, and one of the jurors were wounded. Assistant District Attorney Gary Thomas was shot and paralyzed.

Davis was not present during the crime, and she was not an active participant in the event. According to officials, Davis was incriminated because the three guns used in the takeover were traced to her. Her supporters charged that she was tried because of her involvement in the campaign to free the Soledad Brothers and because of her ties to the Jackson family. Davis spent time with the family, and she exchanged letters with George Jackson while he was incarcerated and eventually becoming romantically involved with him. In addition, Davis served as a mentor to Jonathan Jackson, who was involved in the Black Panther Party and was developing a political consciousness Davis helped nurture.

ACTIONS TAKEN BY THE CRIMINAL JUSTICE SYSTEM

Once police officials realized that three of the guns used in the crime were registered to Davis, a Marin County judge issued a warrant for her arrest on charges of first-degree murder and kidnapping, and then a federal judge issued a warrant for arrest for interstate flight to avoid prosecution. She was placed on the FBI's Ten Most Wanted list, and Director J. Edgar Hoover personally called for her arrest (Steiniger, n.d.). Davis left San Francisco and went into hiding. One scholar suggested she did this because she knew she would not receive fair treatment from the police or the criminal justice system if she turned herself in for questioning and subsequently went to trial. This author stated that Davis feared for her life should she come face to face with the FBI agents who were looking for her (Major, 1973).

In her autobiography, Davis talks about this period on the run from the FBI, and the constant fear that she would be apprehended. Despite reports that Davis was trying to go to Cuba and had been seen in her hometown of Birmingham, Alabama, and in Canada; she reported that she spent time in Los Angeles and Chicago before going to New York where she was eventually apprehended by FBI agents (Davis, 1974).

While searching for Davis, the FBI arrested and questioned her sister, Fania Jordan, and went to Birmingham to question friends and family members about her whereabouts (Aptheker, 1975; Major, 1973). They also searched offices of the Black Panther Party and the Soledad Brothers' defense committee. Agents also went to Miami after hearing Davis was planning to go to Cuba (Meyer, 1970).

Davis was staying at the Howard Johnson Motor Lodge in Manhattan with a friend, David Poindexter. She was arrested at the hotel by FBI agents on October 13, 1970, as she approached her hotel room. She was arraigned on federal charges of interstate flight to avoid prosecution, and she was denied the opportunity to post bail and be released. At the arraignment, there was tight security in the courtroom with reporters who were admitted by passing through metal detectors and being frisked (Meyer, 1970). Poindexter was charged with harboring a fugitive (Meyer, 1970).

At the arraignment, Davis was represented by John Abt, who also served as general counsel for the Communist Party; and Margaret Burnham, Davis's childhood friend, who was also an attorney with the National Association for the Advancement of Colored People (NAACP) Legal Defense Fund. Davis was released from federal custody on her own recognizance and was immediately taken into custody by New York State.

Davis was taken to the New York Women's House of Detention in Greenwich Village. Regular protests were held outside of the jail demanding Davis's release on bail (Aptheker, 1975). Defense committees were formed all over the United States to show support for Davis and to help her defense team secure her release on bail. While incarcerated, Davis was initially housed in the section of the jail for mentally ill inmates, because jail administrators said they feared for her life and had no other means of protecting her. Davis went on a two-week hunger strike to protest the solitary confinement. Other female inmates joined her as a symbol of solidarity and protest. A federal judge ruled that Davis was being held in solitary confinement because of her political beliefs, and ruled that she should be transferred to the general inmate population. Once Davis was back in the general population, she interacted with the other women in the jail, discussed their cases, and talked about the political and social movements in which she was involved (Davis, 1974).

Authorities tried to have Davis extradited to California to stand trial. Her attorneys filed petitions to block her extradition but were unsuccessful. Justice Harlan, of the United States Supreme Court, decided that Davis could be extradited to California. On December 22, 1970, jail officials told Davis that her attorneys had arrived to speak to her about blocking extradition, and instead she was placed in a car and driven from New York to an Air Force base in New Jersey (Major, 1973). Davis's transfer to California was conducted with tight security measures to prevent possible flight or assistance from outsiders. The Holland Tunnel in New York was closed as she was transferred to New Jersey, and she was flown to California in a California Air National Guard plane (Major, 1973).

Once Davis was in California, her attorneys again tried to secure her release on bail. A petition with 35,000 signatures from people around the United States in support of bail was submitted to the judge, but the request was denied (Aptheker, 1975). In denying bail, Judge Arnason cited a section of the California Penal Code, which stated that bail could not be granted in a capital case in which there was a high presumption of the defendant's guilt (Aptheker, 1975). Coretta Scott King (the widow of Martin Luther King Jr.), the Reverend Ralph Abernathy, and Congresswoman Bella Abzug all petitioned the judge on Davis's behalf, but bail was still denied (Ginger, 1974).

Davis and Ruchell Magee were being tried as codefendants. The National United Committee to free Angela Davis had been formed, and the group was active in bringing attention to the case and in mobilizing support for Davis's release. California Superior Court Judge Richard Arnason was assigned to the case (Major, 1973).

On February 18, 1972, the California Supreme Court ruled that the death penalty was unconstitutional. Davis's defense team was hopeful this ruling would remove the grounds for her being held without bail because her case would no longer be a capital one. The defense again filed a motion for release on bail on the grounds that Davis was no longer being tried for a capital offense. Bail was finally granted, but the judge issued a long list of restrictions, which Davis's supporters protested. Many of the restrictions were intended to limit protest activities around the courthouse and to limit Davis's communication with the public. Davis and her attorneys protested these restrictions, arguing that they violated Davis's constitutional rights to free speech (Aptheker, 1974). The defense eventually negotiated with Judge

Arnason and agreed to some restrictions, such as Davis being prohibited from speaking to the media about the case.

Three other pretrial motions were filed by the defense: (1) for Davis to serve as cocounsel, (2) for the Davis and Magee cases to be tried separately, and (3) for a change of venue (Ginger, 1974). All of the motions were granted. Davis and Ruchell Magee were to be tried in separate cases, and the trial was moved from San Francisco to San Jose, California (Ginger, 1974).

MEDIA COVERAGE

It was through the media that Davis first became a public figure over her dismissal from UCLA. A student, who was actually a FBI informant, published an article in the student newspaper stating that the philosophy department had hired a Communist, and the *San Francisco Examiner* later ran a story revealing the alleged member of the Communist Party to be Angela Davis. This story is what prompted the University of California, Board of Regents, to question Davis's political affiliation, for her to confirm that she was a member of the Communist Party, and for her to later be dismissed from her duties (Ginger, 1974). Davis's dismissal from UCLA was reported in national newspapers such as the *New York Times* and the *Times-Herald* and in magazines such as *Newsweek* (Steiniger, n.d.). News reports and editorials raised questions about academic freedom (Berthelsen, 1969; Kraft, 1969). Long before this crime was committed (Davis was acquitted), Davis was a public figure because of her involvement with the Black Panther Party, the campaign to free the Soledad Brothers, and her dismissal from UCLA.

Davis's crime received international media coverage (Brown, 1992; Major, 1973; Steiniger, n.d.). Aptheker (1975) said that "detailed, graphic accounts of the action on August 7 at the Marin Civic Center in San Rafael lit up television screens that same night, and were spread across the front page of every California newspaper by the next morning" (p. 18). Initial media reports did not link Davis to the shootout at the Marin County courthouse, but reports had mentioned an "unidentified accomplice" who reportedly helped plan the crime (Aptheker, 1975). There was also a report that Jonathan Jackson had visited his brother in prison earlier in the week, and there were questions about whether George Jackson knew the inmates involved in the shootout (Aptheker, 1975).

Aptheker (1975) further reported that "two days later—on August 9—the associate warden at San Quentin, James W. Park, called a news conference to announce that he was beginning a full-scale investigation to determine whether or not the incident at the Marin Civic Center was, in fact, part of some 'wild plot to free the so-called Soledad Brothers'" (p. 19). The media promoted the idea that the takeover was linked to the movement to free the Soledad Brothers and that Davis was involved. A news reporter at the scene of the takeover said that he heard one of the prisoners shout "free the Soledad Brothers by 12:30," which was offered as evidence of the connection with the Soledad Brothers, as was Jonathan Jackson and Davis's visits to George Jackson (Aptheker, 1975, p. 20). Within two days of the takeover, the media reported that criminal justice officials suspected that Davis was involved.

The incident became even more highly publicized in the media when Davis was on the run from the FBI and after her arrest. During this period, criminal justice system authorities utilized the press, such as when Davis was placed on the FBI's Ten Most Wanted list. Posters with Davis's picture, stating she should be considered armed and dangerous, were put up around the United States (Ginger, 1974; Major, 1973).

Thousands of phone calls came in to law enforcement officials from people reporting they had seen Davis in places all over the United States and in foreign countries. Once Davis was captured in New York City, President Richard Nixon gave a televised address in which he congratulated J. Edgar Hoover, the FBI Director, for the capture of the "dangerous fugitive" Angela Davis. The criminal justice system used the media to emphasize that Davis presented a flight risk, that she was intimately connected to the crime at the Marin County courthouse, and that her political affiliations meant she had no respect for the laws of the United States.

The media played a dual role in the case, being utilized by both criminal justice system authorities and Davis's supporters. It is hard to determine what role the media would have played had Davis not already been a public figure because of her dismissal from UCLA and her involvement with the Soledad Brothers' defense committee. Both the mainstream press and publications that were considered radical followed the case from the time of the takeover to Davis's acquittal.

The mainstream press coverage reviewed for this chapter was from the *New York Times* and the *Times-Herald* (now the *Washington Post*). The papers frequently cited Davis's political affiliation when reporting about her. One editorial, "The Angela Davis Tragedy," talked about Davis's promise as an intellectual and political leader. It then suggested that it would be a tragic waste if Davis had crossed the line to violence to advance the causes in which she believed ("Angela Davis," 1970). Articles reporting on the incident frequently cited Davis's political affiliation, referring to her as a "militant black Marxist and member of the Communist party" ("Official Disputes,"1970), a "black militant and Communist ousted from the UCLA faculty" ("Angela

Davis is Charged," 1970), the "missing California militant" ("Missing California," 1970), and a "young black militant" (Charlton, 1970). The media repeatedly noted that Davis was black, a Communist, and militant.

Paradoxically, at the same time the coverage used such adjectives to describe Davis, it also seemed to question the extent to which the crime was linked to political activities or was part of a larger political statement. Two articles published in the *Times-Herald* within a two-day period offered two different theories of the incident. The first article, published ten days after the takeover, presented it as part of a political movement, and led with the headline, "Shootout at California Court Marked Start of a New Revolutionary Front." The author reported someone shouting "we are the revolutionaries" during the escape attempt, (Aarons, 1970, p. A1) and quoted Huey Newton, leader of the Black Panther Party, as saying Jonathan Jackson "should have and would have been my successor" (Aarons, 1970, p. A1).

Aarons said, "To the radical movement, the event at San Rafael . . . is fast becoming a revolutionary milestone—a watershed in America's progress toward its own Battle of Algiers" (Aarons, 1970, p. A1). Another statement suggested the shooting induced "the real fear that the state's, and possibly the nation's, courthouses could become the battleground for a form of guerrilla warfare aimed at freeing black or white 'political prisoners'" (Aarons, 1970, p. A5). Aarons ended the article by questioning whether the event was part of a larger revolutionary movement or was a crime committed by Jonathan Jackson acting alone.

Two days later, Aarons wrote another article with a more nuanced tone. He interviewed George Jackson who denied knowing what his brother had planned to do. Jackson said, "The only reason I would have attempted to dissuade him would be that I know the guards here . . . how vicious and diabolical. I knew they would have fired on the crowd in complete disregard of anyone's life. All restraints are trained out of them during in-service training" (Aarons, 1970, p. A6). In the same article, the warden of San Quentin, Louis Nelson, said of the crime, "I thought it was just a dangerous escape attempt . . . militants believe if they do this under the guise of revolution, it makes them heroes or it becomes legal." A different article quoted Associate Warden James W. Park as having said, "To me . . . these men were using this talk to vent their own orneriness. They are nothing but hoodlums and troublemakers. They were hoodlums in their own communities before they got here" (Caldwell, 1970). In some media accounts, there was a deliberate attempt to separate the crime from any type of legitimate movements for social change.

The tone of each article was shaped by the experts chosen to be interviewed. The first article quoted two high-profile figures in radical causes: Huey

Newton, leader of the Black Panther Party, and Tom Hayden, one of the Chicago Seven. The other articles, quoting criminal justice officials from the Department of Corrections, supported the theory that the takeover was an ordinary crime, devoid of political meaning or motivation.

Davis supporters used the media to highlight that she was a black woman who was being charged and tried because of her political beliefs. Her supporters also used the media to garner support for their cause and to mobilize people who would petition politicians on Davis's behalf. The black community newspaper the *Los Angeles Sentinel*, the Los Angeles–based paper the *Free Press*, and the San Francisco–based *People's World* all denounced the way the police handled the search for Davis by saying they were targeting the black community.

Upon Davis's arrest, an international movement mobilized to protest her arrest, and the media gauged these activities closely and offered commentary about whether Davis was a political prisoner or a criminal. The organizations and groups mobilized in Davis's defense utilized the media to rally public support for her release on bail. When the sheriff in charge of holding Davis stated that he thought she should be released on bail, he was asked to hold a press conference stating this and he agreed (Aptheker, 1975).

THE TRIAL

At her arraignment, Davis said, "I stand before the court as the target of a political frame-up, which, far from pointing to my culpability, implicates the state of California as an agent of political repression" (Aarons, 1971). Davis chose to assist in her own defense as a member of her counsel team, which included Howard Moore Jr., a civil rights attorney; Leo Branton Jr.; Margaret Burnham, a childhood friend of Davis; Doris Walker; and Sheldon Otis (Aptheker, 1975).

The jury selection process took over two weeks. Defense Attorney Moore questioned some jurors about whether they could render a fair verdict to a black woman who was a Communist (Aptheker, 1975). Davis's attorneys emphasized that many of the witnesses in the case would be black and Communists. Timothy (1975) reported that the defense did not want the jury to be shocked by the people they would encounter during the trial.

The jury foreperson wrote a book about her experiences while serving on the Davis trial (Timothy, 1975). She described how all of the prospective jurors called to report to jury duty were searched upon entering the courthouse. There were over 100 jurors called, and they were kept in a separate room and watched the voir dire over closed-circuit television. The lengthy jury selection process caused the composition of the jury to become more homogeneous, as students and blue collar workers were unable to sacrifice the time and wages to remain in the pool. One potential juror was a black woman, Janie Hemphill, who was questioned extensively by the prosecution (Aptheker, 1975; Timothy, 1975). Her husband owned a nightclub that went out of business and at one time had a violation of liquor license laws. The prosecution aimed to discredit Hemphill, and she was ultimately dismissed as a juror by the prosecution. The defense team spent extensive time researching the backgrounds of the potential jurors in an attempt to draw those who would be the most open-minded and would listen to the evidence impartially. Ultimately, an all-white jury comprised four men and eight women.

Davis gave the opening statement in the case, mentioning that a jury had recently acquitted the Soledad Brothers because they understood they were being tried as political prisoners. Davis tried to draw a connection between the Soledad case and her own, and she reassured the jury that she had faith they would render a just decision.

Davis was charged with three different counts: conspiracy, kidnapping, and murder. Initially, the prosecution intended to present the motive for the conspiracy and kidnapping as an attempt to free the Soledad Brothers from San Quentin prison, which was where they had been transferred. The prosecution then revised its approach; Davis was motivated by her love for George Jackson, and she had essentially committed a crime of passion. As evidence of the relationship between Davis and Jackson, the prosecution presented letters the two had written to each other professing their deep love, affection, admiration, and respect. In addition, the prosecution wanted to present Davis's diary as evidence of her relationship with Jackson (Aptheker, 1975; Ginger, 1974; Major, 1973). The defense protested admission of the diary, arguing that it was private and irrelevant to the case. The judge eventually ruled that an edited version of the diary could be submitted into evidence.

The trial lasted three months. The prosecution called over 100 witnesses in the case, and the defense presented only twelve. After thirteen hours of jury deliberation, on June 4, 1972, the jury acquitted Davis of all charges (Aptheteker, 1975).

SOCIAL, POLITICAL, AND LEGAL ISSUES
OF DAVIS'S CASE

Most of the published accounts of the trial were written by Davis supporters, which may present a bias in her favor regarding the information available about the case. Nothing written by police or prosecutors involved in the case was found. Perhaps the most neutral party writing about the trial was Mary Timothy, the jury foreperson, although her assessment of the case resembled much of the other published material.

The crime was committed during a period of great unrest in the California prison system, particularly between black and white inmates and between black inmates and white guards. The crime was also the height of the indeterminate sentence, when inmates were given a sentence with a wide range of potential time to be served with actual release dates determined by parole boards. For instance, an inmate could be serving a sentence of two to fifteen years for aggravated assault charges. Such a system fostered a sentiment among black inmates that they were treated in an arbitrary and capricious manner by the prison system and that it was virtually impossible for them to receive justice when sentenced and particularly once incarcerated.

The political and social upheaval occurring in the broader society that had manifested in the Black Power, women's, antiwar, and student movements, was symbiotically linked to social and political movements within the prison system. Growing segments of prisoners claimed they were political prisoners because they were tried by a criminal justice system that was part of the larger racist and classist American society. The Black Panther Party called for all black prisoners to be considered political prisoners and demanded that they be treated in accord with the Geneva Convention. Prisoners came to be viewed as a similarly marginalized segment of society in need of a voice and mobilization for change.

Davis's trial was inextricably linked to the social and political changes of the era. Scholars have suggested that she was tried because of her involvement with the Black Panther Party and her membership in the Communist Party. Huey Newton, head of the Black Panther Party, spoke at Jonathan Jackson's funeral and issued a revolutionary call (Major, 1973). Jackson's mother and sister both said he died for the "cause of the people," but they denied that Davis was involved (Major, 1973).

Scholars have referred to Davis's trial as a political prosecution, and Davis was immediately embraced as a political prisoner (Ginger, 1972). One scholar prefaced his discussion of the Davis trial with an overview of other high-profile cases involving issues of race, politics, and social change. Davis's trial was analogous to other "political trials" such as the Scottsboro Boys, Adam Clayton Powell, and H. Rap Brown (Major, 1973). The political implications of Davis's case stem not only from her activities in groups that criticized the existing social structure and advocated social and political change, but from the time and place in history in which her case occurred.

DAVIS'S IMPACT ON POPULAR CULTURE

A "Free Angela Davis" campaign sparked worldwide attention. The case was deeply embedded in social and political issues, as discussed earlier, as well as in popular culture. Davis's case occurred during the emergence of the counterculture and women's, antiwar, and student movements. Her case was embraced as a symbol of government repression and attempts to stifle dissent.

The issues that emerged during Davis's trial were already infused into popular culture at the time of her trial, and Davis became a symbol of these issues. A broad array of high-profile individuals joined the campaign on Davis's behalf, including actors Ossie Davis, Dick Gregory, and Jane Fonda; musicians Pete Seeger and Aretha Franklin; boxer Muhammad Ali; and author James Baldwin (Steiniger, n.d.).

Writings by high-profile prisoners involved in the Black Panther Party and other political movements that were considered radical were published around the time of Davis's case. Eldridge Cleaver wrote *Soul on Ice* while incarcerated in Folsom State Prison in California, and it was published in 1968. *Soledad Brother: The Prison Letters of George Jackson* was published in 1970. Huey Newton wrote *To Die for the People* in 1972. These works were self-reflective about their experiences as black men in the United States and in the prison system, and they were critical of the larger social system. When Davis was imprisoned at the New York Women's House of Detention, she had ten copies of Jackson's book *Soledad Brother* sent to her. Prison officials originally told her she would have to leave whichever books she received at the jail, and Davis saw this as an opportunity to supplement the jail library with books of political significance (Davis, 1974).

CONCLUSION

The Davis case became part of the narrative of oppressed people who were entangled in a criminal justice system that was considered unjust. Davis was one of a group of political prisoners who were tried for their beliefs and affiliations rather than for any actual crimes they committed. The Davis case provides an interesting reflection of the social and political era in which it occurred, and how the media are a vehicle for defining crime and justice issues.

REFERENCES

Aarons, L. F. (1970, August 17). Shootout at California court marked start of a new revolutionary front. *Times-Herald*, pp. A1, A5. ProQuest Historical

Newspapers, the *Washington Post*. Retrieved January 23, 2004, from http://www.washingtonpost.com

Aarons, L. F. (1970, August 19). 2 views of courthouse tragedy. *Times-Herald*, p. A6. ProQuest Historical Newspapers, the *Washington Post*. Retrieved January 23, 2004, from http://www.washingtonpost.com

Angela Davis is charged in judge's death. (August 16, 1970). *Times-Herald*, pp. 1, A10. ProQuest Historical Newspapers, the *Washington Post*. Retrieved January 23, 2004, from http://www.washingtonpost.com

The Angela Davis tragedy. (October 16, 1970). *New York Times*, p. 34. ProQuest Historical Newspapers, *New York Times*. Retrieved January 23, 2004, from http://www.nytimes.com

Aptheker, B. (1975). *The morning breaks: The trial of Angela Davis*. New York: International Publishers.

Berthelsen, J. (1969, September 29). Firing of red stirs furor at UCLA. *Times-Herald*, p. A6. ProQuest Historical Newspapers, the *Washington Post*. Retrieved January 23, 2004, from http://www.washingtonpost.com.

Brown, E. (1992). *A taste of power: A black woman's story*. New York: Pantheon Books.

Caldwell, E. (1970, August 24). Courthouse shootout linked with radical movement and killing of black inmates. *New York Times*, p. 40. ProQuest Historical Newspapers, *New York Times*. Retrieved January 23, 2004, from http://www.nytimes.com

Charlton, L. (1970, October 16). F.B.I. seizes Angela Davis in motel here. *New York Times*, pp. 1, 32. ProQuest Historical Newspapers, *New York Times*. Retrieved January 23, 2004, from http://www.nytimes.com

Davis, A. Y. (1971). *If they come in the morning: Voices of resistance*. New York: The Third Press.

Davis, A. Y. (1974). *Angela Davis: An autobiography*. New York: International Publishers.

Ginger, A. F. (Ed.). (1974). *Angela Davis case collection*. Dobbs Ferry, NY: Oceana Publications.

James, J. (1998). *The Angela Y. Davis reader*. Malden, MA: Blackwell Publishers.

Kraft, J. (1969, October 7). Reagan-led firing at UCLA may radicalize quiet campus. *Times-Herald*, p. A6. ProQuest Historical Newspapers, the *Washington Post*. Retrieved January 23, 2004, from http://www.washingtonpost.com

Major, R. (1973). *Justice in the round: The trial of Angela Davis*. New York: The Third Press.

Meyer, K. E. (1970, October 15). Miss Davis denied bail in extradition action. *Times-Herald*, pp. A1, A3. ProQuest Historical Newspapers, the *Washington Post*. Retrieved January 23, 2004, from http://www.washingtonpost.com

Missing California Militant. (1970, August 17). *New York Times*, p. 23. ProQuest Historical Newspapers, *New York Times*. Retrieved January 23, 2004, from http://www.nytimes.com

Nadleson, R. (1972). *Who is Angela Davis? The biography of a revolutionary*. New York: Wyden.

Official disputes Miss Davis's suit. (1970, November 4). *New York Times*, p. 52. ProQuest Historical Newspapers, *New York Times*. Retrieved January 23, 2004, from http://www.nytimes.com

Steiniger, K. (n.d.). *Free Angela Davis: Hero of the other America*. German Democratic Republic: National Council of the National Front of the German Democratic Republic.

Timothy, M. (1974). *Jury woman*. San Francisco: Glide Publications.

Tomasson, R. E. (1970, November 6). Hearing set here on Davis arrest. *New York Times*, p. 36. ProQuest Historical Newspapers, *New York Times*. Retrieved January 23, 2004, from http://www.nytimes.com

Von Hoffman, N. (1970, November 27). Letters from Soledad. *Times-Herald*, pp. B1, B4. ProQuest Historical Newspapers, *Times-Herald*. Retrieved January 23, 2004, from http://www.nytimes.com

7

The My Lai Massacre:
A Mixed Reaction to Tragedy

Renate W. Prescott

OPERATION TASK FORCE BARKER

On the morning of March 16, 1968, the men of Charlie Company attacked the subhamlet, My Lai 4, of Son My village, believing that they were going to engage the Viet Cong 48th Local Force (LF) Battalion.[1] Charlie Company commander Captain Ernest L. Medina told his company during their briefing the night before that the villagers would be absent, having gone to their early morning market. But, instead of enemy soldiers, they found old men, women, and children. As they began their sweep into the hamlet, they killed several villagers who were on their way to work in rice fields. Along the paths leading to the hamlet they encountered children, and one soldier dropped to a kneeling position and shot and killed them. Inside the hamlet, the 1st Platoon, under the direction of Lieutenant William L. Calley, rounded up the villagers in large groups and killed them with machine guns, pushing the bodies into a deep irrigation ditch nearby. The elderly, who could not leave their beds, were shot inside their homes. Infants were shot in their mothers' arms. Women were raped and then shot, one with an M-16 rifle jammed inside her vagina. Several bodies had the letter "C" for Charlie Company carved into their chests (Bilton and Sim, 1992, p. 129).

Photograph of My Lai massacre originally published in *Life*. The village was originally misidentified as Son My, as initial press reports confused the attacked village with the refugee camp to which the survivors of the massacre were taken. (Courtesy of Library of Congress)

For four hours and without any kind of resistance or enemy fire, soldiers killed hundreds of civilians. By the American count, three enemy rifles were seized, and 128 Viet Cong and a few civilians were killed that day; however, the Vietnamese survivors placed the number of lives lost much higher at 504.[2] The mission, officially named "Task Force Barker" after its commander, Lieutenant Colonel Frank A. Barker, would thereafter be known to the world as the "My Lai Massacre," in which the commanding officers of Charlie Company encouraged, and in some cases, participated in the killing of civilians.

Of the twenty-eight officers involved with Task Force Barker that the Peers Panel recommended for court-martial, thirteen were charged. Barker, who was killed in a helicopter crash three months after the massacre, left many questions about that day unanswered.[3] The commander of the Americal Division, Major General Samuel W. Koster, who has since been appointed superintendent of West Point, was demoted and stripped of his Distinguished Service Medal; he retired soon thereafter. By the time Medina and Calley faced their courts-martial three years later in 1971, most of the soldiers

The My Lai Peace Park monument. (Photo by Renate Prescott)

of Charlie Company had already returned to civilian life and technically no longer fell under the jurisdiction of the military court system. Colonel Henderson was acquitted at his court-martial after witnesses failed to remember events surrounding that day. The enlisted men who participated in the massacre were given immunity in exchange for their testimony, and those still in the military were discharged. Medina was found innocent of all charges, but his upcoming promotion was halted; his rising-star career in the military had ended. Calley was found guilty of killing twenty-two civilians and assault with intent to murder a Vietnamese child. He was sentenced to life in prison with hard labor, but this verdict so angered the American public that President Nixon interfered with the court system; Calley served only three days in the stockade at Fort Benning, and until he was set free he had spent less than four years under house arrest.

THE AMERICAL DIVISION

In the wake of the January 1968 Tet Offensive during the Vietnam War, coastal Quang Ngai Province, which was a known problematic Viet Cong stronghold, became part of a larger mopping up action assigned to the 11th Brigade, which was one of three brigades that came under the Americal Division commanded by Major General Koster. The newly formed 11th Brigade had also just been assigned a new commander, Colonel Oran Henderson. The brigade, along with Charlie Company, had only recently arrived in Vietnam in December 1967. Thus, the 11th Brigade had no combat-seasoned commanders, and the men of Charlie Company had little or no direct combat experience. The commander of Charlie Company, Medina, was a career army officer who had risen through the ranks. As a former enlisted man, he preferred to be a buddy rather than to hold professional distance from his men, and his men respected and admired him. Under his command were three young lieutenants who had little or no combat experience: 2nd Lieutenant William L. Calley of the 1st Platoon, Lieutenant Stephen Brooks of the 2nd Platoon, and Lieutenant Geoffrey LaCross of the 3rd Platoon. Medina, however, did not like Calley, and he often singled him out in front of the men, calling him "sweetheart" or "Lt. Shithead" (Beidler, 2003). Calley, straight out of Officers Candidate School (OCS), was a poor leader who did not have the respect of his men. Instead, he often found himself in pointless arguments with them. His men complained that "he couldn't read no darn map and a compass would confuse his ass" (Hersh, 1970, p. 21). This lack of overall experience and leadership capability throughout the chain of command was to become the downfall of Charlie Company, who had been in-country only three months at the time of the massacre.

Colonel Henderson's Briefing

On the evening of March 15, 1968, Henderson briefed Medina of his mission, telling him that they would be entering Son My village the next morning to rout the 48th LF Battalion that had been operating in the area with the aid of the sympathetic populous. It was to be Henderson's first combat mission in Vietnam. Medina, in turn, briefed his men, assuring them that they would at last be engaging the enemy. Charlie Company had sustained several losses from sniper fire, mines, and booby traps; and they were eager for revenge. In the three months that Charlie Company had been in-country, they had experienced six devastating losses from booby traps and mines, but they had not yet engaged the enemy in a fire fight. The night before the operation, they had just had a service for George Cox, a popular sergeant who had been killed the previous day by a booby trap. Directly after the service they were briefed by Medina, and he had promised them revenge.

Quang Ngai Province and the Phoenix Program

"Task Force Barker" was part of the larger "Operation Muscatine," which had turned large areas of Quang Ngai Province into free-fire zones, which meant anyone caught inside a free-fire zone would automatically come under enemy fire. It was not uncommon for entire hamlets to be removed to so-called safe areas outside these free-fire zones, called "strategic hamlets." But the villagers, whose lives and identities were tied to the land, habitually returned to tend to their crops and to worship their village ancestors. The Vietnamese, who buried their dead in the rice fields believing that their very spirits entered into the rice they ate, were thus tied to the land in ways that the Americans could not comprehend.[4]

The people of Quang Ngai Province had a reputation for being sympathetic to the Viet Cong and were not to be trusted. They had a history of actively resisting occupation, reaching as far back as the French occupation that lasted from the eighteenth through the twentieth centuries (Ho Chi Minh's Defense Minister, Phan Van Dong, and four other generals were born in Quang Ngai Province). To the people of Quang Ngai Province, the Americans were imperialist invaders and occupiers of their homeland—not the liberators from communism that the Americans liked to believe. Son My also had the reputation of being "probably the most violence-ridden area in all of South Vietnam"(*Newsweek*, 1969, p. 36). Operation Muscastine was also a part of the larger "Phoenix Program," which was initiated by the CIA. The Phoenix Program, known by its Vietnamese name "Phuong Hoang," was designed for the U.S. Army to destroy the Viet Cong's presence in the south and to undermine the people's support. Most of the program's operatives were South Vietnamese soldiers [Army of the Republic of Vietnam (ARVN)]. Phoenix quickly gained its reputation as an assassination program with a primary mission to demoralize the Viet Cong and its sympathizers by terrorizing the villagers who might be assisting the Viet Cong. In the Quang Ngai Province alone, Phoenix operatives "had already drawn up a black book—a list of suspects—for every village in the province. In three months, they claimed, an estimated [796] people had been captured or killed under the program" (Bilton and Sim, 1992, p. 89). Villagers were regularly picked up, beaten, tortured, and never seen again. Or they were sent to the notorious prison island, Con Son, off the coast of South Vietnam; there they were tortured and few never returned home.

Medina and his men were eager for this mission. Son My village had been nicknamed "Pinkville" by the soldiers because it was shaded pink on the maps, which indicated a high-density population. They knew that the area civilians were sympathetic to the Viet Cong, and thus the smiling men and women in black pajamas were viewed with suspicion by the American soldiers. The war in Vietnam was not an easy one to fight. The illusive Viet Cong seldom made themselves visible. It was a frustrating way to fight a war and tensions remained high, especially for the grunts who were constantly on patrol "humping the boonies." It was impossible to know who the enemy was, to separate villager from Viet Cong, when most of the time the two were one and the same. On the eve of the assault, Charlie Company's strength was down 50 percent, having lost men to mines and booby traps, and yet the people in the villages walked the same paths without harm (Hammer, 1971, p. 245). Face-to-face combat was rare. Most contact came from sniper fire, and over 60 percent of casualties suffered by American soldiers during the Vietnam War were from stepping on well-hidden land mines. In 1969, one-third of the casualties in Americal Division were caused by booby traps (Newsweek, 1969, p. 37). The Viet Cong often recruited entire villages, but the American soldiers, who came from a different cultural construct, often could not bring themselves to shoot at women and children. Inevitably, however, because of a frustrating lack of encounters with the enemy and casualties from booby traps, Charlie Company was increasingly getting out of control. Rape became a common occurrence, and shooting civilians and asking questions later seemed to become standard procedure.

March 16, 1968

The day following Medina's briefing, in the early morning hours, Charlie Company entered the subhamlet of My Lai 4 in Son My village. They were told it was "hot" and to expect heavy fighting. What they found instead were a few old men and mostly women and children. With the soldiers entering the hamlet were Sergeant Ron Haeberle and Specialist/5 Jay Roberts, both photographers of the 31st Public Information Detachment. These two men moved about freely throughout the ensuing massacre, taking pictures and recording forever on film the events of that day.

Primed for a fight, the soldiers found no Viet Cong. Instead, there was a lot of shooting but no return fire and a lot of confusion. What seemed like men with weapons hiding in a field turned out to be women carrying bamboo poles. They were shot on sight. Women and children were herded out of their "hootches" into several large groups. They were all shot, and they either fell or were pushed into a large irrigation ditch behind them. Roberts reported that outside the village there was a pile of bodies. A small child was holding the hand of one of the dead, probably his mother. A soldier dropped to a kneeling position and fired on him and killed him. Haeberle noticed a man and two small girls walking toward the group of soldiers: "They just kept walking toward us . . . you could hear the little girl saying, 'no, no.' All of a sudden the GIs opened up and cut them down" (Hersh, 1970, p. 55).

The civilians verbally protested, but none put up a physical fight. They knew that if they ran they would be shot. Some hollered, "No VC. No VC" (Hersh, 1970, p. 50). Varnardo Simpson said, "My mind just went. The training came to me and I just started killing. Old men, women, children, water buffaloes, everything. We were told to leave nothing standing. We did what we were told, regardless of whether they were civilians. They was the enemy. Period. Kill . . . I cut their throats, cut off their hands, cut out their tongue, their hair, scalped them. I did it. A lot of people were doing it and I just followed. I just lost all sense of direction" (Bilton and Sim, 1992, p. 130).

Calley told one of his men, Private Paul Meadlo, "You know what I want you to do with them," referring to a group of civilians they had rounded up. When Calley returned later, he asked Meadlo, "Haven't you got rid of them yet? I want them dead" (Hersh, 1970, p. 50). When another soldier who was ordered to kill the rounded up villagers with a machine gun could no longer fire, more than once Calley manned the machine gun himself to finish the job.

Meadlo became consumed with what he had done. The following day as he was sweeping the area for land mines, Calley ordered him to discontinue sweeping. Within minutes, Meadlo tripped a land mine, which blew off part of his foot. As he was being evacuated, he screamed at his lieutenant, "Why did you do it? Why did you do it? This is God's punishment for me, Calley, but you'll get yours! God will punish you, Calley" (Bilton and Sim, 1992, p. 165).

Pham Phon, his wife, and three children survived the massacre by playing dead. "I tell my wife and my kids, slip into the canal when GI [*sic*] not looking. We watch for our chance and we do that. So then the GI begin [*sic*] to shoot at the standing people and at the sitting people on the banks of the canal. They fall into the canal and cover us with their bodies. So we were not wounded, myself, my wife, and my two sons. My little daughter, only seven years old, she was wounded in the arm when GIs shoot [*sic*] into the canal when they heard the people groaning and making much noise" (Taylor, 1970, p. 125).

Throughout the morning, Haeberle and Roberts freely roamed about the village taking pictures, not taking part in the killings, but did nothing to prevent them or protest the other soldiers' actions. In one particular photograph published the following year in *Life* magazine, a young girl is seen buttoning her blouse. Moments earlier some of the soldiers had tried to rape her. When that proved unsuccessful, she was pushed toward a group of women and children and the entire group was shot. Haeberle said, "Guys were about to shoot those people. I yelled 'Hold it,' and shot my picture. As I walked away, I heard M16s open up. From the corner of my eye I saw bodies falling, but I didn't turn to look" ("Americans Speak Out," 1969). Haeberle later explained that "killing them seemed like a good idea, so they did it. The old lady who fought so hard was probably a VC. . . . Maybe it was just her daughter" (Hersh, 1970, p. 68).

Roberts also recounted his experience of that day. He saw a wounded child standing, staring in shock. He later stated that as he saw Haeberle focus his camera to take a picture, a soldier came up and shot the child. Haeberle looked shocked as he saw the child killed through his camera lens. In another photograph, which showed a boy about seven or eight years old covering a younger boy to protect him, a soldier kept firing at them until they were dead. Another soldier who was there that day, Charles West, expressed annoyance over a photographer being there at all and protested later to Haeberle that he thought it was wrong for him to be taking pictures. He later recalled of that incident that "He [Haeberle] had taken a whole lot of pictures of this. I stressed that I thought it was wrong that people should be walking around taking pictures of dead bodies" (*Life*, 1969, p. 44).

Acts of Compassion and Defiance

There were, however, acts of compassion from the soldiers who were sweeping through the hamlet. When a family was discovered hiding in a bunker, three American soldiers took them to the edge of the village and told them to run. Another elderly couple was also taken to the same road and told to flee. At another place, an ARVN soldier who was with Charlie Company saved the life of a boy who was blind in one eye. He told his American counterparts that he was too small and blind to bother with (Bilton and Sim, 1992, pp. 161–162).

Some of the enlisted men resisted participating. Psychiatrist Robert Jay Lifton later interviewed a soldier at My Lai who "had not fired nor even pretended he was firing"(Lifton, 1973, pp. 57–59). Lifton believed that his identification as a loner who set himself apart from the other men sustained him. Herbert Carter shot himself in the foot to get himself medevaced out of the carnage. Michael Terry witnessed "One officer [who] ordered a kid to machine gun everybody down. But the kid just couldn't do it. He threw the machine gun down and the officer picked it up" (Bilton and Sim, 1992, p. 245). Michael Bernhardt, who would later testify against Calley and Medina at their courts-martial, also refused to fire on the villagers: "It was point-blank murder. Only a few of us refused. I just told them the hell with this, I'm not doing it. I didn't think this was a lawful order" (Wingo, 1969, p. 41). Robert Maples, who at Calley's trial stated that when Calley told him to shot a group of civilians, said he responded with "I refuse" (Tiede, 1971, p. 73).

Not everyone condoned the killings that day. Warrant Officer Hugh Thompson, a helicopter pilot who was flying over the area to support the ground troops, was disturbed enough to file a report about what he had seen. He landed his helicopter several times that day to rescue villagers, telling his crew to train their guns on the soldiers if they made a move toward the children. Thompson stated later that he spoke with a lieutenant, requesting to rescue people hiding in a bunker. The lieutenant responded that the only way to get them out was to throw in a hand grenade. Thompson went into the bunker anyway and guided out several old men, women, children, and babies. "My crew and I were by that time very mad and upset" (Belknap, 2002, pp. 74–75). Thompson was awarded the Distinguished Flying Cross for heroism in October 1969 for "'disregarding his own safety' to rescue fifteen children hiding in a bunker 'between Viet Cong positions and advancing friendly forces'" (Hersh, 1970, p. 119). The commendation, however, was backdated July 1968 to make it appear as if the army acted swiftly to commend him for his actions. In reality, there were no Viet Cong in the area that day, and Thompson placed the helicopter between American soldiers and the civilians whom they were killing. Realizing the award was a sham for the military to cover their own indecisiveness regarding the events that day, Thompson later threw the medal away. Thirty years later, he and his two crew members were sincerely recognized for their heroism, and, in 1998, they received the Soldier's Medal for their act of heroism.

When Thompson complained to commanders about what he had witnessed, Henderson was directed to investigate. He questioned several soldiers who were at My Lai 4, asking whether they had seen any wanton killing of civilians. All denied that anything out of the ordinary had occurred at the hamlet. Henderson seemed satisfied and dug no deeper. However, Henderson was flying overhead in a command helicopter that day and must have either seen what was occurring or heard the action reports over the radio. Everyone else in the helicopters that day could clearly see what was happening and heard the reports over the radio, so it would have been impossible for Henderson to not have known about the killings. He was to become the highest ranking officer to face a court-martial for his attempted cover-up of the massacre.

Days later, Ronald Ridenhour, a helicopter pilot from another company, was flying over the site and noticed that the hamlet was completely desolate. As they were flying overhead, the men saw something in a field and moved in closer to see what it was. "It was a woman, spread-eagled as if on display. She had an 11th Brigade patch between her legs as if it were some type of display, some badge of honor. We just looked; it was obviously there so people would know the 11th Brigade had been there. We just thought, 'What in the hell's wrong with these guys? What's going on?'" (Hersh, 1970, pp. 87–88). Then they spotted a man running below, a Viet Cong. The helicopter pilot could have shot him but instead let him go. When Ridenhour asked why the pilot let him go, he replied that the villagers had enough of a rough time of it over the last few days. It was that incident that prompted Ridenhour to begin asking the men of Charlie Company what had happened. To his surprise, the men were forthcoming, almost eager to relieve themselves of their burden.

Ronald Ridenhour: The Whistle-Blower

The men involved began talking about the incident at My Lai, and what the 11th Brigade had done soon became common knowledge. Ridenhour had previously spoken with his friend, Charles Gruver, who told him, "We went in there and killed everybody" (Bilton and Sim, 1992, p. 215). The incredulous Ridenhour repeatedly asked him if he really meant "everyone." Gruver replied, "We shot 'em. Lined 'em up and shot 'em down. Three hundred, four hundred—I don't know how many" (Bilton and Sim, 1992, p. 215). Ridenhour asked others what happened, and Larry LaCroix added that Calley manned the machine gun himself when the gunner refused to continue (Bilton and Sim, 1992, p. 216).

When Ridenhour went home in December 1968, he talked to several friends about the incident but was advised to forget about it; but he could not. With the help of an old friend and high school teacher, he composed a letter and sent nine copies by registered mail to Senators Edward Kennedy, Eugene McCarthy, and J.W. Fulbright; President Richard Nixon; and to five members of the Arizona delegation (Ridenhour's home state)—Senators Barry Goldwater and Paul J. Fanin, and Representatives Sam Steiger, John J. Rhodes, and Morris Udall. The letter was also sent to members of Congress, the Pentagon, the Joint Chiefs of Staff, the U.S. Department of State, and to the Armed Services Committee Chairman, Mendell Rivers. Out of these correspondences, only Morris Udall and Mendell Rivers signaled any interest. Ridenhour stated in his letter how he had first learned of the events surrounding the incident at My Lai and how he at first did not believe it until he heard so many people talk openly about it that "it became impossible for me to disbelieve that something rather dark and bloody did occur sometime in March 1968 in a village called 'Pinkville' in the Republic of Vietnam" (Peers, 1979, p. 7). Ridenour placed the blame squarely on Lieutenant William Calley and Captain Ernest Medina, as well as on several enlisted men who had confided in him about the events at My Lai.

Haeberle, meanwhile, was discharged out of the army and had returned stateside, showing his pictures in a slide show to civic organizations in Cleveland, Ohio. Incredibly, no one seemed alarmed by the pictures; some thought they were fake. When the U.S. Army Criminal Investigation Division (CID) came to claim the pictures, Haeberle gave them a copy and told them there was another role of film, probably unprocessed, back at the base in Vietnam. When they looked, the film was still sitting in the back of a desk drawer unprocessed, just as Haeberle said.

THE AMERICAN PRESS AND PUBLIC REACTION

The first press reports went unnoticed. SP/5 Roberts, who had been in the village all morning and had witnessed the mass killings, gave Charlie Company only partial credit. He filed in his report for the 11th Brigade that "the infantry company led by Captain Ernest Medina engaged and killed fourteen VC and captured three M-1 rifles, a radio, and enemy documents while moving toward the village" (Hersh, 1970, p. 78). The *New York Times* merely reported that two Americal Division companies (Bravo and Charlie Companies) had "caught a North Vietnamese unit in a pincer movement, killing [128] enemy soldiers," stating only that "the United States soldiers were sweeping the area" (Kihss, 1968). Brigade press officer 2nd Lieutenant Arthur Dunn noticed the high VC count and low ammunition catch and thought the reason was because an artillery round had hit the villagers. However, he suspected the report "was fishy," and said, "If I had known there was a massacre and let somebody write about it, I would have lost my job" (Hersh, 1970, p. 78).

The first hint that anything was amiss was in a small press release dated September 5, 1969, by the Georgia press. It read, "First Lt. William Calley Jr. is being retained on active duty beyond his normal release date because of an investigation being conducted under Article 32 of the Uniform Code of Military Justice. First Lt. Calley, who was to have been separated from the army on September 1969, is charged with violation of Article 118, murder, for offenses allegedly committed against civilians while serving in Vietnam in March 1968" (Hersh, 1970, p. 128).

On November 20, 1969, the *Cleveland Plain Dealer* printed Haeberle's pictures. That same day CBS reported the story on its evening news. The following day the *New York Post* printed four pictures, and the *New York Times* printed one picture the next day. The men involved began talking. Four days later, Paul Meadlo, who had cursed his lieutenant, was wracked with guilt and publicly confessed to the killings on television. When CBS reporter Mike Wallace asked him why he shot civilians, Meadlo answered, "Why did I do it? Because I felt like I was ordered to do it, and it seemed like that at the time I felt like I was doing the right thing, because I lost buddies, I lost a damn good buddy, Bobby Wilson, and it was on my conscience. So after I done it I felt good but later on that day it was gettin' to me" (Bilton and Sim, 1992, p. 262). He told Wallace that he killed about 350 people and that "they were begging and saying, 'No, No.' And their mothers were hugging their children, but they kept on firing. Well, we kept on firing. They was waving their arms and begging" (Bilton and Sim, 1992, p. 262).

Time magazine reacted swiftly, calling the massacre "My Lai: An American Tragedy" (1969). When the *Cleveland Plain Dealer* published the photos November 20, 1969, the paper received more than 250 calls; 85 percent expressed disapproval of the photographs being published. "Your paper is rotten and anti-American," and "How can I explain these pictures to my children?" (Hersh, 1970, p. 152). The *Washington Post* declared in one of its headlines, "Frustration Could Have Caused Alleged Viet Killings" (1969).

However, it was the December 5, 1969, publication of the Haeberle's photographs and the accompanying story in *Life* magazine that generated a public outrage. In an informal poll, the *Wall Street Journal* found that many Americans did not believe the event took place; some wondered, "why all the publicity?" The *Washington Star* featured one of the pictures on its front page and was promptly branded by the public as obscene. The *Chicago Tribune* wrote, "Americans should not be deceived by the contemptible lamentations that we are all guilty and that our troops in Vietnam have been brutalized by the war and are just as inhuman as the Communists" (Hersh, 1970, p. 142). John Knight of *Knight Newspapers* wrote, "The indiscriminate killings at Song My may now dramatize the larger question of why we remain in Vietnam" (Hersh, 1970, p. 141).

In a *Minneapolis Tribune* poll, 49 percent of 600 interviewed people believed that the reports of My Lai were false. Forty-three percent said they were horrified, but then decided it was not true. Only 12 percent believed there was a massacre (Belknap, 2002, pp. 130–131). In a *Time* magazine survey, out of 1,600 people polled, 65 percent believed such incidents were bound to happen in a war. Only 2.8 percent of Americans expressed disapproval over what had occurred. *Time*, however, stated that "America must itself stand in 'the dock of guilt and conscience for what happened at My Lai'" (Belknap, 2002, pp. 131).

Two weeks after the publication of Haeberle's pictures, *Life* magazine readers from around the nation responded to them. Five veterans (four Vietnam veterans) wrote in defense of Charlie Company. Vietnam veteran James Jones from Montgomery, Alabama, wrote, "It's not a game. If you're going to fight, fight. The responsibility is on the Vietnamese people. They are alike, they dress alike, and look alike" (Wingo, 1969, pp. 46–47). Captain Thornton Boyd from Monterey, California, denied the massacre: "I can speak from experience as a company commander in Vietnam that, given discipline, an American military unit could never be involved in the atrocities that have been alleged" (Wingo, 1969, p. 46). Colonel Ray Smith, a Vietnam veteran from Fort Sill, Oklahoma, wrote, "War is hell, as I know very well, having fought in two of them, including a year in Vietnam. But I know, and you know, that even if this incident happened as alleged, it is an isolated incident and not American policy" (p. 47). Vietnam veteran Richard McMillan, from Columbia, South Carolina, responded, "There will be two extremes: those who want immediate withdrawal, and those who want to drop the bomb. The people in between still don't give a damn about the whole thing" (p. 47). Veteran Roger Eckert from La Mesa, California, felt differently: "Having been a Marine, a devoted American, a true believer in our great country, I took the massacre as one would the death of his child. The pictures in your issue was [*sic*] like a knife in my heart" (p. 46).

Professor Harry Fletcher from Montgomery, Alabama, lashed out at the press: "I think the whole thing has been blown out of proportion. I believe the credibility gap is the inability of people to believe the [television] commentators. There is an obvious campaign waged to show the United States as immoral" (Wingo, 1969, p. 46). John Malagrin from Baltimore, Maryland, wrote, "As Agnew said so accurately, the press can make national issues overnight. I now see other reports of so-called tragedies popping up. I believe a new communist tactic is occurring and they know they can rely on the liberals in the press as suckers" (Wingo, p. 47). Mrs. Norris Breaux from Crowley, Louisiana, pleading for the case of ignorance, responded, "The news media weren't satisfied until the story was told over and over and the whole world knew of it and had their comments published. I believe that the public does not have to know every detail. I vote to send competent politicians to Washington to run the affairs of government. I applaud Vice

Present Agnew and now hope he says more against television, radio, and magazines" (p. 47).

However, Sherri Soltow, from Killeen, Texas, reached deeper into the core of the situation when she wondered, "Is it because they weren't white, round-eyed Americans that their deaths are so unimportant to so many?" (Wingo, 1969, p. 47). Glenn Butler from Omaha, Nebraska, went further and wrote that "The whole world is guilty—the Army as an institution and the government as representative of the American people. I feel bitter about it. It lowers the image of America throughout the world. It lowers whatever we strive for in Vietnam" (Wingo, p. 47).

It seemed that in the minds of the American people, had the press not reported the massacre then the incident would never have had to be acknowledged; most Americans reacted as if they did not want to know and were now angry that they were forced to know. Louisiana Congressman John Rarick consistently described My Lai as the "massacre hoax," and he warned, "the American people are daily becoming more aware that the news media is being used as a weapon of psychological warfare against them" (Hersh, 1970, p. 156). Senator Allen Ellender, also from Louisiana, decided to tell the press that they (meaning the civilians at My Lai) "got just what they deserved" (Hersh, 1970, p. 156). No one could decide if the atrocities were a hoax or fact, if the civilians were at fault, or if the news media were at fault for reporting the massacre.

INTERNATIONAL PRESS REACTION

Reactions in the international press were mixed. Germany, wary to say much after its own war atrocities of World War II, distanced itself with a cautious reaction: "Son My was an isolated incident in no way comparable to Hitler's declared policy of genocide" (*Newsweek*, 1969, p. 36). Although the photographs Haeberle took were first printed in the *Cleveland Plain Dealer* free, he began charging for the privilege to print them. The German magazine *Stern* paid $7,000 to print the photographs, and in their haste had to print them in black and white. In all, Haeberle collected over $35,000 for the sale of his pictures to the London *Sunday Times*, Germany's *Stern* magazine, and Swedish, Australian, and South African newspapers (Belknap, 2002, p. 120).

In England, there were violent demonstrations against the killings in My Lai. But, in an editorial printed in the *Daily Mail*, columnist Bernard Levin blamed the American press: "The men already charged, and others who may be charged, are already being tried and found guilty by television and newspapers there. If television networks and the press wanted to demonstrate beyond argument Vice President Agnew's charges of irresponsibility and of patronizing elitism, they could hardly have gone further than in their behavior in the last few days" (*Newsweek*, 1969, p. 36). Another view was expressed, however, in the *Daily Mirror*: "When a soldier says, Yes, I shot babies and God punished me; then a war is lost" (*Newsweek*, 1969, p. 36).

The *Le Morde* newspaper of France presented the good that came out of the publicity: "Other countries should not look down on America, which at least is bringing the perpetrators to a public trial for the Song My massacre. It is hoped that all military nations have the same courage. How many Song Mys—by no means all of them American—have there been since Lidice and Oradour?" (*Newsweek*, 1969, p. 36).

The most strident reaction came from South Vietnam. In their eagerness not to upset their American ally, the South Vietnamese newspaper carried denials of any massacre occurring. "The South Vietnam Defense Ministry yesterday called 'completely untrue' reports that U.S. soldiers carried out massacres in Quang Nai Province in March, 1968" (*Washington Post*, 1969, p. A11). Yet, the village chief who reported the massacre counted at least 300 to 400 civilian lives lost; the figure was later revised to 504. It was not until much later that South Vietnamese government officials accused its army of failing to protect its own people.

THE PEERS PANEL INQUIRY

In November 1969, the U.S. military assembled a panel, headed by Lieutenant General William R. Peers, to investigate what went wrong in My Lai. Peers and his staff flew to Vietnam in December to visit My Lai, even taking Hugh Thompson, a helicopter pilot who came upon the My Lai massacre in progress, along with them. At the beginning of his investigation, Peers doubted Ridenhour's letter, but he soon realized through the testimony of witnesses, both Vietnamese and American, that the accusations were true. The panel's findings indicated clearly that throughout the entire chain of command, from colonels to lieutenants, officers lost control over their men who raped, tortured, and executed the villagers. The Peers Panel submitted its report on March 14, 1970, concluding that "there were serious deficiencies in the actions taken by officials in the Americal Division, the 11th Brigade, and Task Force Barker, after the incident at Son My, and that those officials did not take appropriate action to investigate or report" (Taylor, 1970, p. 167).

From the recommendation of the Peers Panel, which came to a close on March 17, 1970, charges were levied against fourteen officers for allegedly covering up the massacre. However, because Barker was killed three months after the massacre, information that would have been vital to the case was lost, and therefore many officers never came to trial.

LIEUTENANT WILLIAM CALLEY'S COURT-MARTIAL

The military charged Calley on September 5, 1970, with several counts for the murder of "an unknown, not less than thirty Oriental human beings"; and for "with premeditation, murder of an unknown number of Oriental human beings, not less than [seventy], males and females of various ages, whose names are unknown . . . by means of shooting them with a rifle." To ensure the chances of a conviction, the court added additional charges: "with premeditation, murder one Oriental human being, an occupant of the village of My Lai 4, whose name and age is unknown, by shooting him with a rifle"; and "with premeditation, murder one Oriental human being, and occupant of the village of My Lai 4, approximately two years old, whose name and sex is unknown, by shooting him with a rifle" (Tiede, 1971, pp. 112–119). The charges came only one day before Calley was to be discharged from the army. Calley was tried first in a court-martial at Fort Benning, Georgia, which lasted from November 17, 1970, until its close on March 29, 1971. Calley's court-martial was one of the longest military courts-martial in history. Prosecutor Captain Aubrey Daniel stated to the court that "the accused is to blame and he should be held criminally responsible. What happened in My Lai is the truth. You can't hide it. You can't cover it up. It exists. The accused appointed himself judge, jury and executioner . . . To make that assertion is to prostitute the name of his country. When he took an oath of an American soldier he was to given a license to slay" (Tiede, 1971, p. 108).

Leading the defense team was George Latimer, a man who secured his reputation from having served as a judge on the Utah Supreme Court. Calley heard about him when he had successfully defended eight Green Beret soldiers against murder charges in another military court-martial. However, Latimer was elderly, hard of hearing, and presented a weak defense. He represented Calley as a soldier who was "only following orders" (Medina's orders), and he tried to shift the blame for most of the killings to Meadlo. Calley, Latimer said, was a victim of too much marijuana smoking, and a war that had gone sour. The defense team argued that "the young Lieutenant had been sold down the river by the press and the White House and the Pentagon as well" (*Newsweek*, 1970, p. 28).

Leading for the prosecution was Daniel, who was convinced that Calley was guilty. Daniel and his assistant, Captain John Partin, interviewed every witness and pored over every document about My Lai. Daniel called over twenty of the men from Charlie Company to the witness stand to give their account of what had happened in My Lai.

Frank Beardslee, a rifleman in the company, testified, "I did not accept the CIB [Combat Infantryman's Badge] on this mission because we met no resistance and the CIB indicates combat action" (Belknap, 2002, p. 157). Many of the witnesses testified that they had either witnessed or participated in the killings. However, what was the most damning for Calley were the witnesses who said they saw him participate in the killings.

Earl Maples, a machine gunner, testified that "Lieutenant Calley [herded] the people he had into the hole and him and Meadlo was firing into the hole and Meadlo was crying" (Belknap, 2002, p. 161). Maples also stated that he saw Calley man the machine gun and shoot "women, babies, and a couple of elderly men" (Belknap, 2002, p. 161).

Charles Sledge, Calley's radio man, testified that he had seen Calley and Meadlo shove people into the ditch and then fired on them. He stated that Calley hit a priest and then shot him in the face, and that he threw a small child into the ditch and shot him (Belknap, 2002, p. 162).

Thomas Turner testified, "when [Calley] approached the ditch, he saw Meadlo and several other GIs firing into it. Calley emptied his weapon, changed clips, and started shooting again . . . Calley systematically executed them" (Belknap, 2002, p. 162).

Paul Meadlo, who was granted immunity for his testimony, stated how his lieutenant asked him why he had not completed his job when he returned to the ditch later: "'We've got another job to do, Meadlo.' . . . He ordered me to help kill the people. I started shoving them off and shooting . . . the people was just laying there with blood all over them . . . they had wounds in the head, in the body, in the chest, in the stomach" (Belknap, 2002, p. 165).

The defense team tried to prove that Calley was incapable of committing premeditated murder; that the killings instead were spontaneous and without premeditation, and that, as psychiatrist Dr. Wilbur Hamman said, Calley "did as he was told, and there was no element of volition" (Belknap, 2002, p. 176).

In his defense, Calley stated that when he arrived in Vietnam, he learned "everyone was a potential enemy," and the casualties his men suffered caused "a deeper sense of hatred for the enemy." He admitted feeling nothing for the Vietnamese, as "they were only gooks" (Belknap, 2002, p. 177). When Daniel pressed Calley about whether he discriminated between villagers and the enemy, Calley responded, "I didn't discriminate between individuals in the village, sir. They were all the enemy, they were all to be destroyed, sir" (Hammer, 1971, p. 273). When Daniel asked about the shooting at the ditch, Calley responded, "There wasn't any big deal, no sir" (Hammer, 1971, p. 276).

During his closing arguments for the army, Daniel refuted Calley's claim to following orders, cautioning the jury, "You must still consider whether a reasonable man should know without a reasonable doubt that any order if received to gather up thirty people, some children and babies, on the north-south trail and summarily execute them just can't be justified. To gather up more than seventy people and put them like cattle in an irrigation ditch and summarily execute them is illegal and the reasonable man knows it" (Hammer, 1971, p. 333).

The trial went to the jury on March 16, 1971, three years after the massacre. Calley was found guilty on all counts with the exception of one, in which the word "premeditated" was changed to "intent." He was sentenced to life in prison with hard labor.

Only days after the trial, President Nixon ordered that Calley be confined to his quarters pending his appeal, promising the public that he himself would review the case. Daniel was outraged and felt certain that the Nixon administration was interfering with the case. He fired off an angry letter to the White House after the trial and expressed shock at the public's outcry, stating that "so many of the political leaders of the nation . . . have failed to see the moral issue or, having seen it, [are willing] to compromise for its political motives" (Belknap, 2002, p. 204). By May 1971, the White House received over 26,000 letters and over 75,000 telegrams—99 percent of them opposed the verdict (Belknap, 2002, p. 265). In 1973, the Court of Military Review rejected Calley's appeal. In February 1974, he was released on a $1,000 personal bond, and his prison time was reduced to ten years. However, in June he was ordered back to the Disciplinary Barracks at Fort Leavenworth, Kansas. But in September 1974, Calley was again released, and, in November 1974, the Fifth Circuit Court released Calley on bail. In September 1975, the Fifth Circuit Court tried to reverse the earlier decision, attempting to return Calley to confinement, but the military announced that they would not attempt to return him to prison. In 1981 the army rejected Calley's appeal for clemency, and today he lives in Columbus, Georgia, working as a manager of his father-in-law's jewelry store.

CAPTAIN ERNEST MEDINA'S COURT-MARTIAL

Medina was tried at Fort McPherson, Georgia. The trial commenced on August 22, 1971, and ended a month later on September 22 with an acquittal. Medina was charged "on or about 16 March 1968, with premeditation, murder [of] an unknown number of unidentified Vietnamese persons, not less than [100], by means of shooting these persons with machine guns, rifles, and other weapons" (McCarthy, 1972, p. 3). Two additional charges were brought against him of shooting a woman and a child. Medina admitted to shooting the woman but as an act of self-defense. He admitted that he could have been "involuntarily" responsible for the death of the child but only because his orders for his men to stop shooting may have come too late. The verdict seems to have been a foregone conclusion. Medina and his counsel, F. Lee Bailey, throughout the trial "yawned, stretched, doodled, slumped, whispered, rolled martyr's eyes skyward, nudged neighboring ribs, cupped mouths to pass sardonic asides" (McCarthy, 1972, p. 5).

No evidence was presented that could prove that Medina had any foreknowledge about the operation. Herbert Carter's testimony that he overhead Barker and Medina talking the night before that they had "found out there wasn't going to be no enemy there" could not be corroborated (McCarthy, 1972, p. 30). Barker was dead and Medina testified that he did not discover the "civilians only" situation until the next day at My Lai 4. Gene Oliver testified that he was who shot the child Medina was accused of killing, and when he was asked why he came forward, he stated that the experience "was something I had to bury" (McCarthy, 1972, p. 39). Yet, when a CID investigator questioned him in 1969 about whether he had seen any direct killings, he replied, "don't remember. If I did, it didn't stick in my memory" (McCarthy, 1972, p. 40). Other men came forward who had suddenly changed their story from the Calley trial. They now "could not recall clearly," or in the case of Louis Martin, "he went to the defense and confessed that he now 'thought' his testimony may have been 'inaccurate and misleading'" (McCarthy, 1972, p. 44).

Michael Bernhardt, who was a star witness at Calley's trial, was put on the stand, and, under Bailey's relentless examination, Bernhardt began to falter. His pretrial interview with counsel Mark Kaddish was thrown back at him rapid fire, his statements taken out of context: "I have the prerogative as an individual of telling the truth or not . . . I don't know whether I'll tell all the truth or not tomorrow . . . I could lie or conceal the truth for principle of justice. . . . What I *think* is [the truth] is what is important . . . I could tell an untruth to preserve not a person but a principle—namely justice" (McCarthy, 1972, p. 46). Finally, a devastated Bernhardt, who was a staunch Republican, was asked whether he ever took part in antiwar demonstrations. When Bernhardt pleaded the Fifth Amendment, Bailey demanded to know, "Are your ideas of truth connected with a subversive group?" (McCarthy, 1972, p. 47). Bernhardt answered "No," and after a short recess the defense counsel coldly requested to withdraw the witness.

Bernhardt left the courtroom in disgust, making an obscene gesture toward Kadish and Medina (McCarthy, 1972, p. 47).

Calley, who had been convicted at his own court-martial, showed up at Medina's court-martial on September 13; however, it seems to have been only for show. Calley pleaded the Fifth Amendment and left. In Calley's own defense, he stated that he was only following orders—Medina's orders— so to show up at his trial as a witness for the prosecution would not have worked anyway, since his jury found him responsible for his own actions.

The only men who were unflappable on the witness stand were helicopter pilot Hugh Thompson and his crewman Larry Colburn. The defense lawyers, however, wondered if the flinch of the Vietnamese woman when Medina turned her over with his foot before shooting her was because she was about to attack him, thereby, justifying his killing her. At one point Judge Howard became impatient and took over the questioning, asking whether the woman could have been standing? Colburn, unflappable, answered, "Oh no" (McCarthy, 1972, p. 72). Thompson, who believed in the war, could not be shaken as easily as Bernhardt. His testimony that he saw "a captain" nudge a Vietnamese woman with his foot could not have been anyone other than Medina. The only question that remained was if she "flinched" before or after he nudged her, indicating that Medina may have acted in self-defense.

With the defense's constant hammering at minutiae, witnesses who were sure about their memories at Calley's trial suddenly could not recall certain events. They could not place Medina at precise locations—was he nine yards away or farther? They could not recall whether Medina said, "That's enough shooting for the day. The party's over" or "That's enough shooting for the day" (McCarthy, 1972, p. 63). Did he call for a cease-fire at 9 a.m. or 11 a.m.? Did he shoot a baby, or did someone "suddenly remember" that it was he and not his captain who shot the infant? Not surprising for the defense and the American public, Medina was found innocent of all charges. He and his attorney, F. Lee Bailey, later appeared together on television as celebrities (the David Frost show) to brag about Medina's new job at Bailey's helicopter plant. Bailey said, "I think Ernie Medina is the right guy to stick in there to make a little company into a huge giant" (McCarthy, 1972, p. 87).

MY LAI AND THE UNITED STATES

Many things went wrong that day in My Lai. Perhaps it was the unusually large number of lives lost that called attention to the massacre. Perhaps it was the total breakdown of the chain of command that resulted in four hours of chaos, horror, and death to men, women, and children that called attention to the massacre. Perhaps it was only the actions of two men, Ronald Ridenhour and Hugh Thompson, who persisted in calling attention to the massacre, reminding Americans that this behavior was an aberration and not normal procedure. My Lai, unfortunately, was not the only place in which atrocities occurred during the Vietnam War. Other hamlets in Son My Village were also attacked that day, only in comparison they did not seem to merit the attention that came to My Lai. Yet, in perspective, of the 3 million men and women who served during the Vietnam War, only a few committed atrocities. Nevertheless, there seemed to be an overall disconnect between Americans and the Vietnamese whom they were bound by military oath to protect. For one, there seemed to be a low regard for life by the U.S. soldiers because the people were Asian. The first charges brought against Calley accused him of killing "Oriental human beings." The Vietnamese civilians treated in American hospitals in Vietnam were commonly given such names as "Bubbles," "Ohio," and "Cyclops" for a Viet Cong soldier who had lost an eye. Vietnamese people were also routinely called "gooks," "slant-eyes," and "slopes." Often the "mere gook" rule applied, meaning Vietnamese life was considered cheap to the Americans. This attitude was itself ironic since it was General Westmoreland who first charged that the Vietnamese viewed life as cheap.

An unidentified soldier from the Americal Division explained, "People back home in the world don't understand this war. We were sent to kill dinks. How can they convict Calley for killing dinks? That's our job" (Time, 1971, p. 21).

The men involved in the killings at My Lai argued that they were following orders. However some refused to participate. Professor Morgenthau said of those who participated, "what that reveals is that in a certain kind of extreme environment, moral standards are totally reversed. What has become sane becomes psychotic and what has been psychotic becomes sane" (Knoll and McFadden, 1970, pp. xii–xiii). Lifton, who counseled some of the men of Charlie Company, said about the question of blame, "My Lai is simply the foot soldier's direct expression of the axiom of fire and terror that his superiors in Washington devise and command behind desks. The real war criminals in history never fire guns, never suffer discomfort" (Knoll and McFadden, 1970, p. 110).

As a result of the publicity surrounding the My Lai massacre, Congressman Ronald Dellums, in 1970, held hearings in which he invited veterans of the Vietnam War to testify about misconduct that they had either witnessed or committed themselves. The hearing became known as the "Winter Soldier Investigation," in which hundreds of veterans testified about what they thought was wrong with the war and its execution. Dellums stated, "we have attempted to shift the focus of veterans from concern for personal guilt to an analysis of institutional responsibility, appropriate to a mass society such as modern America. We concluded that for veterans who were raised on a spiritual diet of unquestioning patriotism and racial and sexual bias, speaking out to denounce policies and acts they were forced to commit as soldiers, represents an important escalation of confidence in their collective ability to act against an institution that had cruelly oppressed them" ("Citizens Commission," 1972, pp. x–xi).

The press did play a significant role in presenting the massacre at My Lai to the public. Most Americans resented the truth and chose to deny it, but others praised the system for allowing the massacre to be publicized. And, of course, an informed public is vital to the health of democracy. It was no easy time for the United States. The massacre at My Lai made the war in Vietnam even more unpopular with the American people, and the massacre at My Lai did more to question why the United States was in Vietnam than the peace movement could ever have done. When the United States finally did pull out in 1975 after having been involved in Vietnam since the end of World War II, over 58,000 U.S. soldiers had died in Vietnam. However, in 1968 alone, at the time of the massacre, over 50,000 Vietnamese civilians had been killed and over a half million had been left homeless because of the war.

The war was reported on each day in the United States. Magazines such as *Newsweek* and *Time* had sections set aside for regular reporting on the war. As Americans sat down to dinner every evening, they saw their soldiers getting shot, killed, and dragged out of battle in body bags. Americans still struggle with the ramifications of their involvement in Vietnam. Because of My Lai, soldiers were treated like lepers and baby killers upon their return home. My Lai did not help their image at all.

Many Americans blame the press for Calley being brought to trial. Without the enormous publicity, they argue that he would have never been charged; he was just doing his job. Yet, when pressed, most of those men who participated in the atrocities admitted their shame. In his study of war crimes, Lifton stated that Americans cannot hide behind the detached psychological or political analysis: "Rather, we must commit ourselves to precisely what our leaders are failing to do: We must confront events like My Lai by reporting them as accurately as we can and interpreting them with whatever wisdom we possess. We must convey the full story of what has been going on in Vietnam, not by simply inundating the American people with grotesque details and thereby mobilizing their resistance to the truth, but by giving form to these details and events within the larger context of the Vietnam War and its causes" (Knoll and McFadden, 1970, p. 109).

Finally, the Vietnamese people had to come to terms with the events at My Lai. The hamlet itself has never been rebuilt. Instead, the people of Son My village have dedicated a Peace Park and built a monument in memory of their friends and relatives. People from all over the world come to visit, including Hugh Thompson and Larry Colburn, the American helicopter pilots who saved some of the children from the massacre. During the courts-martial, the villagers were declared "unnamed," and the cited number of those killed was inaccurate; however, in the Peace Park at My Lai 4, a plaque memorializes each of the 504 villagers by name who died that day.

NOTES

1. My Lai 4 is one of four hamlets within the village of Son My. The original Vietnamese name for the village (renamed by the Saigon government) is Tinh Khe village. My Lai 4 (renamed by the American military) is actually the subhamlet, Tu Cung. The military called the area collectively "Pinkville."

2. Two days after the operation, the division newsletter proclaimed that "TF Barker Crushes Enemy Stronghold." However, because only three weapons were reportedly captured, many Americal soldiers privately acknowledged that this inequity between the high body count and captured weapons signaled something much different from what the newsletter proclaimed.

3. Captain Earl Michels who commanded Bravo Company and was part of the ground action at My Lai and was also killed in that helicopter crash with Barker.

4. After the killings, the soldiers actually camped out in a graveyard, a sacred place in Vietnamese culture, and spent the night there among shrines and graves.

REFERENCES

Beidler, P. (2003). Calley's ghost. *Virginia Quarterly Review, (79)*1, 37. Retrieved from http://www.virginia.edu/vqr/viewmedia.php/prmMID/8376

Belknap, M. R. (2002). *The Vietnam War on trial.* Lawrence, KS: University Press of Kansas.

Bilton, M., and Sim, K. (1992). *Four hours in My Lai.* New York: Penguin.

Citizens Commission of Inquiry. (1972). *The Dellums committee hearings on war crimes in Vietnam.* New York: Vintage Books.

Hammer, R. (1971). *The court-martial of Lt. William Calley.* New York: Coward, McCann, and Geoghegan.

Hersh, S. M. (1970). *My Lai 4.* New York: Random House.

Kihss, P. (1968, March 17). *New York Times.* Front Page.

Knoll, E., and McFadden J. (1970). *War crimes and the American conscience.* New York: Holt, Rinehart, and Winston.

Lifton, R. J. (1973). *Home from the war.* New York: Simon and Schuster.

McCarthy, M. (1972). *Medina.* New York: Harcourt Brace Jovanovich.

The Nation. (1969, December 5). *Time*, p. 23.

The Nation. (1971, April 12). *Time*, pp. 15–21.

Newsweek. (1969, December 12). pp. 83–84.

Newsweek. (1970, February 2). p. 28.

Peers, W. R. (1979). *The My Lai inquiry.* New York: Norton.

Quang Ngai General Museum. (1998). *A look back at Son My.* Department of Culture and Information.

Taylor, T. (1970). *Nuremburg and Vietnam: An American tragedy.* New York: Random House.

Tiede, T. (1971). *Calley: Soldier or killer?* New York: Pinnacle Books.

Washington Post. (1969, November 23). pp. A11–A14.

Wingo, H. (1969, December 5). Americans Speak Out on the Massacre at My Lai. *Life*, pp. 36–45.

8

Charles Manson and the Tate-LaBianca Murders: A Family Portrait

Marie Balfour

The summer of 1969 was a remarkable period in American history that defined a generation and rocked the nation. Over the span of a month and a half, the nation was riveted to the news, beginning with the coverage of Senator Edward Kennedy and the Chappaquiddick incident and ending with the Woodstock music festival. The summer of 1969 has become famous for other reasons as well. On July 20, Buzz Aldrin and Neil Armstrong became the first men to walk on the moon. Yet, it was the disturbing events of August 9 and 10 that would remain in the headlines for years to come.

THE MANSON MURDERS

Late in the evening on August 8, 1969, four members of the Manson Family arrived at 10050 Cielo Drive in Los Angeles County, California. After parking the car and cutting the telephone wires, Manson Family members Charles Watson, Susan Atkins, Patricia Krenwinkel, and Linda Kasabian entered the property armed with some rope, three knives, and a gun. After ordering the girls to hide, Watson murdered eighteen-year-old Steven Parent, who was in his car getting ready to leave. Leaving Kasabian to stand watch, Watson, Atkins, and Krenwinkel entered the house where

Manson on his way to court to face charges in
the murder of actress Sharon Tate and six others.
(AP/Wide World Photos)

they proceeded to attack and brutally murder the people inside. Sharon
Marie Tate-Polanski, the twenty-six-year-old wife of movie producer Roman
Polanski, was found on the floor of the living room tied by a rope around
her neck to international hair stylist, thirty-five-year-old Jay Sebring. Tate
was eight months pregnant. The body of Roman Polanski's friend, thirty-
two-year-old, Voytek (Wojciech) Frykowski, was found near the porch; and
the body of Abigail Anne Folger, the twenty-five-year-old heiress to the
Folger coffee fortune, was found in the grass. Before leaving, one of the killers
printed the word "PIG" on the porch door in Sharon Tate's blood. The
killers returned to the rest of the Manson Family at Spahn Ranch in the Simi
Hills; they learned the names of their victims the following day during a
television broadcast.

On the morning of August 9, 1969, when housekeeper Winifred Chapman
arrived for work, she discovered the house in disarray and the living room
spattered in blood. The first body Chapman saw was Parent, who was lying
in his car; she ran down the driveway to alert the neighbors and call the
police. When the Los Angeles Police Department (LAPD) arrived soon after,

they found the bodies of five victims. The murder scene was gruesome: Tate had been stabbed sixteen times, and the coroner would later determine from the autopsy that she had been hanged for a short period of time; Sebring had been stabbed seven times and shot once; Folger had been stabbed twenty-eight times; Frykowski had been stabbed fifty-one times, bludgeoned thirteen times, and shot twice; and Parent, who was on the premises visiting the caretaker, had been shot four times, and had a defensive slash wound on his wrist. Despite the horrific brutality of the crimes, there was little time for the Los Angeles community to absorb the shock, for a similar murder occurred on the following evening.

Frustrated by the "messy" way in which the Tate murders had happened, Charles Manson decided to join his Family on the evening of August 9, 1969. According to Kasabian's testimony at the trial, Manson ordered her to drive through Los Angeles, and he repeatedly ordered her to stop so that he could scout out a house with occupants to murder. On this particular night, Manson was accompanied by Watson, Krenwinkel, Leslie Van Houten, Susan Atkins, Linda Kasabian, and Steve Grogan. After selecting a house on Waverly Drive, Manson entered the house first, tying up Leno and Rosemary LaBianca. When Manson returned to the car, he told Watson, Van Houten, and Krenwinkel to hitchhike back to Spahn Ranch. Atkins would later add that Manson had told the three to "paint a picture more gruesome than anybody had ever seen" (Bugliosi and Gentry, 1974, p. 247). When Leno and Rosemary LaBianca's bodies were discovered the next day, Leno was found with his hands tied behind his back with a leather thong, a pillowcase over his head, and the electrical cord of a large lamp around his neck. When the pillowcase was removed, a small kitchen knife was found lodged in Leno's throat. A two-tined carving fork was sticking out of his stomach, and the word "WAR" had been carved into his skin. He had been stabbed twelve times, and there were fourteen additional wounds from the carving fork. Rosemary LaBianca was found on the floor of the bedroom, also with a pillowcase and electrical cord around her neck. She had been stabbed forty-one times. Again, words had been written in the victims' blood: "Death to Pigs" was found on the living room wall, "Rise" was near the front door, and "Healter Skelter" was found on the refrigerator door.

Within hours after beginning the search at the Tate residence, the LAPD had what they thought was a plausible motive: drugs. Friends of both Folger and Frykowski admitted to police that they had been steady users, along with Sebring. Frykowski was known for using cocaine, mescaline, marijuana, and LSD; Folger, along with Frykowski, were both found to have had methylenedioxyamphetamine (MDA) in their bloodstream at the time of their death. In searching the premises, police found cocaine and marijuana in Sebring's car. Expecting to find a drug deal gone wrong as the motive, police began checking all known drug connections generated from Frykowski and Sebring's habits. Police also interrogated William Garretson, the caretaker at the Tate residence, and they had Garretson take a polygraph. Garretson repeatedly stated that he had heard nothing throughout the night; he was released from custody after passing the polygraph test.

Another team of LAPD officers worked on the LaBianca murders. Cooperation between the two groups was limited despite the similarities of the two cases. For their part, the LaBianca detectives were also attempting to find some motive for the killings. With the exception of Rosemary's wallet and wristwatch, nothing was found to be missing from the house. The LaBianca detectives attempted to find leads; they looked into neighborhood activities and investigated Leno's financial records. Although they uncovered information relating to a huge debt run up over racehorse betting, nothing relating to Mafia connections could be established. The LaBianca detectives concentrated their efforts on a former neighbor with previous arrests, including one for attempted murder.

At the time of the first progress reports, the Tate detectives were still concentrating on the possibility of a drug motive. In the LaBianca report, there was a mention of the Beatles album *SWBO 101*, better known as the *White Album*, on which there were songs entitled "Helter Skelter," "Piggies," and "Blackbird," which included the lyrics "arise, arise" (Bugliosi and Gentry, 1974, p. 101). Unbeknownst to them, the LaBianca detectives had hit upon an important piece of information that would later become useful in explaining Manson's conspiracy theory. However, pursuing numerous leads, neither the Tate nor LaBianca detectives were any closer to finding the murderers than they had been at the beginning of their respective investigations.

THE MAN BEHIND THE MURDERS

Born "no-name Maddox" on November 12, 1934, Manson spent the majority of his youth being shuffled between relatives, neighbors, and juvenile detention centers. His mother, Kathleen Maddox, was a teenage prostitute, who was incapable and unwilling to care for a child. Married for a short time to William Manson, he gave her son his name. "No name Maddox" was now Charles Milles Manson. After Kathleen finished serving a sentence for armed robbery, Manson lived with his mother until he was twelve, when she had him sent to the Gibault School for Boys. Manson spent his teenage years in a number of institutions, and he committed his first federal offense in 1951 after escaping from a boys' school in Indiana. Arrested for driving a stolen car across a state line, Manson was remanded to a federal training school for boys in Washington, DC, until he came of age. Due to numerous disciplinary infractions while serving his time, Manson's time was extended. He was nineteen years old when he was eventually paroled on May 8, 1954.

On the outside again and now an adult, Manson met and married a waitress named Rosalie. Less than a year later, Manson was back in federal court in California, this time with a pregnant wife in tow. The presence of a pregnant wife must have been reassuring to the court. Rosalie's condition, combined with a court-appointed psychiatrist's favorable recommendation, Manson was given five years probation. However, unable to stay in one place for long, Manson skipped town and headed east. He was eventually caught in Indianapolis and returned to Los Angeles in March of 1956. Initially sentenced to three years, Manson attempted to escape one month before his parole hearing after he learned that his wife was living with another man. Manson did not escape and was given another five years' time; his wife filed for divorce and retained custody of their son.

Manson spent the majority of his twenties either breaking the law or in jail. Pimping, check forgery, and grand theft auto had Manson back in prison for ten years. While awaiting federal prosecution on the forgery charges, Manson married a woman named Leona who had told his parole officer she was carrying Manson's child. The parole officer had initially managed to get Manson a suspended prison term, but after Manson returned to pimping and violated his probation, he was sent to the U.S. Penitentiary in Washington State during July 1961. Divorce came soon after, but not before Charles Luther Manson was born.

While incarcerated in Washington, Manson became interested in Scientology, which he would later combine with his own ideas into the philosophy that became the Manson Family. Prison records state that besides his interest in Scientology, Manson's only other permanent interest was music. Manson taught himself to play the guitar and drums, and he wrote some eighty or ninety songs while in prison. Manson's obsession with the Beatles was sparked while incarcerated in Washington. "It didn't necessarily follow that he was a fan. . . . He told numerous people that, given the chance, he could be much bigger than the Beatles" (Bugliosi and Gentry, 1974, p. 202). Manson also learned how to play the steel guitar from fellow inmate Alvin Karpis, a former member of the Ma Barker gang. Paroled on March 21, 1967, Manson is reported to have asked to stay in prison; he seemed to prefer institutional life to that on the outside.

Following his parole, Manson was granted permission to go to San Francisco, and during the coming months in the Haight-Ashbury section of San Francisco, Manson began collecting his Family members.

MANSON'S CONTROL

Manson wandered through San Francisco following his 1967 release from prison; he used music, drugs, and love to gain a following among the hippies who lived there. Describing her first encounter with Manson, Lynette (Squeaky) Fromme said of Manson, "'Up in the Haight . . . I'm called the gardener,' he said. 'I tend to all the flower children' . . . He had the most delicate, quick motion, like magic as if glided along by air, and a smile that went from warm daddy to twinkely devil" ("The girl," 1975). During his time in Haight, Manson gained a grand piano from an "admirer." He traded the piano for a beaten up bus, which would eventually serve to take Manson and his followers out of Haight. By the time he left, Manson had an entourage that comprised the core of the Family, including Susan Atkins and Patricia Krenwinkel. Surviving on what they could scrounge from "garbage runs" and credit cards donated by Krenwinkel, the Family eventually settled at Spahn Ranch outside Los Angeles, where their numbers continued to grow.

Spahn Ranch was run-down but frequently used as a movie set. Given permission to stay on the property by the owner, George Spahn, who was elderly and blind, the Family helped with ranch chores. While cooking and cleaning for Spahn, the Manson girls also served as his eyes and ears. Lynette Fromme grew especially close to Spahn. Although not a direct participant in the Manson murders of 1969, Fromme would eventually attempt to assassinate President Gerald Ford in Sacramento in 1975. "One of Manson's shrewdest, toughest, and most slavishly obedient followers," Fromme was assigned to tend to Spahn in the hope that she would eventually inherit the ranch upon his death ("The girl," 1975). It was from Spahn Ranch that Manson sent his Family out to commit the Tate-LaBianca murders of 1969.

Manson's control over the Family stemmed from a combination of charisma, intelligence, and an ability to "work the system." Manson was able to see and understand what his Family needed: Security, faith, a father figure, and a leader. Dr. David Smith, who worked in a free clinic in San Francisco's Haight-Ashbury district, had the following to say about Manson and the Family:

A new girl in Charlie's Family would bring with her a certain middle-class morality. The first thing that Charlie did was to see that all this was torn down. The major way he broke through was sex . . . If they had hang-ups about it, then they should feel guilty. That way he was able to eliminate the controls that normally govern our lives. (O'Neil, 1969, p. 26)

The way in which Manson exerted his control was evasive and difficult to pinpoint. Rarely giving directions, Manson would "suggest" something, and it would be done. Some of the Family members believed Manson could read their thoughts, and some thought he was the second coming of Jesus Christ. Arrested during the Barker Ranch raid, Manson listed his aliases as "Jesus Christ" and "God" (Bugliosi and Gentry, 1974, p. 180). During her grand jury testimony, Atkins said of Manson, "Charles Manson changes from second to second. He can be anybody he wants to be. He can put on any face he wants to put on at any given moment" (Bugliosi and Gentry, 1974, p. 246). Manson's adaptability and his ability to proselytize his sermons and philosophies to the Family gave him immense power over their actions. The heavy use of LSD among the Family members, a drug that is known to lower inhibitions and make the user more susceptible to suggestion, also indicates another manner in which Manson reached his target audience. Manson attempted to break down the existing moral conscience of his Family by encouraging "creepy-crawls." Manson would send out Family members dressed in dark clothing to enter occupied houses at night with the instructions to rearrange items, steal small trinkets, and play mind games on "the establishment."

THE MANSON FAMILY

Invariably, the young men and women that composed the Manson Family were searching for something. Mostly middle-class youth who had run away from home or broken with the establishment, they found alternately a father figure, a brother, a leader, and a Christ-like quality in Charles Manson. Manson's prison records have noted that he could get something from everyone, and he had a remarkable talent for adapting himself to all situations. Using these talents along with his music, drugs, and sex, Manson's Family grew. Safe in the knowledge that Manson was indeed a "Christ-like figure," his Family members became capable of murder.

Before falling in with the Manson crowd, Charles Denton Watson had been an academically talented high-school athlete. Although active in his Methodist church, Watson became involved in drugs after moving away for college. Dropping out of North Texas State University while in his third year, Watson fell in with the Manson Family while they were living with Dennis Wilson. Eventually moving away to sell dope with a girlfriend, Watson rejoined the Family in time to participate in the Tate-LaBianca murders. After participating in the murder of a worker at Spahn Ranch, Watson fled back to Texas in October 1969, and it was from there that Watson fought extradition to California.

Patricia Krenwinkel's change from a quiet, normal girl to one of a member of the Manson Family was quite abrupt. Originally from the Los Angeles area, Krenwinkel's parents separated during her teens. After half a year of college in Alabama, she moved to Los Angeles and got a job at an insurance agency. "She abandoned her car in a Manhattan Beach parking lot in September 1967, quit her job without picking up her paycheck, and went off with Charlie Manson" (O'Neil, 1969, p. 26). In charge of the Manson Family "garbage runs," Krenwinkel would go through grocery store trash bins to find food for the Family. Although Krenwinkel never provided a handwriting sample before the trial, scribbles on her legal pad showed the words "Healter Skelter," misspelled in the same way as had been found at the scene of the LaBianca murders.

Susan Atkins, who had a strained relationship with her family, was a particularly important piece of the puzzle surrounding the initial inquiry into the Tate-LaBianca murders. Her father had left home to look for work, and her mother had died when she was fifteen years old. When Atkins was getting into trouble with the police, "her father complained that the courts were 'too lenient' because they let her out of jail" in the first place (Roberts, 1970, p. 40). Dropping out of school, Atkins sold magazine subscriptions and waited tables. After serving a short jail sentence and probation for armed robbery, Atkins moved back to San Francisco where she began working as a topless dancer. One of Manson's most loyal devotees, Atkins would become the driving source of information that would return a grand jury indictment on the Manson Family members for the Tate-LaBianca murders.

Linda Drouin Kasabian was born and raised in Biddeford, Maine. She dropped out of high school in her sophomore year and was married and divorced within a year. Marrying again, this time to Bob Kasabian, Linda had her first child in 1968. Trouble in the marriage sent Linda back to the East Coast, but Bob convinced her to join him in Los Angeles. Moving to be with Bob Kasabian, Linda met a Manson Family member through a friend, and she left her husband to join the Family. At the Family's urging, she returned the next day to steal money from her friend, which she then turned over to Manson. Kasabian's participation in the Tate-LaBianca murders was limited, having been chosen to come along because she was the only Manson Family member with a valid driver's license.

Leslie Van Houten, although only charged with the LaBianca murders, was tried with Manson, Krenwinkel, and Atkins. Although she was initially convicted with the other Manson Family members, Van Houten was granted a second trial her defense lawyer disappeared during the trial. When the second trial ended in a dead-locked jury, she was given a third trial that ended in conviction and the sentence of life imprisonment.

Van Houten came from the same broken family atmosphere as the other Manson girls. Her parents divorced when she was in her early teens, and she grew up in the Los Angeles area and had eventually discovered the drug scene. She met Manson Family members Catherine Share and Robert Beausoleil in 1968; she was introduced to Manson and the Family and never left.

Beausoleil was born in Santa Barbara, California, in 1947. Originally a musician, Beausoleil was also called "Cupid" for his good looks and ease in attracting women. Before meeting Manson, Beausoleil had starred in a Kenneth Anger film called *Lucifer Rising* (1973) and also wrote the music for the short cult film. Also, Beausoleil sang backup on Frank Zappa's first album *Freak Out* (1966). Beausoleil met Manson while he was living with Gary Hinman—the same man he would later be convicted of killing.

THE INVESTIGATION

While the autopsies were being done on the Tate murder victims, LAPD detective Sergeant Jess Buckles was approached by two detectives from the Los Angeles Sheriff's Office (LASO), Sergeant Paul Whiteley, and Sergeant Charles Guenther. They were investigating the homicide of thirty-four-year-old music teacher Gary Hinman in Topanga Canyon. Whiteley and Guenther thought the LAPD would be interested for several reasons. First, Hinman had been violently stabbed to death, and the words "political piggy" had been written on the wall in his blood. Although the body had been discovered on July 31, the LASO officers believed the victim had been murdered several days earlier. LASO had arrested a young hippie by the name of Robert Beausoleil driving Hinman's car, and a knife was found in the wheel well. Although Beausoleil had been in custody at the time of the Tate murders, it was possible he was not the only one responsible for the Hinman murder. "Beausoleil had been living at Spahn's Ranch, an old movie ranch near the Los Angeles suburb of Chatsworth, with a bunch of other hippies. It was an odd group, their leader, a guy named Charlie, apparently having convinced them that he was Jesus Christ" (Bugliosi and Gentry, 1974, p. 62). However, the LAPD detective Buckles, firmly convinced that the Tate murders had a drug connection, disregarded the information from the LASO detectives.

As part of their investigations into the Hinman murder and a string of car thefts, the LASO raided Spahn Ranch in the middle of August and arrested close to forty members of the Manson Family. However, problems with the warrant resulted in their release. When another raid in mid-October netted the same individuals in Inyo County at the Barker Ranch, this time for car thefts and arson, LASO officers finally got a break. During the three-day search of the Barker Ranch, Inyo County officers found two girls who were fleeing the Family. One was a young woman, Kitty Lutesinger, who was pregnant with Robert Beausoleil's child. Knowing she was connected to Beausoleil, the LASO officers drove to interview her in Inyo County, where she provided information that connected Susan Atkins and the Manson Family not only to the Hinman murder but also to the Tate murders (Bugliosi and Gentry, 1974, p. 114). Lutesinger also provided the names of other Family associates who had been involved with the Family during the recent months.

Working from information provided in Lutesinger's interview, the La-Bianca detectives began looking for a Straight Satan motorcycle gang member. According to Lutesinger, Manson had tried to recruit members of the Straight Satan gang to join the Family to be personal bodyguards for Manson. Only one had taken the bait, and the rest of the Straight Satan members had not been impressed by the idea. Danny DeCarlo had lived with the family on and off for several months. DeCarlo was able to link Manson, Beausoleil, Atkins, and several other Family members to the Hinman murder. He also provided information about the supposed murder of a Black Panther Party member named Bernard Crowe, who had been shot by Manson after threatening retaliation against the Family. Manson had shot Crowe, and his friends dumped the body in Griffith Park near the LaBianca residence. Although DeCarlo and Family members would mention that Manson had killed Crowe, what they did not know was that Crowe had lived. Crowe, who did not belong to the Black Panther Party, testified during the guilt phase of Manson's trial.

Once Atkins had been implicated in the Hinman murder through Lutesinger's interview, she was moved to the Sybil Brand Institute where she told fellow inmates about her participation in the Hinman and Tate murders. Atkins provided enough detail to her dormitory mates Virginia Graham and Ronnie Howard to convince them that she was truly involved. As the LAPD was gathering the story behind the Tate-LaBianca murders from DeCarlo, Graham, who had been transferred to another jail, and Howard were both attempting to tell the authorities what they knew. By the time Howard was able to get her message to the LAPD, they already knew what she wanted to tell them, having learned of the connection between the Family and the Tate-LaBianca killings through Lutesinger and DeCarlo.

The information provided by Atkins and Lutesinger was enough for the police to begin putting together a sketch of the events surrounding the Tate-LaBianca murders. Arrest warrants were issued for Charles Watson, Patricia Krenwinkel, and Linda Kasabian. Manson and Atkins were already in custody. Watson fought extradition from Texas, and although Kasabian waived extradition proceedings and was immediately returned to California from where she surrendered in New Hampshire, Krenwinkel also fought extradition from Alabama (Bugliosi and Gentry, 1974, p. 220). As part of a deal to spare her from a death sentence, Atkins testified before the grand jury. Convinced by her first defense lawyer that it was in her best interest to cooperate, the grand jury indictment was, to a large extent, the result of Atkins's testimony. With the combination of information garnered from Lutesinger, DeCarlo, and Atkins's first-person narrative, indictments were returned on Manson, Watson, Krenwinkel, Kasabian, and Atkins on seven counts of first-degree murder and one count of conspiracy. Leslie Van Houten was also indicted on two counts of first-degree murder and one count of conspiracy. The prosecution suffered a setback when, following a meeting with Manson, Atkins recanted her grand jury testimony, fired her lawyer, and refused to cooperate.

Having lost Atkins's cooperation, the prosecution's star witness became Kasabian. Kasabian had professed her desire to testify since the beginning, and she was considered a better witness than Atkins since she had not physically killed anyone, although she had been present at the Tate murders and had driven the car on the evening of the LaBianca murders. In return for her testimony, Kasabian was granted immunity and was not charged in any of the Manson murders.

"THE DEFENSE RESTS"

By the time the Manson trial was over, the jury had been sequestered for almost nine months, and the defense team for Manson, Atkins, Krenwinkel, and Van Houten had changed composition numerous times. Throughout the trial, Manson kept demanding that he be allowed to represent himself, and although each time his request was denied, Manson was undoubtedly the driving force behind the defense.

Out of a multitude of lawyers willing and eager to represent him, Manson finally chose Irving Kanarek, "whom he regarded as the most obstructionist and time-consuming lawyer in Los Angeles, in hopes of badgering the judge into allowing him to defend himself" ("Manson's shattered defense," 1970, p. 45). The Manson girls went through a multitude of lawyers during the trial. Whenever a lawyer would try to separate his client from the rest of the Family, by way of requesting a psychiatric examination or by utilizing a defense tactic not approved by Manson, within days the Family member would request a new lawyer.

After the prosecution rested in the case, the defense immediately rested without attempting to call any witnesses or present any evidence. This rest was mainly because the lawyers of the three Manson girls had heard that their clients intended to take the stand, to "confess" to the murders, and to absolve Manson of all responsibility. When the girls were given a chance to take the stand out of the presence of the jury, they refused. Only Manson took the stand to "rap" about his philosophies, but he ultimately refused to repeat his testimony in front of the jury.

During the trial, Van Houten's lawyer disappeared. Ronald Hughes, who had been one of the first lawyers to visit Manson in jail, had been Van Houten's counsel since the start of proceedings. Hughes had the dubious distinction of having never tried a case before being selected as part of the Manson defense. When Hughes failed to show up in court after a weekend break at the beginning of December 1970, new counsel was appointed for Van Houten. Hughes's body was found months later in a creek bed near where he was known to go camping. Although the body was too badly decomposed to determine the cause of death, there is significant speculation regarding the nature of Hughes's death and the possibility of the Family's involvement. Because of Hughes's disappearance, Van Houten would eventually be granted a retrial.

The Manson case was prosecuted by Vince Bugliosi of the Los Angeles District Attorney's office. Bugliosi wrote the most comprehensive narrative regarding the Manson murders, *Helter Skelter: The True Story of the Manson Murders* (1974). Although preliminary hearings were done before a separate judge, the trial itself was heard before Judge Charles H. Older. Older, in refusing Manson's repeated requests to represent himself, became Manson's target inside the courtroom on several occasions. Removing the defendants repeatedly for disturbances in the courtroom, Manson on one occasion leaped over the defense table towards Older with a pencil in hand, screaming, "In the name of Christian justice, someone should cut your head off!" (Bugliosi and Gentry, 1974, p. 286).

THE FINAL TALLY

The Tate murders were committed by Charles Watson, Patricia Krenwinkel, Susan Atkins, and Linda Kasabian on Manson's orders. For the LaBianca murders, Watson and Krenwinkel were accompanied by Leslie Van Houten for the actual killings, while Manson participated long enough to tie up the LaBiancas. Also along in the car that night were Atkins, Kasabian, and Steve Grogan. Of the participants, Manson, Krenwinkel, Atkins, and Van Houten had a joint trial that resulted in seven counts of first-degree murder and one count of conspiracy to commit murder for each of Manson, Krenwinkel, and Atkins. Van Houten was convicted of one count of conspiracy to commit murder and two counts of first-degree murder in the deaths of

Leno and Rosemary LaBianca. During the Manson trial, Watson was fighting extradition from Texas, which in effect guaranteed that he would have a separate trial from Manson and the girls. Although his ploy worked and Watson arrived in California too late to be tried with Manson and the girls, he was convicted during a separate trial of seven counts of first-degree murder and one count of conspiracy. Kasabian was granted immunity in return for her testimony at the Manson trial.

Although the Manson Family members were all given death sentences for their 1971 convictions, they were not executed. Under California law, death sentence cases must be automatically appealed. If no technical errors are found at the end of the appeal process, the conviction and death sentences are allowed to stand. However, in early 1972, the California State Supreme Court ruled that the death penalty was unconstitutional under the state's constitution which prohibits "cruel and unusual punishment." This ruling, which predated *Furman v. Georgia* (1972) by only a few months, commuted the sentences of all the inmates on California's death row to life imprisonment. Although California has since reinstated the death penalty, it is not a retroactive statute. The Manson Family members remain in prison, even though they have come up for parole multiple times.

MANSON'S MUSIC AND MOTIVE

One of Manson's goals after leaving prison in 1967 was to produce an album of his songs and guitar music. Believing he could be bigger than the Beatles, Manson used his connections in San Francisco to mingle with people in the movie and music industries. One man he befriended was talent scout Gregg Jakobson, whom Manson met through Dennis Wilson of the Beach Boys. After twice picking up the same two women hitchhiking in the spring of 1968, Wilson returned home one evening to find the girls, Manson, and other Family members in his house. Wilson was intrigued by Manson for a few months, but eventually severed the relationship. Before he did, however, he introduced Manson to Gregg Jakobson. Jakobson was intrigued by Manson's Family but not enough to join. In an effort to promote what he saw as Manson's musical talent, Jakobson introduced Manson to Terry Melcher who was in the music production business. At the time, Melcher was living at 10050 Cielo Drive, the house that would eventually gain infamy as the site of the Tate murders.

Although Jakobson encouraged Melcher to record Manson's songs, Melcher was not interested. It was discovered during the pretrial investigation that during Manson's time with Dennis Wilson, Manson had actually gone with Wilson to drop Melcher at his house on at least one occasion. This was particularly important information because it showed that Manson had previously been to the scene of the Tate murders. Melcher, unimpressed, had this to say about Manson's music:

There were forty or fifty of them; . . . they were everywhere, mostly young women, and they all seemed to be part of the same group, they all sang together with Charlie Manson. He played a guitar, and it seems to me some of the girls were playing tambourines. . . . The type of music they were doing and the whole setting itself was rather peculiar to the pop music business, to say the least. (Gilmore and Kenner, 2000, p. 78)

Melcher decided not to pursue things, and Manson's music career never got off the ground. Manson's obsession with music did not fade, however. Throughout the course of the trial, numerous witnesses would testify to Manson's obsession with the Beatles and his peculiar interpretation of the Bible chapter Revelation nine. To Manson, the release of the 1968 *White Album* by the Beatles was proof that Manson and the Beatles were connected. Reinterpreting the lyrics of songs, Manson felt that the Beatles were calling to him across the Atlantic Ocean, telling him to get ready for the revolution. Manson's reply was to be in the form of an album; the album that Terry Melcher would not produce.

Chapter 9 from the book of Revelation was an integral part of Manson's interpretation of the Beatles' *White Album* and their call to him.

Then the fifth angel blew his trumpet, and I saw a star that had fallen from the sky to the earth. It was given the key for the passage to the abyss. It opened the passage to the abyss, and smoke came up out of the passage like smoke from a huge furnace. The sun and the air were darkened by the smoke from the passage. Locusts came out of the smoke onto the land, and they were given the same power as scorpions of the earth. They were told not to harm the grass of the earth or any plant or any tree, but only those people who did not have the seal of God on their foreheads. (*The New American Bible*, 1987, 9:1–4)

In Manson's interpretation, the locusts were "beetles," and the abyss was a hole in the desert where Manson would lead his Family when the war came upon them. The passage continues on to describe the locusts, which were said to have "chests like iron breastplates," which Manson took to be the Beatles's guitars. According to various witnesses, Manson believed that he was the fifth member of the Beatles and that they were calling to him through the *White Album* to tell him to make ready for the war that was coming.

In a twisted explanation of the Beatles' music, Manson believed that the *White Album* foretold the coming of a race war. Whereas the police initially believed the Tate murders to be drug related, the motive presented at trial was completely different. The Manson trial motive was one of "Helter Skelter." Not only were the words "Helter Skelter" found written on a door at the Spahn Ranch, they were also written and misspelled as "Healter Skelter" in Leno LaBianca's blood on the wall of the LaBianca home.

Among the circumstances implicating Manson in the Tate-LaBianca murders are his frequently proclaimed prophesies of Helter Skelter. Predicting a war started by blacks "ripping off" white families in their homes, Manson stated that "Blackie" (the blacks) would revolt against and kill the "Pigs" (the white establishment). From 1968 through the summer of 1969 Manson told various people about Helter Skelter .... He said Helter Skelter "was coming down fast" and that he "would like to show the Blacks how to do it." (People v. Manson, 1976)

Believing that blacks were taking too long in starting the race war, Manson believed that he could initiate the war that he thought was coming. Manson spoke of a cave beneath Death Valley, to which only he knew the entrance. There, the Manson Family would hide while "Helter Skelter" came down. The following excerpt from the trial testimony of former Family member Paul Watkins describes Manson's ideas:

As we are making the music and it is drawing all the young love to the desert, the Family increases in ranks, and at the same time this sets off Helter Skelter. So then the Family finds the hole in the meantime and gets down in the hole and lives there until the whole thing comes down. (Testimony of Paul Watkins, 2003)

To facilitate the start of these race wars, after Manson tied up the LaBiancas and took Rosemary LaBianca's wallet, he had Kasabian hide the wallet in a bathroom at a gas station in a black neighborhood. Manson had hoped that a black person would find the wallet, use the credit cards, and thus murders would be pinned on the black community. Unfortunately for Manson, when Kasabian hid the wallet in the bathroom on the evening of August 10, 1969, it went unnoticed and undiscovered for months until being recovered on December 10 by an attendant cleaning the toilet. However, the particular gas station where the wallet was hidden was not even in a black neighborhood, as pointed out by one of the defense attorneys at the trial. Yet, the prosecution was able to prove that the gas station was in the vicinity of Pacoima, which is a black ghetto in the San Fernando Valley (Bugliosi and Gentry, 1974, p. 494).

Although other motives have been questioned, "Helter Skelter" was the motive used in court to prove the link between Manson, his Family, and the murders. Prosecutor Bugliosi's cocounsel at the beginning of the trial,

Aaron Stovitz, encouraged the use of another motive during the trial, before he was pulled off the case due to time constraints. In Stovitz's opinion, "Manson ordered the killings to convince police the Hinman's murderer was still loose on the streets and that it was not Beausoleil. That's why it was important for Susan Atkins to write 'pig' in blood at the Tate home" ("Helter Skelter," 1976). At the Hinman murder scene, "political piggy" had been written on the wall. The connection had to be clearly visible if the police were to realize that the killer was still on the loose. LAPD did tie the Hinman murder to the Tate-LaBianca murders but not in a manner that exonerated Beausoleil.

MEDIA COVERAGE OF THE MURDERS AND TRIAL

The Tate-LaBianca murders sparked immediate and intense media coverage. Following the discovery of the bodies through the end of the trial, the media played a large part in what has since become known as one of the most convoluted and mystifying trials in American history. On August 10, 1969, the *Los Angeles Times* headlines read, "'Ritualistic Slayings' Sharon Tate, Four Others Murdered"; and the *New York Times* headlines read, "Actress Is Among 5 Slain At Home in Beverly Hills." The following day, as Tate's husband Polanski returned to the United States from London, new headlines reported the discovery of the LaBiancas. The *Los Angeles Times* connected the Tate and LaBianca murders at a time when even the LAPD was disavowing any connection with "2 Ritual Slayings Follow Killing of 5," "New Murders in Silverlake; Fresh Tate Clue."

Throughout the investigation, the media, with even less evidence than the police, misrepresented details of the crime and reported satanic overtones. The towel used to write "Pig" on the door at the Tate residence, when thrown back into the living room by Atkins, landed on Sebring's head. The towel became a "hood" in the media, leading *Newsweek* magazine to report dealings with black magic and voodoo. Speculation by friends indicated "that the murders resulted from a ritual mock execution that got out of hand in the glare of hallucinogens" ("Crime: The Tate Set," 1969). In the LaBianca case, the *Los Angeles Times* stated that "XXX" had also been carved into Leno's skin, when in reality only the word "WAR" was found (Torgerson and Thackrey Jr., 1969). However, because of the amount of evidence released to the media, the police had difficulty retaining even a minimum of information to use during polygraph examinations. Eventually the police were forbidden to discuss the cases outside of work.

Whereas Sharon Tate had achieved only minor stardom during her lifetime, she was critically acclaimed in death. Studios re-released some of her earlier movies, including *Valley of the Dolls* (1967) and *The Fearless Vampire Killers* (1967). The Hollywood jet set worried about the murders due to the proximity and the identity of the victims. The presence of drugs at the scene led to mass disposal of paraphernalia throughout the area. Quoted in *Life*, a film figure stated, "Toilets are flushing all over Beverly Hills; the entire Los Angeles sewer system is stoned" (Bugliosi and Gentry, 1974, p. 45).

As time went on and the trial began, the media coverage picked up again. The media played off of the American public's view of the trial and the defendants. Three young women and an older man were on trial for these brutal murders. As the information behind the identities of the defendants grew, the public recoiled at the knowledge: drugs, sex, violence, and the mind control of an older charismatic ex-convict. Articles were written about a band of hippies, known as the "Manson Family," living in Death Valley. Police were first told about the Family's possible connection to the Tate-LaBianca murders while interviewing a Family member involved in yet another murder case from Topanga Canyon, California.

Once all of the suspects were in custody, the state began building its case. Jury selection began on June 15, 1970, approximately ten months after the murders. Immediately sequestered following selection, the jury members were allowed only limited access to media sources in an attempt to guarantee the Manson Family members a fair and impartial trial. Jury members were allowed to read newspapers only after all articles and headlines pertaining to the Manson Family and the trial had been removed. When the trial finally began, the defendant's antics in the courtroom, as well as the actions of the Family members holding their vigil outside the court building, attracted continuous media attention. After Manson's lawyer initially requested and was denied a change of venue for the trial, the judge issued a "gag order" to limit the amount of press that would be associated with the trial. With the gag order in place, no one associated with the trial was allowed to discuss it. This occurred too late to stop the publication of Susan Atkins's tell-all "confession" interview. First a newspaper exclusive and eventually a book, the deal went through the evening before the "gag order" was issued (Bugliosi and Gentry, 1974, p. 262). For the general population, however, all they had to do was turn on the television or the radio to hear about the trial.

With the publication of Atkins's story, the media actually made a significant contribution to the prosecution's case. Atkins provided details about leaving the scene of the Tate murders in which the murderers changed in the car and then stopped and tossed the bloody clothing over the side of the canyon road. Using the Atkins' story as a guide, a Los Angeles television crew from KABC-TV retraced the killers' route. "They found three sets of clothing: one pair of black trousers, two pairs of blue denim pants, two black T-shirts, one dark velour turtleneck, and one white T-shirt which was spotted with some substance that looked like dried blood" (Bugliosi and Gentry, 1974, p. 267). The clothing would later be identified as having come out of the Family's communal clothing pile in Manson's bus.

Even President Richard Nixon commented on the Manson trial. Standing in the federal building in Denver, Colorado and complaining that the press had made Manson a glamorous hero, Nixon said, "Here was a man who was guilty, directly or indirectly, of eight murders without reason" ("Justice: A bad week," 1970, p. 7). Although he immediately issued a retraction, the damage was done. Newspaper headlines claiming, "Manson Guilty, Nixon Declares," appeared across the country. Manson himself managed to gain access to a newspaper in the courtroom and displayed it to the jury before a bailiff pulled it away. The motion for a mistrial was denied, and the trial continued.

Outside the courthouse, the circus continued. Clustered on the street corner were some of the Manson Family girls. Following the lead of the defendants inside, they carved Xs into their foreheads, and shaved their heads, yet again demonstrating the hold of Manson over his Family. The girls even vowed to set themselves on fire if Manson was sentenced to death ("Jury votes death," 1971).

MANSON IN THE MEDIA TODAY

More than thirty years have passed since the Tate-LaBianca murders and the sentencing of their killers. But Manson and the Family have stayed in the headlines. An internet search will yield millions of websites listing Manson, his music, and the Family. Manson admirers can order T-shirts with his face on them, join his fan club, and even correspond with him. Incarcerated in California's Corcoran Prison, Manson still receives a great deal of fan mail from people wanting to join the Family. In 1999, Manson was contacted by Kansas political science professor Robert Beattie to help in his Newman University class. Manson provided Beattie with a forty-five minute interview that the students used to hold a mock trial (Charles Manson, 1999).

Numerous tell-all books by the defendants, other Family members, jurors, and the prosecutor, Vincent Bugliosi, have set out varying renditions of the motives, the facts, and the teachings of Manson. A CBS television movie *Helter Skelter*, which was initially released in 1976 and starred Steve Railsback as Charles Manson, has been authorized for a remake. "CBS's first adaptation of 'Helter Skelter' was the highest-rated telecast of the 1975–1976 television season" (de Moraes, 2003). Currently in post-production (2004), the newer version stars Jeremy Davies as Manson, and is described by the executive producer as focusing "on who Manson is, why he did what he did, and how he got people to kill for him" (Andreeva, 2003). Manson's music, drawings, and writings are also highly sought after. Music groups, including Guns 'N' Roses and the Beach Boys, have recorded Manson's lyrics. The group Nine Inch Nails purchased the infamous Tate mansion and turned it into a recording studio called "Le Pig." Marilyn Manson recorded parts of the album *Portrait of an American Family* (1994) at the Nine Inch Nails's studio.

Though he dislikes being labeled a "hippie," Manson's image throughout the trial was exactly that. During the age of American free love, the notions of peace, flower power, and a flourishing drug culture were permanently warped by the actions of Manson's Family. Particularly disturbing to the American psyche was the realization that one charismatic individual could warp the minds of average middle-class youth, and murder without guilt became possible. The strength of the American collective revulsion is evenly balanced by the allure of what Manson preached against and by the twisted meaning that free love came to embody. The Tate-LaBianca murders instilled fear into the establishment. Yet, the fear that remains etched on the American consciousness even today is not so much a result of the murders themselves, but rather revulsion to the nature of Charles Manson and the seemingly carefree manner in which the Manson Family murdered.

REFERENCES

Andreeva, N. (2003, August 4). CBS focusing on Manson for 'Skelter' redo. *Hollywood Reporter, 379,* 1(2).

Anger, K. (Producer/Director). (1973). *Lucifer rising* [Motion Picture]. United States: Mystic Fire.

The Beatles. (1968, November 22). *White Album* [Record]. U.K.: Capitol Records.

Bugliosi, V., and Gentry, C. (1974). *Helter Skelter: The true story of the Manson murders.* New York: W.W. Norton and Company.

Charles Manson offers his help in teaching political science course. (1999, March 16). *Kansas News.* Retrieved February 25, 2004, from http://cjonline.com/stories/030299/kan_manson.shtml

Crime: The Tate set. (1969, August 25). *Newsweek,* p. 24.

de Moraes, L. (2003, August 5). With 'Helter Skelter' remake, CBS again gives evil the eye. *Washington Post,* p. C7.

Emerson, B. (2004). Cielo Drive. Retrieved February 1, 2004, from http://www.cielodrive.com/

Furman v. Georgia, 408 U.S. 238 (1972).

Gilmore, J., and Kenner, R. (2000). *Manson: The unholy trail of Charlie and the family.* Los Angeles: Amok.

The girl who almost killed Ford. (1975, September 15). *Time, 106*(11), pp. 8–12, 17–19.

Jury votes death for Manson, girls. (1971, March 30). *Sacramento Union News*, pp. A1, A9.

Justice: A bad week for the good guys. (1970, August 17). *Time, 96*(14), pp. 6–8.

Keys, L. (1976, June 13). 'Helter Skelter' lawyer sees movie role as wry disguise. *(Pasadena) Star News*, p. A14.

Linder, D. (2003). Famous trials: The trial of Charles Manson. Retrieved February 1, 2004, from http://www.law.umkc.edu/faculty/projects/ftrials/manson/manson.html

Manson, Marilyn. (1994, July 19). *Portrait of an American family* [CD]. United States: Interscope Records.

Manson's shattered defense. (1970, November 30). *Time, 96*(22), p. 45.

The new American bible. (1987). Grand Rapids, MI: Catholic World Press.

O'Neil, P. (1969, December 19). The wreck of a monstrous 'Family'. *Life, 67*(25), pp. 20–31.

People v. Manson, 61 Cal. App. 3d 102 (1976).

Polanski, R. (Producer). (1967). *The fearless vampire killers* [Motion Picture]. United States: Warner Home Video.

Roberts, S. V. (1969, August 10). Actress is among 5 slain at home in Beverly Hills. *New York Times.* pp. 1, 63.

Roberts, S. V. (1970, January 7). Manson cult: Broken-family product. *Chicago Today.* p. 40.

Robson, M. (Producer), and Weisbart, D. (Writer). (1967). *Valley of the dolls* [Motion Picture]. United States: Twentieth Century Fox.

Testimony of Paul Watkins in the Charles Manson trial. (2003). Retrieved February 25, 2004, from http://www.law.umkc.edu/faculty/projects/ftrials/manson/mansontestimony-w.html

Torgerson, D. (1969, August 10). 'Ritualistic Slayings' Sharon Tate, four others murdered. *Los Angeles Times,* pp. A1, A18, A19.

Torgerson, D., and Thackrey Jr., T. (1969, August 11). 2 ritual slayings follow killing of 5. *Los Angeles Times*, pp. A1, A3.

Turner, M. (2004). *Charlie Manson.Com.* Retrieved February, 1, 2004, from http://www.charliemanson.com/home.htm

Zappa, F. (1966). *Freak out: Mothers of invention* [Record]. United States: Rykodisc, Massachusetts.

9

The Attica Trials:
A Thirty-year Pursuit of Justice

Sidney L. Harring and George W. Dowdall

The uprising at Attica Prison in 1971 and the political trials that followed represented an era of increasing politicization of the American prison. The civil rights movement, the Vietnam War, the student movement, and the law and order politics of the 1960s all had an impact on the men and women in prisons. Not only were politically astute leaders of the black and student movements in and out of prison themselves, but much of the prison population was increasingly politically aware. Eldridge Cleaver's book *Soul on Ice,* Alex Hailey's the *Autobiography of Malcolm X,* and other books had a profound impact on politics both inside and outside of prisons. Recurring political trials such as the trial of the Chicago Seven were on the evening news. Black, Hispanic, Native American, and white political organizations such as the Black Panther Party, Weathermen, and the American Indian Movement had members both inside and outside of prison, as radical political action came to routinely result in prison time.

The election of President Richard Nixon in 1968 was a victory for the forces of "law and order" that had promised a "crackdown" on crime and led to a "war on drugs" and a "war on crime"—the domestic versions of the Vietnam War. Police tactics became increasingly militarized; legislatures passed new laws such as New York's Rockefeller Drug Laws that provided much longer prison sentences—up to life for possession of drugs. Prisons then, as they are now, were almost entirely filled by minorities, which made prisons a fertile ground for political organizing.

By the end of the 1960s, there was unrest in prisons all over the United States. In California, San Quentin Prison had a major strike in 1970. Also in 1970, three inmates at Soledad Prison in California where shot dead by a guard; an event widely believed by inmates to have been planned in advance.

THE ATTICA UPRISING AND THE RETAKING OF THE PRISON

These political and racial tensions came together in September 1971 in an explosive mix at Attica Correctional Facility in New York; Attica is a maximum security prison about forty miles east of Buffalo, New York.[1] Attica appeared to observers at the time as a fairly typical maximum security prison that was similar to the other five prisons operating in New York State. Inmates lived in cells that were six feet wide by nine feet long, with all the buildings enclosed by a thirty-foot-high wall. Attica held 2,243 inmates; about 20 percent had been convicted of homicide, manslaughter, or murder; and 10 percent were serving life sentences or awaiting execution. Unlike prisoners of the previous generation, many of Attica's inmates grew up on the streets of inner city ghettos, and the inmates often thought of themselves as political prisoners rather than common criminals. Although rehabilitation of these inmates composed part of the official rhetoric of Attica, the reality of everyday life centered on confinement within an institution devoted literally to maximum security. Education or training programs were rarely available for those who wanted them.

"Security" has continued to be the dominant theme: the fantasy of reform legitimatized prisons but the functionalism of custody has perpetuated them .... For inmates, "correction" meant daily degradation and humiliation: being locked in a cell for 14 to 16 hours a day; working for wages that averaged 30 cents a day in jobs with little of no vocational value; having to abide by hundreds of petty rules for which they could see no justification. It meant that all their activities were regulated, standardized, and monitored for them by prison authorities and that their opportunity to excise free choice was practically nonexistent: their incoming and outgoing mail was read, their radio programs were screened in advance, their reading material was restricted, their movements outside their cells were regulated, they were told when to turn lights out and when to wake up, and even essential toilet needs had to be taken care of in view of patrolling officers. (New York State Special Commission on Attica, 1972, p. 2)

Medical care was poor. Sick call was held behind a screen but in the cellblock with little privacy. While doctors dispensed pills for simple ailments, long-term care and care for serious illnesses was either inadequate or nonexistent.

Built into daily life was a series of deprivations and humiliations that ranged from inadequate health care, an absence of recreation, bad food, and shabby clothing to the threat of violence, unwelcome sexual advances, menial work paid for at a fraction of regular wages, and despair at ever being paroled. In many ways, Attica approached the perfect definition of a "total institution," providing twenty-four-hour-a-day and seven-day-a-week conformity to an absolute authority and an unwavering mass routine of life (Goffman, 1961). Incarceration in a total institution for years at a time must have had a great impact on a person's sense of self. Any inmate of such an institution might experience daily life as enormously frustrating, but one factor made it almost unendurable: The perception and reality of racism.

Race shaped every facet of daily life. Black inmates came to increasingly resent the degrading racism of white guards. Black prisoners could be routinely "written up" for minor disciplinary infractions and be locked up for weeks in the "hole." As social relations deteriorated, inmates became increasingly organized. A prison, in the best of times, is a difficult social organization and one in which inmates have many forms of organization and control that are invisible to their guards.

Black and Hispanic inmates did not have access to the best prison jobs, and jobs were important sources of power and social gratification in prison. Whites worked the good jobs as clerks, runners, and in the officers' kitchen. Blacks and Hispanics worked in the shops and factories and cleaned the floors.

There were religious grievances as well. Black Muslims, in particular, were denied the right to practice Islam. The food being prepared in the prison kitchen was beyond their control, and conditions made it impossible to observe dietary requirements. Prison cooks were rumored to secretly put pork in many dishes, forcing devout Muslims to not eat any form of food that they could not clearly identify. Muslims were denied access to members of the clergy; however, these privileges were long granted to Catholic, Protestant, and Jewish prisoners. Muslims were denied leave from their work assignments on Friday afternoon to attend religious services. These adversities forged a strong Muslim culture within the prison: Muslim prisoners were highly disciplined and organized to protest these injustices.

In the fall of 1971 at Attica, the inmates had a sense that they had little to lose. They were serving hopelessly lengthy sentences in a prison with poor and deteriorating conditions. With daily tensions on the rise, the relationships between inmates and guards got worse, as did the interracial tensions among inmates. The heavily black and Hispanic inmate population, many from the New York City area, which was hundreds of miles away, was watched by a staff of 543 white guards from rural or small towns. "In the end, the promise of rehabilitation had become a cruel joke. If anyone was rehabilitated, it was in spite of Attica, not because of it" (New York State Special Commission on Attica, 1972, p. 4).

The Riot

In 1971, there was little evidence of organized planning of a revolt at Attica. Instead, the underlying tension exploded in a series of unplanned events that cumulatively brought about the capture of the prison by its inmates. A police force that was itself poorly organized reacted and took back the prison under circumstances that guaranteed great loss of life.

Events during the late summer of 1971 had led to an atmosphere charged with the threat of violence. Just as in the society outside the prison, organized protests against what were seen as inhumane conditions began to occur more frequently. Increasingly militant prisoners had drawn up a manifesto of demands, many surprisingly moderate, but they found little reason to think that prison authorities would respond to them. Correctional officers thought that their authority was being undermined, and mutual suspicion and fear became widespread.

In such an atmosphere, small events can lead to catastrophic outbursts. A misunderstanding among some inmates had escalated into a confrontation between the inmates and guards, and one guard was struck by a soup can thrown by a prisoner. On the next day, September 9, in A Block, which was one of four major sections of the prison, an altercation led to several prisoners attacking an officer who was trying to get them to return to their cells after breakfast. The prisoners broke free and began running through the cellblock on a violent rampage. Things might have ended there had a locked gate's bad weld not broken under pressure, which had allowed the inmates access to a control area known as "Times Square," which contained keys to other gates. The inmates began opening cellblocks and attacking correctional officers; one officer, William Quinn, was murdered. Resistance by the prison's guards was minimal, and within a few hours 1,281 inmates had seized control of much of the prison and had taken over forty hostages with most congregating in the yard in D Block.

Prison officials were unable to respond quickly enough to quell the uprising; insufficient manpower, an inadequate communication system, and no plan for dealing with a large uprising contributed to the outcome. A later investigation would reveal that this was not a planned rebellion but more of a spontaneous riot. Apparently there had been some talk among prisoners of a sit-down strike, but there was no prior evidence of anyone taking over the prison. Prison officials and, after a time, New York State Commissioner of Corrections Russell Oswald, began negotiating with those prisoners who emerged in the yard as leaders. A hastily assembled force of state police, correction officers, and county sheriffs kept watch outside of the prison walls. The media also began to gather outside with press and film crews from all over the world eventually reaching the site.

After a period of disorganization and anarchy, the emerging leaders of the rebellion began to negotiate in earnest. A fifty-yard buffer, or no-man's-land (termed the "DMZ," or demilitarized zone), separated inmate spokesmen and state authorities; communication between the two sides initially involved shouting across that space. Commissioner Oswald rushed from Albany to take charge of the scene. Several notable journalists, lawyers, and politicians joined the negotiations as observers. Herman Schwartz, a professor of law, and Arthur O. Eve, an assemblyman, had come from Buffalo, and they were allowed by the commissioner to visit the inmates in D yard; Oswald, Schwartz, and Eve returned together for a second visit and they were accompanied by reporters and television cameras. The leaders in D yard began to discuss demands and talk with observers who continued to visit them. Tom Wicker, associate editor and columnist for the *New York Times*, joined the team of observers and later wrote one of the most important eyewitness accounts of the uprising and retaking of the prison (Wicker, 1975).

By Saturday afternoon on September 11, the observers had formulated a twenty-eight-point list of prisoner demands that were deemed acceptable by Commissioner Oswald; the list included reforms that addressed many of the sources of tensions. Some of the demands were unchanged from the language used by the prisoners and observers. For example: "6) Allow all New York State prisoners to be politically active, without intimidation or reprisal"; and "7) Allow true religious freedom" appeared as both the observers' proposal and as a proposal acceptable to Commissioner Oswald. Others were different. For example, the observers stated, "Apply the New York State minimum wage law to all work done by inmates. STOP SLAVE LABOR." The proposal acceptable to Commissioner Oswald stated, "Recommend the application of the New York State minimum wage law standards to all work done by inmates. Every effort will be made to make the records of payments available to inmates." Although Oswald held firm on the issue of criminal amnesty, he agreed that there would be no administrative reprisals or criminal charges that dealt with property damage during the rebellion (New York State Special Commission on Attica, 1972, pp. 250–258).

Retaking the Prison

A few hours later, the "Twenty-Eight Points" that Commissioner Oswald found acceptable were rejected by the prisoners because the list did not include criminal amnesty. Rumors about reprisals circulated among the inmates that made further negotiation almost impossible. Criminal amnesty became the critical issue; many of the prisoners feared that a wave of mass prosecutions would follow the retaking of the prison. A few of the inmates were also worried about their involvement in the murder of Officer William Quinn on the rebellion's first day and in the murders of several prisoners during the following days. On Sunday, September 12, as negotiations failed, the outside observers and eventually Commissioner Oswald requested that Governor Nelson Rockefeller come to the prison. By Sunday evening, Rockefeller declined, instead approving the retaking of the prison by force with as little violence as possible.

At 7:40 a.m. on Monday, September 13, the commissioner's ultimatum was read to the prisoners in D yard. The prisoners' response came about an hour later: eight blindfolded hostages with knives to their throats were paraded across the catwalks. If a slim hope of a peaceful resolution had existed, it was now gone. At 9:30 a.m., the prisoners formally rejected the ultimatum, and sixteen minutes later, the assault on the prison began with tear gas being dropped on inmates in D Yard by a state police helicopter.

What happened next is best described in the often-cited words of the Special Commission that investigated the events at Attica:

Forty-three citizens of New York State died at Attica Correctional Facility between September 9 and 13, 1971. Thirty-nine of that number were killed and more than 80 others were wounded by gunfire during the 15 minutes it took the State Police to retake the prison on September 13. With the exception of Indian massacres in the 19th century, the State Police assault which ended the four-day prison uprising was the bloodiest one-day encounter between Americans since the Civil War. (New York State Special Commission on Attica, 1972, p. xi)

One correctional officer had been killed on the first day of the uprising, and several prisoners had been murdered by their fellow inmates; the remaining thirty-nine deaths were from police bullets. The conditions under which the prison was retaken virtually guaranteed a very high loss of life, despite specific orders to use minimum force. The police forces that retook the prison used weapons such as shotguns, which were likely to cause numerous casualties. Police and correctional officers had no training in this type of assault, and they did not seek assistance from other forces, including the military, which was trained. Police feared that the inmates were heavily armed, and over 1,400 weapons were confiscated after the retaking of the prison. Correctional officers participated in the takeover, despite orders from the governor to not do so for fear of revenge against prisoners, and these officers were responsible for several deaths. Rumors quickly spread that guards had their throats slit, but no evidence was found to support this charge.

After the resistance ended, the occupying forces secured the prison and forced the prisoners to strip naked before returning to their cells. In the ensuing hours, prisoners were brutally beaten by state employees, and reports of torture were alleged. Medical treatment of the wounded was delayed for four hours by inadequate planning; and although no prisoner died as a result of the delay, many prisoners suffered unnecessarily from excruciating wounds. An inventory of prisoner injuries taken several days after the retaking of the prison found that 45 percent of the prisoners had broken bones as well as other signs of the reprisals against them.

MEDIA COVERAGE OF ATTICA: AN "EXPLOSION OF RHETORIC"

A unique aspect of the events at Attica was the extraordinary media coverage. Television cameras were allowed into the prison when the commissioner and several observers began negotiations. The result was characterized by one observer as "an explosion of rhetoric"; prisoners stated their grievances while state officials attempted to justify their actions.

Media from around the world covered the uprising and retaking of the prison, and much of the retaking was photographed by state police using still and video cameras. These images were published in newspaper and television accounts all over the world, and shaped the public perceptions of Attica. Years later, the images found their way into several powerful documentary films such as *Attica* and *Ghosts of Attica*. Tom Wicker's first-person account of his role as an observer provided the basis for the film *Attica*.

Initial coverage of the prison retaking tended to follow the arguments presented by state officials. On the day immediately following the state police assault on Attica, the *New York Times*, one of America's most influential newspapers published the following: "In this worst of recent American prison riots, several of the hostages—prison guards and civilian workers—died when convicts slashed their throats with knives. Others were stabbed and beaten with clubs and lengths of pipes." The following day, the *Times* commented, "The deaths of [the hostages] reflect a barbarism wholly alien to our civilized society. Prisoners slashed the throats of utterly helpless, unarmed guards whom they had held captive through around-the-clock negotiations, in which the inmates held out for an increasingly revolutionary set of demands." The *New York Daily News* ran a story with the headline, "I saw seven throats cut" (New York State Special Commission on Attica, 1972, pp. 455–456).

Days later, newspapers would run stories that confirmed that all nine dead hostages had died from bullet wounds as part of the massive assault by state police forces. However, the false media images of revolutionary prisoners slitting hostage throats had already been burned into the public consciousness; those persisting images would shape the ensuing trials.

New York State convened a Special Commission on Attica, also known as the McKay Commission, which was named after New York University's law school dean who was named to chair the commission. The commission interviewed sixteen hundred inmates, four hundred correctional officers, and two hundred and seventy officers of the New State Police. The commission also had access to autopsy reports and other physical evidence. The commission's report (New York State Special Commission on Attica, 1972) and books by observers such as *New York Times* journalist Tom Wicker (1975) provide a virtually complete account of the events. What happened in the retaking of the prison is not in doubt, but its political meaning remains controversial to this day.

THE POLITICAL CHARACTER OF THE PROSECUTIONS

Governor Nelson Rockefeller of New York was one of the leading Republican politicians in the United States, and Rockefeller had clear presidential ambitions. His reputation was at stake, and it required vindication. Accordingly, the Attica prosecutions were directed by Assistant Attorney General Anthony Simonetti, who had been appointed special prosecutor along with a large staff of prosecutors handpicked from around New York State and a much larger staff of police investigators. The police investigations were biased from the start. Although state police had fired almost all of the 3,000 shots, state police investigators led the investigation, which was a clear conflict of interest. Moreover, from the start, the investigation was focused on crimes committed by unarmed inmates to the exclusion of the crimes committed by armed state police and prison guards; evidence clearly showed that state police and prison guards had killed dozens of people and tortured hundreds more.

This bias aside, the investigation proceeded in an uneven and incompetent manner. The evidence was in chaos, as thousands of witnesses remembered fluid and complex events in very different ways. The inmates, as well as the officers, were all dressed alike, and individual identifications were uncertain at best. A few inmate "stooges" were promised immediate release if they testified against fellow inmates. Evidence was deliberately distorted in a one-sided way to overemphasize inmate actions and exonerate guard actions.

Three years into the trials, Malcolm Bell, an assistant prosecutor, resigned his position in protest of the political nature of the prosecutions and submitted a lengthy report to Governor Hugh Carey—the new governor of New York who was a Democrat. Bell detailed the bias and misconduct in the special prosecutor's office. Carey appointed a commission, the Meyer Commission, which was named after its chairperson. The Meyer Commission reported some months later that the prosecution was riddled with bias and other problems, and the commission recommended that Carey appoint a new special prosecutor to begin investigation into the state's misconduct as well. Carey reacted by "closing the book" on the Attica case by ending all the criminal prosecution. The case was over. By this time, former Governor Rockefeller was now Vice President of the United States with no political authority left in New York State.

THE ATTICA BROTHERS LEGAL DEFENSE AND THE FAIR JURY PROJECT

A unique aspect of the Attica trials was the organization of the defense efforts— the Attica Brothers Legal Defense (ABLD). The ABLD assembled a legal staff, raised funds to support their efforts, publicized the defense view of the trials and its political agenda, and led demonstrations in support of the defendants in Buffalo and in New York City. The ABLD assumed that the inmates' defense should not be a narrow legal response to the charges against them, but rather a broad effort to promulgate their version of the rebellion and advance their political views about the need for radical change throughout United States.

The team of lawyers who began to work for ABLD included the famous radical lawyer William Kuntsler (defense lawyer for the Chicago Seven and other antiwar radicals of the 1960s), Ramsay Clark (former Attorney General of the United States and a spokesperson for radical social change), and David Kairys (at the beginning of a career as a civil rights and constitutional lawyer). Other attorneys who worked on the trials included Elizabeth Fink, who for several decades conducted an effort on behalf of civil damages for the inmates of Attica.

ABLD also helped launch an effort that became known as the Fair Jury Project, which was designed to deal with the extraordinary challenges the Attica Brothers faced as criminal defendants. The initial indictments against the defendants were brought in Wyoming County, which is the county in which Attica is located. All the defendants were serving time after convictions for very serious crimes. Most were African Americans and Hispanics from New York City who were about to be tried in a virtually all-white upstate county at a time of high-racial tension. Television, radio, and print coverage of the uprising had blanketed western New York with indelible images of violence, and rumors had circulated that the prisoners had tortured hostages and slit their throats. Attica Prison was one of the largest employers in Wyoming County, and many potential jurors had ties to the prison.

The Fair Jury Project conducted a telephone survey of Wyoming County that established empirically that many potential jurors would have a difficult time in providing the defendants with a fair trial. Potential jurors admitted that they could not follow a judge's instructions to ignore the enormous pretrial publicity or presume that the defendants were innocent of the charges until proven guilty. The survey helped support defense arguments for a change of venue, but the court ruled that the trials would be moved to nearby Erie County and not to New York City, as the defense had argued.

A storefront in downtown Buffalo was used as the base of operations for ABLD, and the legal team worked several blocks away out of separate offices. In addition, an office was opened in New York City, both to influence the national media and to provide services for those brothers who came from downstate New York. Other ABLD offices functioned for a time in several other cities, including Detroit, Michigan, and Oakland, California.

The Fair Jury Project studied the jury pool of Erie County and used statistical analysis to show that its composition was skewed toward being disproportionately white, middle-aged men. The composition again posed major difficulties for the defendants' chances of a fair trial by a jury of peers (Levine and Schweber-Koren, 1977). Staff from the jury commissioner's office verified that potential female jurors were being excluded because of improper use of a "women's exemption" allowed at that time under New York law. A series of charts made clear that the Erie County jury pool was anything but a reasonable cross-section of the community from which it was drawn. A motion submitted by the defense led to 97 percent of the existing Erie County jury pool to be thrown out; this was perceived as a major victory for the defense.

A telephone survey of 651 registered voters was conducted by the Fair Jury Project to help defense lawyers assess which individuals might be most likely to set aside their prior opinions about prisoners and the uprising and follow the judge's instructions to presume innocence. The survey results provided a snapshot of contemporary opinion about the trials, indicating widespread bias against the defendants. As one press release from the ABLD summarized, "The results of the study not only show strong and pervasive prejudice against black people, persons who seek change, and persons accused of crime—all leading to the conclusion that most people in Erie County could not function as impartial jurors if called to sit on these cases." The survey found that 69 percent of the potential jurors blamed the prisoners for the killing of forty-three persons, and 19 percent still believed the rumors that the hostages had been castrated or had their throats slit. Most people viewed strong protest as unjustified, and about a third would imprison black militants and radicals solely for their beliefs. About 50 percent believed prison conditions to be excellent or satisfactory.

The survey findings were combined with courtroom analysis of potential juror body language and response to voir dire questions in an effort to help select a "fair jury." This part of the project was led by Jay Schulman, a social psychologist who had previously used these techniques in picking a jury for the Harrisburg, Pennsylvania, trial of Catholic antiwar activists (Hunt, 1982; Schulman, Shaver, Colman, Emrich, and Christie, 1973). ABLD staff sat at the defense table during jury selection in an attempt to guide attorneys in their decisions about which potential jurors to challenge "for cause" or which to deselect for other reasons.

THE SIX ATTICA CRIMINAL TRIALS

Sixty-two inmates and one prison guard were indicted by a grand jury in Wyoming County, the rural county where Attica Prison was located, for 1,289 alleged crimes that ranged from assault to murder. Only eight of the sixty-two inmates were ultimately convicted. John Hill was the only inmate convicted of murder for the death of Officer William Quinn; Officer Quinn's death occurred during the initial taking of the prison. Joseph Pernasilice, also charged in Quinn's murder, was acquitted, but he was convicted of the lesser crime of attempted assault.

The evidence at this trial reflected the difficulty of these cases. Quinn, a young man, had died tragically with a wife and children left behind. He was the only guard killed, which clearly indicated that the inmates had no plans to kill guards in the uprising. Rather, Quinn had been at the wrong place at the wrong time; he was in a stairwell as hundreds of excited inmates pushed past him. Some of the testimony was that he fell; other testimony was that he was pushed or trampled accidentally. Still, other testimony indicated that Hill and Pernasilice had beaten Quinn with different and inconsistent descriptions of the weapon used. In the end, the jury believed that Hill had beaten Quinn to death.

The special prosecutor's years of investigation and preparation collapsed in poorly presented cases (Light, 1995). One government witness, a prison employee, had positively identified an inmate as holding a flare gun in a tunnel during the riot. A defense lawyer asked the witness if he had ever called inmates "niggers." The prison employee admitted that he had but qualified that he only did so when it was appropriate in the context of their rehabilitation. The lawyer then asked the officer to describe how that word contributed to rehabilitation. The jury acquitted—such testimony could have no credibility.

In one trial, several inmates were charged with the murder of inmate "snitches." The testimony was inconsistent, and inmates had been offered various inducements to testify. The jury did not believe the witnesses and acquitted.

The trials were still proceeding at the time Special Prosecutor Malcolm Bell wrote his memo to Governor Carey. Carey not only ended the trials, but he pardoned the seven Attica Brothers who had been convicted—and commuted the twenty-years-to-life sentence of John Hill. If the prison guards and state troopers were not to be punished for firing the 3,000 shots that killed forty inmates and guards or for torturing Big Black and the hundreds of other inmates, it was not fair to punish John Hill for killing William Quinn. Nothing in these results represented justice from any standpoint.

THE CIVIL CASES

The Attica civil cases, filed by inmates and hostages, are some of the most complex and lengthy civil suits ever filed against New York State (Light, 1995). The most important of the early lawsuits, *Inmates of Attica Correctional Facility v. Rockefeller*, was filed immediately after the retaking of the prison while inmates were being tortured. The United States Court of Appeals for the Second Circuit issued what is still considered a landmark opinion denouncing the use of force by corrections officers:

The beatings, physical abuse, torture, running of gauntlets, and similar cruelty—was wholly beyond any force needed to maintain order. It far exceeded what our society will tolerate on the part of officers of the law in custody of defenseless prisoners. . . . [T]he mistreatment of inmates in this case amounted to cruel and unusual punishment in violation of their Eighth Amendment rights. (*Inmates of Attica Correctional Facility v. Rockefeller*, 1971)

Inmates of Attica Correctional Facility v. Rockefeller was part of a wide range of lawsuits filed by prisoners in the 1970s that created a new category of human rights law: the law of prisoners' rights. Prisoners today live under improved prison conditions because of this litigation. It is now clear that a prisoner still maintains substantial rights as a citizen while incarcerated. Hundreds of lawsuits about prisoners' rights to medical care—safe working conditions; improved "housing" conditions; access to lawyers, courts, reading materials, and the media; religious freedom; and due process rights in prison discipline—were all litigated in the wake of the Attica litigation. Attica prisoners had taken a stand that prisoners needed to be respected as U.S. citizens and as human beings.

Other lawsuits seeking to remove indicted inmates held in segregated housing units and to block prison disciplinary hearings against inmates for their role in the uprising were not successful.

Other cases went through the courts for many years. The twenty-eight hostages and/or their families that were killed or injured in the uprising filed many lawsuits. All except one of these lawsuits were dismissed on a technicality: as state employees they were barred from filing lawsuits for damages if they had accepted workmen's compensation. Most of the state employees had taken such checks—they were working people with no money to live on—without realizing that such acceptance would bar filing lawsuits. The widow and daughter of Herbert Jones were the only officer's family members to prevail; they had not accepted their checks and were awarded $550,000 plus interest. This left the families of the officers feeling bitter: the state denied them the right to sue for their injuries on the technicality of workmen's compensation law.

Fourteen inmates sued in the Court of Claims for injuries sustained in the uprising; nine inmates were awarded about $1.5 million in damages. These cases moved at a proverbial snail's pace. Inmate Peter Tarallo complained in 1983 that his life had been shortened by his injuries in the Attica retaking and that he would not live to see any money. His estate was awarded $164,000 in 1989—eighteen years after the uprising and after Tarallo was, as he had feared, dead.

In 2001, the inmate class action suit was settled almost thirty years after the retaking of the prison. This complex lawsuit sought damages of $2.8 billion from Governor Rockefeller, Corrections Commissioner Oswald, Attica Warden Mancusi, Deputy Warden Pfiel, and other state officials for violation of prisoner rights, excessive force, unrestricted firepower that caused death, serious injury, and suffering (Light, 1995). The case had a complicated legal history and was tried in Buffalo in 1991. Ten more years of appeals and negotiations passed before a settlement was agreed to in 2001. The 502 inmates would share $8 million, apportioned by the judge into five categories, depending on the degree of their injuries. More than half fell into the lowest category, receiving what can only be called a token payment of $6,500. The other half received either $10,000, $25,000, or $31,000 for the relatives of inmates who had died. Fifteen inmates received the highest award of $125,000. Elderly men and their families came to court for the settlement. They told stories that many had not told since they left Attica, but all of them agreed that it was important that the case was settled. The world would know that the New York State had committed serious crimes against them at the retaking of Attica prison.

THE LEGACY OF ATTICA

What impact did the Attica trials have? A year after the uprising, the McKay Commission argued,

Unless the cry to "Avenge Attica" can be turned to reforms that will make repetition impossible, all effort will have been in vain. Change should not be lightly under-taken, but the status quo can no longer be defended. The only way to salvage meaning out of the otherwise senseless killings at Attica is to learn from this experience that our Atticas are failures. The crucial issues remain unresolved; and they will continue unresolved until an aroused public demands something better. (New York State Special Commission on Attica, 1972, p. xxi)

Now, decades later, prison reform appears to be grappling with remarkably similar issues. Racial inequality remains at the heart of the U.S. criminal justice system, and prisons still incarcerate a far larger proportion of minorities than would be expected from population size alone.

One of the legacies of the Attica trials was the impact of the ABLD. Though not the first trials to use expert social science research techniques to challenge potential jury composition or selecting juries, the Attica trials set a new standard for those efforts. At a minimum, the ABLD led a successful effort to change the venue from Wyoming County to Erie County (Buffalo), which probably enabled the defense to mount a more successful political struggle. Several of the Attica Brothers credited the ABLD with helping them win their trials. The ABLD efforts also delayed several of the criminal trials until a new governor took power in Albany and set in motion the eventual dismissal of indictments. Beyond the Attica trials, these jury techniques would be used in other trials, and expert consultation on jury selection would become a significant new part of American courtroom practice.

The United States in the post-Attica period has five times as many people in prison and most of them still minorities. New York State currently has seventy-four prisons; in 1971, there were sixteen. Sentences now are two or three times longer then they were in 1971. Violence in prison is still prevalent, and guards, still mostly white, mistreat inmates (Butterfield, 2003, May 8).

The war on crime, going strong since 1968, shows no sign of abatement, except that some politicians have noted its high cost. In New York State, there has been significant discussion of the need to repeal the draconian Rockefeller drug laws that played such a major role in the growth of the prison population. But, thus far, there has been no successful effort to repeal the laws, and the prison population remains large and continues to grow.

Attica reminds us of how high the costs of this mass reliance on imprisonment can be, with up to 3 million Americans imprisoned at any given moment. Prison is difficult institution to administer and is a violent social institution. The goal of rehabilitation, established with the first prisons in the United States, is as elusive as ever.

NOTE

1. The best account of the events at Attica is the New York State Special Commission on Attica in 1972; much of this chapter is based on the commission's findings.

REFERENCES

Butterfield, F. (2003, May 8). Mistreatment of prisoners is called routine in the U.S. *New York Times*, p. A11.

Cleaver, E. (1967). *Soul on ice.* New York: McGraw-Hill.

Goffman, E. (1961). *Asylums.* New York: Anchor.

Hunt, M. (1982, November 28). Putting juries on the couch. *New York Times Magazine*, p. 70ff.

Inmates of Attica Correctional Facility v. Rockefeller, 453 F.2d 12 (1971).

Kairys, D., Schulman, J., and Harring, S. (1975). *The Jury system: New methods for reducing prejudice.* Philadelphia: National Jury Project and National Lawyers Guild.

Levine, A. G., and Schweber-Koren, C. (1977). Jury selection in Erie County: changing a sexist system. *Law & Society Review, 11,* 43–55.

Light, S. C. (1995). The Attica litigation. *Crime, Law & Social Change, 23,* 215–234.

Malcolm X. (1964). *The autobiography of Malcolm X.* New York: Grove Press.

National Advisory Commission on Civil Disorders. (1968). *Report of the national advisory commission on civil disorders.* New York: Bantam.

New York State Special Commission on Attica. (1972). *Attica: The official report of the New York State special commission on Attica.* New York: Bantam Books.

Schulman, J., Shaver, P., Colman, R., Emrich, B., and Christie, R. (1973). Recipe for a jury. *Psychology Today, May,* 37–84.

Wicker, T. (1975). *A time to die.* New York: Quadrangle.

10

The Execution of Gary Gilmore: Restarting the Killing Machine

Timothy M. Sledd

Imagine the death penalty as a very large and heavy machine. The machine has many moving parts that emit a drone and vibrate the ground. Power to the machine is controlled through a switchboard manned by very specific individuals and entities. These select few have coded keys (knowledge of law, legislative power, or political clout), without which the machine cannot run. In 1972, the U.S. Supreme Court silenced the killing machines in the United States. However, four years later, the Court decided a group of cases that allowed the machines to be turned back on. Gary M. Gilmore, a career criminal and convicted murderer, heard the drone, felt the vibrations, and, to the world's surprise, did not beg for his killing machine to be silenced, but rather he challenged those at the controls to use the machine to kill him first.

This chapter discusses Gary Gilmore and why he committed the murders that ultimately led to his execution. Because of the critical importance the national debate concerning the death penalty played in the fervor to restart the killing machine, this chapter reviews a brief discussion of the legal context of Gilmore's case. The polarization of public opinion concerning the death penalty proved to be fertile ground for headlines in newspapers, magazines, and television news. The media's role in Gilmore's death will be addressed. Finally, the chapter discusses the social impact of Gilmore's death wish.[1]

It has been said that in comedy, timing is everything. This not only holds true for comedy but also tragedy—Gilmore's fame is due to the timely mixture of his heinous nature, the U.S. Supreme Court's attention to the death penalty, a heated public debate, and combustible media attention. Not only did Gilmore face down the machine, he provided the ignition to the machine that has not stopped since.

THE MAKINGS OF MURDER

Gilmore's murders were senseless and heinous. His first victim was forced to lay face down on a service station bathroom floor before being shot execution style. His second victim was shot in the head but did not die instantaneously; Gilmore left the man to bleed to death. Such brutal and deliberate killings were just the proverbial tip of the iceberg in Gilmore's rough life. What existed beneath the surface, buried deep in his mind and history, was a past that created the killer.

Gilmore's Childhood

Gilmore was born in 1940 and was named Fay Robert Coffman, because his father, Frank Gilmore Sr., was running from the law. Gilmore Sr. was a "One-Hundred percenter," or a traveling salesman who would go door to door offering to sell services or products in exchange for payment up front. Instead of delivering the products, the conmen would keep 100 percent of the money and flee (A&E, 1996).

Gilmore Sr. had a violent and suspicious relationship with his wife, Bessie. An alcoholic, Gilmore Sr. was prone to fits of rage, and much like a tornado plowing across the plains states, Frank would beat anyone who stepped in his way. Not only was Gilmore Sr. violent, but he would also leave the family for extended periods of time with little support. It is believed that Gilmore Sr. had families "scattered all over the nation" (Gilmore, 1994).

Bessie did not provide much comfort for the children. Bessie would not let the children touch her. She was highly superstitious believing that she and her family were cursed by ghosts. Her children were told of the Mormon rituals of blood atonement. Mikal, Gilmore's youngest brother, described a scenario where Bessie believed she saw a ghost in Gilmore's room and therefore concluded that the ghost possessed him. Bessie used her belief that Gilmore was possessed by the ghost to justify his later troubles and eventual execution (Gilmore, 1994).

In 1948, Bessie convinced Gilmore Sr. to settle down in Portland, Oregon. There he created a legitimate business compiling and publishing regulations, ordinances, and statutes regarding building construction. This did not quench Gilmore Sr.'s thirst for alcohol, nor did it stop the violent beatings of the boys. Gary was the most frequent target of his father's violence. He was beat with razor straps and clinched fists (A&E, 1996). According to Mikal, Gilmore did not succumb to the abuse easily. He would fight back and resist, which usually compounded Gilmore Sr.'s anger and abuse (Gilmore, 1994).

Gilmore's Early Criminal Life

Gilmore's defiance of authority and fearlessness of the law began early and was unrelenting. Gilmore exhibited a thorough disregard for rules, structure, and the well-being of others. Gilmore was known for fighting in school, talking back to teachers, and bullying other students (Gilmore, 1994). Gilmore enjoyed his reputation as a troublemaking risk-taker. He would prove his fearlessness to friends by standing on a railroad bridge as trains approached. When there seemed to be no time left, Gilmore would jump from the bridge into the water below. Gilmore demanded similar bravery from his friends. Mikal retold a story of Gilmore and his friends shooting guns near a swimming hole. Gilmore threw a gun into the water near a sharp rock then dared his friends to jump in and get it. When one of the friends landed on the rock, gashed his leg, and required assistance to get out of the water, Gilmore laughed mockingly (Gilmore, 1994).

It was not long before Gilmore's passion for taking risks manifested itself in the form of criminality. In 1955, Gilmore dropped out of school at the age of fourteen. He stole anything he wanted, including beer and cigarettes. By the age of fifteen, Gilmore was frequently drinking alcohol, using drugs, stealing cars, and running a car theft ring.

The Institutionalization of Gilmore

Gilmore not only despised authority, but he learned at an early age how to manipulate the system. For example, Gilmore and some of his friends were arrested by local police for throwing rocks through a school's windows. Gilmore Sr. hired a private investigator and a lawyer to argue that Gilmore had been out of town; all of which was fabricated. Gilmore was taught a lesson that the legal system could be controlled regardless of guilt or innocence (Gilmore, 1994).

Later, in 1955, Gilmore would stand accused of stealing cars, repainting them, and then selling them. Gilmore Sr. stood in court and pleaded with the judge, claiming Gilmore was an unwitting accomplice. The judge released

Gilmore into his father's custody. Such freedom would not last long. Within a couple of weeks Gilmore had committed a similar car theft and the judge was no longer willing to be lenient. Gilmore was sentenced to MacLaren's Reform School for Boys (Gilmore, 1994).

Gilmore entered MacLaren with a certain degree of mischievousness and a disdain for authority—reform school proved to be an education in delinquency. "Reform schools disseminate certain esoteric knowledge. . . . They sophisticate. A kid comes out of reform school and he's learned a few things he would otherwise have missed . . . he identifies . . . with the people who share the same esoteric knowledge, the criminal element," Gilmore reported in an interview. While at MacLaren, Gilmore found himself serving time in maximum security, and he liked it. As Mikal states, Gilmore's "penchant for hard time punishment became a pattern that would hold true for my brother for the rest of his prison career" (Gilmore, 1994, p. 155). After a year at MacLaren, Gilmore had served his time and was released.

Gilmore was frequently in and out of jail. After another of his favorite offenses, stealing cars, Gilmore was placed in Oregon State Correctional Institution. While serving a subsequent sentence, a pivotal event occurred that scarred Gilmore: Gilmore Sr. died. Gilmore was not allowed to attend the funeral and by all accounts protested by going on a rampage destroying everything in his cell (A&E, 1996). He then attempted suicide and was violent toward prison staff.

His release and rearrests were closely timed. Once, in 1962, he was arrested for driving without a license. Eventually, Gilmore assaulted and robbed a man for mere dollars. The prosecution in that case sought extended punishment due to their prognosis that Gilmore was a danger to society and repeat offender (Gilmore, 1994). In 1964, Gilmore received a fifteen-year sentence for assault and robbery. Because his actions caused him to be defined as a dangerous member of the prison population, Gilmore was separated from maximum security and placed on the drug Prolixin. This drug had the effects of making Gilmore act like a zombie, "drooling" and with flatten affect (A&E, 1996). On a visit, Bessie witnessed her swollen son and convinced the facility to take Gilmore off of the drug.

Prolixin was but one of the painful experiences Gilmore would face in jail while serving his sentence. His younger brother, Gaylen, was brutally attacked in Chicago. Because he was unable to afford adequate medical treatment, his injuries lasted for an extended period. Eventually, he attempted to have the damage repaired through surgery, but instead he died. Gilmore had to face the death of another member of his family while incarcerated. Bessie, however, was able to pay prison guards overtime to escort Gilmore to Gaylen's funeral (Gilmore, 1994).

Gilmore spent a significant amount of time in solitary confinement after Gaylen's death. While confined, he practiced drawing, read classical literature, and discovered a talent that won him the opportunity for an early release in 1972 to attend art school. Gilmore was intimidated by the youth of the students at the art school. Within a month, Gilmore was arrested and convicted of armed robbery.

Violent behavior and suicide attempts forced the Oregon State Correctional System to decide whether to put Gilmore on Prolixin again or to transfer him out-of-state to a maximum security prison in Illinois. In early 1975, Gilmore's pleas to avoid Prolixin resulted in his transfer across the country to Illinois.

The move to Illinois was lonely and painful for Gilmore. His family was unable to travel the distance to visit him. Gilmore began a pen pal relationship with his cousin, Brenda. She was able to convince a parole board to release Gilmore early to her custody. On April 9, 1976, Gilmore was released to Brenda's custody where he would be able to work for his uncle, Vern Damico, in the shoe repair business (A&E, 1996). At the age of thirty-six, Gilmore traveled to Provo, Utah, to live with his cousin and establish a new life.

Life, Labor, and Love

By the time of his last release from jail, Gilmore had been in prison for nearly half of his life. He had been institutionalized, which meant he had very limited job skills and a difficult time conforming to the requirements of good citizenship. Utah had a conservative moral code derived from its Mormon heritage. During the time that Gilmore worked in Damico's shoe repair shop, Damico had to chastise Gilmore repeatedly for lewd comments made toward female customers (A&E, 1976). Gilmore would make sexual references without realizing the social reprehensibility of his actions. The difficulty in adjusting wore on Gilmore. He retreated to drinking alcohol and stealing. His compulsive behaviors toward self-gratification were beginning to drive his actions again.

Gilmore met a nineteen-year-old woman named Nicole Barrett. Barrett, a young mother, had been married and divorced three times. The woman, half Gilmore's age, provided him with nurturing, drugs, and alcohol; the things Gilmore desired the most. Gilmore drank often and in great quantities. He also began to take headache medication. The combination of pain medications and alcohol caused Gilmore to have violent mood swings. After only two months of intense dating and living together, the mood swings and Gilmore's theft of some guns caused Barrett to decide to leave Gilmore. Barrett recalls that she felt Gilmore was going to get in trouble again, and this time it would not end peacefully. Flight was the only way to ensure her own safety (A&E, 1996).

When Barrett left Gilmore in July 1976, his life seemed to spiral out of control. His lack of money, alcohol abuse, mood swings, and Barrett's absence caused Gilmore to become immensely angry. Barrett hid from Gilmore for over a week. Gilmore searched tirelessly for her. Eventually, Gilmore went to Barrett's mother's house (Ramsland, 2004). He demanded to know where Barrett was. No one would tell him, but Barrett's sister, April, decided to ride along with Gilmore in his new truck. April was young and strung out on drugs. She had no idea where they would be going or what Gilmore would do next.

A STRING OF MURDERS

Max Jensen was a twenty-four-year-old law student and a Mormon. He was a family man with a young wife and infant daughter. Jensen was working the late shift alone at the Sinclair Service Station in Orem, Utah, the night of Monday, July 19, 1976. That night business was slow, which made the service station Gilmore's target (Mailer, 1979).

Gilmore needed money. He was fuming after finding out that, because no one would co-sign for his truck, his truck was likely to be repossessed. He also needed money to take April to see *One Flew over the Cuckoo's Nest* (Mailer, 1979). As he drove by the Sinclair Service Station, Gilmore reported that it looked empty except for the attendant. In an interview given to *Playboy* magazine, Gilmore told Barry Farrell that as he approached the service station he not only had the intent to rob the service station, but he also intended to kill the attendant.

At 10:30 p.m., Gilmore parked his truck around the block from the Sinclair Station. He told April that he was going to run and use the phone. April remained in the truck. Jensen was performing some routine duties when Gilmore entered the service station. Gilmore ordered Jensen to empty his pockets, give him his money, and hand over the coin changer attached to Jensen's belt. Jensen complied without a fight. Gilmore was not satisfied. He ordered Jensen to kneel in the bathroom. Gilmore placed the gun against Jensen's head and pulled the trigger while saying, "This one's for me." He fired a second shot into Jensen's head saying, "This one's for Nicole."

The blood from Jensen's body got on Gilmore's pants. Distracted by this, when he left the service station, he missed a large wad of cash left on the desk (A&E, 1996). He returned to April, who was waiting in the truck parked around the block. Gilmore and April went to the movies. Because April was having flashbacks from the LSD and could not stand to view the movie, the two then moved on to Gilmore's cousin Brenda's house. Brenda reported noticing that Gilmore was overly agitated and concealing his clothing from her (Mailer, 1979). Further agitated by Brenda's incessant questioning, Gilmore took April to the Holiday Inn to spend the night. There, he made several sexual advances toward her, which were rebuffed. Gilmore did drugs and drank with little concern about the murder he had committed earlier in the night.

Another Mormon man, who was soon to be a father, would be Gilmore's next victim. Ben Bushnell managed the City Center Motel, an establishment that was not very far from Damico's house (Gilmore, 1994). On Tuesday, July 20, 1976, the day after the Jensen murder, Bushnell's pregnant wife accompanied Bushnell to the Motel.

That same day, Gilmore was having some mechanical problems with his truck. The truck was an irritating factor in Gilmore's life. He could not afford it, no one would co-sign for it, the salesman let him purchase it on threat of repossession, and, to end all, it did not run well. The day after killing Max Jensen, Gilmore took his truck to a gas station, close to Damico's home, for repair. The attendant told Gilmore that the repair could take as long as twenty minutes to fix. Gilmore decided to "do a little visiting" (Mailer, 1979, p. 249).

Gilmore walked a short distance from the gas station and saw the City Center Motel. He entered the office and was greeted by Bushnell. After they exchanged greetings, Gilmore drew his gun and shot Bushnell in the head. Gilmore located the cash box from behind the counter, grabbed it, and began to leave. As he did so he paused, noticing that Bushnell was groaning and moving; the shot in the head had not killed this man as quickly as the man the night before. Bushnell's wife heard a pop, thought there must be children with balloons in the office, and ventured into the office to see. There she observed a tall man with a goatee holding the cash box, preparing to leave. She next observed her dying husband lying face down on the floor bleeding from his head. Gilmore fled (Mailer, 1979).

As he walked away from the motel, Gilmore emptied the cash box into his pockets. He tossed the empty box into some bushes. Realizing he should get rid of the murder weapon too, he grabbed the gun by its barrel and shoved it into a bush. Something caught the trigger and the gun went off. The bullet went through Gilmore's left hand between his thumb and index finger, tearing his flesh. This injury would prove to be damning evidence of Gilmore's guilt.

Bleeding and in intense pain, Gilmore rushed into the gas station restroom. Norman Fulmer, the gas station attendant, noticed the trail of blood. When Gilmore exited the restroom, Fulmer watched Gilmore get into his truck and drive it erratically. Fulmer had heard over a police scanner that an aggravated assault and robbery had occurred at the motel, so Fulmer called the police dispatcher. Fulmer conveyed a description of Gilmore, the truck's license plate number, and the general direction in which Gilmore was heading. The pursuit was on.

CATCHING THE KILLER

Gilmore drove to a friend's house and asked to be driven to the airport. The friend did not comply. Gilmore made a call to Brenda's house to see if she could be of any assistance. Once she had determined where Gilmore was, she phoned the police and told them. Later, she would tell interviewers that they suspected Gilmore had killed someone on Monday night, killed someone else on Tuesday night, and she wanted him stopped before Wednesday came around (A&E, 1996).

Gilmore grew impatient and drove away from his friend's house. With SWAT teams mobilized, the police began setting up roadblocks. Once Gilmore was spotted in the white truck, police followed him and eventually commanded him to stop. Gilmore was ordered to exit the vehicle and lay on the ground. As he did, the truck rolled forward through a fence and into a field. Gilmore was read his rights and only said, "Be careful of that hand. It's been hurt" (Mailer, 1979, p. 268).

The brief interlude of freedom in Gilmore's life was now over. Strangely, it ended directly in front of Barrett's mother's house. Nicole Barrett was able to witness the arrest of her former lover who was now accused of murder.

THE TRIAL

Much like his arrest, Gilmore's trial went down without a fight. The prosecution charged Gilmore with first-degree murder, and, if successful, the prosecution vowed to seek the death penalty to prevent Gilmore from being a further danger to society or other inmates. The trial began on Tuesday, October 5, 1976. Admitted as evidence was the FBI's examination of the cartridge expelled when Gilmore fired the gun into Bushnell and the cartridge of the bullet that went through Gilmore's hand; the FBI concluded that the two cartridges had been fired from the same gun. The prosecution called Peter Arroyo, who positively identified Gilmore as the man he saw fleeing the scene of Bushnell's murder immediately after Bushnell had been shot (Mailer, 1979).

After the prosecution had presented its evidence and rested, the judge asked Gilmore's defense team if they wished to present any evidence: They did not. The defense rested. Gilmore was livid. He felt that he was being railroaded into pleading guilty, and he wished to take the stand and claim insanity as a defense. Gilmore's defense team refused to allow Gilmore to take the stand, because their own doctors had concluded that Gilmore was not insane at the time he murdered Ben Bushnell.

Gilmore requested that the court allow him to take the stand despite his counsel's advice. The court, in attempting to determine if Gilmore understood the ramifications of taking the stand, such as being subject to prosecution cross-examination and presentation of rebuttal evidence, asked Gilmore several pointed questions. After much discussion between Gilmore, the court, and defense counsel, Gilmore withdrew his request to take the stand.

In closing arguments, the prosecution reiterated that the shot that killed Bushnell had been fired while the gun was placed directly against his head. There was not an errant shot intended to merely intimidate Bushnell; this shot was meant to kill the young man. The defense merely argued that the evidence did not satisfy the requirements of overcoming all reasonable doubt, and that the facts, as laid out by the prosecution, were "ridiculous" (Mailer, 1979, p. 432).

On October 7, 1976, at about 10:13 a.m., the jury began deliberating the guilt or innocence of Gary M. Gilmore. At 11:30 a.m. the jury returned. They found Gilmore guilty of murder in the first degree. The next phase was the sentence hearing, which took place after a lunch recess.

The prosecution presented testimony of Gilmore's violence toward inmates and staff during his previous incarcerations. Additionally, a detective on the Jensen murder case was called to testify that he believed Gilmore had been the culprit in that homicide, as well. The defense allowed Gilmore to take the stand to plea for his life. Gilmore was walked through the time period when Bushnell was murdered and the defense attempted to defang the prosecution's closing arguments heard earlier in the day. However, once Gilmore was on the stand, the prosecution seized the opportunity to cross-examine him. The prosecutor made Gilmore recount shooting Bushnell in vivid detail. The impression left on the jury was a lasting one (Mailer, 1979).

The jury returned a sentence of death. The judge asked Gilmore if he had a preference of method of execution. Gilmore responded, "I prefer to be shot" (Mailer, 1979, p. 447). Thus, it was determined that Gary M. Gilmore was to be executed by the State of Utah by means of a firing squad.

THE EXECUTION

Gary Gilmore made it very clear by his actions that he did not fear death. As a young boy, he played chicken with trains. As an inmate, he attempted suicide on numerous occasions. As a murderer, he walked boldly into businesses and coldly shot two men with little regard for potential retaliation. As a condemned prisoner, Gilmore stared the killing machine down and dared the authorities to use it. Nicole Barrett attributes Gilmore's concession of his death sentence to his lack of fear of death (A&E, 1996).

Others, like Mikal Gilmore and their cousin Brenda, contend that Gilmore's antics, fight to die, and suicide attempts are indicative of Gilmore's fear of living. Gilmore had spent most of his life incarcerated. His last stint of freedom provided enough time for him to fall in love and lose his love. Facing the remainder of his life in prison may have proven too much for Gilmore to bear. In a tape-recorded message to Barrett, Gilmore speaks of wanting to die to get out of his "bum life" (A&E, 1996).

Gilmore's desire to die was plagued by his inability to kill himself. Once, Gilmore coerced other inmates to join in a suicide pact with him because the prison would not make his dentures fit well. They all agreed to slit their wrists at the same time. When they did, many of the inmates injured themselves badly, but Gilmore only scratched himself (A&E, 1996). Likewise, toward the end of his life, Gilmore entered into another suicide pact. This time, he and his former lover, Nicole Barrett, were to take an overdose of pills at midnight. Nicole followed through with her pact and ingested the pills at midnight. Gilmore waited until closer to morning to take his pills, leading some to speculate that he wanted Nicole to die, but for someone to find him and save him (Ramsland, 2004). Demanding the state carry out his execution allowed Gilmore to control the end of his life while letting someone else kill him.

On the night of January 16, 1977, Gilmore ate, drank smuggled whisky, and downed handfuls of pills, which had made him high. Gilmore's attorney had arranged for a call to be placed, during which Gilmore's favorite musician, Johnny Cash, would sing Gilmore a song (A&E, 1996).

The next morning, Gilmore, Lawrence Schiller, Damico, and Gilmore's lawyer were led by authorities to an old cannery located on the prison property. Within the cannery, a curtain was placed twenty-five feet in front of a chair. The curtain contained five slender openings through which the firing squad could aim. The chair was on a small platform and surrounded by sandbags. It had nylon-padded straps to secure Gilmore. Gilmore was placed in the chair and strapped down. By all accounts, he was jovial and fearless. His heart was located and a white paper target was placed directly over it for the firing squad to aim at and shoot. When asked if he had any last words, he responded, "Let's do it." A black corduroy hood was placed over his head. The firing squad took its mark; four of the rifles were loaded with live ammunition, the fifth contained a blank so that each shooter could believe he did not shoot Gilmore (Ramsland, 2004). After the firing squad shot Gilmore, blood ran out of his body and within seconds he was dead.

THE DEATH PENALTY DEBATE

Some may ask the following questions: Why is Gary Gilmore different from any other murderer? Why is he so relevant to U.S. criminal history? The answers lay more in Gilmore's timing than in his person or offenses. Had Gilmore's offenses been committed several months earlier, the death penalty would not have been an option. Had Gilmore resisted his death penalty through rigorous appeals and protests, it is possible that someone else would have been the first to be executed in the country since 1967. In that case, Gilmore would not be a topic of discussion; just another inmate or victim of the death penalty. However, the timing of his crime, conviction, and sentencing placed him at the front of the line to be executed, and that made him a focal point of the national debate over the death penalty.

The legal situation surrounding the death penalty was at its most complicated in the late 1960s and 1970s. One must understand that the reason Gilmore became popular was because of his timely falling into the fertile soil of an intense legal debate. What follows is an explanation of how the debate raged.

Furman v. Georgia

The United States is the last remaining "western democracy" to retain the death penalty as a form of punishment (A&E, 1996). The retention of the death penalty has not been without a fight. The highest court of the land, the U.S. Supreme Court, has found itself battling over the issues surrounding the death penalty for nearly 200 years. Until 1972, the Court had not found a constitutional problem with the government's choice of executing murderers. However, in 1972, the Court was presented with cases arguing that the death penalty, as it was being applied by state statutes, constituted cruel and unusual punishment, and therefore was a violation of the Eighth Amendment of the U.S. Constitution. To the shock of most people the Court agreed, as evidenced by the decision in *Furman v. Georgia*.

When the Court decided *Furman*, it did not find that the death penalty was a per se violation of the Constitution's prohibition of cruel or unusual punishment. The Court held that if sentencing statutes provided for a penalty of death, which could be applied arbitrarily or capriciously, or there was a substantial risk of such application, then the statutes violated the Eighth Amendment because the statutes do not "comport with human dignity" (*Furman v. Georgia*, 1972, p. 304). The Court declared that the existing state statutes were not in compliance with the Eighth Amendment because they created a substantial risk that the death penalty would be arbitrarily or capriciously imposed. The power to the killing machines was turned off.

Immediately the ripples of the *Furman* decision incited a national debate regarding the propriety of the death penalty. *Furman* did not resolve the central issue of the constitutionality of executions. The Court had been cautious not to speak too broadly in creating a moratorium on the death penalty. Their caution stemmed from deep concerns about federalism. Traditionally, the states were allowed to create legislation, define morals, and handle criminals without interference from the federal government. Portions of the national discourse over the death penalty focused on federalism; that is, whether the Supreme Court could tell the states not to utilize the death penalty. Several southern states (Georgia, North Carolina, and Texas, among others) quickly set out to improve their death penalty statutes to remove or lessen the risk of arbitrariness in its application and capriciousness so that they could then challenge the moratorium and resume executions.

The other side of the national debate felt assured that the death penalty had been silenced forever. Strong evidence supporting this view was the practical effect of *Furman* in invalidating nearly forty state death penalty statutes and overturning close to 600 death sentences. "The decision was front-page news with headlines of a size usually reserved for the declaration of war" (Rivkind and Shatz, 2001, p. 74). Much of the language contained in the *Furman* majority opinion was interpreted as "anti-death penalty" and proclaimed to be defining the shift in modern morality and decency away from killing criminals. Justice Brennan said boldly,

The calculated killing of a human being by the State involves, by its very nature, a denial of the executed person's humanity . . . grounded upon the recognition of human fallibility, that the punishment of death must inevitably be inflicted upon innocent men, we know that death has been the lot of men whose convictions were unconstitutionally secured in view of later, retroactively applied, holdings of this Court. The punishment itself may have been unconstitutionally inflicted, yet the finality of death precludes relief. (*Furman v. Georgia*, 1972, p. 290)

Justice White stated what he felt was a near truism: "I begin with what I consider a near truism: that the death penalty could so seldom be imposed that it would cease to be a credible deterrent or measurably to contribute to any other end of punishment in the criminal justice system" (*Furman v. Georgia*, 1972, p. 311).

Justice Marshall's views breathed much hope into the anti-death penalty perspective. Not only did Marshall argue that the death penalty failed to satisfy any of its six justifications (retribution, general deterrent to crime, prevent recidivism, encourage guilty pleas, eugenics, and reducing state expenditures), he also argued that American society had evolved in decency past a point where executions where morally acceptable. "Even if capital punishment is not excessive, it nonetheless violates the Eighth Amendment because it is morally unacceptable to the people of the United States at this time in their history" (*Furman v. Georgia*, 1972, p. 360).

The slow pace at which cases proceeded through the legal system provided further false hope for the anti-death penalty perspective. The states were quickly working to restore power to killing machines during the four-year moratorium. One method by which they sought to achieve this end was arguing that their revised statutes satisfied the *Furman* mandate against arbitrariness and capriciousness.

Gregg, Woodson, and Jurek

North Carolina, Georgia, and Texas all allowed juries to sentence men to die during the moratorium period. Each state allowed the appeals to be taken through the legal system ending with the U.S. Supreme Court. Rather than being relegated to a "dwindling minority," the states were responding with assertions that the majority of U.S. citizens were in favor of the death penalty (Rivkind and Shatz, 2001).

The U.S. Supreme Court found itself faced with a long line of cases marching toward its doors, requesting resolution. Three men—Troy Gregg, James Woodson, and Jerry Jurek—had their appeals heard by the Court on the same day. Gregg was sentenced to die under Georgia's revised death penalty statute, Woodson was sentenced to die under a North Carolina statute, and Jurek was sentenced to die in Texas.

Gregg's case would provide the voice of the Court. The Court stated clearly that the federal court's job is not to be a representative body of the democracy and because of this, federal courts should give great deference to state legislatures' decisions surrounding decency and morality. Therefore, if the states' statutes met constitutional guidelines in assuring no substantial risk of arbitrary and capricious application, the states would be free to determine if death was the appropriate sanction for the crime. Georgia's revised statute corrected the flaws found in the *Furman* decision and thus, the Court determined it was valid. Gregg could lawfully be executed.

Woodson challenged North Carolina's statute, claiming it violated the Eighth Amendment. North Carolina's statute provided for mandatory death sentences in first-degree murder convictions. The Court was not satisfied with North Carolina's statute. Finding three constitutional shortcomings to the North Carolina Statute, the Court sent the case back to the state for further proceedings. Woodson's life was spared by the Court.

Jurek's life was in the Court's hands next. He, too, was arguing that Texas's statute was cruel and unusual. However, the Court found that the narrow definition of capital murder provided by the statute limited the risk of arbitrary and capricious application, and therefore was a constitutional application of the state's sovereign power. Jurek could also lawfully be executed.

The Court's decisions in *Gregg*, *Woodson*, and *Jurek* provided the states with the ability to restart their killing machines. The decisions also gave clearer guidelines concerning the required procedures when seeking to apply the death penalty. Utah was a state with strong public support for the death penalty. When the Court decided *Gregg*, prosecutors and juries across the state were quick to realize they now had the ultimate form of punishment at their disposal.

Gilmore had made a critical mistake by killing Bushnell and Jensen in the summer of 1976. His lawyers would be precluded (even if he wanted them to) from citing the moratorium as a defense for his life. The timing of his conviction and sentence to die placed him in the middle of a public debate over the propriety of the death penalty.

Utah had sentenced Gilmore to die. Some believed there might be a way for public opinion to stop the killing machine. Gilmore, however, was reluctant to try. He refused to allow his attorneys to file appeals on his case. Gilmore's attorneys had planned on taking his case up on appeal anyway, but Gilmore fired them. Gilmore's insistence on receiving the sentence handed down by the jury made him the center of the argument raging in the public concerning the humanity of the death penalty.

THE MEDIA'S ROLE IN GILMORE'S DEATH

Having waived all appeals, Gilmore's execution was to take place within sixty days after his sentencing (Ramsland, 2004). The initial date was to be November 15, 1976. Such expediency meant that Gilmore would be the first person to be executed in the United States in ten years. The media, which understood the public's interest in the death penalty, swarmed in on the Gilmore case.

Gilmore hired an attorney, Dennis Boaz, to fight in support of his execution. Boaz agreed to be Gilmore's attorney if Gilmore would let him write

Gilmore's story. Boaz proclaimed that he would be a writer first and an attorney second (Mailer, 1979, p. 549). This attitude paved the way for the media to obtain information concerning Gilmore's case. Boaz was critical to the release of information because the media were prevented from entering the prison to interview Gilmore.

Many factors made Gilmore's situation very attractive for the media. First, Gilmore refused attempts to save his life. This oddity struck a chord with the public, and made easy headlines. Mikal Gilmore stated that during the last few months of Gilmore's life, one could not find a major magazine or newspaper that did not have Gilmore's face on it and life history within it. *Newsweek* ran Gilmore as a cover story. *Time* magazine did a story followed by one in *Life* magazine (Mailer, 1979).

Next, major national newspapers, such as the *New York Times* and the *Los Angeles Times,* picked up on the sensitivity of the public perceptions of the death penalty. Not only did the pending execution of Gilmore fuel a rampant dialogue in the communities of Utah, but a national dialogue was also alive and all eyes were on Gilmore. Before Gilmore was executed, international notoriety was achieved when the *London Daily Express* and certain Swedish reporters paid top dollar for interviews. The media reported that the American Civil Liberties Union (ACLU) was interested in stopping Gilmore's execution, and the media followed the ACLU's movements throughout the legal system. The local papers published pleas from reverends and rabbis calling for humane treatment of Gilmore. Such a debate and willing public dialogue excited the media.

Finally, the nature of the events that occurred in Gilmore's last months kept the attention closely on him. Gilmore spoke openly about his desire to die and openly challenged the system to do its duty. By denying his appeals, Gilmore acted outside the norm and provided fodder for news media. When Gilmore, upset that his execution date was too far away, had attempted to commit suicide by overdosing on pills, the media had fresh material to discuss. After the jail banned Gilmore from having contact with Nicole Barrett because she had smuggled, in her vagina, the thirty-five pills with which Gilmore had attempted to kill himself, he then went on a hunger strike. Such antics kept the media present and thirsty for headlines.

When Gilmore's execution was stayed pending review by the Utah State Board of Pardons, Gilmore attended the hearing and spoke for himself. The hearing room was filled with microphones and video recording equipment. Gilmore played up to the media, telling the board that he took his sentence "literal and serious" (A&E, 1996). He proceeded to tell the reverend and rabbis from Salt Lake City to "butt out" of his life. Gilmore asserted determinedly that it was his life and his death and that he was not going to ask for any pardons or stays (A&E, 1996).

When the Utah State Board of Pardons proclaimed that Gilmore's life should not be spared, the news media printed Gilmore's fate in large print. On December 2, 1976, Bessie Gilmore filed a request for stay to the U.S. Supreme Court, claiming to be "next friend" of Gilmore. The Court granted a stay to determine if Bessie had standing to halt the execution. Gilmore was upset with his mother's maneuver. Using the media, Gilmore wrote a statement telling his mother to stay out of the matter and let him die. On December 13, 1976, the U.S. Supreme Court lifted the stay and the sentencing judge set January 17, 1977, as the new execution date (see *Gilmore v. Utah*, 1976). Such tension and a building crescendo of events kept the media's mouth watering (A&E, 1996).

With the desire to break the news, speak with authority on the issues, or have the ultimate rights to the story came a monetary price. Damico sold the rights to the movie, life story, book, "and everything" for $50,000 to Lawrence Schiller, a Hollywood film producer. Schiller conducted continuous interviews with Gilmore and his family, compiling a wealth of details concerning the life, crimes, and plight of Gilmore. Schiller's findings were penned into a book, *Executioner's Song*, by Norman Mailer. In graphic detail, Mailer's 1,056-page book chronicled a version of Gilmore's life and death. It received critical acclaim for its portrayal of the condemned to die, but it is best known for winning the Pulitzer Prize in 1980. More than three years after his death, Gilmore was continuing to envelop the media's attention.

During the last few months of his life, interviews to newspapers went for $500 each (Mailer, 1979). According to Gilmore's cousin Brenda, everything was sought after by the media and others interested in profiting from Gilmore's execution (A&E, 1996). Mikal Gilmore told interviewers that the media, legal, and commercial powers had created a situation where the only possible satisfying ending was Gilmore's execution (A&E, 1996).

The commercialization and media saturation of Gilmore's situation created what some referred to as a "media circus" (A&E, 1996). According to the former assistant warden of the prison holding Gilmore, a special request was made to the Federal Aviation Administration to make the air ways over the prison restricted air ways after a media helicopter attempted to fly into an inmate recreational yard to shoot pictures of the cell area in which Gilmore stayed. On January 16, 1977, more than 300 media representatives arrived at the prison to report Gilmore's execution. The prison officials had to organize the media and protesters in special locales to avoid disruption (A&E, 1996).

The media were able to report several events over the last twenty-four hours of Gilmore's life. The ACLU received another stay of execution that was promptly overturned by the Tenth Circuit Court of Appeals. Finally, on the morning of January 17, 1976, the media were able to report that Gary Gilmore had been shot dead by the firing squad.

According to Mikal Gilmore, the media showed up because it had wanted all along to see a "man have his heart riddled with bullets." Gilmore had become a spectacle, more than a mere murderer, and more than a merely condemned prisoner. He was the fuel for the debate, the headlines; he was the key to the killing machines (A&E, 1996).

SUMMARY AND CONCLUSION

The bullets that pierced Gilmore's heart, not only ended the life of a heinous career criminal, they served as evidence that the killing machines were still functional. A ten-year silence was shattered by the explosion of the rifle shots, and, even after the sound of the explosion had ceased, the drone and vibration of the killing machines could be heard and felt.

The killing machines have grown increasingly efficient as time has gone by. From 1977 to 1995, approximately 300 executions occurred. Between 1995 and 2004, nearly 600 executions have taken place ("William Wickline," 2004). One man's fear of living has enabled the execution of hundreds.

NOTE

1. The information contained within this chapter is synthesized from several sources, primarily, *Shot in the Heart, Executioner's Song,* Crimelibrary.com, and *Gary Gilmore: A Fight to Die.*

REFERENCES

A&E (Producer). (1996). A&E Biography. *Gary Gilmore: A Fight To Die* [Television broadcast].
Furman v. Georgia, 408 U.S. 238 (1972).
Gilmore, M. (1994). *Shot in the heart.* New York: Doubleday.
Gilmore v. Utah, 429 U.S. 1012 (1976).
Gregg v. Georgia, 428 U.S. 153 (1976).
Jurek v. Texas, 428 U.S. 262 (1976).
Mailer, N. (1979). *Executioner's song.* Boston: Little, Brown and Company.

Ramsland, K. (2004). Retrieved February 1, 2004, from http://www.crimelibrary. com/notorious_murders/mass/gilmore/index_1.html?sect=2

Rivkind, N., and Shatz, S. (2001). *Cases and materials on the death penalty.* St. Paul, MN: West Group.

"William Wickline Scheduled to Die." (n.d.). Retrieved February 29, 2004, from http://web.amnesty.org/library/index/ENGAMR510402004

Woodson v. North Carolina, 428 U.S. 280 (1976).

11

The Trial of Joan Little: An Inmate, a Jailer, and a First-degree Murder Charge

James R. Acker

Joan (pronounced and occasionally spelled "JoAnne" or "Joanne") Little, a twenty-year-old black woman, was incarcerated in the small town of Washington, North Carolina, during the summer of 1974. She was thrust into the national limelight after she fatally stabbed Clarence Alligood, the 62-year-old white jailer who was working the graveyard shift in the Beaufort County Jail on August 26 and 27 of that same year. She was charged with first-degree murder, which was a crime automatically punished by death under North Carolina law. There were no eyewitnesses to the killing, and thus no explanation—other than Little's—for the condition in which Alligood's body had been found, locked in the jail cell from which Little had escaped. Alligood had suffered multiple stab wounds from an ice pick, including one that penetrated his heart. His lower body was nude, save only for the socks adorning his feet. A small pool of seminal fluid had collected on his leg. It soon became obvious that this would not be a routine murder prosecution.

Americans, in the time following the Watergate scandal, had exhibited a deep distrust of government and government officials. Many citizens, particularly African Americans, waited impatiently for the day when their civil rights would be recognized, not just as abstract legal promises but also in mainstream activities, including involvement with the U.S. criminal justice system. Southern states were under particular scrutiny on racially charged matters. In the mid-1970s, women's issues were at the focal point, having gathered momentum in the wake of the decision in *Roe v. Wade* (1973) and spurred on by aggressive campaigns targeting reform of antiquated and misogynistic rape and sexual assault laws. The death penalty had been dealt a severe blow by the U.S. Supreme Court's ruling in *Furman v. Georgia* (1972), which had invalidated capital punishment statutes across the United States on procedural grounds. Nevertheless, capital punishment had resurfaced with a vengeance amidst strident public debate in North Carolina and elsewhere.

Thus, the stage was set for the murder trial of Joan Little, a case smoldering with so many urgent social issues that its symbolic significance threatened to obscure the individuals caught up in it.

It was a case whose elements were novelistic, almost surpassing the novel in intrigue, for what novelist can construct a believable set of circumstances that contains so much mystery and at the same time bears so importantly on five crucial questions? In a sexual assault, does a woman . . . have the right to kill her . . . attacker? Is the level of decency in North Carolina and the nation above the spectacle of human executions? What recourse does a prisoner in jail have to the brutality of jail authorities? How has the lot of the black citizen changed in the rural South? And finally . . . how new is the New South? (Reston, 1977, p. x)

So turgid was the case with overarching social implications that, as she approached her trial, Little felt compelled to protest that, "I am nobody's cause . . . I am on trial for my life before a judge and jury" (Simms, 1975, p. 21). Nevertheless, it was foreordained that many fundamental assumptions of American social justice would be on trial along with Joan Little.

A KILLING AT THE BEAUFORT COUNTY JAIL

Joan Little was born in 1954 in Washington, North Carolina, the county seat of Beaufort County, nestled between the Pamlico and Tar Rivers in the eastern, tobacco-rich part of the state. The small town was often referred to as "Little Washington" to avoid confusion with the nation's capital, which the locals volunteered with a wink and a grin. One of nine children, Little proved during early adolescence to be more than her mother could handle. Her habitual truancy and streetwise behavior caused her mother to invoke the authority of the juvenile court to have Little committed to training school at age fourteen. In an eerie portent of the future, Little took flight from the training school, sought out relatives in New Jersey and

Philadelphia, and did not return to her North Carolina home until she was eighteen years old. She almost immediately became involved in minor scrapes with the law, including several arrests and a conviction for shoplifting. She got into more serious trouble in January 1974 (Harwell, 1979, pp. 21–30).

With her brother Jerome, she was arrested and charged with breaking and entering into three residences in a Beaufort County trailer park and stealing televisions, a rifle, appliances, clothing, and other belongings worth more than $1,300. She was convicted following a jury trial in June 1974 and sentenced to serve seven to ten years in the Women's Prison in Raleigh. At her own request, she was confined in the Beaufort County Jail immediately following her trial. She hoped to secure release from jail on bond pending appeal of her convictions, and she preferred staying close to home to being transferred to the Women's Prison.

The Beaufort County Jail had been constructed only three years earlier. It was a modern facility located on the ground floor of the courthouse. Little was locked up in the women's section of the jail, which was maintained separately from the men's quarters. The women's section consisted of only two cells, each roughly seven feet by five feet, including a narrow cot, a sink, and a toilet. All of the jailers were men. Clarence Alligood had been employed at the jail for over a year. A former farmer and truck driver, who stood nearly six feet tall and weighed a sturdy 200 pounds, Alligood had been married for forty-four years and was the father of six children (Harwell, 1979, pp. 3941). Little was of modest stature, just five feet three inches tall and weighing one hundred and twenty pounds ("Rape or Seduction," 1975).

Alligood reported to work at the jail for the 10 p.m. to 6 a.m. shift on the evening of August 26, 1974. By this time, Little had been incarcerated for nearly three months following her trial. The facility was not overly encumbered by formal rules and regulations, and the staff and inmates intermingled somewhat casually. While Alligood was making his rounds, Little asked him if she could use the telephone in the jailers' office. Alligood readily assented. He accompanied her from her cell to the office, where another inmate, a teen-aged boy named Terry Bell, was having a soft drink. Little placed her phone call at about 10:30 p.m. Several people were in and out of the office while she conducted her conversation, but at one point, after Alligood had stepped out to assist a woman swear out an assault warrant, Little and Bell apparently were left alone. Little may even have been completely alone in the office for a brief period; a period of some significance because an ice pick—the very ice pick with which Clarence Alligood was stabbed to death—was routinely kept in a desk drawer in the office.

The ice pick had proven useful in removing gum, paper, and other objects that occasionally were jammed into cell door locks (Harwell, 1979, pp. 55–60).

Alligood returned Little to her cell by 11 p.m. At around 2 a.m., a police officer stopped by the jail and dropped off some fast food for an appreciative Alligood. Just before 3 a.m., Alligood visited police dispatcher Beverly King in her office, and asked if all of the sheriff's deputies (who frequently paid visits to the jail with arrestees while engaged in other business) had gone for the night. She replied that they had, and Alligood left her office and returned to the jail area. Alligood's body would be discovered a little over an hour later, shortly after 4 a.m., by a police officer who was seeking assistance with processing an intoxicated woman whom he had brought to the women's section of the jail.

Alligood's body was found locked in Little's cell, slumped to the side on a blanket that had been folded on the floor. His body was nude from the waist down, except for the socks on his feet. Blood marked his temple. His glasses lay on the floor. Additional blood was on one of his legs, as was a string of fluid that, on later analysis, proved to be "teeming with spermatoz[o]a" (Reston, 1977, p. 11). His pants were clutched in one of his hands. The other hand loosely cupped the ice pick that had been the source of the eleven stab wounds in his body, including one that had pierced the wall of his heart. Fast-food wrappers and part of a sandwich were found in the women's cellblock area. Alligood's shoes were outside of the locked cell. Little's bra and negligee, as well as a blanket, had been tied to the bars of the cell. Neither Little nor Alligood's keys were anywhere to be found.

ARREST AND PRETRIAL PROCEEDINGS:
THE CRIMINAL JUSTICE SYSTEM RESPONSE

Confusion reigned in the immediate aftermath of the killing. An all points bulletin (APB) was issued that announced the homicide and Little's escape from jail. Sheriff Ottis (Red) Davis turned his attention to finding a replacement set of keys, so the inmates could be released from the facility's jail cells in case of an emergency. A rescue squad and a doctor were summoned, Alligood's death was confirmed, and his body was removed from the jail cell. A police photographer had first taken pictures of the cell and the body, but the camera's flash attachment malfunctioned which resulted in only a few poor-quality photographs. A sheriff's deputy had removed the ice pick from Alligood's hand and handed it to another officer, who simply slipped it uncovered into his back pocket. State Bureau of Investigation agents who traveled from Raleigh to the Beaufort County Jail were dismayed to learn that, before their arrival, the local authorities had already cleared the jail cell of all belongings and scrubbed its four walls thoroughly, leaving the cell spotless.

Rumors abounded that an order would be sought declaring Joan Little an outlaw, (which under an anachronistic North Carolina law would soon be declared unconstitutional), which would have authorized citizens and law enforcement officials alike to kill her on sight. That drastic measure was not taken and nevertheless would have proven futile because Little managed to elude capture. She hid out for nearly a week following her escape in the ramshackle home of Ernest (Paps) Barnes in the black section of Little Washington, just six blocks from the jail (Harwell, 1979; Reston, 1977). Margie Wright, a local activist, learned of Little's whereabouts and contacted Golden Frinks, who was actively involved with the Southern Christian Leadership Conference. She also called Jerry Paul, an attorney who was known for his work in civil rights cases, who had grown up in Washington, North Carolina.

A former football player at East Carolina University and a graduate of the University of North Carolina Law School, Paul had since taken up residence in Chapel Hill. During the dead of night and disguised with a wig, Little was smuggled out of Paps Barnes's house and delivered to Paul's waiting car. Paul drove her to his home and allowed her to take refuge there. Three days later, on the Tuesday after Labor Day, Paul negotiated Little's surrender and delivered her amidst much media fanfare to the North Carolina State Police in Raleigh. It was agreed that she would not be returned to the Beaufort County Jail, but that she would instead be taken to the Women's Prison in Raleigh to await trial.

The district attorney serving Beaufort County, William Griffin, sought an indictment for first-degree murder, a crime that required proof of a premeditated and deliberate killing. The Beaufort County Grand Jury quickly obliged, although two years later the U.S. Supreme Court would declare North Carolina's mandatory death penalty for first-degree murder unconstitutional (*Woodson v. North Carolina*, 1976). However, in 1974, the first-degree murder charge signified that Joan Little would die in the state's gas chamber if convicted. This threat did not appear to be an idle one. At the time, North Carolina had the country's largest death row, with more than sixty prisoners awaiting execution (King, 1974).

Little's bail was set at $115,000 dollars, with $100,000 for the murder charge and an additional $15,000 appeal bond on the breaking and entering and larceny convictions that accounted for her presence in the Beaufort County Jail. This amount was well beyond Little's means, and she would remain incarcerated for six months following her arrest. However, as news of the first-degree murder charge spread—along with the vague outlines of her defense that she had wrestled the ice pick away from Alligood following a sexual assault and killed him in self-defense—Little's cause not only commanded the support of legions of social activists, but it attracted significant financial backing as well. Morris Dees, legal counsel for the Southern Poverty Law Center in Alabama, an organization that fought race discrimination and championed causes including the rights of prisoners and jail inmates, learned of Little's plight and, after consulting with Jerry Paul, launched a major fundraising campaign for the Joan Little Defense Fund. Dees's solicitation letter, which featured a reprint of a December 1, 1974, *New York Times* article about the case (King, 1974), had reached over 2 million people. More than $350,000 would be raised on Little's behalf by the end of the trial. Making use of a portion of these donations, Little posted bail and gained pretrial release on February 27, 1975 (Harwell, 1979; Reston, 1977).

The legal wrangling over the case had begun shortly after Little's arrest. Jerry Paul assembled a team of lawyers that eventually included himself; his associate Karen Galloway, who had just graduated from law school and was the only black and only woman among the attorneys; Morris Dees; Marvin Miller, a civil rights attorney from Washington, DC; and three additional North Carolina lawyers. The defense team comprised more than just lawyers, however. With the money raised for the Joan Little Defense Fund, Paul also brought in several social scientists who helped lay the foundation for a change of venue motion, jury consultants who created sophisticated profiles for identifying favorable jurors and studied body language to help screen out undesirable jurors, and even a psychic who had a hand in jury selection and in preparing Little for trial. An initial priority for the defense was to remove the trial from Beaufort County to a different part of the state.

To bolster the argument for a change of venue, the social scientists completed surveys of residents of Beaufort County, surrounding counties in eastern North Carolina, and elsewhere in the state. Their aim was partly to help make the case that it would be impossible to obtain an impartial jury in Beaufort County because of the massive publicity surrounding the killing and its aftermath. But, it also was to show that Little could not receive a fair trial anywhere in the eastern part of the state because so many people in that region harbored racial prejudices and regressive attitudes about women and sexual assault. Following a lengthy hearing, Judge Henry McKinnon granted the change of venue motion. The judge's written order relied almost exclusively on the evidence concerning prejudicial publicity. However, instead of moving the trial to a neighboring county in eastern North Carolina, he took the unusual step of relocating it to Raleigh. Positioned in the central, Piedmont region of North Carolina and an urban center with a cosmopolitan population as well as being the state capital, Raleigh was light years removed from Little Washington. The defense considered securing this change of venue as crucial to their chances for an acquittal (McConahay, Mullin, and Frederick, 1977, p. 206).

THE MEDIA'S INFLUENCE

As evident by the change of venue order, media coverage had already had a direct impact on the case. The defense had shown, among other things, that news reports in eastern North Carolina were significantly more likely than in other parts of the state to emphasize the multiple stab wounds that Alligood had received and to minimize aspects of the killing that could be considered more favorable to the defense; such as that Alligood's body was found partially nude, that there was evidence of recent sexual activity, and that Little maintained that she had killed in self-defense (Reston, 1977, pp. 193–195). From the very outset, however, press coverage fueled and largely defined the case, blurring the lines between substance and image until they were virtually indistinguishable. Following the trial, Jerry Paul would unabashedly admit that he "'had to create [Joan Little] totally . . . You could let people see only so much of her. If they saw too much, the mask would slip away'" (Reston, 1977, p. 113). To this end, for example, he was not above planting a copy of *To Kill a Mockingbird* in Little's hands for the benefit of news photographers and otherwise deliberately attempting to manipulate press reporting ("Personality Sketches," 1975a). For his part, District Attorney William Griffin complained, "The media shaped this case. There's no doubt about it" (Harwell, 1979, p. i).

The case did not begin to capture national attention until several months after the slaying, when the *New York Times* ran a December 1, 1974, story entitled, "Killing of Carolina Jailer, Charged to Woman, Raises Question of Abuse of Inmates" (King, 1974). Earlier press coverage was primarily local, beginning the day after the killing, when the *Washington (NC) Daily News* ran a story and an editorial entitled "Brutal Murder," in which Alligood was proclaimed as "a man who gave his life in the line of duty," and he was hailed as "a good man" (Reston, 1977, p. 22). The story neglected to mention the compromising circumstances in which Alligood's body had been found. Those details were not announced publicly for a full week until the release of the report of the physician who had examined Alligood's body in the jail cell, which noted his state of partial undress and "a string of what appeared to be seminal fluid" on his thigh (Harwell, 1979, pp. 106–107). This revelation cast the case in an explosive new light, although news of it spread slowly until a *New York Times* story was published ("National Issues," 1975a), which was promptly exploited in the Southern Poverty Law Center's mass mailing and fundraising campaign.

The ensuing coverage by the *Times* decried Little's case as evidence that "Justice in North Carolina is Once More Old South," citing its "archaic" outlaw statute, "a string of controversial criminal prosecutions of politically active blacks," the state's large death row population, and its "deteriorating, almost paralyzed prison system" ("Old South," 1975a). A *New York Times Magazine* article dubbed Little's impending first-degree murder trial as "a *cause celebre* combining the issues of civil rights, women's rights and prisoners' rights" (Reston, 1975, p. 38). *Newsweek* noted, "what might have been a little-noticed, small-town murder trial [has turned] into a national crusade among women's and civil-rights organizations" (Footlick and Smith, 1975). An article in *The Progressive* argued that "interracial rape has been the quintessential political act for more than [300] years" in the South, and that Joan Little's jury would "be asked to think the unthinkable: first, that the rape of a black woman by a white man is indeed a crime; and second, that a black woman is justified in killing a white man for exercising what would once have been considered his prerogative" (Pinsky, 1975b, p. 9). Radical activist Angela Davis intoned in a *Ms.* magazine article that Joan Little was "one of the most recent victims in" the "racist and sexist tradition" of the United States, where she was "black and a woman, trapped in a society pervaded with myths of white superiority and male supremacy" (Davis, 1975, p. 74).

Meanwhile, several publications with traditionally black readership editorialized about Little's plight. *Jet* quoted the Reverend Ralph Abernathy, Martin Luther King Jr.'s successor as the president of the Southern Christian Leadership Conference, as saying, "I ask North Carolina, if there was a white woman who had stabbed a Black man who was attempting to rape her, would that white woman be on trial today? That white woman would be given a medal of honor. Well, hell, we think as much of our women as white men think of their women" ("Abernathy Supports Little," 1975a). Two weeks later, pictured smiling and comfortingly scratching a dog behind its ear, Little appeared on the cover of *Jet*, under the grisly heading, "Joan Little Fights to Avoid Death Sentence" ("Little Fights Sentence," 1975b).

Julian Bond, a member of the Georgia House of Representatives and the president of the Southern Poverty Law Center, wrote in the *Black Scholar* that Joan Little's "story is one of the most shocking and outrageous examples of injustice against women on record" (Bond, 1975, p. 31). Another article in the *Black Scholar* inveighed that "it is important that we understand and argue that Sis. Joanne Little is not on trial, but rather the [United States] and its system of justice which is rooted in and ruled by class and race . . . [w]e must recognize and respect the social reality that Sis. Joanne Little is a symbol of black womanhood in resistance everywhere against rape and against all other dehumanized and dehumanizing acts and assumptions negative to their freedom and human fullness" (Karenga, 1975, p. 41). *Freedomways* proclaimed that it "adds its voice to the many who are outraged by the unjust prosecution of [twenty]-year old Joanne Little who has committed the threefold 'crime' of being [b]lack, a woman, and defending herself against rape by a racist jailer" (1975, p. 87). The editor of *Essence* demanded to know, "What is the worth of a Black woman's virtue in 1975?" The lament continued: "Not only is Jo Anne [*sic*] Little on trial, we all are. For she represents [b]lack [w]omanhood and our collective chance to affix forever in the consciousness of America that our virtue has been redeemed after centuries of abuse. If the price must be blood, so be it, for we are precious, our sex a gift to be given, but never again taken with but token resistance" (Gillespie, 1975, p. 37).

Joan Little's defense team capitalized on this wave of pretrial publicity by holding press conferences and making television appearances and seizing every opportunity to associate their client with broader issues of racial and sexual exploitation, dehumanizing conditions of incarceration, abuses of the death penalty, and other themes of social injustice. Prosecutor Griffin was reduced to wondering aloud whether, under the circumstances, "the state could get a fair trial" (Reston, 1977, p. 123). John Wilkinson, hired by the Alligood family as a private prosecutor to assist Griffin in presenting the case against Little, complained that, "There was profound disgust in Beaufort County for its portrayal in the national press as a bunch of intolerant, ignorant slobs like the characters of Caldwell's *Tobacco Road*" (Reston, 1977, pp. 166–167). The glare of national and even international publicity would only intensify as the case proceeded to trial.

THE MURDER TRIAL OF JOAN LITTLE

The trial commenced in Raleigh on July 14, 1975. Hundreds of Little's supporters marched through the downtown area, chanting "Free Joan Little," and "One, two, three. Joan must be set free. Four, five, six. Power to the ice pick. Seven, eight, nine. Should have done it a thousand times" (Carroll, 1975a, 1A). More than 400 media representatives vied for fewer than forty seats made available for the press in the Wake County Courthouse (Sitton, 1975, p. 4). Judge Hamilton Hobgood, a respected and experienced judge known for his even temperament, was handpicked by the chief justice of the North Carolina Supreme Court to preside over the trial (*News and Observer*, 1975a, p. 8I).

The first two weeks of the trial were consumed by jury selection. Because it was a capital case, prospective jurors were screened carefully by both sides about their views on the death penalty. Although prosecuting attorneys relied on traditional questions to inform their exercise of peremptory challenges, the defense employed a variety of jury-selection techniques that were anchored on a mathematical model portraying ideal jurors that had been constructed by the social scientists on the defense team. Trouble erupted on the second day of the trial when Judge Hobgood grew impatient with Jerry Paul's reliance on this model while questioning a prospective juror about her magazine reading habits. Hobgood advised Paul, "I am just busting up your system right now," and then cleared the courtroom of potential jurors. Following extensive pleading to be allowed to continue, Paul exploded, ultimately resulting in his being cited for contempt of court and a two-week jail sentence served at the trial's conclusion.

MR. PAUL: The only reason I can see that your Honor is now cutting us off is because we are gaining an advantage and your Honor is favoring the State and your Honor is proceeding in such a manner to insure [*sic*] Joan Little's conviction.
COURT: All right, you got that in the record.
MR. PAUL: And at this point we ask your Honor to recuse yourself because I don't think you are capable of giving Joan Little a fair trial and I don't intend to sit or stand here and see an innocent person go to jail for any reason and you can threaten me with contempt or anything else, but it does not worry me.
COURT: All right, you got that in the record.
MR. PAUL: And to sit there and say like the queen of hearts off with the heads because the law is the law is to take us back a hundred years.
COURT: All right.
MR. PAUL: It is apparent I'm quite disgusted with the whole matter, whole matter of ever bringing Joan Little to trial anyway. There has been one roadblock after another and one attempt after another to railroad Joan Little and I am tired of it. Now we intend to ask these questions and you can sustain the objections if you want to but the appellate court cannot make a ruling on whether or not they were proper questions unless the questions are asked.
COURT: All right, you have said that twice. I haven't said you couldn't ask the questions. (*Paul v. Pleasants*, 1977, pp. 580–581)

Paul continued asking his voir dire questions. Several days later, when the jury was finally in place, the twelve chosen jurors were a remarkable lot. Five members were under age thirty. Five were black. Among the eight women were two who worked in a vegetarian restaurant. Only two white males were seated, one (the eventual foreman of the jury) worked in a stereo shop, and the other, a lawyer who had been a law school classmate of defense team member Karen Galloway (Nichols, 1975b; Reston, 1977). One juror, "a white, middle-aged farmer's wife," was excused at mid-trial when her mother-in-law suffered a heart attack (Nichols, 1975c, p. 1). She was replaced by an alternate, a young black man. The jury that would decide Little's fate comprised six whites and six blacks.

The state began presenting evidence on July 28, 1975. Various celebrities, including Julian Bond, Angela Davis, and comedian and social commentator Dick Gregory, made appearances throughout the trial. However, the number of protestors rapidly dwindled, and major demonstrations failed to materialize. The trial nevertheless did not fail to produce fireworks. Judge Hobgood was kept busy applying sanctions to other defense lawyers in addition to Paul. He ordered Morris Dees removed from the case after Dees approached a prosecution witness during a court recess and exhorted her to reconsider the testimony she had given (King, 1975b; Nichols, 1975d). Radical defense attorney William Kunstler later was denied permission to enter the case as a replacement for Dees, whereupon he sarcastically commented, "I'm glad to see the quality of justice in North Carolina has not improved." Hobgood ordered Kunstler to be seated "or you'll be on the fifth floor," which was the location of the jail. Kunstler brusquely replied, "Take me up there. What you're doing down here is outrageous." Hobgood proceeded to make good on his threat, holding Kunstler in contempt and jailing him for two hours (Carroll, 1975b, p. 5B).

In the absence of eyewitnesses to the killing, the prosecution's case was circumstantial. The state's theory was that Little had surreptitiously removed the ice pick from the desk drawer in the jailers' office while placing her phone call on the night of August 26, subsequently lured Alligood into her cell on the promise of providing him with sexual favors, and then stabbed and killed him so she could escape from the jail. Prosecutors attempted to portray Little as a cool and calculating killer who was anxious to escape the jail so she could be reunited with her lover. The defense, however, capitalized on the shoddy police investigation following the killing, and through cross-examination of the involved officers painted "a picture of confusion and disorganization, as well as lost, overlooked and destroyed evidence and failure to take notes or photographs or to search thoroughly for fingerprints" (King, 1975c, p. 6).

Most observers were not surprised when, at the conclusion of the state's case, Judge Hobgood ruled that insufficient evidence of premeditation and deliberation had been offered to allow the first-degree murder charge to be presented to the jury. District Attorney Griffin suffered Hobgood's rebuke when he complained, "Without all the publicity and public clamor this case would go to the jury on a first-degree-murder charge" (Nichols, 1975e, p. 1). Although the ruling meant that the threat of capital punishment had been eliminated, the jury would still be allowed to consider the lesser-included charge of second-degree murder, which was punishable by up to life imprisonment. The defense thus renewed its quest to persuade the jury that Little had killed in self-defense after Alligood had forced her to perform oral sex at the point of the ice pick.

To begin its case, the defense offered the testimony of three black women who reported that Alligood had fondled them or made sexually suggestive remarks while they had been inmates in the Beaufort County Jail (Nichols, 1975f). A forensics expert from New York had jurors "openly laughing" at the sheriff department's inept crime scene investigation as he explained "that fingerprints might have been lifted from an ice pick that had been stuffed in a deputy's pocket; that photos were 'inferior'; and that evidence may have been contaminated by being thrown together in a pillow case" (Nichols, 1975g, p. 19). Still, everyone sensed that these witnesses were little more than preliminary to the testimony that would follow. Joan Little was called to the witness stand to be examined by Jerry Paul on August 11 as the fifth week of the trial began.

In response to questioning, Little testified that Alligood had come to her jail cell several times during the early morning hours of August 27, 1974. She recounted that she was wearing her nightgown. Alligood told her that she "looked real nice" and that he "wanted to have sex" with her (Reston, 1977, p. 294). Alligood was called away, but he returned sometime later with "a silly-looking grin on his face" (Reston, 1977, p. 295). He took off his shoes in the outside corridor and then let himself into the cell. He advanced on her and removed her gown. As he took off his pants, she had noticed that he was holding an ice pick in his hand. He then forced her head to his penis. After she performed oral sex on him, Alligood loosened his grip on the ice pick, Little wrestled it away from him, and in the ensuing struggle she stabbed him numerous times. As Alligood slumped over the bunk, bleeding, Little hurriedly got dressed and ran out of the cell, slamming the door behind her. She grabbed the keys from the cell door and escaped into the night through a basement exit (Reston, 1977, pp. 296–306). Little broke down at one point during her testimony and a recess was called to allow her to regain her composure. Two of the black women on the jury wept openly (Nichols, 1975h).

William Griffin then began his cross-examination, a "wheedling, battering" interrogation that spread over two separate days (King, 1975d, p. 68). Griffin attempted to establish that Little had become desperate during her incarceration in the Beaufort County Jail to reestablish contact with her lover, Julius Rodgers, who she feared had abandoned her. He tried to paint her as having loose morals and as having traded sex for money or favors on prior occasions. He suggested that she had invited Alligood into her cell after removing the ice pick from the desk in the jailers' office earlier in the evening. The heart of his cross-examination, however, centered on the specifics of her story regarding the killing. He hammered away at her admitted lack of resistance to Alligood, a tactic that may have backfired as it culminated in the following dramatic exchange:

GRIFFIN: He had not threatened you, had he, had he said anything except make a proposition to you?
LITTLE: He said some things later.
GRIFFIN: He had not threatened you; he had not said he was gonna hurt you; all he said to you in effect was that he wanted to have sex with you, is that right?
LITTLE: Yes sir.
GRIFFIN: And you didn't holler, you didn't scream, you didn't fight him off, is that right?
LITTLE: No I did not, but if you had been a woman you wouldn't have known what to do either, you probably wouldn't have screamed either, because you wouldn't have known what he would have done to you. (Reston, 1977, p. 310)

Closing arguments to the jury began on August 13, after additional testimony was elicited from a few minor defense witnesses and a rebuttal witness for the prosecution. During seven hours of prosecution and defense arguments, Little was "alternately characterized . . . as a heroine guided by Divine Providence and a calculating killer who lured Clarence Alligood into her cell and slew him 'at the moment of ecstasy'" (King, 1975e, p. 10). "It was court as theater, a day of strutting, Southern lawyering that left at least one juror in tears" (Nichols, 1975i, p. 1). Judge Hobgood delivered a lengthy charge to the jury, detailing the elements of second-degree murder as well as instructions about when deadly force is justifiable as self-defense. The jury began deliberating shortly after 10:30 a.m. on August 15. After a trial that had lasted five weeks, they needed only seventy-eight minutes to return to the courtroom with a verdict. The jury foreman stood and stated firmly, "Not guilty."

THE TRIAL'S AFTERMATH: THE INVOLVED
PARTIES AND ENDURING LESSONS

Joan Little remained free following her acquittal until December 1975, when the appeal of her breaking and entering and larceny convictions was finally rejected (*State v. Little*, 1975) and she was required to begin serving her seven-to-ten-year prison sentence. In the interim, she appeared at a Black Panther Party rally in Oakland, California, where she was hailed as "the symbol of black womanhood" ("Black Panthers," 1975a). She was scheduled to appear on national television on the *Today* show, but she had overslept, unexpectedly leaving host Barbara Walters without her advertised featured guest (Reston, 1977, p. 327). She served nearly eighteen months of her prison sentence before being approved for a work release program in May 1977 ("Work Release," 1977). However, she absconded in October of that same year and was arrested in December in Brooklyn, New York, following a high-speed car chase ("Auto Chase," 1977). After fighting extradition, she was returned to North Carolina and incarcerated again before her parole in July 1979 (Lescaze, 1979). Ten years later, she was arrested in New Jersey while driving a car with stolen license plates and charged with additional minor offenses (Saxon, 1989). She has remained out of the public eye since 1989.

Little's lead defense counsel, Jerry Paul, began a hiatus from his law practice following Little's acquittal and took to the lecture circuit to deliver speeches. He was roundly criticized for remarks he made to a *New York Times* reporter two months after the conclusion of Little's trial. During that interview, Paul said "he still believes in Miss Little's innocence. But he says it is almost irrelevant that the whole trial process has nothing to do with justice. He uses the words 'illusion' and 'charade.' He says that he simply 'bought' Miss Little's acquittal, and it cost $325,000" (King, 1975a, p. 23). Paul further suggested that the prosecution had been inept and had overlooked potentially damning evidence including a newspaper clipping that Little had used as a bookmarker in the Bible she kept in her jail cell. "The clipping . . . depicts, in a drawing and text, how a woman named Jael lured the leader of an army opposing the Israelites to her tent, 'gave him comfort, and let him rest. Then, as he slept,' the text goes on, 'she took a huge nail and drove it through his temples,' killing him" (King, 1975a, p. 23). The analogy to Alligood's slaying is unmistakable, yet prosecutors, Paul pointed out, failed to take advantage of the evidence, although it had been in their custody. Paul's remarks were later branded as "cynical" and "arrogant" ("Judicial Nihilism," 1975b), and some questioned whether they may have jeopardized the pending appeal of Little's breaking and entering and larceny convictions ("Little Charade," 1975). Paul later resumed his law practice, although he was admonished for subsequent ethics violations (Chandler, 2000; *State v. Joyner*, 1978), and ultimately was disbarred in 1987 (In the Matter of Paul, 1987).

For others involved in the trial, life slowly returned to normal, or at least as normal as circumstances allowed. Clarence Alligood's widow and son expressed disappointment in the verdict and believed that the intense publicity had produced an unfair trial ("Alligoods Dissatisfaction," 1975b). Lead prosecutor William Griffin similarly "believed news accounts of the trial have been biased in favor of the defendant" ("New Bias," 1975), and he said that he did what he thought was right. "This case had to be tried to show that publicity should not prevent a case from coming to trial" (Nichols, 1975j, p. 5B). Judge Hobgood complimented the attorneys involved in the trial for their work, but before the verdict he had opined that the evidence presented was "not as strong" as in most murder trials over which he had presided (Nichols, 1975j, p. 5B). Defense attorney Karen Galloway, whose closing argument to the jury may have been the strongest of all delivered at the trial, returned to practicing law and later became the first black woman judge in Durham County, North Carolina (Reston, 1977, p. 320).

Although Joan Little's case had an undeniable "mythic quality" (National Review, 1975, p. 924) and was hailed by some as the preeminent civil rights trial of the 1970s (Roche, 1975), it receded to obscurity almost as rapidly as it had captivated the nation during the summer of 1975. The case had no discernible impact on general jail conditions or on the specific issues confronting women inmates. The case failed to make a difference in public attitudes about capital punishment and appeared to have had no lingering significance in racial politics. Its one arguable contribution may have been to solidify a woman's right to use deadly force to defend against a sexual assault. Even that message is blurred, however, because Alligood's stabbing death was not sought to be justified in the name of preventing a sexual violation but rather as an act of self-defense after the sexual act had been consummated. One commentator concluded resignedly, "The Joan Little case would have a legacy not of benefits and accomplishments but of bitter memories, disappointments, and broken spirits" (Harwell, 1979, p. 283). Today, when few people recognize Joan Little's name or recall the facts of her case, that assessment is an unfortunately fitting epitaph to a tragedy that once reverberated in America's conscience.

REFERENCES

Abernathy leads 2,000 in support of Joanne Little. *Jet, 48*(5), pp. 48–49.

Alligoods express dissatisfaction. (1975b, August 16). *The News and Observer (Raleigh)*, p. 5B.

Bond, J. (1975, March). Self-defense against rape: The Joanne Little case. *The Black Scholar, 6*, 29–31.

Carroll, G. (1975a, July 15). 500 stage courthouse rally. *The News and Observer (Raleigh)*, pp. 1A, 5B.

Carroll, G. (1975b, August 5). Kunstler is jailed for 2 hours. *The News and Observer (Raleigh)*, p. 5B.

A case of rape or seduction? (1975a, July 28). *Time, 106*(4), p. 19.

Chandler, L. (2000, September 12). Incompetence among defense lawyers one problem with death penalty. *Charlotte Observer*, p. 1B.

Davis, A. (1975, June). JoAnne Little: The dialectics of rape. *Ms. 3*(12), 74–77, 106–108.

The editors. (1975). *Freedomways, 15,* 87–88.

Footlick, J. K., and Smith, V. E. (1975, February 24). Joan Little's defense. *Newsweek, 85*(8), 86.

Furman v. Georgia (1972). 408 U.S. 238.

Gillespie, M. A. (1975, April). Getting down. *Essence, 5,* (12), 37.

Harwell, F. R., Jr. (1979). *A true deliverance.* New York: Alfred A. Knopf.

In the Matter of Paul (1987). 353 S.E.2d 254 (N.C. App.), cert. denied, 356 S.E.2d 779 (N.C.), cert. denied, 484 U.S. 1004 (1988).

Joan Little fights to avoid death sentence. (1975, May 8). *Jet, 48*(7).

Joan Little held after auto chase with N.Y. police. (1977, December 8). *Washington Post*, p. A9.

Joan Little on work release. (1977, May 3). *New York Times*, p. 36.

Joanne Little saga. (1975, August 29). *National Review, 27*(33), 924.

Judicial nihilism. (1975b, October 25). *New York Times*, p. 28.

Karenga, M. R. (1975, July–August). In defense of Sis. Joanne: For ourselves and history. *The Black Scholar, 6,* 37–42.

King, W. (1974, December 1). Killing of Carolina jailer, charged to woman, raises question of abuse of inmates. *New York Times,* p. 41.

King, W. (1975a, October 20). Joan Little's lawyer scorns legal system and says he "bought" her acquittal. *New York Times*, p. 23.

King, W. (1975b, July 30). Joan Little loses defense lawyer. *New York Times,* p. 40.

King, W. (1975c, August 2). Lost evidence in slaying scene is conceded at Joan Little trial. *New York Times,* p. 6.

King, W. (1975d, August 13). Defense closes for Joan Little. *New York Times,* p. 68.

King, W. (1975e, August 15). Prosecutor and defense present final arguments in Joan Little trial; case likely to go to jury today. *New York Times*, p. 10.

Lescaze, L. (1979, July 10). Joan Little, free in N.Y.: "It feels good to be out." *Washington Post*, p. A10.

Little charade? (1975b, November 3). *Time, 106*(3), 62.

McConahay, J. B., Mullin, C. J., and Frederick, J. (1977). The uses of social science in trials with political and racial overtones: The trial of Joan Little. *Law and Contemporary Problems, 41,* (1), 205–229.

Miss Little appears on the coast and thanks the Black Panthers. (1975a, August 28). *New York Times*, p. 14.

News bias charged in Little trial. (1975c, August 15). *The News and Observer (Raleigh)*, p. 5B.

Nichols, R. (1975a, July 13). National issues engulf unlikely N.C. celebrity. *The News and Observer (Raleigh)*, pp. 1I, 5I.

Nichols, R. (1975b, July 24). Joan Little trial jury seated. *The News and Observer (Raleigh)*, pp. 1, 9.

Nichols, R. (1975c, August 5). Little's calls pursued. *The News and Observer (Raleigh),* pp. 1, 5B.

Nichols, R. (1975d, July 30). Judge bans lawyer in Joan Little case. *The News and Observer (Raleigh),* pp. 1, 11.

Nichols, R. (1975e, August 7). Charge is reduced in Joan Little trial. *The News and Observer (Raleigh),* pp. 1, 18.

Nichols, R. (1975f, August 8). Ex-inmates testify in Little case. *The News and Observer (Raleigh),* pp. 1, 4.

Nichols, R. (1975g, August 9). Jury examines bloodstains. *The News and Observer (Raleigh),* p. 19.

Nichols, R. (1975h, August 12). Joan Little says stabbing followed forced sex act. *The News and Observer (Raleigh),* pp. 1, 10.

Nichols, R. (1975i, August 15). Lawyers end arguments; case goes to jury today. *The News and Observer (Raleigh),* pp. 1, 5B.

Nichols, R. (1975j, August 16). Verdict comes quickly. *The News and Observer (Raleigh),* pp. 1, 5B.

Paul v. Pleasants, 551 F.2d 575 (4th Cir.), cert. denied, 434 U.S. 908 (1977).

Personalities sketch of Joan Little trial. (1975a, July 13). *The News and Observer (Raleigh),* p. 8I.

Pinsky, M. (1975a, March 9). Justice in North Carolina is once more Old South. *New York Times,* p. 6.

Pinsky, M. (1975b, April). In the heat of the night. *The Progressive, 39*(4), 9.

Reston J., Jr. (1975, April 6). The Joan Little case. *New York Times Magazine,* pp. 38–46.

Reston J., Jr. (1977). *The innocence of Joan Little: A Southern mystery.* New York: Times Books.

Roche, C. S. (1975, August 11). Judge Hobgood living up to his reputation. *The News and Observer (Raleigh),* p. 6.

Roe v. Wade, 410 U.S. 113 (1973).

Saxon, W. (1989, February 26). Joan Little, tried for killing jailer in 1974, is arrested in New Jersey. *New York Times,* p. 34.

Simms, G. (1975, May 8). Joan Little fights to avoid death sentence. *Jet, 48*(7), 20–24.

Sitton, C. (1975, July 6). Joan Little murder case: The making of state's cause celebre. *The News and Observer (Raleigh),* p. 4.

State v. Joyner, 239 S.E.2d 883 (N.C. App. 1978).

State v. Little, 219 S.E.2d 494 (N.C. App. 1975), cert. denied, 220 S.E.2d 621 (N.C.).

Woodson v. North Carolina, 428 U.S. 280 (1976).

12

The Life and Trial
of Francine Hughes:
Beyond the Burning Bed

Suzanne M. Enck-Wanzer

On March 9, 1977, Francine Hughes poured gasoline on and around the bed of her sleeping, intoxicated ex-husband James "Mickey" Hughes, threw a lit match under the bed, and fled the house with her three children. Panicked and confused, she drove quickly without a destination in mind— as she explained in her trial seven months later, "I decided that the only thing for me to do was just get in the car and drive. . . . Just go. And not let anyone know where I was at. Just leave everything and never, never turn back" (McNulty, 1980, p. 5). Rather than disappearing, however, Hughes drove to the Ingham County Sheriff Department and cried out, "I did it. I did it. I did it" (McNulty, 1980, p. 6).[1] These three words encapsulated a wide variety of emotions and actions for Hughes—she had indeed just killed her ex-husband, but she had also escaped twelve years of continuous (and well-documented) abuse, fear, and torture; and, she had offered her children an opportunity to escape the cycle of familial violence that had filled their young lives. In addition to the specific deeds of March 9, the successful defense of Francine Hughes nearly a year later ignited hope for victims nationwide that battered women who defend themselves might find mercy in the American judicial system.[2]

Removed from the context of a life with James Hughes, Francine Hughes's crime was quite simple. Factually, she never denied killing her husband, nor were any of the events of March 9 contested save one: the question of whether Francine Hughes's actions constituted a premeditated act of vengeance. Or were they, as argued by her defense team, the acts of a woman driven temporarily insane after enduring more than a decade of abuse and threats? Such questions fueled Hughes's trial, the contemporaneous public debates, and subsequent public culture and legal dialogues about the nature and limits of "self-defense" in domestic violence cases. To be sure, had Francine Hughes been convicted of murder, her story would have drifted into the shadows of American criminal lore—a lesson reiterated that there is often no escape from a life filled with domestic violence. As Dawn Bradley Berry stated, "as recently as the 1970s, most judges followed the predominant social trend and ultimately based their decisions on the idea that 'family matters' were outside the jurisdiction of the court. They felt [as some still do] that the power of the law ended at the threshold of the home" (Berry, 2000, p. 155).

Although the courts had failed Francine Hughes (repeatedly) prior to the death of James Hughes, her eventual acquittal in an era of tremendous skepticism regarding gendered violence and women's rights represented a change in social attitudes toward violence against women. To better understand the wide array of issues at stake with regard to the Francine Hughes murder trial, this chapter begins by detailing the tumultuous lives of Francine and James Hughes; next, it offers an overview of her trial as a means of discussing how her acquittal became her legal legacy; and finally, the chapter extends the implications of Hughes's acquittal to explore the aftermath of the jury's decision and the inferences for American narratives of legal mores and women's place(s) in society.

A LIFE OF ABUSE

At the heart of this volume is the role of American crimes and trials in our public culture. In many instances, the crimes and trials detailed within these pages belong clearly to the defendants—who did what to whom and why? In the case of Francine Hughes, a person acquitted of the crimes charged to her, the interesting questions shift from those that explore the acts she committed (the purported crimes) to an inquiry into why she was exonerated and how she might come to represent (and give hope to) the women of a culture replete with gendered violence. Thus, to more fully appreciate the trial and acquittal of Francine Hughes, one must grasp the remarkable circumstances guiding her path toward the trial.

Born in the mountains of Kentucky to Walter and Hazel Moran in 1947, Francine was named for the "French chanteuse who was singing on the radio as her mother sat dreaming of her unborn child" (Darling, 1980, p. E1). Later, when Francine was five years old, the Moran family moved to Michigan in search of a more prosperous life. Working in onion fields and later in various factories, the "good life" eluded the Moran family; but Francine was described by all who knew her as having a great deal of dignity and personal pride. A successful student, Francine flourished in her early English classes and yearned to someday overcome her "stigma of poverty" (McNulty, 1980, p. 41). By the time she entered junior high school, as her household responsibilities necessitated that she care for her siblings, Francine's standards for group acceptance and personal success were shifting—she dreamed primarily of getting married, having her own children, and living the life of a nurturing wife and mother.

At the age of fifteen, Francine met eighteen-year-old James Hughes. Within the year, Francine quit high school and married Hughes. The couple retreated to James's hometown of Dansville, Michigan, and they moved in with his parents, Flossie and Berlin Hughes. Living in a small house with James's parents and three siblings, Francine found her days as a newlywed cramped and overwhelming. A few weeks after their wedding and beginning their new life in the Hughes's family home, James physically assaulted Francine for wearing clothes he thought were too sexy. James pushed her onto the bed, ripped her pants from her body while accusing her of flirting with other men, and forced her to have sex. With these acts, James provided a template for the pattern of abuse that would become all too common in their marriage—upset by a perceived violation of his expectations (ranging from a tucked-in shirt to a late return home), James would verbally degrade Francine and abuse her physically, coerce her into having sex, and then fall asleep as if everything was normal.[3]

As the physical beatings, emotional torment, and sexual abuse escalated throughout the Hughes's relationship, a variety of complicating factors converged over the next decade to create a feeling of entrapment for Francine. Among these factors, as a high-school dropout, Francine had few job marketable skills that would enable her to support her growing family. Moreover, James forbade any full-time employment for Francine, demanding instead that she stay home to raise their children. James's infrequent work history, combined with his tendency to use his paychecks to buy beer rather than staples, made putting food on the table nearly impossible. As Francine was repeatedly told by social service workers, she was not eligible for food stamps or other aid because she was not the "head of household," and James's pride kept him from applying for assistance himself. Beyond this sheer financial insecurity, James refused to use birth control; with three children and after Francine was denied birth control pills by her Catholic obstetrician, she became pregnant with a fourth child and was thus further entrenched in her restrictive household and abusive life. Ultimately, the only way for Francine to become the "head" of her household and secure food for her children was to divorce James. In July 1971, out of sheer desperation and hope for a better life for her children, she filed for divorce.[4]

In the weeks following their divorce, Francine moved away from the small town of Dansville and returned to Jackson in an attempt to start anew. Over the next six months, James tried repeatedly to bring Francine and his children back to his family home—he promised to join Alcoholics Anonymous and attend church with his parents; he vowed that the violence would end; he threatened to sue Francine for custody of their children—none of these efforts were successful in bringing Francine back to Dansville. However, one afternoon after visiting Francine and the children in Jackson, James left after an angry argument and proceeded to drive recklessly into oncoming traffic. This near-fatal accident left James radically disabled and in position to exact constant support and attention from his family.

Flossie and Berlin Hughes placed a tremendous amount of guilt on Francine and insisted that she return to Dansville to help care for her children's father. Reluctantly, Francine moved into a vacant apartment neighboring the Hughes family household and consequently returned to a life of fear, exhaustion, and hopelessness. While James's recovery was slow (confounded by his agenda of entrenching further his familial support system), he eventually regained his former strength, physically, and his former attitude toward Francine—before long, the abuse (both bodily and emotional) resumed, and Francine found herself trapped back in Dansville.

Over the next four years, James engaged in verbal and physical attacks against his wife almost daily. As McNulty relayed, "escape was constantly in Francine's thoughts" (McNulty, 1980, p. 139). But, even if Francine could have escaped from the house with the children, James held all of the money, the keys to their car that she had bought with money earned through various part-time jobs, and threatened to find and kill her if she ever left him again. In any given week, the beatings became so intense that Francine would sprint to her in-laws' house and hide in their basement or closets to buy a few minutes of respite from the violence. As Francine realized repeatedly, her situation was beyond assistance: Flossie and Berlin could not force James to stop the abuse, and they often denied the severity of the violence even while staring it directly in the face; her neighbors were not willing to intervene and help her family; her own mother could not handle the stress of housing

Francine and the kids; and the police were not compelled to arrest James without witnessing the strikes on his wife.

Significantly, by the end of James Hughes's life, the Dansville police had accumulated a thick file of reports documenting their many trips to the Hughes's house. Although many of these reports contained observations of bruises and cuts on Francine's face, broken items throughout the house, and statements from James indicating threats to kill Francine after the police departed, none of these visits resulted in an arrest of James Hughes, except for a few instances when James assaulted a police officer. Criminal justice standards of the 1970s and early 1980s did not allow police to arrest abusers under a judgment of "probable cause"; rather, as officers repeatedly informed Francine Hughes, while she was free to file her own complaint against James Hughes in Lansing, they were not empowered to arrest someone without personally witnessing the assaults.[5]

In 1975, Francine was able to convince her husband that she should return to community college as a means of supplementing their household income potential. By government standards, James had been found "permanently disabled" after his accident; as such, he refused to return to work, leaving Francine to support herself, the four children, and James on her paltry welfare benefits, which she only continued to receive because the welfare department was unaware that the two were cohabitating again. James spent his monthly disability benefits on himself—visiting the Wooden Nickel saloon around the corner from their home, buying cases of beer, and enhancing the car that he had taken from Francine. Promising that her attendance at college would not interfere with her duties of maintaining the household, caring for James, and raising the children, Francine entered Lansing Business College under a federal grant to study administrative services.

From September 1976 through March 1977, Francine attended classes and excelled. According to McNulty's biography, this was one of the few times in her life that Francine could remember feeling proud. As she gained self-esteem and job skills, however, her relationship with James became more tense and abusive. The violence hit a nadir on March 9, 1977, when Francine returned home ten minutes late from school, and James confronted Francine because she planned to feed TV dinners to the children. With nothing else in the house to feed her four children, Francine proceeded to cook the dinners and within minutes, James "bounded across the room, turned the oven off, and hit her across the face. Then he crowded her against the stove, cursing her. 'No-good slut. I told you you weren't fixing TV diners [*sic*] and you ain't gonna!'" (McNulty, 1980, p. 175). Like other attacks, it seemed senseless and unprovoked; unlike other attacks, Francine saw a look in his eyes that suggested he had no intention of ceasing.

As the assaults elevated, James started to strike her repeatedly, throwing her around the house and advising her that her days as a student were over. To underscore this decision, he forced Francine to burn her schoolbooks and assignments, doused her in beer, and continued to hit, kick, and thrash Francine about the house while their children looked on in horror. Their daughter, Christy, ran to her grandparents' house and called the police, asking them to save her mother. As usual, when the police did arrive (about twenty minutes later), they offered little support. According to Francine Hughes's account of the evening,

The cops didn't say much. One of them scolded him and told him that talking like that and hitting me was a bad thing to do. James said he was going to kill me. The cop said, "You're going to kill her? Where do you think that will get you?" I was thinking, "This is a waste of time; a waste of your time, officer, and a waste of my time; of everybody's time. The minute you leave James can do anything he wants to me. You know it; I know it. Above all, he knows it!" (McNulty, 1980, pp. 179–180)

Before leaving, the police offered to take her to a relative's house in Ingham County for respite; since her only relatives within the county limits were James's parents, the offer was hollow.

After the police departed, James followed through on his threats to continue the assaults. After throwing the children's dinners around the kitchen, James forced Francine onto the floor by her hair and held her face over the food forcing her to clean up the mess. Once she finished scraping food from the carpet and walls, James poured the garbage onto Francine and demanded that she clean the room again. This routine repeated until James forced Francine to acknowledge that her dreams of education were quashed; he then demanded a freshly cooked dinner to be served in the bedroom. After eating, James forcibly raped Francine and then fell asleep.

With only three of her children home at the time, Francine sat on the couch with them and tried to think through her options. As she had learned from experience, leaving was not a viable choice and neither was staying. After thirteen years of excruciating torment, physical abuse, and fear, Francine Hughes stood at a crossroads. The weight of saving herself and her children was upon her like never before, and she acted. She told her children to go to the car and then brought a gasoline can into the kitchen. She proceeded to pour gasoline onto and around James, threw a match onto the fuel, and fled the house. When police and firefighters arrived on the scene, there was nothing they could do to save James Hughes—James's still intoxicated corpse was found, asphyxiated by the intense smoke, and all they could do was extinguish the fire.

MURDER ON TRIAL

The charges brought against Francine Hughes were twofold: first-degree murder and murder while perpetuating another crime. The first count against Hughes held that on March 9, 1977, with malice aforethought, she willfully, deliberately, and with premeditation intentionally killed James Berlin Hughes. Under this charge, jurors also could find her guilty of a lesser degree such as second-degree murder or manslaughter if they determined that her actions were not premeditated. The second count against Hughes held that she murdered James Berlin Hughes while perpetrating, or attempting to per-petrate, the crime of arson. Unlike the first count, there could be no mitigating this charge—jurors had two choices: guilty or not guilty.

Hughes's lawyer, Aryon Greydanus, repeatedly argued before Judge Michael Harrison to drop the second charge due to its redundancy. Allegedly, Harrison's initial response to this request was a resounding denial with the added comment, "After all, what kind of woman would burn up her husband?" (McNulty, 1980, p. 213). Feeling that this comment and Harrison's repeated refusals to consider his motions demonstrated a bias against his client, Greydanus requested that Harrison recuse himself from the trial. Harrison denied having made such a statement, balked at claims that he was biased, and refused to step down from the case. Subsequently, the chief judge of the circuit court declined to hear a motion on this issue and preliminary court meetings went forward with Harrison as overseer.

Five days before the trial was scheduled to begin, Judge Harrison requested a meeting with Hughes and her attorney. Rather than bringing Hughes to the meeting, Greydanus called the prosecuting attorney, Martin Palus, and requested his presence at the conference. Although Harrison maintained that he held no bias against Hughes, he acknowledged that he may have made a comment that sounded prejudiced (as was revealed to him by a clerk who overheard the initial statement to Greydanus) and would therefore step down from the trial. The result was a one-week postponement of the Hughes trial and the placement of Judge Ray C. Hotchkiss to preside over Francine's case. Once again, Greydanus pled for the court to dismiss the second charge brought against Hughes—Hotchkiss concurred that the count of "murder by arson" was redundant and reduced the state's charges against Hughes to first-degree murder (and the potential for lesser findings).

By the start of Hughes's trial, public opinion (both positive and negative) of her act was brimming. In support of Hughes, the plights facing battered women in the United States were being pushed into public news commentar-ies; a feminist defense team sponsored by the National Organization for Women (NOW) was assembled in Michigan to assist with her case; and

NOW's advocates were joined by Lansing's local chapter of the National Lawyers Guild who formed a "Francine Hughes Defense Committee." Although the Committee "was careful to say that they neither advocated nor condoned murder . . . they held that women confronted with violence have a right to defend themselves" (Jones, 1996, p. 282). Although there were waves of support from sources unknown to Francine Hughes (but quite familiar to the broader problem of domestic violence), the few who knew Francine personally (e.g., her neighbors) were reluctant to get involved with her case. As many potential witnesses relayed to Greydanus, "We have to live here. It's not our business" (McNulty, 1980, p. 207).[6]

On Monday, October 24, 1977, the case of *People v. Francine Hughes* opened at 10 a.m. in a Lansing, Michigan, courtroom. Pulling a jury of twelve women and two men, the prosecution unfurled their case, arguing that Francine Hughes had killed her husband, not in a moment of heightened duress, but after deep reflection and planning. To build their case, the prosecution offered evidence that Francine had had an affair with another man. The murder, they suggested, was part of Francine Hughes's plan to run away with her lover. Indeed, the prosecution did establish that Francine Hughes had engaged in an affair with another man—a police officer named George Walkup who she met while attending community college in Lansing. While separated from James, Francine and Walkup dated briefly until she learned that he was a married. Later, while Francine was in jail awaiting trial, Walkup and Francine began to correspond once again. However, as the defense demonstrated through Francine's testimony and corroborating witnesses, this second liaison ended abruptly when Francine learned that Walkup was still married.

The most damning evidence regarding this accusation was correspondence exchanged between the two while Francine was in jail. Writing letters to Walkup that described her longing for mutual and healthy intimacy, Hughes wrote in great detail of her capacity for passion. Thinking that he was finally divorced, Hughes allowed herself the hope that someday she might find love with George Walkup. Ultimately, though, her desires for a relationship based in true romance and genuine love were dashed when Walkup committed suicide, leaving behind a public scandal and the letters from Francine Hughes for the police to discover and the prosecution to use against her.

In the end, these accusations of a torrid affair did little to sway her adjudicators. What did threaten to compel the jury, however, was that rather than killing James Hughes in the "heat of the moment" or in the midst of a physical struggle, Francine had waited for several hours after that evening's abuse subsided before pouring gasoline on his bed. During these hours, the prosecution argued, she had time to plan the murder and diagram her escape. Why, the prosecution demanded, would a woman so afraid of her ex-husband not run away rather than kill him? The assistant prosecuting attorney Lee Atkinson said, "The best personal advice I could have given Mrs. Hughes is that, while I don't know the answer, the alternative is not to commit murder" (McNulty, 1980, p. 1). This sort of response became the rallying cry for those hoping to keep Francine in jail—there was no doubt that Francine Hughes was abused by James Hughes for over a decade, but there must have been an alternative to killing him.[7]

The prosecution called several police officers and even two of the Hughes's children to testify. In all but one of the statements, the fact that James Hughes had beaten his wife for years was reiterated. The only person to contest that James had a violent relationship with Francine was his mother, Flossie Hughes. As she took the stand, she vehemently rebutted that she "'wasn't ever aware of him beating up on her'" (McNulty, 1980, p. 235). Flossie went on to testify: "I have knowed [sic] of them having fights, but I don't know what was the cause or who was afighting who. I didn't see nobody hit the other. Afterwards she would tell me, 'It's more my fault than his. He was the one that would have the bruised places and the cut places. I never seen none [sic] on her'" (McNulty, 1980, pp. 235–236). Despite police statements to the contrary, Flossie further swore that her son had never hit her, broke into her house, or threatened to kill Francine in her presence.

The prosecution called most relevant police personnel to testify on Francine's behalf. During the questioning, they attempted to demonstrate that, although James Hughes was repeatedly violent toward his wife, Francine Hughes could have left if she had wanted to leave. Additionally, the prosecution tried to demonstrate that Francine Hughes had been remiss for not traveling to Lansing to file a complaint each time she called the police to her home. Indeed, Francine had only traveled to the Lansing courthouse once to file a complaint. During this meeting, she was told that since daily alcohol consumption was part of James's pattern of abuse, the justice system could not intervene; rather as the court informed her, she was expected to enroll her ex-husband in an alcohol treatment program to help with her problem of abuse.[8]

The prosecution rested after calling approximately fifty witnesses to the stand. When the case was turned over to the defense, there was little left to reveal except for the depth of Francine's terror and hopelessness. Although most of the police officers questioned were called by the prosecution, one former officer, Mohammad Abdo, offered stinging testimony on behalf of the defense regarding the tenacity of James's violence. As one of the officers who had been assaulted by James, Abdo was one of the few who ever put James Hughes in jail. He recounted the evening, six years earlier, when he was called to the block where both of the Hughes families resided. When asked if he tried to restrain James from hitting his wife and mother, Abdo confirmed that he had and explained the situation in this way:

He [James Hughes] was on his back and I was holding down his right arm and holding his head. He was so violent that he was banging his head on the ground. I was holding his head trying to keep him from banging it. He turned to bite me. I grabbed his arm and he picked me up off the floor with one arm. I held his shoulder, his right arm, and his head, and when he tried to bite me, apparently his mother thought we were going to hit him and tried to interfere. (McNulty, 1980, p. 249)

The fact that Hughes could lift this 200-pound police officer into the air spoke volumes to the jury regarding his potential to inflict harm upon his ex-wife.

The defense proceeded to unfurl a picture of Francine Hughes's life as unbearable. Francine testified to the many, many episodes of physical violence against her, her mother-in-law, and their pets. She spoke somberly of the black eyes, swollen lips, and bruised ribs common in her life. She told the court about the day when James Hughes wrung the neck of their daughter's kitten, killing it in front of their young child. She described the time when James forced the family dog to give birth to her puppies in the bitter winter snow and then refused to allow the wallowing, bloated pet into the house and about how the dog and all of its pups died an agonizing death in the backyard, as their children, who were too young to understand the concept of death (let alone killing), sobbed in their bedroom. She portrayed, in detail, the events of the evening leading up to James Hughes's death, stating, "'Day after day it got worse. I felt like I couldn't breathe. I had a tight feeling in my chest. I don't think I could ever make anyone understand how much I have been through and how much I have hurt'" (McNulty, 1980, p. 258).

Again, the prosecution, on cross-examination of Francine, returned to the one important question—why did Francine kill James rather than leaving while he was asleep in the bedroom? Palus, the prosecutor, attempted to demonstrate that Francine Hughes acted in a spirit of vengeance. He pressed her to explain why the abuse on March 9 was worse than the abuse she had been experiencing for the past dozen years. After considering this, she responded, "'I don't know, Mr. Palus. I just . . . it was just everything over the years; everything that had happened. . . . Don't you understand Mr. Palus? . . . It wasn't because twelve years ago he gave me a black eye. It was everything that happened. Everything! Everything!'" (McNulty, 1980, p. 267).

Rather than trying to demonstrate that Francine Hughes had acted in defense of herself and her children, Greydanus pushed for a different strategy: temporary insanity. Ann Jones explained the decision in this way:

The method of the murder made the plea of self-defense problematic. Traditionally, deadly force in self-defense is supposed to be exerted against comparable deadly force. One man lunges at another with a knife. The second clubs the first with a tire iron he happened to have in his hand, killing him. That's self-defense. But sneaking up on a sleeping man to set his room on fire seems to be another kind of move altogether. (Jones, 1996, p. 288)

Especially given the hours that had elapsed between the attack and rape of Francine Hughes and her subsequent act of arson, her legal team felt it unlikely that a plea of self-defense would be well-received. Breaking from the legal traditions of the 1970s, Greydanus argued that "Hughes suffered temporary insanity not for any reasons familiar to legal tradition but because she was a battered woman" (Jones, 1996, p. 289). For one of the first times in legal history in the United States, the defense now commonly known as "battered woman syndrome" was fashioned successfully.[9]

Based on psychiatric interviews of Hughes, Greydanus created a representation of his client, demonstrating that after years of abuse, fear, uncertainty, and frustration, she experienced "psychological decompensation." As argued by clinical psychiatrist Dr. Arnold Berkman, Francine Hughes's diagnosis was "borderline syndrome with hysterical and narcissistic features" (McNulty, 1980, p. 270). In layperson's terms, Berkman claimed that for "people with borderline syndrome, when a certain kind of stress impinges on them . . . at a particular time those people can fall apart" (McNulty, 1980, p. 270). Another psychiatrist, Dr. Anne Seiden, complemented this view and asserted that Francine Hughes was in a state of "ego fragmentation" that began "when she crouched in the corner of the kitchen with garbage smeared in her hair and told James she wouldn't go to school anymore" (McNulty, 1980, p. 272). Even the prosecution's rebuttal witness, though disagreeing that Francine was temporarily insane under medical standards, ended his testimony by asserting, "I do not think that her actions represented premeditation and planning. In other words, she did not sit back and think, 'I'm going to kill my husband now!' It was an impulsive thing that happened" (McNulty, 1980, p. 276).

After eight days of arguments and a little over five hours of deliberation, the jury in *People v. Francine Hughes* returned with their verdict—not guilty by reason of temporary insanity. Repeated stories of years of abuse and torture, integrated with strong support from three expert psychiatric witnesses, combined to convince twelve jurors that Francine Hughes had not planned to kill James Hughes on that night; rather, she was accepted as a "battered woman" who had been pushed to the brink of her own sanity. Upon exiting the courthouse the next day, someone handed her a bouquet of roses with a card that said astutely, "To a battered rose who blooms again" (McNulty, 1980, p. 285).

According to Martha R. Mahoney (1991), the decision in the Francine Hughes case set "legal precedent" in four different ways. First, she killed her abuser while he was sleeping rather than as he was imminently threatening her; second, she claimed "temporary insanity" brought on by years of abuse; third, the jury was permitted to hear evidence that she had been routinely and severely beaten (arguably, putting the victim—James Hughes—on trial); and finally, and most significantly, she was acquitted (Mahoney, 1991, p. 126). Complicating this legal success, Jones argued that while the acquittal was morally correct (i.e., Hughes should not have been convicted of murder), it represented a "hollow victory" because Hughes's defense resorted to a sanity plea rather than challenging the status quo of legal logic (e.g., what constitutes "self-defense" and "reasonable" fear) (Mahoney, 1991, p. 289). Indeed, even Hughes's lawyer admitted in a posttrial interview that contrary to being "precedent shattering . . . the only significance of the Hughes case lay in the social conditions surrounding it, in the 'enormous amount of women who are undergoing this type of abuse in the United States'" (Jones, 1996, p. 289). In short, while Hughes's acquittal did break the norms of either convicting or committing women who kill their abusers—there remained serious philosophical problems with the fact that she had to resort to this desperate act and the methods by which she was acquitted. It is these problems that speak to the very core of the American justice system's treatment of women.

SELF-DEFENSE AND BATTERED WOMAN SYNDROME

Upon Francine Hughes's acquittal and release from prison there erupted a media flurry of commentary, both commending the jury for striking a victory for battered women everywhere in America and condemning the jury for making it "an open season on men" (Gillespie, 1988, p. 10). To be sure, Hughes's defense team took a risk by arguing "temporary insanity," and this decision is one that continues to be debated and questioned. The risk, argue many feminist legal theorists, was not only one of calculation (i.e., Hughes could have lost the case), but, more significantly, one of principle (i.e., pathologizing women who are battered). This sort of ambivalence is located in a variety of cultural responses to and extensions of the Francine Hughes murder trial ranging from popular media representations of domestic violence to challenges to the foundations of our legal system.

As mentioned earlier, the trial of Francine Hughes began as national (and international) attention to violence against women was on the rise. In the United States, the first shelters for abused women, modeled after programs in England, were opening in a handful of cities. For Francine Hughes, this was too little information too late; although battered women's shelters were on the rise when she killed James, they were still few and far between and widely unpublicized to low-income women in rural areas.[10] In light of the Hughes trial, increased attention fell upon the plight of battered women and the growing victims' rights movement more broadly. Jones documents an array of articles in widely distributed periodicals ranging from *Ladies' Home Journal* to *People* magazine, published in the few years leading up to Hughes's trial. In the wake of her trial, by the end of 1977, the *New York Times* had "carried forty-four articles on wife beating, ranging from stories about hotlines and shelters to trials of women who had murdered their assaultive husbands" (Pleck, 1987, p. 182). As Charles P. Ewing (1987) reveals, "It was not until the 1970s that the plight of the battered woman was identified as a significant social problem worthy of major scientific and scholarly attention" (p. 7).

Furthermore, just prior to Hughes's trial, in March of 1977, a North Carolina woman (Joan Little) was cleared of murder charges after stabbing the jailer who sexually assaulted her. ABC's Sylvia Chase, who covered Hughes's story on the weekend news, noted, "Michigan feminists hoped to make Francine Hughes 'a symbol for battered women, the way Joan Little became a symbol for rape victims'" (Jones, 1996, p. 289). As Lenore Walker relayed, "Back then [in 1977 specifically], while stories of battered women who had been killed by their abusive husbands or boyfriends were commonplace, it was far less common to hear about battered women who struck back.[11] But obviously some did, and then had no voice with which to speak of their reasoning for harming or killing their batterers in self-defense" (Walker, 1989, p. 9). This influx of public awareness about domestic violence in general and Hughes's case in particular equipped an American audience to be open to thinking more sympathetically about the abuse endured by Hughes and millions of other American women.

To be sure, this deluge of public support did not happen in a vacuum. Rather, the Hughes murder trial and the battered women's movement were contextualized within a public dialogue and growing comprehensive crime victims' rights movement.[12] With the first crime victims' compensation program established in California in 1965, the decade leading up to Hughes's trial included a variety of state and national commissions charged with studying crimes and their consequences. By 1975, the National Organization of Victim Assistance (NOVA) was founded, and it offered a clearinghouse of information for grassroots groups working on behalf of various crime victims (including battered women and rape victims). Such efforts to give voice to victims primed an American public (and probably Hughes's jury) to recognize Francine's status as a victim herself.

While Hughes awaited trial in the Ingham County jail, she reported that she received many letters from people wanting to lend their support and compassion. As McNulty conveyed, the letters and news coverage of her case "comforted [Hughes] by letting her know that people cared about her" (McNulty, 1980, p. 201). Although Hughes benefited personally from a surge of public awareness, publicity of her case also sparked a backlash from people purportedly concerned for the lives of abusive men. According to Jones's research, a "neighbor who had once pulled James off Francine when he was beating her in the yard . . . thought that Francine 'should sit in prison the rest of her life. . . . If she gets out of this . . . there'll be a lot of dead guys lying around'" (Jones, 1996, pp. 289–291).

This simultaneous public demand for more comprehensive responses to victims of domestic violence coupled with a fear of vigilante justice at the hands of battered women sent a ripple of skepticism throughout the mediated accounts of domestic violence—the Hughes trial in particular. Both *Time* and *Newsweek*, for example, subsequently marked their concern of a surge of women killing their husbands and claiming self-defense. As Jones surmised, "the real significance of the Francine Hughes case was this: it marked the turning point in the development of a feminist issue, the beginning of the backlash, the moment at which the anxious social fathers said 'Enough!' and closed ranks to turn it all around" (Jones, 1996, p. 291). Furthermore, by couching Francine's experiences in the language of victimhood, her defense team laid the groundwork for future victims of domestic violence to be understood likewise.

Most people today who know of Francine Hughes's trial and abuse have gleaned their insight from NBC's made-for-television movie, *The Burning Bed*, which was directed by Robert Greenwald. Based closely on McNulty's biography of Hughes and starring Farrah Fawcett as Francine, this movie aired on October 8, 1984—the first day of National Domestic Violence Awareness Week. Although not playing in movie theaters, *The Burning Bed* experienced brisk video store rentals in the 1980s and was the highest rated program the week it aired and the fourth highest rated television film ever in the year it debuted ("Series," 1984, p E7).[13] More significantly, it could be argued that this film was the first of a genre of movies privileging domestic violence as an issue to be taken seriously by the cinema and by society, while simultaneously reinforcing the notion that victims are isolated when it comes to escaping abusive relationships.

Wendy Kozol contended that "since the 1970s, when the [mass] media first began discussing domestic violence, they have typically depicted it as a problem of the 'private sphere' and focused on the women involved, either blaming them for the abuse or championing them as lone heroines fighting lone villains" (Kozol, 1995, p. 648). Though referring specifically to the news media's depictions of domestic violence, Kozol's words ring true with relation to American cinematic portrayals of battered women, especially in the shadow of Francine Hughes's trial. H. F. Waters and L. Wright stated, "Since women can no longer count on men to rush to their rescue, they're saving themselves. They take charge of their own cases and reverse their bum raps. They cajole, demand, infiltrate, investigate and settle scores. They literally push back" (Waters and Wright, 1991, p. 74). Although some may not agree with Waters and Wright's tenor that such images are necessarily empowering, the image of abused women taking matters into their own hands is common to a genre of movies depicting domestic violence.

Most American movies that represent the plight of an abused woman end with a singular glance at solving domestic violence: a dead abuser. This narrative has been played out in an array of movies since Hughes's trial— *Independence Day* (Robert Mandel, 1983), *Fried Green Tomatoes* (Jon Avnet, 1991), *Mortal Thoughts* (Alan Rudolph, 1991), *Sleeping with the Enemy* (Joseph Ruben, 1991), *Dolores Claiborne* (Tayler Hackford, 1995), *Sling Blade* (Billy Bob Thornton, 1996), *The Rainmaker* (Francis Ford Coppola, 1997), *Crazy in Alabama* (Antonio Bandares, 1999), *In the Bedroom* (Todd Field, 2001), and *Enough* (Michael Apted, 2002)—usually at the hands of the abused woman herself (or someone acting on her behalf), the propensity for films to offer closure only through the most extreme "justice" is both intriguing and problematic. If *The Burning Bed* stands apart as one of the first movies to tackle head-on the social issue of domestic violence, it also provided a model for talking about battered women's justice in American public culture. If the national statistics—that up to 6 million women are battered each year at a rate of one woman every seven seconds—are accepted, responding to this widespread system of abuse can certainly seem overwhelming (Berry, 2000, pp. 7, 8).

Although most domestic violence movies situate the violence within the family unit and present it as a problem of men abusing women, there is no sense of salvation unless the women involved—the victims—can escape their plights and save themselves by relying on a hyperbolized personal heroism and a concomitant dependence on retributive violence. Quickly, they fall in line with the "rugged individualism" theme with which American viewers so easily identify. Although this type of theme might be inspiring or thrilling in other genres of movies (e.g., westerns, space adventures), it is especially pernicious to focus on individual solutions devoid of social interactions or responsibilities when dealing with a violence so pervasive in American culture.

The anxiety produced by the acquittal of Francine Hughes, coupled with increased representations of women killing their abusers, spoke and continues to speak to larger fears regarding changes in legal standards and challenges to male privilege. Even Maria Roy, founder of New York City's Abused Women's Aid in Crisis conveyed in a *New York Times* article that "the publicity the acquittals have received presents a danger because of the tendency some women may have to see that as a solution" (Quindlen, 1978, p. B4). Clearly, no one would argue that women resorting to such final measures are the best solutions; just as clearly, such representations and anxieties demonstrate a need to more thoroughly think through how the U.S. criminal justice system addresses battered women.

Thus, in turning finally to how the Hughes case fits into wider discussions regarding pragmatic justice for battered women, the chapter returns to the controversial decision for Francine Hughes to plead "temporary insanity." Gillespie asserted that this defense runs "the very real risk of years of mental commitment that very well may be worse punishment than a prison term" (Gillespie, 1998, p. 76). For example, just prior to Hughes's killing of her ex-husband, another long-term victim of domestic violence, Roxanne Gay of Camden, New Jersey, stuck a knife in the throat of her abusive husband (a defensive linebacker for the Philadelphia Eagles) while he slept. In Gay's case, law enforcement records showed that she too had requested police assistance over twenty times in their three-and-a-half-year marriage and, despite various injuries, her husband was never arrested. Although the murder charges against Gay were ultimately dropped, it was only after she "had been shuffled off to a New Jersey state hospital for the insane, officially listed as paranoid schizophrenic" (Jones, 1996, p. 287).

Although the danger of interment in a psychiatric facility is quite real for women who kill their abusers, the principle of the "insanity" defense is potentially more troubling. This distinction mirrors divisions between delineations made between "justification" and "excuse" defenses. Those who support "justification" rationalizations (e.g., "self-defense") argue that an act is warranted due to particular circumstances; however, the excuse defense, "like insanity or heat of passion, focuses on the actor; it is a finding that the act, though wrong, should be tolerated because of the actor's particular characteristics or state of mind" (Schneider, 2000, p. 135). Such pathologizing of battered women keeps the critical focus on the victim rather than on the abusive mate and thus, attention on reacting to domestic violence rather than preventing it.

Additionally, as Ewing explained, "for the most part, when battered women kill their batterers, they do so for a rational reason: namely, to protect themselves from further physical or mental suffering" (Ewing, 1987, p. 46). What this indicates—that women who kill their abusers tend to do so based on a reasoned response to continued trauma—is that rather than acting out of a moment of disassociation or insanity, they are usually reacting reasonably based on years of embodied experience. Lenore Walker pointed to the common legal definition of self-defense as a "reasonable perception of imminent danger" (Walker, 2000, p. 202). As a key crafter of the now widely cited terms that get circulated as reasons for women's decisions to remain in violent relationships ("Learned Helplessness" and "Battered Woman Syndrome"), Walker insisted that it "would be a reasonable perception for that woman [with a history of abuse] to believe that serious bodily harm or death is imminent primarily because she has been threatened with death and previously suffered bodily harm when he acted in the same way" (Walker, 2000, p. 203).[14] By taking seriously that abused women tend to act in ways that are uniquely adaptive to the violence in which they have been ensnared, one might also view women who are battered as especially capable of gauging their own level of danger as well as its imminence.

Such challenges to the definition of "self-defense" can be located elsewhere in Feminist Jurisprudence scholarship in arguments against the "reasonable man" standard that grounds a wide variety of legal expectations and exceptions.[15] Arguments against such standards are "premised on the view that the traditional boundaries and definitions of self-defense, as a form of justification, were sex biased and shaped by male experience" (Schneider, 2000, p. 135). Says Bender said, "Today we are taught to consider women reasonable when they act as men would under the same circumstances, and unreasonable when they act more as they themselves or as other women act" (Bender, 2000, p. 63). Thus, cosmetic changes to the "reasonable man" standard do little to challenge the foundations of what is considered reasonable and unreasonable and realistic and unrealistic. In fact, a shift in terminology (e.g., toward "reasonable person") could do more damage to the sexism pervasive in the criminal justice system by offering the appearance of neutrality while continuing to support traditional models of prudence. Instead, based on Hughes's case and others like it, scholars working in the realm of Feminist Jurisprudence strive to reconstruct legal standards of "reasonableness" to root the concept in a model of responsibility and care consistent with the experiences of many women.

The problem facing legal scholars is complex to be sure. Elizabeth Schneider, drawing upon the judicial opinion of Judge Claire L'Heureux Dubé of the Canadian Supreme Court explained the paradox clearly:

By emphasizing a woman's "learned helplessness," her dependence, her victimization, and her low self-esteem, in order to establish that she suffers from "battered woman syndrome" the legal debate shifts from the objective rationality of her actions to preserve her own life to those personal inadequacies which apparently explain her failure to flee from her abuser. (2000, p. 141)

As the Hughes trial illustrates manifestly, convincing a jury that a woman has been abused severely enough to warrant exceptional fear and anxiety is to create a depiction that is difficult to combine with a portrayal of a person acting rationally in accord with one's reasonable fears of impending danger. It is this with disjuncture that legal scholars working in the realm of domestic violence policy continue to wrestle.

Three years after her acquittal, Francine Hughes was interviewed by the *Washington Post* and questioned about the legacy she left behind and the life she anticipated before her. Hesitant to view herself as influential to the battered women's movement or any movement, Hughes noted that "there were those who, at the time of the trial, saw her on the barricades, a representative of oppressed women everywhere. 'I thought that was kind of funny,' [she continued] 'I don't know what they expect of me. I was just a housewife then. And I'm just a housewife now'" (Darling, 1980, p. E1). Though "just" a housewife, Francine Hughes's life (from childhood to the fateful moment when she killed her ex-husband, James Hughes) speaks volumes about the complicated nexus of oppressions that keep battered women in abusive relationships. Likewise, her ability to save herself and her children, despite enormous pain and suffering, demonstrated clearly the capacity for women to listen and trust their ability to reason in even the most unreasonable situations.

Just as Hughes's acquittal resonated throughout various feminist groups and victims' rights advocates, the aftermath of her case did not end there for Hughes—she needed still to raise her children and make peace with her actions. Although James was capable of attacking Francine without clear immediate repercussions, it is Francine who continues to live with the pain that she inflicted on him. As she told Darling, only after igniting the fire in James's bedroom "did it hit me. 'My God, what are you doing!' The fumes of gas caught with a roar and a rush of air slammed the door with tremendous force, almost catching my hand. I ran for my life'" (Darling, 1980, p. E1). The double edge of this statement ought not be lost—whereas

Francine Hughes once was trapped in a cycle of trying to run away from her life and to escape the pain, her drastic actions on March 9, 1977, afforded her an opportunity to run to an existence in which she could determine her range of life and potential for human growth.

NOTES

1. Faith McNulty's book, *The burning bed: The true story of an abused wife,* offers the most comprehensive source of information about Francine Hughes's life and introspections. A contributor to the *New York Times,* McNulty relays Hughes's life from her move to Michigan until the end of her court case, including extensive quotations from the trial transcripts. Most of the facts cited in this chapter are taken from McNulty (1980).

2. In addition to offering hope to battered women, Francine Hughes's successful defense fit into a growing movement for "victims' rights" more broadly speaking.

3. Indeed, for James Hughes, this pattern probably was thought to be "normal." Growing up in a violent household, he learned early on that women were to be subservient to men.

4. Significantly, it was Francine's need to care for her children, not a heightened concern for her own safety and well-being, that motivated this decision for divorce. Such prioritizing is quite consistent with patterns of other abused women. See, for example, Walker (2000).

5. Machaela M. Hoctor (1997) indicates that most states now have "mandatory arrest laws" in which police are empowered to arrest misdemeanor abusers without a warrant (based on probable cause of violence). Hoctor argues that "by making domestic violence a crime against the state, mandatory arrest will take the criminal justice system's focus off the victim and place it where it belongs—on the person who has violated the laws" (Hoctor, 1997, p. 648).

6. Such a response is consistent with a larger public perceptions that domestic violence is a private problem, one that should be taken care of within the bonds of the familial.

7. An article in the *Washington Post* sums up this position by arguing that the larger problem with Francine Hughes's actions was that she "took it upon [herself] to administer justice and [she] did not make the punishment fit the crime" (Cohen, 1977, p. B1).

8. This sort of assumption that alcoholics will quit engaging in violent behaviors once they "sober up" often pervades cultural constructions of domestic violence and subsequent responses and treatment programs. However, without commitment to building healthy relationship skills, anger management, and purging male privilege, even the driest alcoholic will still likely be abusive.

9. Lenore Walker (1984), one of the leading forensic psychologists in the field, defines a "battered woman" as "a woman who is repeatedly subjected to any forceful physical or psychological behavior by a man in order to coerce her to do something he want her to do without any concern for her rights" (Walker, 1984, p. xv). Battered

Woman Syndrome, then, is the term that describes the psychological patterns experienced by battered women wherein a woman feels the violence is her fault; is unable to place the blame elsewhere; fears for her life and/or children's lives; has a belief that her abuser is omnipresent/omniscient (Walker, 1984, pp. 95–97).

10. To be sure, this lack of access to shelters for battered women in rural areas continues still today.

11. Today, statistics indicate that one-third of female homicide victims in the United States are murdered by a current or former intimate partner whereas approximately 3 percent of male homicide victims died at the hands of a current or former female intimate partner (Bachman and Saltzman, 1995, p. 4).

12. See, for example, Karmen (1990).

13. Tracking calls to domestic violence shelters after the airing of *The Burning Bed,* "Gail Martin, vice chair of the National Coalition Against Domestic Violence [said that] 'the response [to the movie] in most states was overwhelming'" (Krebs, 1984, p. 8).

14. Walker bases a great deal of her psychological judgments on the notion of "learned helplessness" which she adapted from psychologist, Martin Seligman. Living with exceptional anxiety and erratic behaving partners, women identified with "learned helplessness" develop coping skills that will give "her the most predictability within a known situation and to avoid things that can send her into the unknown" (Berry, 2000, p. 38).

15. As Leslie Bender asserts, although legal scholars have attempted to equalize principles by shifting rhetorically from a reasonable man standard of care to a reasonable person standard, "changing the word without changing the underlying model does not work" (Bender, 1993, p. 62). Specifically, based on Carol Gilligan's influential studies of "women's care," Bender problematizes "reason" as a gendered concept—a male gendered concept.

REFERENCES

Bachman, R., and Saltzman, L. E. (1995). Violence against women: Estimates from the redesigned survey. In *Bureau of Justice Statistics Special Report: National Crime Victimization Survey.* Washington, DC: U.S. Department of Justice.

Bender, L. (1993). A lawyer's primer on feminist theory and tort. In D. Kelly Weisberg (Ed.), *Feminist legal theory: Foundations* (pp. 58–74). Philadelphia: Temple University Press.

Berry, D. B. (2000). *The domestic violence sourcebook.* Los Angeles: Lowell Books.

Cohen, R. (1977). Vigilante justice back in women's movement. *The Washington Post,* p. B1.

Darling, L. (1980, November 5). Ring of fire. *The Washington Post,* p. E1.

Ewing, C. P. (1987). *Battered women who kill: Psychological self-defense as legal justification.* Lexington, MA: Lexington Books.

Gillespie, C. K. (1988). *Justifiable homicide: Battered women, self-defense, and the law.* Columbus, OH: Ohio State University Press.

Hoctor, M. M. (1997, May). Domestic violence as a crime against the state: The need for mandatory arrest in California. *California Law Review 85*, 643–700.

Jones, A. (1996). *Women who kill.* Boston: Beacon Press.

Karmen, A. (1990). *Crime victims: An introduction to victimology.* New York: Springer Publishing Company.

Kozol, W. (1995). Fracturing domesticity: Media, nationalism, and the question of feminist influence. *Signs 20*, 646–667.

Krebs, P. (1984, November 30). "Burning bed" prompts flood of calls. Off our backs: a women's newsjournal, p. 8.

Mahoney, M. R. (1991, October). Legal images of battered women: Redefining the issue of separation. *Michigan Law Review, 90*, 1–94.

McNulty, F. (1980). *The burning bed: The true story of an abused wife.* Toronto: Bantam Books.

Pleck, E. (1987). *Domestic tyranny: The making of social policy against family violence from colonial times to present.* New York: Oxford University Press.

Quindlen, A. (1978, March 10). Women who kill their spouses: The causes, the legal defenses. *New York Times*, p. B4.

Schneider, E. M. (2000). *Battered women and feminist lawmaking.* New Haven, CT: Yale University Press.

Series, *Burning Bed* Win Big for NBC. (1984, October 18). *The San Diego Union Tribune*, p. E7.

Walker, L. E. A. (1989). *Terrifying love: Why battered women kill and how society responds.* New York: Harper Perennial.

Walker, L. E. A. (2000). *The battered woman syndrome.* New York: Springer Publishing Company.

Waters, H. F., and Wright, L. (1991, November 11). Whip me, beat me . . . and give me great ratings. *Newsweek*, pp. 74– 75.

13

John Wayne Gacy Jr.: The Killer Clown

Dennis J. Stevens

On May 9, 1994, John Wayne Gacy Jr., better known as the "killer clown," had his last meal: Fried chicken, fries, strawberry shortcake, and a coke (Sullivan and Maiken, 1983, p. 4). Gacy's last supper cost the state eighteen dollars and twenty-six cents. Chef Bill Deloria prepared Gacy's meal at Catcher's Tap near Stateville Penitentiary. The chef commented, "I don't think it's an honor [to serve Gacy, but somebody's gotta do it]" (Feldmann, 1992). Illinois prison officials described Gacy's demeanor as "chatty . . . talking up a storm." In a telephone interview before the execution, he told a *Knight-Tribune* reporter, "There's been [eleven] hardback books on me, [thirty-one] paperbacks, two screenplays, one movie, one off-Broadway play, five songs, and over 5,000 articles. What can I say about it?" But of course, he quickly protested, "I have no ego for any of this garbage" (Lohr, n.d.). Gacy had been convicted of murdering young boys and burying most of them under his home in Norridge, Illinois, a suburb of Chicago.[1]

Just after midnight on May 10, 1994, Gacy was executed by lethal injection. For his last words, Gacy said. "Kiss my ass" (Sullivan and Maiken, 1983, p. 6).

The best way to describe Gacy is that he was a real bogeyman—the evil symbol of the closest human monster that anyone could create even in his or her worst nightmare. Although some are unsure about his activity and might snicker a bit, Gacy was a mysterious molester who hid behind a clown's face. Gacy was a madman with a deadly desire for young victims (Whiteside, 1993). Some days, Gacy ravaged and killed more than one victim. In total, there were thirty-three young men whom Gacy abducted, tortured sexually, and murdered, often using their own undergarments as weapons. Many professionals believe there were many more victims.

Few people who knew Gacy before his arrest suspected he was anything other than a sexual predator. After all, many saw Gacy as a respected member of the chamber of commerce, a performing clown (Pogo or Patches) at neighborhood children's parties, a precinct captain in the Democratic party (he once had his picture taken with former First Lady Rosalyn Carter), and the owner of a contracting business. Gacy worked hard to make his community a better place (Bell, 2003).[2] At his home, he sponsored weekend barbecues and other events that were the talk of the town. On one occasion, over 300 guests attended one of his legendary parties (Mendenhall, 1995). How could this caring impressive businessman and neighbor be one of the most prolific serial killers in U.S. history? (Lohr, 1998). To say that there was a dark side to Gacy is an understatement.

Factually, his victims, at least those who lived to tell their story, such as Jeffrey Ringall, also liked Gacy—at first. In May 1978, Jeffrey Ringall returned to Chicago from a vacation in Florida. Visiting a few singles' bars on Chicago's northside, Ringall's path was blocked by a black Oldsmobile parked in an alley way. Ringall thought the driver was a police officer since the vehicle had the appearance of an undercover Chicago police vehicle. A heavy-set man leaned from the driver-side window and complimented Ringall on his unseasonable tan. Small talk, chilly weather, and the promise of a joint (marijuana) got Ringall into that automobile. Before they finished the joint, the heavy-set man shoved a rag doused with chloroform over Ringall's mouth. Ringall lost consciousness. When he awoke a few times during the ride, the man covered his mouth again and again.

Ringall recalled the man sitting naked on the floor before him in a bedroom of a house or an apartment, but he was not sure. He remembered a number of varying-sized dildos that the stranger pointed out to him. He was told in explicit detail how each would be used on his body. The next morning, Ringall awoke, fully clothed under a statue in Chicago's Lincoln Park. It was as though he'd dreamt everything—a nightmare, until he stood. Piercing pain riveted his body, and for a moment he was embarrassed since most of the pain emanated from his private parts—all his private parts.

Was he alive—he asked himself and no one at the same time? Painfully, he made his way to his girlfriend Susan's nearby apartment. She called an ambulance that took Jeffrey to Northwestern Memorial Hospital, one-half mile away. Jeffrey remained hospitalized for six days. During his stay, he reported the incident to the Chicago police. They doubted his story. However, the doctor's report confirmed skin lacerations, severe anal penetration, burns, and permanent liver damage caused from chloroform. It came as no surprise that Ringall also suffered severe emotional trauma. The lead investigator thought that since the evidence was shaky, the police would not be able to initiate an investigation even though they now accepted, in part, the story told to them by Ringall. A few years later, a junior investigator involved with the Ringall case recalled hearing of a similar attack on another young man, but he failed to follow up for fear of being "labeled a homosexual lover" (Chicago Police Department Investigator's Report, 1983). Later, Jeffrey Ringall staked various locations including freeway entrances until he spotted Gacy's car. He demanded an investigation since he now had Gacy's license plate number. However, the authorities declined to prosecute Gacy because of a lack of evidence. Jeffery Ringall was, indeed, fortunate to be alive.

GACY'S YOUTH

Chicago's Irish population, along with Mr. and Mrs. John Wayne Gacy Sr., marked the day with celebration; it was St. Patrick's Day and the Gacys welcomed their first son into the world at Edgewater Hospital in 1942 (Linedecker, 1980). Gacy had two sisters: Joanne was two years older, and Karen was two years younger. He had a typical childhood, with the exception of a rocky relationship with his father (Sullivan and Maiken, 1983). Gacy Sr. was an alcoholic who physically and verbally assaulted his children. Like most children, the young Gacy loved his father and wanted to gain his approval and attention, but he failed to win him over (Cahill and Ewing, 1986). Nonetheless, young Gacy knew he was different from other kids. When he was six, for instance, he took his mother's underwear and hid them under his front porch (Cahill and Ewing, 1986). Gacy grew up scared of other kids and was horrified at the sounds of fire engines. Also, he was born with an enlarged bottleneck heart, a serious condition that made him very weak as a child (Cahill and Ewing, 1986). His weight had also become a problem. In a period of about three years, he was hospitalized several times with heart trouble.

While growing up on the northside of Chicago, all of the Gacy children were raised Catholic, and they all attended Catholic schools until the eighth grade. John Wayne Gacy Jr. was neither an exceptional student nor a poor student. Most liked him and few teachers ever had a harsh word to say about him. Gacy was sociable, and he had a group of friends who often followed his lead when he was around. He liked to play baseball and seemed most happy when he pitched, but due to poor health, he could not play often or for very long. However, Gacy was actively involved with Boy Scouts. A grade-school classmate described Gacy as a fellow who got along with everybody and had a positive view on most things.[3] Often, other classmates revealed that young Gacy spend more time at home than most kids, but few offered any plausible explanation. However, Gacy had no close friends.

Gacy was struck in the head with a playground swing when he was eleven years old (Linedecker, 1986). He suffered from blackouts until he was sixteen. A doctor diagnosed him with a blood clot on the brain and corrected the condition with medication; the blackouts ceased immediately. As long as Gacy took medication, he felt fine. Some writers imply that this injury was a causal factor associated with his later years of murder, yet there is little evidence to support their claims. Then, too, there were indicators revealing young Gacy had engaged in cruel "experiments" with animals before the swing accident through some of his own conversations years later with others (officers, caseworkers, and inmates) while incarcerated.[4]

Gacy attended Carl Schurz High School and was an undistinguished student. He also worked part time at the A&P as a clerk throughout some of his high school years. Later, Gacy would tell his first wife that he was hauled out of the school in a straitjacket "a couple of times" after becoming uncontrollably enraged. Gacy transferred from Schurz to Cooley Vocational High and then to Prosser Vocational, but he never graduated with his class of 1960 (Bell, 2003). His high school records showed Gacy received below average grades and some of the notes in his folder showed that teachers said he rarely paid attention in class; his history teacher said he was a chronic day dreamer.[5] Another source revealed that one reason Gacy attended three different high schools was because there were complaints of a sexual nature against Gacy by younger students.[6] In those days, it was rare to discuss sexuality, let alone sexual predators, even among school counselors.

Gacy's general attitude on life was positive, but students and teachers noticed his absences from class and school functions. One explanation was that Gacy was actually shy around new friends; there was not enough time to concentrate on new friendships. Yet, some speculate that young Gacy was often active in the gay community along Clark Street and Diversey Avenue, adjunct to Lake Michigan—a "regular," they say, in some of the bars that were a short bus ride down Fullerton Avenue from all three high schools.

A supporting piece of evidence was an article in the *Chicago Magazine*, dated in the late 1980s. A retired Chicago police officer's daily "work diary" was buried in the officer's attic. After the officer's natural death, his wife sat in the attic and read the accounts of the officer's early police career. In 1958, the officer was part of a team investigating the murder of a young man in the city's Clark and Diversey area. The officer visited what he called a "gay bar" situated near the ally on Clark Street, where the body of a grade-school child was discovered. The officer talked to a young man whom he described with the distinctive features of John Wayne Gacy Jr., the officer's wife said. She said that she was dumbfounded by the description detailed by her husband. The description of the young man questioned and released by her husband years before resembled the pictures of Gacy seen on television and in the newspapers. The officer wrote that young Gacy was sent home since the officer believed that "this young man wandered into the bar looking for a phone." The murder is still an open case in the city.

Gacy left Chicago for Las Vegas when he was seventeen years old. Some say he left with an older man whom he had met from the Clark and Diversey area. While in Las Vegas, he worked part-time as a janitor for the successful Palm Mortuary. Unhappy in Vegas, Gacy returned to Chicago and enrolled in Northwestern Business College. This time he graduated and with some distinction. One of his instructors wrote that Gacy was an excellent student and had the ability to be successful at business.

Gacy was considered very smooth by many of his instructors and had little trouble gaining employment with Nunn Bush Shoe Company. He excelled and was transferred to Springfield, Illinois, to manage a men's clothing outlet for the company.

In 1964, Gacy married Marilyn Myer, a coworker of his at the Nunn Bush Shoe Company. Shortly after the wedding, the newlyweds relocated to her hometown of Waterloo, Iowa. Marilyn's father prompted the move by offering Gacy a position in the family's franchise of Kentucky Fried Chicken restaurants. In 1966, Gacy accepted management of the Meyer's chicken franchise. He and Marilyn had a son and a daughter. Gacy was well-known and respected in the community by his neighbors and business associates (Reinitz, 2000). However, John Wayne Gacy Jr. was an impatient man who was stopped by the police frequently for traffic offenses. Some of his employees say that he also drank often on the job, or appeared to be drunk. Some suggested he was nervous because he received a draft notice for the military, and he was sure, despite his two children, the government was going to draft him and deploy him to Vietnam. Many claimed, including Marilyn, that Gacy was a "control freak" with serious issues.

SEXUAL CHARGES AGAINST GACY

In 1968, Gacy was indicted on sodomy charges after a seventeen-year-old boy reported "deviate sex acts" consisting of an attempt to coerce the youth, who was also an employee of Gacy's, into homosexual acts during the late summer of 1967 (Bell, 2003).

Mark Miller, a young man who worked for Gacy, claimed Gacy had tied him up and forced him to have anal sex with him ("All things horror," 2003). Gacy denied the charges. Gacy's response was that he had political enemies who framed him because he was running for president of a local community organization (Linedecker, 1986). Later Gacy claimed Miller wanted to have sex for money.

Eventually, Gacy pled guilty but not before he hired Dwight Andersson to attack Miller. Gacy gave Andersson $10 plus $300 more to pay off his car loan if he carried out the beating (Bell, 2003). Andersson lured Miller to his car and drove him to a wooded area where he sprayed mace in his eyes and attacked him. Miller fought back, breaking Andersson's nose. Miller ran to safety and called police. When Andersson was arrested, he told police that Gacy's hired him to beat up Miller. An additional offense was charged against Gacy. Gacy was ordered to undergo a psychiatric evaluation. The evaluation demonstrated characteristics consistent of antisocial personality disorder (Bell, 2003). However, Gacy was shown to be competent to stand trial. Nonetheless, the psychological examiner concluded that no medications or treatment could help Gacy. Gacy was sentenced to ten years (the maximum sentence for sodomy) at the Iowa State Men's Reformatory at Anamosa, a medium security facility. The psychological evaluation became part of Gacy's presentence investigation (PSI), which was part of his permanent record and in his file at the Iowa Department of Corrections.

Gacy was a model prisoner and served eighteen months at the Men's Reformatory before he was granted parole on October 18, 1971. Evangelist G.W. Bessette recalled Gacy as a "man who found the path of truth," and Bessette wrote a letter of recommendation for Gacy's parole (Iowa Department of Corrections, 2003).

Several months after Gacy's release, Jason, an inmate at Anamosa, told a caseworker that Gacy had sexually assaulted him on the day that Gacy had received Marilyn Gacy's divorce papers.[7] Gacy phoned Marilyn and told her that he did not want to see his children (Cahill and Ewing, 1986). After the telephone call, Gacy assaulted Jason in his own cell. Gacy returned later and the sexual assault lasted all night and on many subsequent occasions, equally as long. Jason also said that Gacy had sexually attacked other inmates before his parole. It was common knowledge among inmates and correctional personnel that Gacy was able to bring illegal contraband such as drugs into prison, had some serious issues about sexuality, and had no respect for himself or others—human life was insignificant to him. It is also curious that Gacy had not received professional intervention while incarcerated, and no disciplinary sanctions were found in Gacy's prison records.

Jason had not come forward previously because Gacy was friendly with the prison staff. Gacy was a prison trustee who worked in the prison library, and he had access to many parts of the prison that were out-of-bounds for most prisoners. When trouble happened in several areas of the prison, the correctional staff relied on Gacy to solve those problems. To hear Jason's description of Gacy, apparently Gacy had manipulated the correctional staff including officers in some way or another, and apparently that provided him a "free hand" or a license to do as he pleased with the younger inmates.

LIFE AFTER PRISON

Gacy headed to his birth town of Chicago when released from prison. He moved in with his mother, and then he went out on his own, making friends with his new neighbors. He found work as a chef in a Chicago downtown restaurant (Cahill and Ewing, 1986). No one knew that Gacy was a convicted sexual offender. Unknown to his parole officer, Gacy was arrested by Chicago police on Feb. 12, 1972—five months after his release from prison—for attempted rape and disorderly conduct (Bell, 2003). Gacy lured a boy into his car at the bus terminal, which was a block from where Gacy worked. The charge reported that Gacy took the boy to his house where he forced him to perform sexual acts. Gacy got lucky when the boy failed to appear in court, and he was set free. Some officers said that it was coincidence that the young boy who was from out of town had disappeared. Nothing more ever came from the case (Cahill and Ewing, 1986).

In 1975, Gacy started his own construction business, PDM Contractors, and he married Carole Hoff, a recently divorced woman whom he met through mutual friends. Carole knew Gacy's past. But she insisted that Gacy was a changed man, and she believed that he would make a good provider for her two daughters. Gacy's home life became a focal point for him as he often stayed home while developing his construction business.

Gacy had a talent for business. According to the *Des Plaines Journal*, Gacy gained contracts by undercutting his competitors' bids. He was able to cut costs by hiring on a number of teenage boys. It was subsequently learned that at least five of these boys were victimized by Gacy. His business continued to grow.

Gacy's second wife divorced him in March 1976. She felt she could no longer cope with the marriage due to her husband's unpredictable moods and bizarre obsession with homosexual magazines (Mendenhall, 1995). The couple did not have children of their own. Other speculation was that he was cruel towards Carole's children, but criminal charges were never filed. Carole and her children could not be found to comment on this matter.

On December 11, 1978, Robert Piest, a fifteen-year-old boy, had finished work at Nisson's Pharmacy in Des Plaines, Illinois. His mother was parked on the street waiting to take him home. Robert Piest ran to her car and asked if she would mind waiting a few moments while he talked to a man about a job; Robert Piest never reappeared. Gacy had recently completed a remodeling job at the pharmacy, and he was identified as the last person who talked to Robert Piest.

THE INVESTIGATION

When investigators ran a background check on Gacy, they were surprised at his earlier conviction. After additional investigation revealed that two young employees of Gacy, Gregory Godzik and John Butkovich, also had disappeared, the police placed Gacy under surveillance. At first, Gacy took surveillance as a joke, playing with the officers as often as possible: he disobeyed traffic laws whenever possible and smoked marijuana in clear view of the officers (Douglas and Olshaker, 1997, p. 105). Gacy invited the officers to dinner at his home. While at Gacy's home, Lt. Joseph Kozenczak of the Des Plaines Illinois Police smelled the telltale odor of decomposition and rotting flesh while in the bathroom when the furnace fan turned on. The officers arrested Gacy on a drug charge and with the aid of a search warrant, they reentered his home. The officers went into the crawl space located beneath the home and smelled the rancid odor, but they decided the source of the offensive odor was a faulty sewage line (Bell, 2003).

At the Des Plaines Police Department, Inspector Kautz inventoried the following evidence taken from Gacy's home:

- a jewelry box containing two driver's licenses and several rings including one which had engraved on it the name Maine West High School class of 1975 and the initials J.A.S.;
- a box containing marijuana and rolling papers;
- seven erotic movies made in Sweden;
- pills including amyl nitrite and Valium;
- a switchblade knife;
- a stained section of rug;
- color photographs of pharmacies and drug stores;
- an address book;

- a scale;

- books such as *Tight Teenagers, The Rights of Gay People, Bike Boy, Pederasty: Sex Between Men and Boys, Twenty-One Abnormal Sex Cases, The American Bi-Centennial Gay Guide, Heads and Tails,* and *The Great Swallow;*

- a pair of handcuffs with keys;

- a three-foot-long two-by-four wooden plank with two holes drilled in each end;

- a six millimeter Italian pistol;

- police badges;

- an eighteen-inch rubber dildo was found in the attic;

- a hypodermic syringe and needle and a small brown bottle;

- clothing that was much too small for Gacy;

- a receipt for a roll of film with a serial number on it from Nisson Pharmacy;

- nylon rope; and

- three automobiles belonging to Gacy, including a 1978 Chevrolet pickup truck with a snowplow attached that had the name "PDM Contractors" written on its side; a 1979 Oldsmobile Delta 88; and a van with "PDM Contractors" also written on its side. Within the trunk of the car were pieces of hair that were later matched to Rob Piest's hair. (Bell, 2003)

Finally, after intense investigation and lab work, police had evidence against Gacy. One ring found at Gacy's house belonged to another teenager who disappeared a year earlier named John A. Szyc.

Based on the evidence, Lt. Kozenczak obtained a second search warrant. This time investigators entered the crawl space and ran soil tests. Officers learned that the Gacy case was more than about two victims, much to their surprise.

On December 22, 1978, Gacy realized that his dark secrets were about to be exposed, and he confessed (Bell, 2003). Shortly into his confession, Gacy waived his Miranda rights and told detectives, "There are four Johns." He later explained that there was John the contractor, John the clown, John the politician, and the fourth went by the name of Jack Hanley. Jack was the killer and did all the evil things (Bell, 2003; Sullivan and Maiken, 1983).

Jack Hanley and John Wayne Gacy had an argument about devolving information about "Jack's" adventures (Douglas and Olshaker, 1995, p. 351). Gacy told investigators that Jack's first kill took place in December 1958, but Jack made it clear that it was January 1972, and the second murder was two years later in January 1974. The investigators accepted the January date and decided that the 1958 date would have made Gacy too young to commit a murder.

GACY'S METHODS OF ATTACK

Gacy confessed that often he would lure his victims into being handcuffed. Gacy told them that he wanted to show a "pair of trick handcuffs" he used in his clown act, claiming there was a special way to unlock the cuffs (Kozenczak and Henrikson, 1992). He dared his victims to break out of the cuffs. Once the youth was securely handcuffed, Gacy followed his "act" with a "rope trick." Gacy inserted a rope around the victim's neck, inserted a stick in the loop, and twisted it slowly like a tourniquet until the victim strangled to death. Often, he would push the victims' undergarments into their mouths, but he enjoyed hearing his victims scream. "But, I didn't want to wake the neighbors," Gacy said. One of his favorite positions was in back of his victims. Gacy penetrated his victims with his penis and often with a large rubber dildo (in associated colors) while tightening the tourniquet (Kozenczak and Henrikson, 1992).

Gacy admitted that he often kept the dead bodies under his bed before burying them in the crawl space or throwing them into the river. Sometimes he pulled the bodies out and stared at his handy work. Sometimes he forgot to remove items from the cavities of his victims, and he experimented on the corpses when he was bored. Once he moved the bodies to the crawl space, he covered them with lime to decompose.

Although Gacy confessed to murder, he could not remember all the details. Often, he would say to the investigators, "You'll have to ask Jack" (Kozenczak and Henrikson, 1992, p. 87). Gacy confirmed to police that he had killed more than one person in a day.

The Crawl Space

The investigators believed Gacy's stories to be the fantasy of a madman until they visited his home and dug up the crawl space under the house and garage. They recovered two bodies: one unidentified victim was buried in the crawl space, and John Butkovich's body was found under the garage. As days passed, the body count grew. Some victims were found with their underwear lodged in their throats, just as Gacy confessed. Others were buried so close together that police believed they were killed or buried at the same time. Gacy would later tell the officers, "I also buried them together because I was running out of room" (Kozenczak and Henrikson, 1992, p. 87).

By December 28, 1978, police removed twenty-seven bodies from Gacy's crawl space. The bodies of Frank Wayne "Dale" Landingin, whose driver's license was later found in Gacy's house, and James "Mojo" Mazzara were discovered in the Des Plaines River. Mazzara's undergarments were lodged in his throat, and the coroner said the obstruction had caused the boy to suffocate.

Gacy told police that he disposed of the bodies in the river because he had back problems from all the digging under his house. During the digging for corpses, the media heard the news, and Gacy's modest home led the national news night after night (Bell, 2003). The house itself became almost as familiar to viewing audiences as the White House.

By the end of January, police and construction crews gutted the house. The search had taken longer than expected due to the freezing winter temperatures. When workmen broke the concrete on Gacy's patio, they discovered the body of a man still in good condition. The unidentified man wore a pair of blue jean shorts and a wedding ring. Robert Piest was still unaccounted for.

With the addition of a body found in the Illinois River, thirty-one bodies had been found. The victim's name was Timothy O'Rourke, and because he was a fan of Bruce Lee, he took his last name and added it to his first name in a tattoo that read "Tim Lee." A friend of the victim's father recognized the tattoo when he read the newspaper and phoned police. Gacy met Tim Lee at a gay bar on Chicago's northside.

Finally, in April 1979, the remains of Robert Piest were discovered in the Illinois River. His body had been lodged along the river, but strong winds dislodged the corpse and carried it to the Dresden Dam locks where it was eventually discovered. Autopsy reports determined that Piest had suffocated from paper towels lodged in his throat. The Piest family filed suit against Gacy for murder for $85 million, and the family also sued the Iowa Board of Parole, the Iowa Department of Corrections, and the Chicago Police Department for negligence.

Police investigators continued to match dental records and other clues to help identify the remaining victims. Nine victims were never identified. Investigators thought that all of the victims were young men with ages ranging from early teens to mid-twenties. Some were young homosexuals looking for "action" at "Bughouse Square" and in the gay bars on Chicago's northside, some were young men who simply disappeared for no apparent reason, and five were employees of PDM Contracting at one point or another.

As the search came to an end, Robert Donnelly came forward and spoke to investigators. The youth's story was similar to the earlier case of Jeffrey Ringall. Robert Donnelly had been abducted at gunpoint by Gacy, chloroformed, tortured, whipped, and raped in December 1977. For reasons only known to Gacy, the lives of Donnelly and Ringall were spared.

Of special concern to prosecutors and investigators was the large map of the United States discovered in a room that Gacy used as an office in his home. "Serial killers always travel a lot, and I can't see where Gacy would be the exception," added Investigator Kozenczak (Burns, 1984). The map was littered with colored pins showing the towns where Gacy had lived, worked, or traveled throughout the years. "There were pins all over the place," recalls Robert Ressler, former head of the FBI's Violent Criminal Apprehension Program (Burns, 1984; Ressler and Shachtman, 2003). Although Ressler says that during subsequent conversations with Gacy, he denied any link between the map and other killings, "I think Gacy's good for more than thirty three," Ressler concluded (Ressler and Shachtman, 2003, p. 48). The FBI implies that many other jurisdictions such as St. Louis, Missouri, and Springfield, Illinois, had suspected that Gacy had sexually assaulted and murdered boys there as well (FBI, 2003).

It is difficult to guess how many victims, other than Jeffrey Ringall and Robert Donnelly, had come forward in Chicago and in other cities where Gacy worked or lived and had their cases declined by the police. It is equally difficult to estimate how many other young men were sexually assaulted and lived but did not report the attack because they did not want the stigma of the attack to complicate their lives. "I personally believe he [Gacy] killed a lot more than thirty three people," wrote Joseph Kozenczak, the former Des Plaines police detective who finally brought Gacy to justice (Burns, 1984; Sullivan and Maiken, 1983). "I think there are other victims out there, but we might never know," Kozenczak continued. Terry Sullivan, one of Gacy's prosecutors, added, "I think there are missing kids out there, and no one has ever tried to link them to Gacy" (Burns, 1984, p. 2). Sullivan admits that one of the most frustrating aspects of Gacy's case was its "enormity." Sullivan, like many other experts, believed there were many victims who had never been discovered. Steven Egger suggests that "[Gacy] started killing when he got to Chicago because he had a base and a comfort zone, his home" (Burns, 1984, p. 3). Although he insisted that Gacy's killings were confined to the Chicago area, Egger revealed that it is not "beyond the realm of possibility" that other victims exist. Other officials contend that more victims exist because Gacy lived, worked, and traveled in various cities across the country before settling down in the Chicago suburbs (Burns, 1984, p. 3).

THE TRIAL

Gacy's trial started on February 6, 1980, in the Cook County Criminal Court Building in Chicago. Gacy was thirty-seven years old. Louis B. Garippo was the trial judge, William Kunkle was the prosecutor, and Sam L. Amirante was the defense attorney hired by Gacy (Illinois Death Penalty, 2003).[8] Gacy claimed he paid $41,350 for his defense during the course of the trial and during the early years of his appeal. However, Cook County taxpayers paid approximately $12.5 million in appeals, trial matters, and incarceration. Gacy was always in a modified segregation unit with an estimated cost to maintain at $76,000 per year. The prosecution took five weeks to present their evidence. The defense called more than 100 witnesses to testify on Gacy's behalf.

The defense strategy was to establish that Gacy was insane and out of control at the time of the killings. To bolster this claim, the defense placed psychiatrists on the stand who had interviewed Gacy before his trial. The prosecution vigorously opposed the notion that Gacy was insane, contending that his claim of multiple personalities was a death-penalty dodge. The jury sided with the prosecution's claim.

The jury deliberated for two hours before finding Gacy guilty of murder. On March 13, 1980, Judge Louis B. Garippo sentenced Gacy to death for twelve murders. Gacy's execution followed the execution of Charles Walker by four years; Walker had abandoned his appeals and became the first person to be executed in Illinois after the U.S. Supreme Court allowed capital punishment to be resumed in 1976 after a four-year hiatus (*Gregg v. Georgia*, 1976). Gacy was the first to be involuntarily executed. Gacy had a respectful funeral, and he was buried in the plot at the head of his father's tombstone (Cahill and Ewing, 1986, p. 172).

SOME OF GACY'S VICTIMS[9]

Johnny Butkovich was seventeen years old, and he enjoyed cars like many young men. He took pride in his 1968 Dodge and continually worked on it because he loved to race it. Requiring money for parts, he took a job with PDM Contractors. Gacy refused to pay Johnny for two weeks of work. Angered, Johnny and two friends went to Gacy's house to collect. An argument erupted. Johnny threatened to tell authorities that Gacy was not deducting taxes from earnings; Gacy was enraged. Finally, Johnny and his friends left. Johnny dropped off his friends at their homes, and he was never to be seen alive again.

Michael Bonnin, also seventeen years old, was not too different from Johnny in that he enjoyed working with his hands. He especially liked carpentry work, and he was often busy with several projects at a time. In June 1976, he had almost completed work on restoring an old jukebox. While on his way to catch a train to meet his stepfather's brother, he disappeared.

Billy Carroll Jr. was the kind of boy who always seemed to be getting into trouble. At nine years old he was in a juvenile home for stealing a purse, and at eleven years old he was caught with a gun. Billy was mischievous and spent most of his time on the streets of the northside of Chicago. At sixteen,

Billy made money by arranging meetings between teenage homosexual boys and an adult clientele; it was thought that one client was Gacy. Billy disappeared suddenly on June 13, 1976.

Gregory Godzik liked his job with PDM Contractors. The money allowed him to buy parts for his 1966 Pontiac, which working on was a time-consuming hobby. He was proud of his car, and although it was a bit of an eyesore, it served Gregory well. On December 12, 1976, Gregory dropped his date off at her house, and he drove towards his home. The following day police found Gregory's Pontiac but not Gregory.

On January 20, 1977, nineteen-year-old John A. Szyc also disappeared much like the other young men before him. He had driven off in his 1971 Plymouth Satellite, and he was never seen alive again. Interestingly, a short while after the young man vanished, another teenager was picked up by police in Szyc's car while trying to leave a gas station without paying. The youth said that the man he lived with could explain the situation. The man was Gacy, and Gacy explained that Szyc had sold him the car earlier. Police never checked the title which had been signed eighteen days after Szyc's disappearance with a signature that was not his own. Szyc had known both Gregory Godzik and Johnny Butkovich (Sullivan and Maiken, 1983).

Eighteen-year-old Robert Gilroy was an outdoorsman, avid camper, and horse lover. On September 15, 1977, he was supposed to catch a bus with friends to go horseback riding, but he never showed. His father, who was a Chicago police sergeant, immediately began searching for Robert. Although a full-scale investigation was mounted, Robert was not found.

FINAL THOUGHTS

Gacy's case history was consistent with government findings associated with other sexual offenders. That is, convicted rape and sexual assault offenders who had served time in state prisons reported that two-thirds of their victims were under the age of eighteen (U.S. Dept. of Justice, 2003). Also, of four datasets that had been analyzed (the FBI's Uniform Crime Reports arrests, state felony court convictions, prison admissions, and the National Crime Victimization Survey), research indicated a sex offender who is older than other offenders who commit violent crimes, generally in his early thirties, and more likely to be white than other offenders who commit violent crimes. However, Gacy's history was also inconsistent with the same government reports that indicated that two thirds of the victims (aged eighteen to twenty-nine, who were Gacy's primary targets) had had a prior relationship with their rapist. Gacy sexually assaulted young men he knew. But more often Gacy criminally violated young men he did not know. For that reason, Gacy was the ugly side of the bogeyman, as his behavioral patterns revealed that he continually possessed, at an early age, the conscious intention to violate young men. He attacked despite the strength, power, or experiences of his victims. It appeared that most of his victims were physically capable individuals, and because Gacy had health issues most of his life, it could be argued that he was engaged in a game or contest to triumph over those stronger than he—somehow drawing on their strength to enhance his own weakness—which is right out of the pages of ancient pagan ideologies. After all, the only prerequisite to becoming a Gacy victim was "availability."

Sexual homicide is an event that has historically electrified public watch-fulness to the work of law enforcement in the United States. Both the public and law enforcement officers have expressed frustration regarding the number of unsolved homicides (Holmes and DeBurger, 1998). Therefore, it should come as no surprise that John Wayne Gacy Jr. arrogantly engaged in the abduction, sexual assaults, and murder of young men for such a long period of time in a city with the resources and pride as only Chicago could muster. However, it took a long time to bring Gacy to the attention of those who could bring him to justice. Maybe because Gacy's victims were young boys, or maybe because homosexuality was at the very core of his attacks, Gacy was not dealt with by the Chicago school system or the Chicago police who refused to hunt him down like other lust murderers such as Jerry Brudos and Ted Bundy (Holmes and DeBurger, 1988). Had the cops and the educators turned a blind eye to male victims?

Even untrained observers can recognize the patterns of criminally violent behavior produced as a person's (as in this case, Gacy's) "general" response involved with the same consistency that persuasion or retreat or self-insulation or humor or defiance is employed by others (Toch, 1997). Why were these people, who engaged in such violent criminal behavior, not stopped when they committed their early crimes? Surely, Gacy's potential towards sexual violence that included his lack of self-control, impulsiveness, risk seeking, insensitiveness, and sexual orientations were witnessed by many who could have made a difference before Gacy's first victim (Gottfredson and Hirschi, 1990). Perhaps it is true that Gacy's crimes were a testament to the passive acceptance of pervasive violence crowding the American experience from the colonial times to our war against terrorists (Holmes and DeBurger, 1998). Gacy's criminal activities revealed that he conducted heinous sexual crimes in the open for all to see while he was in high school and even before high school. Gacy's behavior appeared to be antisocial at an early age as he came to the attention of school personnel and law enforcement many times during his youth.

Even after Gacy's first arrest when he had been professionally examined, it was revealed that he had antisocial tendencies and represented a danger to society.[10] Nonetheless, Gacy was granted parole by the Iowa Department of Corrections. In no way should U.S. criminal justice professionals or school officials who work among serious offenders be blamed since most criminal justice professionals rarely produce policy. That is, police and correctional professionals do not control law enforcement and correctional systems but rather the politicians and the courts do (Stevens, 2003). Furthermore, alleged criminals and dangerous offenders have more rights under the U.S. Constitution than most responsible Americans (Stevens, 2001). Yet, Gacy was able to avoid detection due to his manipulative abilities and to the slipshod policies of the politicians. Even after Gacy was officially considered a huge danger, he was able to move around the United States at will. If sexual offender registration requirements for violent offenders had been in place, Robert Piest and many others might have lived long enough to watch their own children graduate college. But for them, that was not to be as they met their destruction alone, begging for their young lives.

Gacy manipulated his victims' helplessness by turning their strength or confidence against them through the use of drugs and restraints such as handcuffs (Stevens, 2001). Continuing along this line of reasoning, it could be argued with a great degree of confidence that criminals like Gacy who possess the intent of sexual homicide from an early age only seek a victim to fulfill their one goal in life: The sexual assault and murder of another human being (Samenow, 1996). Thus, these criminals continually survey their social environment to seek prey (Stevens, 2001). Their other life functions such as eating, working and sleeping hold the one purpose of bringing them closer to their goal—criminally sexual violence. How can they be stopped?

RECOMMENDATIONS

It is easier to be critical of the problems within the U.S. criminal justice system than to resolve them. But, it becomes apparent to question if early invention had been avoided by educational personnel, who had a suspicion about Gacy, and by the criminal justice community, which actually knew of his criminal intent early on. In other words, through proactive education and proactive policing could Gacy have been stopped? Because educators are not expected to be trained to discover antisocial behavior among youngsters, the possibility of integrating the community policing efforts as a problem-solving strategy with youngsters in classroom as a preventive police philosophy should be considered. That is, police problem-solving initiatives could be part of the educational process for students of all ages. Officers could instruct students on how to solve problems—the problems of living and working in a democratic society. They could participate in mutual problem-solving sessions that empower students and officers to resolve mutual issues. School violence might even be reduced through this process. Officers would instruct appropriate courses, and when antisocial behavior is revealed, they would address it or refer those cases to an appropriate caseworker who possesses the skills to aid students towards quality lifestyle decisions and to provide, when necessary, appropriate (correctional) supervision to aid students in altering antisocial behavior. "School" officers would be educated similar to teachers; the officers would hold appropriate certifications, and a college degree, training, and language skills would be necessary to provide a professional classroom experience for students. Caseworkers and those in correctional systems would engage in a mutual association towards professional supervision practices with the single aim of public safety.

Another recommendation evolving from this work is to remove the handcuffs of limited power from correctional and law enforcement personnel to protect potential victims from predators such as Gacy. For example, the Sexual Predator Act of Kansas (SPAK) represents one of the most important devises leading to pubic safety within correctional systems associated with incarcerated sexual offenders. SPAK empowered the state's attorney general to bring civil commitment actions against individuals who are within ninety days of release from criminal confinement and who are deemed, through a review process, to be at high risk for repeat offenses (Des Lauriers, 2002). Through a civil commitment process, sexual offenders like Gacy could be committed to a Sexual Predator Treatment Program for treatment until it is determined by treatment staff and the court that those sexual offenders are no longer high risk. Gacy would not have been released from his previous incarceration in Iowa if a similar devise was enacted in that state. It is recommended that sexual predator acts similar to the one in Kansas be enacted in every jurisdiction to aid those sexual offenders who continue to be at risk. Sexual predators are only referred to treatment after serving their prison sentences; the purpose of the treatment is to change their thinking and their life options, and generally those programs last approximately two years after prison time is served. In conclusion, it is recommended that punishment, education, and intervention are the most practical and efficient means that society has at its disposal for the moral training of children, even the children who become criminally violent offenders (Athens, 1992; Mednick, 1977; Stevens, 2001).

Gacy was crude and brutal about his bisexuality and other matters. He enjoyed shocking people that he thought might disapprove of his preference for young boys to satisfy his sexual appetites. To amuse himself between victims, Gacy arrogantly kept personal property or trophies of his victims (Hazelwood and Michaud, 2001). He lacked any sensitivity for his violent sexual crimes or held any regard for his victims. For instance, he told a reporter after his conviction that "the only thing I'm guilty of is running an unlicensed cemetery" (Fox and Levin, 1994, p. 233). Maybe his execution was a reasonable solution. However, what weighs heavily on some minds is that Gacy's carnage might have been prevented had the state allocated money to create preventative strategies rather then spending the millions to kill him.

NOTES

1. Gacy's address was 8213 Summerdale, Norridge, Illinois. At the time of his arrest by Cook County Sheriff's office, Gacy was five feet and nine inches tall, weighed 218 pounds, his eyes were blue, and his hair was gray.

2. Note: Bell's (2003) accounts seem to be the most valid and consistent with the literature regarding Gacy. The author's dates, places and events are well-documented. Bell's source is recommended for further information regarding John Wayne Gacy Jr.

3. Personal Communication. Informant wishes to remain anonymous.

4. The writer was a prison teacher and group leader at Stateville Penitentiary and Joliet Correctional near Chicago from 1984–1987 at a time when Gacy and Richard Speck were both incarcerated there.

5. Personal Communication.

6. Personal Communications with former high school students who attended schools also attended by Gacy.

7. Personal communication. However, this story cannot be substantiated with other evidence. It appears likely that these events took place given all the information presented.

8. Amirante graduated from Loyola University of Law (Chicago) in 1974, immediately taking the position of assistant public defender in Cook County Illinois. Four years later he joined the firm of McLennon, Nelson, Gabriele & Nudo, where he was assigned to the Gacy case. From 1978 to 1980, Amirante prepared the Gacy murder case for trial. Amirante started his own law practice in 1981 and returned to school to complete his education at National Judicial College and The American Academy of Judicial Studies. In 1988, Amirante was appointed Associate Judge of the Circuit Court of Cook County, the position he still holds.

9. Information in this section is from Bell (2003).

10. Antisocial personality disorder can be defined as:

    1. A pervasive pattern of disregard for and violation of the rights of others occurring since age fifteen, as indicated by three (or more) of the following:

        A. Failure to conform to social norms with respect to lawful behaviors as indicated by repeatedly performing acts that are grounds for arrest.

B. Deceitfulness, as indicated by repeated lying, use of aliases, or conning others for personal profit or pleasure.

C. Impulsivity or failure to plan ahead.

D. Irritability and aggressiveness, as indicated by repeated physical fights or assaults.

E. Reckless disregard for safety of self or others.

F. Consistent irresponsibility, as indicated by repeated failure to sustain consistent work behavior or honor financial obligations.

G. Lack of remorse, as indicated by being indifferent or rationalizing having hurt, mistreated, or stolen from another.

2. The individual is at least age eighteen years of age.

3. There is evidence of Conduct Disorder with onset before age fifteen.

4. The occurrence of antisocial behavior is not exclusively during the course of Schizophrenia or a manic episode.

REFERENCES

All things horror. Retrieved October 1, 2003, from http://allthingshorror.tripod.com/gacy.html

American Psychiatric Association. (1995). *Diagnostic and Statistical Manual of Mental Disorders, DSM IV* (4th ed.). Washington, DC: Author.

Athens, L.H. (1992). *The creation of dangerous violent criminals.* Chicago: University of Illinois Press.

Bell, R. Court TV's Crime Library. Retrieved October 1, 2003, from http://www.crimelibrary.com/serial/gacy/gacymain.htm

Burns, T. H. (1984). John Wayne Gacy. Retrieved from http://www.suburbanchicagonews.com/joliet/prisons/executed/gacy6.html

Cahill, T., and Ewing, R. (1986). *Buried dreams: Inside the mind of a serial killer.* New York: Bantam Books.

Chicago Police Department Investigator's Report. (1983). Chicago Police Department Archives.

Des Lauriers, A. (2002, October). Kansas' sex offender treatment program. *Corrections Today, 64*(6), 118–120.

Douglas, J., and Olshaker, M. (1995). *Mind hunter: Inside the FBI's elite serial crime unit.* New York: Pocket Star Books.

Douglas, J., and Olshaker, M. (1997). *Journey into darkness.* New York: Scribner.

Federal Bureau of Investigation. Retrieved October 1, 2003, from http://foia.fbi.gov/gacy.htm

Feldmann, M. (1992). Cook: No honor in preparing last meal. *Suburban Chicago Newspaper.* Retrieved October 1, 2003, from http://www.suburbanchicagonews.com/joliet/prisons/executed/gacy1.html

Fox, J. A., and Levin, J. (1994). *Overkill—mass murder and serial killing exposed.* New York: Plenum Press.

Gottfredson, M. R., and Hirschi, T. (1990). *A general theory of crime.* Stanford, CA: Stanford University Press.

Gregg v. Georgia, 428 U.S. 153 (1976).

Hazelwood, R., and Michaud, S. G. (2001). *Dark dreams*. New York: St. Martin's Press.

Holmes, R. M., and DeBurger, J. E. (1988). *Serial murder: Studies in crime, law and justice* (Vol. 2). Newbury Park, CA: Sage.

Holmes, R. M., and DeBurger, J. E. (1998). Profiles in terror. In R. M. Holmes and S. T. Holmes (Eds.), *Contemporary perspectives on serial murder* (pp. 5–16). Thousand Oaks, CA: Sage.

Illinois Death Penalty. Retrieved January 15, 2004, from http://www.illinoisdeath-penalty.com/gacy.html

Inmate Records from the Iowa Department of Corrections. 420 Watson Powell, Jr. Way, Des Monies, Iowa, 50309.

Kozenczak, J., and Henrikson, K. (1992). *A passing acquaintance*. New York: Carlton Press.

Linedecker, C. (1980). *The man who killed boys: The John Wayne Gacy, Jr. Story.* New York: St. Martin's Press.

Lohr, D. (n.d.) *Crime Magazine. An encyclopedia of crime.* Retrieved October 1, 2003, from http://crimemagazine.com/boykillergacy.htm

Mednick, S. (1977). A biosocial theory of the learning of law-abiding behavior. In S. Mednick and K. Christiansen (Eds.), *Biosocial bases of criminal behavior.* New York: Gardner.

Mendenhall, H. (1995). *Fall of the house of Gacy.* West Frankfort, IL: New Authors Publication.

Ressler, R. K., and Shachtman, T. (2003). *I have lived in the monster: Inside the minds of the world's most dangerous serial killers.* New York: St. Martin's Press.

Samenow, S. (1996). *Before it's too late.* New York: Basic Books.

Serial killer Gacy's art for sale on the Internet. Local police say victims of former Waterloo man's crimes should get profits. (2003, April 2). *Waterloo Courier.* Retrieved October 1, 2003, from, http:// www.wcfcourier.com/articles/2000/04/02/export888.txt

Shelden, R. G. (2001). *Controlling dangerous classes: A critical introduction to the history of criminal justice.* Boston: Allyn Bacon.

Stevens, D. J. (2001). *Inside the mind of the sexual rapist.* New York: Author's Choice.

Stevens, D. J. (2003). *Community policing in the 21st century.* Boston: Allyn & Bacon.

Sullivan, T., and Maiken, P. (1983). *Killer clown.* New York: Grosset and Dunlap.

Toch, H. (1997). *Violent men: An inquiry into the psychology of violence.* Washington, DC: American Psychiatric Press.

U.S. Department of Justice (2003). Bureau of Justice Statistics. NCJ 163392. Retrieved October 1, 2003, from http://www.ojp.usdoj.gov/bjs/abstract/soo.htm

Whiteside, J. (1993). The bogeyman in all our nightmares. *Herald-News.* Retrieved October 1, 2003, from http://www.suburbanchicagonews.com/joliet/prisons/executed/gacy1a.html

Ted Bundy:
The Serial Killer Next Door

Gary Boynton

THE CRIMES

Pleasantly handsome, piercingly intelligent, Ted Bundy was a master manipulator, a silver-tongued charmer who lured women to their deaths, confounded police pursuers, and clogged the court system for nearly a decade. The exact number of women killed by Bundy will never be known, but the estimates range from 30 to 300 ("Did Bundy Kill 300?," 1982). Because of the large number of victims and the media's sensational coverage of this case, Bundy became one of society's best-known serial killers.

A one-time Boy Scout and an "A" student, Bundy seemed headed for a sterling career in Republican politics in Washington State, and he even served as assistant director of the Seattle Crime Prevention Advisory Committee. Perversely, he was the author of a pamphlet instructing women on rape prevention (Lamar, 1989). Bundy also worked at Seattle's Crisis Clinic and earned his degree in psychology (with honors) at the University of Washington before attending law school at the University of Utah (Rule, 1980a, p. 30).

Bundy's reign of terror began in Seattle in 1974. On January 4, eighteen-year-old Joni Lentz was brutally attacked while sleeping in the large home she shared with several roommates. Although she was found in a coma, lying

Bundy's appearance in court just before he was sentenced to die. He is criticizing the media for its coverage of his trial. (AP/Wide World Photos)

in a pool of blood and having been sexually violated with a broken bed rod, Lentz survived the assault.

On January 31, Lynda Ann Healy, a University of Washington law student and part-time weather reporter, disappeared from her basement bedroom in Seattle's University District. Her parents called the police—the police found her pillowcase and sheets soaked in blood.

Throughout 1974, young women disappeared from college campuses and other locations around Washington, Oregon, and Utah. All of them were slender, white, and wore their hair parted in the middle. They all disappeared in the late afternoon or evening (Lohr, 2002).

Two of the missing women, Denise Neslund and Janice Ott, were each last seen on July 14, 1974, at Lake Sammamish State Park in Issaquah, which is twelve miles east of Seattle. Several other women who were at the park that Saturday told investigators that they had been approached by a handsome young man with his arm in a sling, who told them that his name was "Ted" ("Another Encounter," 1974).

On November 8, 1974, Bundy attempted to kidnap eighteen-year-old Carol DaRonch from a shopping mall in Salt Lake City, Utah. She escaped and was able to provide investigators with a description of the man and his vehicle, a tan Volkswagen. A similar vehicle was reported to have been speeding away from where a teenager named Debby Kent was last seen before she disappeared from Bountiful, Utah.

After his bungled abduction attempt, Bundy apparently stopped killing for four months, before he resumed in Colorado, where he abducted and murdered four more young women. After first being arrested and convicted of attempted kidnapping in Utah, and then being charged with murder in Colorado, Bundy escaped twice.

On June 7, 1977, while awaiting trial for the murder of Carolyn Campbell in the Garfield County Jail, he received special privileges to use the Pitkin County Courthouse library in Aspen. He escaped by jumping from a second-story window. He was recaptured eight days later while trying to leave town in a stolen car.

Almost seven months later, on December 30, 1977, Bundy escaped again. In the intervening months he had eaten very little food and had shed thirty pounds, which was enough to allow him to shimmy through a small hole where a light fixture had been in the ceiling of his cell in the Garfield County Jail. He then crawled into the closet of his jailer's apartment and waited before casually walking out of the front door. It took jailers nearly fifteen hours to realize he was gone. After making his way to the Midwest, he boarded a plane to Florida.

By January of 1987, Bundy was renting an apartment near Florida State University. He supported himself by committing petty thefts; he grew a beard, and went by the alias Chris Hagen. However, he was not content with his new freedom, and he could not control his murderous impulses (Lohr, 2002).

Bundy killed three victims in Florida. On the night of January 14, 1978, he bludgeoned and strangled to death Margaret Bowman, 21, and Lisa Levy, 20, in the Chi Omega sorority house at Florida State University in Tallahassee. Two other coeds, Karen Chandler, 21, and Kathy Kleiner, 20, survived his attacks. Less than a month later, he killed his final victim, a twelve-year-old Lake City, Florida, girl named Kimberly Leach (Lohr, 2002).

Bundy's four-year killing spree, which began in Washington State and continued in Utah and Colorado, finally came to an end in Florida, when he was caught in a stolen Volkswagen bug. However, the story of serial murderer Ted Bundy was just beginning.

THE ACTIONS OF THE CRIMINAL JUSTICE SYSTEM

Law Enforcement

Bundy's assault on Lentz and the disappearance of Healy were both investigated by detectives from the Seattle Police Department. The detectives were unable to find a motive or a viable suspect in either case, and they were unable to link the two cases together.

Investigators learned that Lentz was a friendly, shy girl with no enemies. They concluded that she had been a chance victim, attacked simply because someone knew she slept alone in her basement bedroom, and perhaps the attacker had seen her through a window and found the basement door unlocked.

In the Healy case, every inch of her neighborhood was searched—including all the dark, leafy ravines of nearby Ravenna Park—both by officers and by dogs from the K-9 unit. No traces of Healy or of her abductor were found; detectives were perplexed.

While these cases were being investigated, detectives from the Thurston County Sheriff's Department were having problems solving the disappearance of Donna Gail Manson, a nineteen-year-old coed, who had disappeared from the campus of Evergreen State College, southwest of Olympia, Washington.

Investigators talked to everyone who new Manson and followed up on every possible lead. They learned that she had been a bright but troubled young woman, who was weighed down with depression and obsessed with death, magic, and the ancient pseudoscience of Alchemy. She was also known to have smoked marijuana daily, to have used other drugs as well, and to have been dating four different men. None of these leads produced a suspect. Detectives considered the possibility that she might have committed suicide, and they even had a psychiatrist evaluate her writings. He concluded, however, that dark thoughts were not unusual for a young woman of her age and that there was no indication that she feared anyone.

When Bundy's next victim, Susan Rancort, disappeared from the campus of Central Washington State College in Ellensburg, a rodeo town that has retained the flavor of the old West, the campus police department investigated. They learned what outfit she was wearing when last seen, and they attempted to retrace her route from a meeting with an advisor back to the dorm where she lived. Somewhere in between was when she had vanished.

As word spread of Rancort's disappearance, other coeds came forward with descriptions of incidents that had vaguely disturbed them. Two of them told of encounters with a tall, handsome man in his late twenties, who had his arm in a sling and asked for their help putting books or packages in his car, a tan Volkswagen. Both had felt uncomfortable with the situation and fled. One had noticed that the car's passenger seat was missing, and the other did not want to get into a stranger's vehicle to start the engine for him (Rule, 1980a, pp. 61–62). As with Bundy's earlier crimes, investigators from Kittitas County and the Central Washington State College Police were unable to locate either the victim or the person who abducted her.

Bundy's next victim, Kathy Parks, disappeared from Oregon State University in Corvallis, which is 250 miles south of Seattle. The investigation into her disappearance was the responsibility of the Oregon State Police Criminal Investigation Unit, which had a lieutenant stationed on the OSU campus. He led a week-long search of the campus but was unable to find any trace of the missing coed or of any suspicious strangers like those reported in Ellensburg. For a while, investigators considered the possibility that Parks had committed suicide, after they learned that she had recently broken up with her boyfriend, was homesick for her native California, and was guilt-ridden over an argument with her father. When no body was found in the nearby Willamette River, where police feared she might have killed herself, they abandoned the suicide theory and concluded that she had been abducted.

Police bulletins with pictures of the four missing girls were now tacked up side-by-side on the office walls of every law enforcement agency in the Pacific Northwest, with smiling faces that looked enough alike to be sisters. Yet, only the commander of the Seattle Police Department's Crimes Against Persons Unit was convinced that Parks was part of the pattern. Other detectives thought that Corvallis was too far away for her to be a victim of the same man who prowled Washington campuses.

Bundy's next victim, Brenda Ball, was last seen in the parking lot of a tavern in Burien, Washington, just south of Seattle. She was talking with a handsome, brown-haired man who had one arm in a sling. The investigation into Ball's disappearance was the responsibility of the King County Police (now Sheriff's Department), which had jurisdiction in the unincorporated areas of Washington State's most heavily populated county. It would not be the last case that would pit Bundy against King County detectives.

When Bundy's next victim, Georgeann Hawkins, disappeared from "Greek Row," a tree-lined street of sorority and fraternity houses just north of the University of Washington, the initial report was taken by a detective from the Missing Persons Unit of the Seattle Police Department. Usually any police department will wait twenty-four hours before beginning a search for a missing adult, but in view of the events of the first half of 1974, the disappearance of Georgeann Hawkins was immediately treated very seriously. Three homicide detectives and the head of the Western Washington State Crime Lab covered ninety feet of the alleyway behind Greek Row on their hands and knees, searching for evidence: They found nothing.

Leaving the alley cordoned off and guarded by patrolmen, they went into the Theta House to talk with Hawkins' sorority sisters and her housemother. They learned that she had last been seen leaving the nearby Beta fraternity house by the backdoor after a quick visit to her boyfriend who lived there, on her way home from a party that she had attended with a sorority sister. It was only forty feet down the alley from the back of the Beta House to the back of the Theta House, but Hawkins never made it that far. The detectives were baffled that she could have vanished within such a short distance.

When the news of Hawkins's disappearance was released to the media, two witnesses came forward with a familiar story: they reported seeing a tall, good-looking man on crutches, carrying a briefcase on Greek Row on the night that Hawkins vanished. Detectives canvassed every house on each side of the street. They found that the housemother at a sorority across the street from the Theta House recalled being awakened by a high-pitched, "terrified" scream in the middle of that night. She figured it was "just kids horsing around" and went back to sleep. No one else reported hearing the scream (Rule, 1980a, pp. 65–69).

With six young women now missing in the Pacific Northwest, the pressure on law enforcement was tremendous. On July 3, 1974, more than 100 representatives from departments all over Washington and Oregon met at Evergreen State College for a day-long brainstorming conference. The law enforcement agencies represented included the Seattle Police Department, King County Police Department, Washington State Patrol, the U.S. Army's Criminal Investigation Department, University of Washington Police, the Central Washington Security Force, Tacoma Police Department, Pierce County (WA) Sheriff's Office, Multnomah County (OR) Sheriff's Department, Oregon State Police, and dozens of smaller police departments.

The investigators noted the striking similarities among all the girls—their age, their appearance, and the circumstances of their disappearance. They also discussed that in two instances a man wearing a sling had been seen in the vicinity around the time that the girls had vanished. Also considered were the possibilities that there might have been more than one perpetrator or that there might be some kind of satanic cult involvement in the disappearances. The latter speculation was fueled by a rash of reports of the apparent ritual mutilation of cattle in the region during this same time period.

The general consensus was that there was not a cult involved but that only one man was responsible for the disappearances. Investigators focused on how the man was able to get his victims to trust him enough so that he could kidnap them without leaving much evidence for investigators. They speculated that perhaps he was, or pretended to be, someone in an occupation that people would automatically trust such as a clergyman, doctor, fireman, or police officer. Or maybe he was, or pretended to be, handicapped in some way and in need of assistance: perhaps a man with his arm in a sling or on crutches?

As the discussion turned to the law enforcement response, it was determined that they lacked the manpower to infiltrate every campus in the Northwest to stop every man dressed like a priest, fireman, or police officer or every man with his arm in a sling or leg in a cast. In the end, the only thing to do was to warn the public with as much media saturation as possible, to ask for information from citizens, and to keep working on every tip that came in (Rule, 1980a, pp. 71–73).

It was less than two weeks after the meeting in Olympia when Bundy's next two victims vanished from Lake Sammamish State Park, which fell under the jurisdiction of the King County Police. They immediately formed a "Ted Squad," based on the name that the young man with his arm in a sling had given to several women at the park that day.

The scope of the investigation drew all of the manpower of King County's Major Crimes Unit, along with Seattle detectives and personnel from the small-town police departments near Lake Sammamish State Park, Issaquah, and North Bend. The "Ted Squad" knew that the disappearances in Issaquah were part of an increasingly familiar pattern. They began interviewing the dozen or more people who had seen "Ted" in the park that day, including the young women he had approached and several individuals who had seen Bundy talking to Janice Ott before she walked away with him.

As a result of the descriptions these people provided, a police artist was able to render a composite sketch of "Ted," which was widely disseminated in the news media. Hundreds of calls came in response to the drawing, but it was hard for investigators to come up with a distinguishing characteristic that would differentiate the real "Ted" from all the other possible suspects who looked like him.

Some of the witnesses even went under hypnosis in the hope that they would remember more. All they could recall was that he sounded well-educated, was tan, and had a memorable smile. Several also noted the strange way that he had stared at the women he had approached. Aside from these few tidbits, the only other thing investigators had to go on was a description of the suspect's car: a tan Volkswagen bug. In the early seventies, such vehicles were very common.

Police closed the 400-acre park and searched the park on foot and horseback along with volunteers from the Explorer Scouts. They also had police divers probe the lake for evidence and helicopters search from above. Planes flew over the vast areas of woodlands surrounding the park to take infrared photos, hoping to find where the two young women might have been buried. No evidence of the victims or of their abductor was found.

The detectives asked a local psychiatrist to draw a verbal picture of the man now known as "Ted." The profile he gave them was of a sexual psychopath, between the ages of twenty-five and thirty-five, who feared women and their power over him, and would at times demonstrate "socially isolative" behavior.

Investigators followed up every lead, even those from psychics, and compiled a long list of possible "Teds." Among the names on that list was that of Ted Bundy, whose name had been given to detectives separately by true-crime writer Ann Rule, who had worked side-by-side with Bundy at the Crisis Clinic, and by Bundy's girlfriend (Rule, 1980a, pp. 77–89).

In early August, 1974, just a few weeks after the disappearances at Lake Sammamish, the remains of Ott, Neslund, and a third young woman believed to be either Manson or Hawkins were discovered by a King County road worker near the side of a service road about two miles from the park. It appeared to investigators that the three young women had been murdered during a crazed sexual frenzy. There was little evidence at the scene, but the similarities between the Washington and Oregon cases quickly caught the attention of investigators in Utah. The three states began working together and soon agreed that one man was committing these murders (Lohr, 2002).

A task force of Seattle and King County detectives was set up in a windowless room hidden between the first and second floors of the county courthouse. The walls were covered with maps of Lake Sammamish and the University District with flyers bearing the missing girls' pictures, and composite drawings of "Ted" (Rule, 1980a, p. 97).

In March 1975, more young female remains were discovered near Taylor Mountain, about ten miles east of the site where the other bodies had been found. The remains were identified as Ball, Healey, Rancourt, and Parks.

As the summer dragged on, the task force began feeding the names of all their possible "Ted" suspects into a county computer. They assigned each list they had—registered owners of Volkswagens, transfer students among all the universities, attendees at a company picnic at Lake Sammamish, released mental patients, and all the names of suspects they had been provided—with a different letter or pair of letters of the alphabet. They then used the computer to produce a list of the twenty-five men whose names appeared on the most lists. Among those twenty-five was Theodore Robert Bundy, whose name appeared on four different lists. Bundy was noted an "AAA" because his name was in the suspect file (List A) three times; a "C" because he was the registered owner of a Volkswagen bug; an "FFF" because he was in three different psychology classes with Healy at the University of Washington; and a "Q" because he was observed by an anonymous citizen driving a Volkswagen bug near where two women disappeared.

The task force detectives decided to concentrate their efforts on Bundy and the other twenty-four men whose names appeared on at least four different lists. A week into this part of the investigation, they received a call from a detective in Salt Lake City informing them of Bundy's arrest for the attempted kidnapping of Carol DaRonch (Keppel and Birnes, 1995, p. 74).

Bundy was arrested when a Utah Highway Patrol officer noticed an unfamiliar, tan Volkswagen bug driving by his home in the Salt Lake City suburb of Granger. The patrolman shined his bright lights to read the license plate. Suddenly, the Volkswagon's lights went out and it took off at high speed. The patrolman gave chase, pursuing Bundy through two stop signs and onto the main thoroughfare. Bundy then pulled over into a vacant gas station parking lot.

Bundy told the officer that he had been to see a movie and had gotten lost, but the patrolman knew that the movie Bundy had claimed to have seen was not playing at the local drive-in.

When the cop asked if he could look in the car, Bundy said, "Go ahead." The officer then saw a small crowbar resting on the floor behind the driver's seat and an open satchel sitting on the floor in front. Using his flashlight, he saw some of the items inside the satchel: A ski mask, a crowbar, an ice pick, rope, and wire. The Utah patrolman placed Bundy under arrest for evading an officer, frisked him, and then handcuffed him (Rule, 1980b).

The patrolman then called for assistance in transporting Bundy and his vehicle. When a Salt Lake County deputy arrived at the scene, there were already three Utah State Police officers with Bundy. The deputy immediately looked in the canvas satchel, in which he found not only the ice pick, crowbar, ski mask, tape, and wire, but also a flashlight, gloves, torn strips of sheeting, another mask made from pantyhose, and handcuffs. He then checked the trunk of Bundy's Volkswagon and found some large green garbage bags.

Bundy was released on his own recognizance after he was booked for evading the officer. But two days later, when a detective was reviewing the arrest reports for the weekend, the name "Bundy" piqued his interest. He recalled that it was the name of a man being considered for the murders of women in Washington, Oregon, and Utah.

The detective noted that the physical description of the man who had just been arrested fit with the details provided by Bundy's ex-girlfriend, and Bundy drove a tan Volkswagon bug. He pulled out the files on the DaRonch and Kent cases, looking for any common threads. Although the handcuffs confiscated from Bundy were a different brand than those used on DaRonch, the investigator wondered just how many men carried handcuffs with them. He also noted that where Bundy had been arrested was not far from where a girl named Melinda Smith had last been seen.

On August 21, 1974, Bundy was arrested on the added charge of possession of burglary tools. The Salt Lake County Sheriff's detectives thought he was responsible for the DaRonch kidnapping, and they suspected that Bundy might well be the man who had taken the three young women missing from Utah.

The investigators obtained permission from Bundy to search his apartment. Because it was a consent search, there was no warrant to limit the scope of the search. In the apartment, investigators found a number of interesting items, including a bicycle wheel suspended from a meat hook with an assortment of knives hanging from it, and a chopping block. There were other items—seemingly innocuous, but meaningful to the ongoing probe—including a map of ski regions in Colorado, with certain areas marked and a brochure from a ski resort in Utah.

Investigators showed mug shots of Bundy, along with those of several other men, to DaRonch and to a teacher who had last seen Kent talking to a stranger before she vanished. DaRonch set aside Bundy's photo, saying that it looked like the man who had tried to kidnap her, but she was not sure. The teacher picked Bundy's photo out immediately without hesitation. When shown a second set of photos by a detective from Bountiful, Utah, DaRonch selected Bundy's picture out of the montage, but she was less certain about photos of Bundy's Volkswagen, which had been cleaned up and repaired since it was impounded.

Bundy was now under the constant attention of law enforcement agencies. His gasoline credit card records and school records were subpoenaed, and Utah detectives contacted his fiancée in Seattle (Rule, 1980a, pp. 120–124). This and other evidence was enough to have Bundy charged with the attempted kidnapping of DaRonch. While free on bail as he awaited trial, Bundy visited the Seattle area. Detectives from King County asked him if they could talk to him about the local murders, but Bundy told the officers that his attorney said, "No." The difficulty that King County detectives had in trying to talk to Bundy was compounded by the fact that they had no specific evidence against him. They found no clothing, jewelry, or other personal items belonging to any of the local victims. For example, Naslund was known to wear six rings at the time of her disappearance, and Ott's yellow bicycle was also never found (McCarten, 1978).

Unlike their Northwest counterparts, investigators in Utah and Colorado did have some physical evidence linking Bundy to some of their victims. Scalp hair found on the front floor of his Volkswagen matched that of Campbell, the nurse who had disappeared from the ski resort in Aspen, Colorado. Pubic hair found in the trunk matched that of Smith, who was slain in Salt Lake City in the fall of 1974. Detectives in Aspen used Bundy's gas credit card records to show that he was in the Aspen area on the day that Campbell disappeared. They also obtained a statement from a woman who claimed to have seen Bundy in the same ski lodge from which the young nurse had vanished. Campbell's nude, frozen body had been found near Aspen six weeks after she went missing. She had been raped and bludgeoned to death. Utah investigators continued to search for links between Bundy, Smith, and at least three other young women who had disappeared or been killed in the Salt Lake area during the fall of 1974 (McCarten, 1977).

A three-day meeting of law enforcement authorities from Washington, Utah, Colorado, and California was held in Aspen to discuss the various murders believed to be linked to Bundy. Officers from California attended, even though there were indications that slayings in their state had no connection with those in the other three. The investigators compared notes and agreed to a cooperative strategy to solve these cases. They kept the meeting quiet to avoid publicity that might endanger the chance of a conviction, should charges be filed in any of the deaths (McCarten, 1975).

A detective from King County's "Ted Squad" informed his colleagues from the other states of his squad's attempts to link Bundy to the crimes in Washington. He also gave them a thumbnail sketch of Bundy's formative years and his relationships with women, including his fiancée, who told of being tied up and choked by Bundy during sex. The detective then outlined the possible connections between Bundy and some of the Northwest victims. Bundy not only had several classes with Healy, but they lived in the same neighborhood and shopped at the same grocery store.

Bundy was known to frequent Evergreen State College to play racquetball, around the time that Manson disappeared. And, most damning of all, he was positively identified by two witnesses at Sammamish State Park and tentatively identified by a third as the man last seen with Ott. Other witnesses from the park were uncertain, describing a man of varying height, build, and hair color.

The detective also bemoaned the lack of physical evidence, telling his colleagues, "All we have is bones." At the conclusion of the conference, one of the Colorado investigators told a detective from Utah, "It looks like the only chance any of us has of tying down Mr. Bundy is your kidnapping case there in Salt Lake City" (Larsen, 1980, pp. 113–123). Unfortunately, he was wrong. Bundy would not be stopped until he was caught in Florida and more young women were dead.

Two-and-a-half years later, when Bundy attacked four coeds in the Chi Omega House at Florida State University, the case was initially handled by both the Leon County Sheriff's Office and the Tallahassee Police Department. A Be On the Look-out (BOLO) bulletin was issued to every law enforcement officer in the area, based on the description given by a member of the sorority who had seen the attacker (Rule, 1980a, p. 238).

Detectives photographed and collected evidence at the crime scene, including hair and fingernail scrapings taken from the victims' bodies, and traces of bark from the oak club used in the assaults. For hours, police searched streets, sidewalks, yards, and garbage cans, looking for the murder weapon. Hundreds of wood chunks and branches lay beneath the old oak trees in the neighborhood, but none were found with blood on them.

A joint task force of detectives from Leon County, Tallahassee, the Florida Department of Law Enforcement, and members of the Florida State University Police investigated the attacks. A member of the university's police force soon received a call from a detective from King County advising him, "You might want to look for a guy named Ted Bundy" (Larsen, 1980, p. 253).

Unlike in the western states, Florida investigators had a great deal of physical evidence to collect and process. This evidence included blood from the victims (which was useful in determining the logistics of the attacks); numerous latent fingerprints (none of which proved to be useful); a piece of chewing gum found in one of the murder victims' hair (which was accidentally destroyed at the crime lab, rendering it useless); and a section of flesh from Levy's buttocks with teeth marks in it. There were also all the sheets, pillows, blankets, nightgowns, and panties belonging to the victims. The killer also left behind a pantyhose garotte on Bowman's neck.

When Bundy's final victim, twelve-year-old Leach, went missing in Lake City, Florida, halfway between Tallahassee and Jacksonville, her parents contacted the Lake City Police Department, who immediately issued a BOLO for her. At the same time, a Leon County detective received a call from a Jacksonville detective seeking help in tracing a white van in which a man had tried to pick up the detective's own teenage daughter. The girl had gotten the license number of the van. The Leon County investigator determined that the license plate had been stolen not far from the FSU campus. He also learned that a white Dodge van matching the one described by the Jacksonville detective's daughter had been stolen from the campus around the same time as the plates. This was the first link between the Tallahassee attacks and the disappearance in Lake City.

The Jacksonville detective arranged to have his daughter and her friend—who had been with her when approached by the strange van—hypnotized, to see if they would enhance their recollections. The teenagers were then separated to assist police artists in putting together sketches based on their hypnosis-aided memories. Both sketches looked amazingly similar. Investigators would also later note how much they looked like mug shots of Bundy.

In the early morning hours of February 15, 1978, a patrolman for the Florida Police Department in Pensacola spotted an orange Volkswagen bug emerging from an alley near a well-known local restaurant. Knowing that the eatery had closed hours earlier and not recognizing the vehicle as belonging to any of the restaurant employees, the officer called in to see if it was stolen. Upon learning that it was, the cop signaled for the driver to pull over. When he did not, the officer gave chase until the car finally pulled over a mile later.

After first refusing to do so, Bundy finally got down on the ground as ordered by the armed officer. As he was about to be handcuffed, he kicked the legs out from under the cop and then hit him. The officer was able to get off one shot from his revolver to get the suspect off of him. Bundy then attempted to flee, but the officer was able to get off another shot and Bundy hit the ground. When the cop checked him to see if he'd been hit, Bundy again leapt up and began fighting. Strangely, all through their struggle, Bundy kept yelling for help. The officer finally subdued Bundy, handcuffed his hands behind his back, and then placed him in his patrol car, where he read him his rights. Bundy, who seemed quite depressed, repeatedly said, "I wish you had killed me" (Rule, 1980a, pp. 251–261).

THE PROSECUTORS

Because Bundy committed his crimes in so many different jurisdictions, many different prosecutors had to get involved. They not only worked with investigators from their own areas, but they also actively participated in the multistate consultations that took place once the connections among the various disappearances and murders became apparent (McCarten, 1975). Prominently involved were the King County prosecuting attorney, whose office had jurisdiction over all the cases in Seattle, as well as those in other parts of the county; the District Attorney of Pitkin County, which includes Aspen; and prosecutors from Salt Lake County. Although the King County prosecutors had the most cases to deal with, they also had the least evidence. The Pitkin County officials were reluctant to prosecute Bundy for the Campbell murder before Salt Lake County had a conviction for his attempted kidnapping of DaRonch, so officials from all three jurisdictions met in Salt Lake City a week before the kidnapping trial (McCarten, 1976). Eight months after Bundy was convicted in Utah, he was charged with the Campbell murder by the Pitkin County district attorney and extradited to Colorado, but he was able to escape from jail there twice and from the murder charge altogether (Lohr, 2002).

In Florida, Bundy fell under the jurisdiction of the Florida State Attorney's Office, which prosecutes all murders in Florida. Two separate teams of prosecutors handled the Chi Omega trial in Miami and the Leach trial in Orlando (Larsen, 1979a).

THE DEFENSE

Over the course of his criminal career, Bundy had twenty-one different attorneys representing his interests. During his kidnapping trial in Salt Lake City he had two very competent and respected defense attorneys in court, and he also frequently consulted with a Seattle public defender, who later went on to become one of that city's most prominent criminal defense lawyers.

In Florida, Bundy acted as his own attorney, assisted by a number of different lawyers. Even so, he bitterly complained that having to prepare for two different trials simultaneously put him in "an untenable and fundamentally unfair position" (Larsen, 1979a).

Before each trial, Bundy and his lawyers flooded the Florida courts with pretrial motions, including two successful motions for change of venue. The trials were moved to Miami and Orlando. During the trials, Bundy often took the lead in questioning key witnesses, and at one point, he fired his legal team and replaced them with a group more to his liking, while assuming greater control over his own defense.

Despite disorganization among and bumbling by his defense team, a number of legal experts thought that Bundy had a shot at an acquittal in the Chi Omega trial in Miami. This view was held despite the fact that Bundy had a disagreement with the most experienced member of his team, after the lawyer worked out a plea bargain, which Bundy vetoed (Larsen, 1979b).

THE TRIALS

Bundy had much in his favor in the DaRonch kidnapping trial in Salt Lake City. He had the support of family and friends, one of the top criminal lawyers in Utah, and a judge with a reputation as a fair-minded jurist. Judge Stewart J. Hanson Jr., of Salt Lake County Superior Court, presided. Because Bundy surprisingly waived his right to a jury trial at the last minute, it was up to Judge Hanson to weigh both the facts and the law.

The key witnesses were the victim and Bundy. DaRonch was not a confident victim. She appeared intimidated by the way Bundy stared at her, and she sobbed during her testimony. Her greatest show of strength was when she pointed at Bundy and identified him as the man who had tried to kidnap her. In contrast, Bundy appeared extremely confident, as he testified on his own behalf. He had an explanation for everything. He said that he had fled the patrolman because he had been smoking marijuana in his car, that he had found the handcuffs in a dump and had no key for them, and that there had been a mix-up on the license plate numbers he had given to a gas station attendant around the time of the abduction attempt.

Judge Hanson took his dual role very seriously and often took it upon himself to ask questions of witnesses. After hearing five days of testimony and argument, and requesting extra security for his courtroom, he spent the following weekend "agonizing" over his verdict. The next Monday afternoon, he announced that he had found Bundy guilty of aggravated kidnapping (Rule, 1980a, p. 161). He then sentenced him to fifteen years in prison (Larsen, 1980, p. 148).

In Florida, Bundy faced two different judges. Judge Edward Cowart of the 11th Circuit, who presided over the Chi Omega trial, decided that he could not seat an impartial jury in Tallahassee, so he moved the trial to Miami. Judge Cowart ran his courtroom like the captain of ship, taking no nonsense from Bundy or any of the attorneys.

The Miami trial could not have been more different from the rather mundane proceedings in Utah. Throughout the trial, Bundy took center stage in his dual roles as defendant and defender. With television cameras in the courtroom and Bundy acting as his own attorney, including cross-examining many of the state's witnesses, it was unlike any trial that had ever come before. Very much aware of the television cameras and other media, he displayed the full range of his complex personality from his charm, intelligence, and wit to his ego, temper, and contempt for authority.

The trial consisted of a parade of lay and expert witnesses for both the prosecution and the defense. The state attempted to link Bundy to the crimes by both circumstantial and direct forensic evidence, while Bundy and his lawyers tried to cast doubt on every element of the state's case.

One of the most crucial elements of the trial was the testimony regarding the bite marks found on one of the victims. The prosecution's expert claimed that the marks had clearly been made by the defendant, and Bundy and his team attempted to question the reliability of such evidence.

The defense's key testimony came from a serologist who had concluded that a semen stain found on a bed sheet belonging to one of the victims came from a man who was a "non-secretor," meaning that his blood type antigens were not secreted into his other bodily fluids. Bundy was a secretor.

When Bundy was convicted, Cowart dispassionately cited the aggravated circumstances in the case, and he sentenced Bundy to death for the murders of Levi and Bowman. He then told Bundy to "take care of yourself. It is a tragedy to this court to see such a total waste of humanity. You'd have made a good lawyer. I would have loved to have had you practice in front of me" (Larsen, 1980, p. 321).

The Leach trial was presided over by Judge Wallace Jopling. After an unsuccessful attempt to seat a jury in Suwannee County, where Leach was killed, Judge Jopling moved the trial to Orlando, in Orange County. There he presided over the trial in a careful, restrained manner.

The trial began with a long and tedious jury selection process. Because of all the publicity from the Miami trial, it took the questioning of over 130 prospective jurors to finally impanel a jury of twelve. Bundy then got off to a bad start by railing against the judge and prosecutor for allegedly wanting a prejudiced jury.

Although there was physical evidence linking Bundy to Leach's murder—footprints, fabric, blood, and semen—the crux of the case came down to credit card receipts putting him in Lake City around the time of the killing, and the testimony of a fireman who identified Bundy as the man he saw leading a young girl into a white van parked in front of Leach's school on the day that she disappeared. Another witness linked Bundy to the knife that was used to kill Leach. Bundy and his defense counsel focused their efforts on attacking the credibility of the witnesses, claiming that their testimony had been tainted by all of the publicity surrounding Bundy.

Bundy, however, was convicted, and Judge Jopling sentenced him to death. He echoed the words of Judge Cowart, telling the defendant, "You have every ability that a young man could expect to have to succeed in your life. May God have mercy on your soul" (Larsen, 1980, p. 336).

RESOLUTION

Bundy was convicted on all charges rising out of the attacks in the Chi Omega House, including two counts of aggravated murder, two counts of assault, and one count of burglary. He was sentenced to death by electric chair.

Bundy was also convicted of the kidnapping and murder of Kimberly Leach. During the penalty phase of the trial, he surprised all onlookers by marrying a woman from Olympia, Washington. He wed Carole Boone in open court after she had obtained a valid marriage license and arranged to have a notary present, along, of course, with the judge (Larsen, 1980, pp. 334–335). Married or not, Bundy was also sentenced to death for the Leach murder, but he did not stop fighting. He filed numerous appeals and received several stays of execution. When his legal remedies were nearly exhausted, he tried to stay alive anyway he could.

After many years of denying his involvement in any of the murders that he was suspected of, he began confessing to some of the killings, while holding back information on others to use as bargaining chips in his attempts to avoid execution. When asked if he had killed thirty women, Bundy taunted, "Put a zero after that" (Millitich, 1989). He also offered himself as a "consultant" on the unsolved Green River Killer cases in Washington State, which were being investigated by some of the same detectives who had served on the "Ted Squad" years before (Keppel and Birnes, 1995, pp. 198–210).

Bundy also did a widely viewed, videotaped interview with a Christian radio psychologist, in which he blamed his aberrant behavior on a life-long addiction to violent pornography. Most investigators familiar with Bundy dismissed his claim as a way to relieve himself of responsibility for his crimes and to win enough sympathy to be kept alive, at least for a while longer.

Bundy's legal appeals and other maneuvers finally ran out. On January 24, 1989, he was executed in Florida's electric chair. Outside the prison, several hundred people gathered, representing both sides of the death penalty debate. Loud cheers could be heard when word of Bundy's death was announced.

MEDIA COVERAGE

Bundy's first few crimes, which at first seemed like isolated incidents, received little if any media coverage. It was not until it became clear to law enforcement that there was a possible link among the disappearances that newspaper and television coverage began to escalate. The turning point was when the two young women vanished from Lake Sammamish State Park on the same day. From then on, the "Ted" story was big news across the Pacific Northwest and eventually on a national level.

When Tacoma native and University of Washington graduate Bundy was arrested in Utah, the Seattle and Tacoma papers became flooded with stories on his arrest and his possible link to the local cases of missing women. Bundy's dramatic escapes from jail only added to the interests of the media and the public. When he eventually was caught in Florida, his story took on a new importance on a national scale. It was in large part due to the extensive press coverage of having both his trials moved to different venues.

The novel combination of television cameras in the courtroom and Bundy's acting as his own attorney turned his two trials in Florida into full-fledged media circuses. The numerous delays and heated debates over his impending electrocution kept the show going. In addition to extensive coverage of Bundy by newspapers, television, and magazines, several books told his story from various perspectives. Former Seattle policewoman-turned-true-crime-writer Ann Rule, who worked with Bundy at the Crisis Clinic and considered him a friend, wrote of it all in *The Stranger Beside Me*, which years later was made into a television movie.

Seattle Times reporter Richard Larsen, who first met Bundy while covering Washington State politics, wrote *Bundy: The Deliberate Stranger*, which was made into a network miniseries. Robert Keppel, King County's lead detective on the "Ted" cases, wrote *The Riverman: Ted Bundy and I Hunt for the Green River Killer* about Bundy's attempts to delay his execution by offering investigators his thoughts on yet another Northwest serial killer. Other books on Bundy included *The Only Living Witness* (Michaud and Aynesworth, 1983), in which he chillingly recounts his crimes to two journalists in the third person, and books by Bundy's former girlfriend and by the final attorney to represent him. The Bundy saga continues to be kept alive by a plethora of web sites, and by true-crime shows on cable television.

RELEVANT SOCIAL, POLITICAL, AND LEGAL ISSUES

Although there had been many serial killers before him, from Jack the Ripper to The Boston Strangler, it was not until Ted Bundy that the term came into the consciousness of American and, indeed, international society. With his cunning intelligence, good looks, charm, and the number and nature of his crimes, he became the archetype for a new breed of killers both in fact and in fiction. Behind his "mask of sanity" lurked a human killing machine totally without empathy or remorse (Cleckley, 1982).

On a national level, the Bundy cases didn't have much of a political impact, other than to add to the public's already high level of fear about violent crime. But, on a local level in Tallahassee, they were an important issue in the election campaign for prosecutor.

A number of significant legal issues did arise from Bundy's murder trials in Florida. Chief among them was the issue of cameras in the courtroom. Bundy's Miami trial was the first major criminal trial to come into American's living room, live and in color. At the time, there was a great deal of debate on the pros and cons of allowing the trial to be televised. Little was settled, as the debate roared on in future trials, including the rape trial of William Kennedy Smith and of course, the O.J. Simpson trial.

Another key legal issue was the bite mark evidence. Although it had actually been first used in an obscure case in the same Miami courthouse where Bundy stood trial, it was the Chi Omega trial that put the spotlight on this new kind of forensic evidence. Despite the defense's attempts to discredit bite mark evidence as unscientific, it played a key role in Bundy's conviction and in many other cases since.

The most significant issue raised by the Bundy cases was the death penalty, because advocates for and against it tried to exploit this case for their position. Death penalty proponents viewed the number and nature of Bundy's acts as the perfect justification for the ultimate penalty, and those opposed to capital punishment argued that the use of Florida's antique electric chair, known as "Old Sparky," amounted to cruel and unusual punishment (Barber, 1989).

SIGNIFICANCE OF THE CASE

The Bundy saga has had a lasting impact on both legal and popular culture. His interstate murder spree helped bring about the creation of the Violent Crimes Apprehension Program (VICAP), which hoped to overcome many of the difficulties in dealing with cross-jurisdictional murder sprees exposed by the Bundy investigation by compiling a national database of reports of such crimes. It also brought a new awareness within law enforcement of both the prevalence and nature of serial homicide (Keppel and Birnes, 1995, pp. 134–158).

On the popular culture front, Bundy in some ways became almost a folk hero. He was played on television by Mark Harmon, who had been named one of *People* magazine's Sexiest Man Alive (Larsen, 1988). While in the spotlight, Bundy drew legions of female fans (Licitis, 1979). He also became a subject of fascination among young people, who were both intrigued and repulsed by the lethal charmer (Thunemann, 1989).

Although other high-profile murder cases continue to dominate the news media and other serial killers have come and gone, it is not likely that we will ever see the likes of another Ted Bundy. At least we can hope we never do.

REFERENCES

Another Encounter with Ted? (1974, August 9). *The Seattle Times,* p. D1.

Barber, M. A. (1989, January 26). Prober, Bundy Deserves to Die. *The Seattle Post-Intelligencer,* p. B1.

Cleckley, H. (1982). *The mask of sanity.* New York: New American Library.

Did Bundy Kill 300? (1982, March 3). *The Seattle Post-Intelligencer,* p. C12.

Keppel, R. D. and Birnes, W. J. (1995). *The Riverman: Ted Bundy and I hunt for the Green River killer.* New York: Pocket Books.

Lamar, J. V. (1989, February 6). "I deserve punishment": Killer Ted Bundy bargains and postures to the end. *Time,* p. 34.

Larsen, R. (1979a, March 11). Bundy faces awesome battles on two fronts. *The Seattle Times,* p. A6.

Larsen, R. (1979b, July 9). Bundy could win, despite bumbling defense. *The Seattle Times,* p. B8.

Larsen, R. (1980). *Bundy: The deliberate stranger.* New York: Pocket Books.

Larsen, R. (1988, May 4). Bundy: Real and Reality. *The Seattle Times/Post-Intelligencer,* p. K1.

Licitis, E. (1979, July 19). Bundy: A fascinated female following. *The Seattle Times,* p. A10.

Lohr, D. (2002, Oct. 6). Ted Bundy: The poster boy of serial killers, Retrieved September 15, 2003, from http://www.crimemagazine.com

McCarten, L. (1975, November 15). Lawmen conclude session on Bundy. *The Seattle Post-Intelligencer*, p. A3.

McCarten, L. (1976, March 3). Bundy case stirs probes in 3 states. *The Seattle Post-Intelligencer*, p. A6.

McCarten, L. (1977, February 6). The Colorado murder case. *The Seattle Post-Intelligencer*, p. A8.

McCarten, L. (1978, August 27). Local Bundy probe stymied. *The Seattle Post-Intelligencer*, p. A1.

Michaud, S. G., and Aynesworth, H. (1983). *The only living witness*. New York: Signet.

Millitich, S. (1989, January 23). Bundy confesses to more killings in an attempt to delay execution. *The Seattle Post-Intelligencer*, p. A1.

Rule, A. (1980a). *The Stranger beside me*. New York: W.W. Norton.

Rule, A. (1980b, September 28). Victim's bones and a siege of horror. *The Seattle Post-Intelligencer*, p. A19.

Thunemann, K. (1989, January 28). Bundy intrigues, repulses youngsters. *The Bellevue Journal American*, p. A12.

Index

About the Editors and
the Contributors

FRANKIE Y. BAILEY is Associate Professor at the State University of New York, Albany. With Steven Chermak, she is co-editor of *Media Representations of September 11* (Praeger, 2003) and *Popular Culture, Crime, and Justice* (1998). She is author of *Out of the Woodpile: Black Characters in Crime and Detective Fiction* (Greenwood, 1991), which was nominated for the Mystery Writers of America 1992 Edgar Award for Criticism and Biography, and *"Law Never Here": A Social History of African American Responses to Issues of Crime and Justice* (Praeger, 1999).

STEVEN CHERMAK is Associate Professor and Director of Graduate Affairs in the Department of Criminal Justice at Indiana University. He is the author of *Searching for a Demon: The Media Construction of the Militia Movement* (2002) and *Victims in the News: Crime and the American News Media* (1995).

JAMES R. ACKER is a professor at the School of Criminal Justice, University at Albany (SUNY). Acker has authored numerous scholarly articles and is coauthor or coeditor of several books including *Two Voices on the Legal Rights of America's Youth*; *Criminal Procedure: A Contemporary Perspective*; and *America's Experiment With Capital Punishment: Reflections on the Past, Present, and Future of the Ultimate Penal Sanction*.

MARIE BALFOUR is a Ph.D. student at the School of Criminal Justice, University at Albany (SUNY).

LINDSEY BERGERON is a Ph.D. student at the Department of Criminal Justice and Political Science, North Dakota State University.

GARY BOYNTON is a freelance true-crime writer, researcher, and teacher. For six years he was Pacific Northwest Correspondent for the Detective Files Magazine Group, and his work has also appeared on several crime-related websites.

JOHNNA CHRISTIAN is Assistant Professor at the School of Criminal Justice, Rutgers University.

GEORGE W. DOWDALL is Professor of Sociology at Saint Joseph's University. His publications include *The Eclipse of the State Mental Hospital*; *Finding Out What Works and Why: A Guide to Evaluating Prevention Programs*; and *Adventures in Criminal Justice Research: Data Analysis Using SPSS*.

SUZANNE M. ENCK-WANZER is a doctoral candidate in the Department of Communication & Culture, Indiana University.

LAURA L. FINLEY, Ph.D., is Adjunct Professor of Sociology at the University of Northern Colorado. She is currently working on a book titled *Piss Off! How Privacy Violations in Public Schools are Alienating America's Youth*. Other publications include "Using Content Analysis Projects in the Introduction to Criminal Justice Classroom (*Teaching Sociology*) and "Teachers' Perceptions of School Violence Issues: A Case Study" (*Journal of School Violence*).

SIDNEY L. HARRING is Professor of Law at the City University of New York School of Law, New York. He is the author of numerous scholarly articles and several books including *Policing a Class Society* and *Crow Dog's Case*.

RENATE W. PRESCOTT is Associate Professor of English, Kent State University–Geauga. Her publications include "We Speak to James: The Narrator/Reader Relationship in Paco's Story" (*Viet Nam War Generation Journal*, April 2002); "Rewriting the Vietnam War: The (re)Construction of Vietnam War Narratives" (Community College Humanities Association, Fall 2000); "The Reliability of the Narrator: Writing Oral History of the Vietnam War" (*Oral History Review*, Summer/Fall 1999); "Teaching the Vietnam War: A Student's Oral History Project" (Ohio Association of Two Year Colleges, Spring 1999); "The Politics of Pain: Family Letters from the Vietnam War" (*Studies in American Culture*, Winter 1997).

JIM SINCLAIR is a lecturer in the School of Information Science and Humanities, The Open Polytechnic of New Zealand. His publications include *Constructing an Online/Electronic Resource: A Pathway*; "An Internet Guide to Communication Resources" (coauthored by Trevor Landers).

TIMOTHY M. SLEDD is a Ph.D. student at the Department of Criminal Justice, Indiana University–Bloomington.

DENNIS J. STEVENS is Associate Professor of Criminal Justice, Salem State College, Salem, Massachusetts. His publications include *Applied Community Corrections*; *Police Stress*; *Applied Community Policing in the 21st Century*; *Case Studies in Applied Community Policing*; *Case Studies in Community Policing*; *Policing and Community Partnerships*; *Inside the Mind of the Serial Rapist*; and *Corrections Perspective Coursewise*.

STEPHANIE N. WHITEHEAD is a graduate student at the Department of Criminal Justice and Police Studies, Eastern Kentucky University.

KEVIN F. WOZNIAK is a financial fraud investigator and is currently working on a book about Lee Harvey Oswald's life.